REAL WORLD ADOBE INDESIGN 1.5

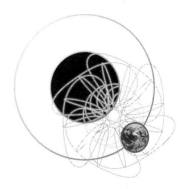

Real World Adobe
InDesign 1.5

by

Olav Martin Kvern

PEACHPIT PRESS

for Jane E. Hawkins and Vonda N. McIntyre

REAL WORLD ADOBE INDESIGN 1.5
Olav Martin Kvern

Copyright © 2001 by Olav Martin Kvern

PEACHPIT PRESS
1249 Eighth Street
Berkeley, California 94710
(800) 283-9444
(510) 524-2178
(510) 524-2221 (fax)

Find us on the World Wide Web at: http://www.peachpit.com
Peachpit Press is a division of Addison Wesley Longman
Real World Adobe InDesign 1.5 is published in association with Adobe Press

Copy Editor: Leona Benten
Indexer: Jan C. Wright
Cover design: Gee + Chung Design
Cover illustration: Mimi Heft
Interior design, illustration, and production: Olav Martin Kvern

ISBN 0-201-35478-0

9 8 7 6 5 4 3 2 1

Printed and bound in the United States of America

I admit it. I absolutely refuse to stop and ask for directions. I'm a guy, so it's probably part of my genetic makeup. The way I see it, if you make enough right turns along the way, you're bound to get where you are going—or at least back to where you started. Yes, I understand that this strategy doesn't always yield the most direct, efficient, or scenic route to my destination, but there is a sense of pride and self-reliance in finally figuring out how to get to your destination on your own. And yes, it drives my wife crazy.

But even with this admission of guilt, there are times that the most intrepid explorers should look to an expert to assist us in finding whatever it is we're looking for. It's times like these I wish Olav Kvern would write *Real World Frequent Flying*. Or *Real World Japanese Food*. Or *Real World Retirement Planning*. I know if I had such a guide written with such clarity and insight, it would certainly make the process of needing to stop and ask directions a more pleasant one.

As it is, graphic designers and production artists the world over can be grateful that Olav's experience lies in the realm of professional publishing and not (necessarily) in the matters I mentioned, because this book contains a treasure trove of information to help you take the absolute fullest advantage of the creative freedom afforded by Adobe InDesign.

In short, this book contains directions that are worth stopping and asking for.

It should come as no surprise to you that *Real World Adobe InDesign* is an expansive look into how Adobe InDesign functions and how you can make best use of it to produce beautiful pages. To say that Olav understands the skills used everyday by publishing and graphic design professionals is an understatement—"guru" is the word that more readily comes to mind. His excellent works, *Real World PageMaker* and *Real World Freehand*, are studied and used daily by thousands of grateful designers to help improve their work and their workflow.

Olav is no newcomer to page layout software, and he's no newcomer to Adobe InDesign either. He has been involved with InDesign from the earliest stages of its development in its pre-beta stage long before InDesign 1.0 shipped. As a product manager for InDesign 1.0 and 1.5, I can tell you with no uncertainty that Olav's feedback to our development team shaped many of InDesign's capabilities.

Olav has produced in *Real World Adobe InDesign* a comprehensive guide that helps you get up to speed quickly with InDesign's new features. Olav's easy, conversational style of writing is both engaging and thorough, making *Real World Adobe InDesign* as useful a starting point for beginners as it is a reference for experts with years of ink under their fingernails. At Adobe, we think so much of Olav's talents that we contracted him to write the excellent *InDesign Scripting Guide* that ships with every version of InDesign worldwide. Suffice it to say that Olav is one of the world's true experts in the area of using Adobe InDesign in a professional publishing environment.

In creating Adobe InDesign 1.5, we endeavored to bring a tool to the graphic designer and production artist that would offer power, flexibility, precision and quality in a way that takes full advantage of modern computing power—and tear down many of the barriers that existing software has imposed on the elegance of graphic design. For the literally thousands of features Adobe InDesign has introduced to the world of graphic design and production, *Real World Adobe InDesign* will expose to you the best ways to take advantage of them. I believe that the information in this book will allow you to unleash the creative potential of InDesign—and of yourself—in ways that have been impossible before now.

This much I can say: *Real World Adobe InDesign* has earned its place—not on my bookshelf—but right beside my mouse. I am certain it will do the same for you.

Wishing you the best and brightest realization of your creative dreams,

David Evans
Senior Evangelist, Adobe InDesign
Adobe Systems, Inc.
Seattle, Washington

CONTENTS

I'm a desktop publishing user—just like you. I've been through the long shifts (some of them longer than 40 hours), entering and editing text, setting type, drawing paths, importing images, and trying to get files to print. On most of those late nights and early mornings, I could have been home in bed if I'd known just one key piece of information. But I didn't. There was no one there to tell me.

I'm here to tell you.

If some piece of information in this book saves you one late night, one early morning, or gets your document to print on the first pass through the imagesetter instead of the second or third, I will have succeeded in my purpose.

InDesign is a watershed of technologies that have, until now, only been at the edge of our page layout "radar": support for OpenType and Unicode, direct export of prepress-quality PDF files, integral PostScript/PDF screen rendering, built-in font management and rasterization, multi-line composition, and optical kerning, solid scripting support on both the Mac OS and Windows platforms, to name just a few of them. Adobe has always said that InDesign is "the future of page layout"—but I think they're selling themselves a bit short. With InDesign, the future is here.

And, to my eye, at least, it looks pretty cool.

A Note About the Text

If you've read *Real World FreeHand*, you'll probably notice that a number of the leads, conclusions, and jokes in this book are the same or similar to text in that book. I hope that this doesn't offend or upset you. Like any other business entity, I have to amortize the high costs of research and development, testing, and marketing of my product. I have no choice—the cost of testing a single silly paragraph, such as the one at the end of Chapter 7, can run into the thousands of U. S. dollars, and requires me to file a special Environmental Impact Statement. Testing leads and conclusions is entirely destructive; we run them into a brick wall at high speed, while special crash test dummies record the impact of metaphors and conceptual explanations. Rest assured that, in the event of an actual rhetorical collision, *Real World Adobe InDesign* will deploy airbags designed to meet or exceed the highest safety standards for any text. No animals were harmed in the development of this title.

Acknowledgments

Thanks to the entire InDesign team at Adobe, for making such a great program, for letting me work on it, and for supporting this book. Special thanks to David Evans for his inspiring foreword.

Jan C. Wright, the Queen of Indexing, produced the superb (and funny) index.

Thanks to Silicon Graphics (SGI)—this book was produced on an SGI 320 workstation running Windows NT4 (because of amount of time it took me to write the book, this system is "last year's model"—you can see newer systems at www.sgi.com). I cannot thank SGI enough for the use of this wonderful system. The Silicon Graphics 1600SW flat panel monitor is without question the best page layout display I have ever seen or used.

Thanks to the Seattle Gilbert and Sullivan Society and their photographer, Ray O. Welch, for giving me permission to use some of their archival photographs as example images. Special thanks to Ed Poole for the free use and abuse of his moustache.

Thanks to Nancy Ruenzel for being a great publisher, to Ted Nace for founding Peachpit Press, and to all of the folks at Peachpit for their patience and support (and did I mention patience?). Special thanks to Cary Norsworthy, my editor, and Kate Reber.

Special thanks to my long-suffering officemates Brett Baker, David Blatner, Jeff Carlson, Glenn Fleishman, Toby Malina, Steve Roth, Agen Schmitz, and Jeff Tolbert.

Finally, thanks to Leslie Renée Simons and to Max Olav Kvern, for their encouragement, understanding, and support.

Olav Martin Kvern
ole@desktopscience.com
Republic of Freemont
Seattle, 2000

1

Workspace

Come on in! Let me show you around. I'll be your tour guide to the world of InDesign. I'm here to tell you what's what, what's where, and how it all fits together. This chapter is all about InDesign's user interface—the myriad windows, palettes, menus, and other gadgets InDesign displays on your screen. It tells you what they all are, and what I call them (this is important, because not everything in InDesign is clearly labeled—as you read through the techniques in this book, you need to know that I mean this button *over here*, and not that button *over there*).

This chapter also contains lots of tips and tricks for working with InDesign's user interface. These are the "little things" that make all the difference between enjoying and hating the time you spend working with InDesign (or any other program, for that matter). The point is to get you up to speed with all of these new tools so that you can get on with your work.

Ready? Let's start the tour.

A note about keyboard shortcuts: Since you can redefine most of the keyboard shortcuts in InDesign, I can't guarantee that your keyboard shortcuts will be anything like mine. And I can't follow every keyboard shortcut in the text with the disclaimer, "…or the shortcut you've defined for this action." So, as you read this, bear in mind that I'm using the shortcuts from the default keyboard shortcut set. If you want to return to InDesign's default keyboard shortcuts, see "Customizing Keyboard Shortcuts," later in this chapter.

Another note about keyboard shortcuts: Quite a few of InDesign's default keyboard shortcuts—especially those for selecting tools—do not use a modifier key (by "modifier key" I mean Command, Control, Option, Ctrl, Alt, Shift, and so on). If you're editing text, you can't use these keyboard shortcuts. If you do, you'll end up entering characters in the text.

The keyboard shortcut to switch to the Pen tool, for example, is "P." If you press the shortcut while the cursor is in text, you'll enter the character "P." If you use InDesign to set type (and I think most of us do), you'll almost certainly want to add a modifier key to the unmodified keyboard shortcuts you use most often.

Unfortunately, you can't modify the "hide all palettes" shortcut. It's hardwired to the Tab key. You also can't switch to the Selection tool (press Command/Ctrl) and then use the shortcut.

Publication Windows

When you open or create an InDesign publication, you view and work on the publication in one or more publication windows (see Figure 1-1). Each publication window gives you a view on a page, spread, or pasteboard area in an InDesign publication. You can have multiple publication windows open on a single publication, and you can have multiple open publications.

The view of the publication you see in a publication window can be magnified or reduced to show more or less detail. Each publication window can be set to a different magnification. Since magnification is primarily a way of moving around in your publication, I'll cover it later in this chapter, in "Publication navigation."

Title Bar At the top of a publication window you'll see the title bar. The appearance of the title bar differs slightly between Macintosh and Windows versions of InDesign. On the Macintosh, you'll see the title (the name of your publication file), close box (click it to close

FIGURE 1-1

Inside a publication window

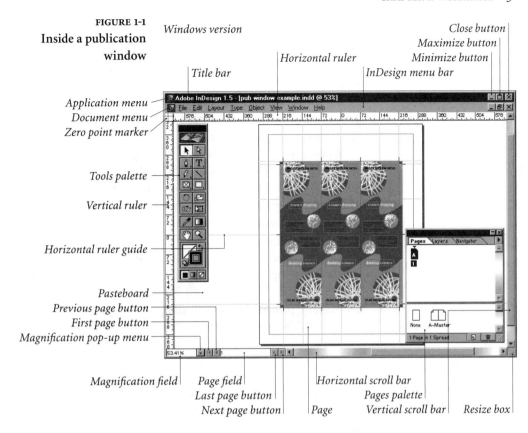

Windows version

Title bar

Horizontal ruler

InDesign menu bar

Close button
Maximize button
Minimize button

Application menu
Document menu
Zero point marker

Tools palette

Vertical ruler

Horizontal ruler guide

Pasteboard
Previous page button
First page button
Magnification pop-up menu

Magnification field   Page field
Last page button
Next page button

Page

Horizontal scroll bar
Pages palette
Vertical scroll bar   Resize box

Macintosh version

Close box

Collapse box
Zoom box

Resize box

the window), and zoom box (click it to expand the publication window to the size of the screen; click it again to return the publication window to its previous size). In Windows, you'll see the title, control menu, and close/minimize/maximize buttons (click them to close, hide, or enlarge a publication window, respectively).

To close a publication window, press Command-W/Ctrl-W (or Ctrl-F4). To close all publication windows, press Command-Option-Shift-W/Ctrl-Alt-Shift-W.

Pasteboard and Page   Like most other page layout programs, InDesign is built around the concept of the pasteboard—an area on which you place pages

*Items stored on the
pasteboard for future use*

Document pages
Pasteboard

and graphic elements. The pasteboard is not a fixed size, as it is in FreeHand or PageMaker, and it's not shared between spreads—each spread has its own pasteboard (as in QuarkXPress). You can use areas of the pasteboard for temporary storage of the elements you're working with—just drag the elements off the page, and they'll stay on the pasteboard until you need them (again, this is just like an old-fashioned layout board).

When objects can extend past the edge of the page, into the pasteboard, they create a "bleed." The objects will be clipped off at the edge of the paper when your commercial printer cuts your printed pages, but sometimes, that's just the design effect you want.

The size of the bleed, the page size, and the size of the paper (that is, the paper size you want to use when you print your final copy) all affect each other. In InDesign, the page size you define in the Document Setup dialog box should be the same as the final size of the document's page after it's been printed and trimmed by a commercial printer. You define the paper size in the Page Setup dialog box (Macintosh) or Printer Properties dialog box (Windows) when it's time to print your publication. When you're printing to an imagesetter, the paper size is a defined area on the imagesetter's film roll (or sheet).

If your publication's page size (without the bleed) is the same as the paper size you've chosen in the Print Options dialog box, you can expect InDesign to neatly clip off any elements that extend beyond the edge of the page. Choose a larger paper size than your publication's page size when you want to print bleeds (choose Letter.Extra when you're printing a letter-size publication with a bleed, for example). If you want to learn how to create new paper sizes for imagesetters (I don't know of any laser printer that can handle custom paper sizes), see "Rewriting PPDs" in Chapter 10, "Printing."

Scroll Bars

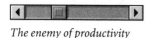

The enemy of productivity

The most obvious, least convenient, and slowest way to change your view of your publication is to use a scroll bar (that is, to click in a scroll bar, drag a scroll handle, or click the scroll arrows). For more on better ways to get around, see "Publication navigation," later in this chapter.

**Page Field
and Page Buttons**

The Page field/pop-up menu and its attached navigation buttons give you a way to get from one page to another. Click the Previous Page button to move to the previous page in your publication, or click the Next Page button to move to the next page. Alternatively, you can click the First Page button to go to the first page in the publication, or the Last Page button to go to the last one.

If you know exactly which page you want to go to, choose the page number from the Page pop-up menu or enter the page number in the Page field.

Magnification Field

Enter a magnification percentage in this field, or choose one from the attached pop-up menu, and InDesign magnifies or reduces the view of the publication you see in the publication window. There are better ways to do this, as shown in "Publication navigation," later in this chapter.

To make the cursor "jump" into the Magnification field, press Command-Option-5/Ctrl-Alt-5. Enter a percentage and press Enter to change the publication window's magnification.

These views aren't the only magnifications available—if you use the Zoom tool, you can achieve any magnification you want. For more on using the Zoom tool, see "Zooming," later in this chapter.

Rulers

Pressing Command-R/Ctrl-R displays or hides InDesign's rulers—handy measuring tools that appear along the top and left sides of a publication window (see Figure 1-2). The rulers are marked off in the units of measurement specified in the Units & Increments Preferences dialog box. The actual increments shown on the rulers vary somewhat with the current magnification; in general, you'll see finer increments and more ruler tick marks at 800% size than you'll see at 12% size.

As you move the cursor, lines in the rulers (called shadow cursors) display the cursor's position on the rulers (see Figure 1-3).

FIGURE 1-2

Rulers

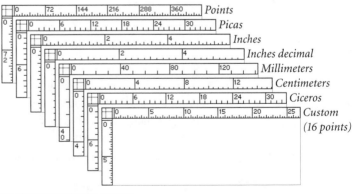

FIGURE 1-3

Shadow cursors

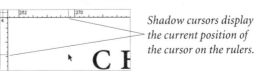

Shadow cursors display the current position of the cursor on the rulers.

The Context menu is the quickest way to change measurement units.

To change the units of measurement used by a ruler, Control-click/Right-click the ruler to display the Context menu. Choose a new measurement system from the menu, or choose Custom to enter a custom measurement increment (if you do this, InDesign displays the Custom Measurement Unit dialog box, where you can enter the measurement unit you want to use).

Zero Point

The intersection of the zero measurement on both rulers is called the zero point. In InDesign, the default location of the zero point is at the upper-left corner of the spread, page, or binding spine (it's an option in the Grids Preferences dialog box). To control the location of the zero point, use the zero point marker (see Figure 1-4).

To move the zero point, drag the zero point marker to a new position. As you drag, intersecting dotted lines show you the position of the zero point. When you've moved the zero point to the location you want, stop dragging. The rulers now mark off their increments based on this new zero point.

To reset the zero point to the default location, double-click the zero-point marker.

FIGURE 1-4
Moving the zero point

Position the cursor over the zero point marker.

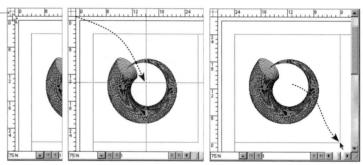

Drag the zero point marker.   When you stop dragging, InDesign moves the zero point.

To lock the position of the zero point, use the Context menu. Point at the zero point, then hold down Control and click (Macintosh) or click the right mouse button (Windows). Choose Lock Zero Point from the Context menu (see Figure 1-5). To unlock the zero point, display the Context menu and choose Unlock Zero Point.

FIGURE 1-5
Locking the zero point

 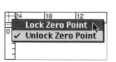 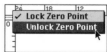

Unlocked zero point.   *Choose Lock Zero Point from the Context menu.*   *Locked zero point.*   *To unlock the zero point, use the Context menu.*

Managing Multiple Windows

InDesign displays a list of open publication windows at the bottom of the Window menu.

If you want to open more than one window on a publication, choose "New Window" from the Window menu. The new window covers the original window, so you'll have to drag and resize windows to see both views at once, or choose Tile Windows from the Window menu (see Figure 1-6). Choose Cascade from the Window menu to stack the open publication windows on top of each other.

To get from an active publication window to an inactive publication window, you can click any part of the inactive window, or you can choose a window name from the listing of open windows at the bottom of the Window menu.

Sometimes it's easier to display pages in multiple windows than it is to scroll or zoom from page to page. I use multiple windows in the following situations:

◆ When I find myself jumping back and forth between two or more locations in a publication.

◆ When I need to copy an object or objects from one page to another page that's several pages away. Dragging the objects from one publication window to another is faster than scrolling and dragging or cutting and pasting.

FIGURE 1-6

Window views

InDesign highlights the title bar of the active publication window.

In either view, you can rearrange and resize windows to create custom views.

Use the Tile view when you want to drag objects from one window to another or from one publication to another.

When you choose Cascade from the Window menu, InDesign stacks up the open publication windows. To bring any window to the front, click its title bar.

When you choose Tile from the Window menu, InDesign arranges the open publication windows to fill the screen (Macintosh) or the InDesign application window (Windows).

♦ When I'm trying to fit copy into a story that spans several pages. I can make one publication window focus on the end of the story, and, as I edit and format text, I can see exactly when the last line of the copy appears at the end of the last text frame (see Figure 1-7).

FIGURE 1-7
Using views for copyfitting

This window shows me the text at the beginning of the story.

With these two windows open, I can quickly see whether deleting these words will make the story fit.

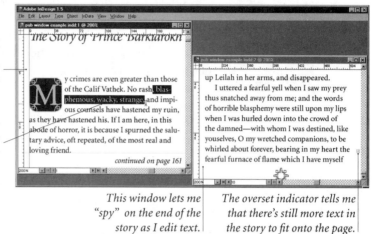

This window lets me "spy" on the end of the story as I edit text.

The overset indicator tells me that there's still more text in the story to fit onto the page.

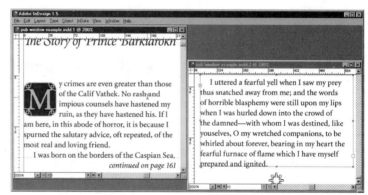

When I delete the text in this window…

…I can see that the story now fits (and the overset text indicator disappears).

There's no trick to removing a view—simply close the window, and the view disappears from your Windows menu.

You can have as many different publications open as you like. You switch from one publication to another by choosing a window name from the bottom of the Window menu, or by clicking on their windows, just as you'd switch among applications.

To close all open windows, hold down Option as you click the Close box (Macintosh) or hold down Shift as you click the Close button (Windows). Or press Command-Option-Shift-W/Ctrl-Alt-Shift-W to close all of the open windows.

InDesign's Palettes

Can you see your page? If not, it's probably due to InDesign's omnipresent palettes—there are plenty of them. Don't rush out to buy a larger screen—you don't have to have all of the palettes open all of the time. The best way to work with InDesign's palettes is to have the minimum number of them open at once, to combine palettes into functional groups, and to learn and master the keyboard shortcuts for working with and navigating through palettes. That's what this part of the book is about.

InDesign's palettes work two ways—they display information about the publication or the selected object or objects, and they provide controls for changing the publication and the objects in it. The palettes are an integral part of InDesign's user interface, and are the key to doing almost everything you can do in the program (see Figure 1-8).

FIGURE 1-8

InDesign palettes

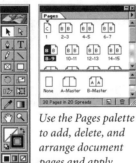

You find tools in—where else—the Tools palette.

Why do I include pictures of the palettes? So you can take the book away from your computer and still be able to see what I'm talking about. It's an attempt at creating a kind of virtual reality—on paper.

Use the Library palette (or any number of Library palettes) to store text and graphics for future use.

The Character palette controls character formatting.

Use the Pages palette to add, delete, and arrange document pages and apply master pages.

The Navigator palette gives you another way to change your view of a publication.

Use the Align palette to align and distribute objects.

When you want text to avoid a graphic, use the options in the Text Wrap palette.

Want to work with objects "by the numbers?" If so, the Transform palette is for you.

Use the Paragraph palette to set paragraph indents, alignment, and other paragraph formatting attributes.

FIGURE 1-8
**InDesign palettes
(continued)**

*Other palettes dedicated to
working with text and type.*

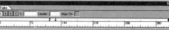

*Paragraph styles and Character
styles can save you lots of time and
trouble. These two palettes are the
key to working with styles.*

*Want to set a tab stop? You'll have to
talk to the Tabs palette.*

*You've heard the rumor, and
it's true: InDesign pushes
the boundaries of user interface design by providing the
Check Spelling palette.*

*Use the Find/Change palette to find
and change text in your InDesign
publications.*

*Palettes for setting the fill
and stroke of the selected
object.*

*Store, edit, and apply
named colors, tints, and
gradients using the
Swatches palette.*

*Library colors, such as
those defined by Pantone,
TruMatch, or Toyo are
stored in InDesign's
swatch library palettes.*

*You can also define
and apply unnamed
colors and tints using
the Colors palette.*

*The options in the
Attributes palette con-
trol the overprinting/
knockout qualities of
the fill or stroke of an
object.*

*Use the Stroke palette
to set the stroke width,
stroke type, and other
stroke attributes.*

*Use the Gradient palette
to control the gradient
ramp and angle of gradi-
ent fills and strokes.*

All About Focus   When a particular window, or field, or control is active, we say it has "focus"—meaning that the gadget is receiving any keystrokes you might press. If you're furiously pressing keys, and yet no text is appearing in the selected text frame, it's because something else—some other window—has focus.

Understanding and manipulating palette focus is very important—especially when you're working with text.

When you choose a menu option or click a button in a palette, InDesign applies the change and returns focus to your page layout. When you press Tab to move ahead one field (or Shift-Tab to move back one field), InDesign applies any change you made and shifts focus to the next (or previous) palette field.

InDesign offers a number of keyboard shortcuts for controlling keyboard focus:

◆ Press Shift-Return/Shift-Enter to apply the value you've entered in a palette field and keep that palette field in focus.

◆ Press Enter/Return to apply a value you've entered in a palette field and return focus to your page.

◆ If you've entered a value in a palette field and decide you don't want to apply it, press Escape/Esc. InDesign changes the field back to whatever it was before you started typing, and keeps the focus on the palette field.

◆ In any of the "list" palettes (the Swatch Library palette, for example), hold down Command-Option/Ctrl-Alt and click in the list. This transfers focus to the list—you can type the name of a list item to select that item from the list (see Figure 1-9).

FIGURE 1-9
Palette lists and focus

Hold down Command-Option/Ctrl-Alt and click to give a list focus.

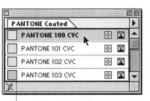 

When a list has focus, InDesign displays a dark border around it.

Once a list has focus, you can select list items by typing—it's often quicker than scrolling.

Displaying and Hiding Palettes

You can use keyboard shortcuts and save yourself lots of mouse movement (see Table 1-1). If a palette's open, but behind other palettes in the same group, pressing the keyboard shortcut brings the palette to the front of the group. To close a palette, click the Close button on the palette's title bar.

Hiding All Palettes. Press Tab, and all of the palettes currently displayed disappear; press it again, and they reappear. This shortcut won't work when you have text selected or have an active text cursor in a text frame (it'll enter a tab character, instead). You'd think that you could use the keyboard shortcut to switch to the Selection tool (hold down Command/Ctrl) and then press Tab to hide the palettes, but you can't.

To display this palette:	Press:
Align	F8
Attributes	None/Alt-W, R
Character	Command-T/Ctrl-T
Character Styles	Shift-F11
Check Spelling	Command-I/Ctrl-I
Color	F6
Edit Dictionary	None/Alt-E, Y
Find/Change	Command-F/Ctrl-F
Gradient	None/Alt-W, G
Layers	F7
Links	Command-Shift-D/Ctrl-Shift-D
Navigator	None/Alt-W, N
Pages	F12
Paragraph	Command-M/Ctrl-M
Paragraph Styles	F11
Story	None/Alt-T, S
Stroke	F10
Swatches	F5
Tabs	Command-Shift-T/Ctrl-Shift-T
Text Wrap	Command-Option-W/Ctrl-Alt-W
Tools palette	None/Alt-W, T
Transform	F9

Zipping and Unzipping Palettes. With all these palettes, it's easy to run out of room on your screen to see anything *but* the palettes. While you can use keyboard shortcut to display the palettes, you might like this better: Macintosh users can shrink a palette down to just its tab and title bar by clicking the zoom box; Windows users can click the Minimize button to do the same thing. You can also double-click the palette's tab.

This is called "zipping" a palette. The title bar stays on the screen (see Figure 1-10). When you want to display the entire palette, click the zoom box again if you're a Macintosh user, or click the Maximize button if you're using Windows. The palette expands to its full size. In addition, you can:

◆ Double-click the tab of the front most palette in a group.

◆ Click the tab of any palette in a group that is not the front most palette in the group.

◆ Press the keyboard shortcut for the palette.

On the Macintosh, you can shrink the palette down to its title bar by double-clicking the title bar. To expand the palette again, double-click the title bar again. In Windows, double-clicking the title bar is the same as clicking the Minimize button or double-clicking a palette's tab.

FIGURE 1-10

Zipping and unzipping palettes

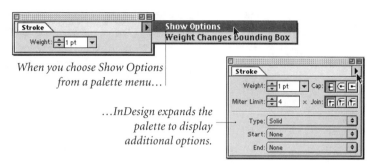

When you choose Show Options from a palette menu...

...InDesign expands the palette to display additional options.

Here's another (and possibly quicker) way to accomplish the same thing. Position the cursor over a palette tab...

...and double-click the tab. InDesign shrinks the palette to the next smaller size (if one is available).

In Windows, you can double-click the palette's title bar to show or hide palette options.

Double-click again, and InDesign shrinks the palette further (if possible).

On the Macintosh you can also shrink a palette down to its title bar.

InDesign displays only the palette's title bar.

To expand the palette, double-click the title bar again, or click the Zoom box.

Double-click the palette's title bar or click the Collapse box.

Displaying options. Many of InDesign's palettes can be set to display all of the available options for a particular feature, or a subset of those options. The Stroke palette, for example, can display all stroke attributes (stroke weight, stroke type, end cap type, join, and arrowheads) or the stroke weight only.

Resizing palettes. To resize a palette, drag the Resize box at the palette's lower-right corner (see Figure 1-11). If a palette doesn't have a Resize box, you can't resize it. In Windows, you can drag the sides of some of the palettes to resize them (this works for the Paragraph Styles, Character Styles, and Pages, and Swatches palettes).

FIGURE 1-11

Resizing palettes

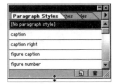

To change the size of a palette, drag the resize box.

In Windows, you can also drag the borders of the palette to resize the palette.

Snapping palettes into position. When you drag a palette near to the edge of another palette, InDesign snaps the edge of the palette you're moving to the closest edge of the other palette. This makes it easy to arrange and resize palettes in relation to other palettes.

Combining and separating palettes. You can rearrange any of the "tabbed" palettes (see Figure 1-12). You can combine many palettes into a single palette, or you can create more palettes than you'll see when you first open InDesign (this is a mind-boggling concept, I know). Why would you want to do this? You could display the Paragraph Styles palette and the Character Styles palette at the same time (rather than having them stacked on top of each other). We all have different ways of working, and tabbed palettes give us a way of customizing InDesign to fit our particular habits and needs.

To combine palettes, drag the tab of one palette into the area at the top of another palette. When you combine two or more palettes, you create a "palette group." A palette group behaves as if it is a single palette—the palettes move, resize, and zip/unzip as a unit.

In any palette group, only one palette can be "on top" at a time; only the tabs of the other palettes in the group are visible. To display another palette in the group, click the palette's tab or press the keyboard shortcut for the palette.

Docking palettes. Another way to customize the layout of InDesign's palettes is to "dock" one palette to another. When you do this, both palettes remain visible (in contrast to combined palettes, where only the uppermost palette is visible), and move, hide, display, or resize as a single palette.

FIGURE 1-12

**Combining or separating
tabbed palettes**

To join two palettes:

Position the cursor over a palette tab.

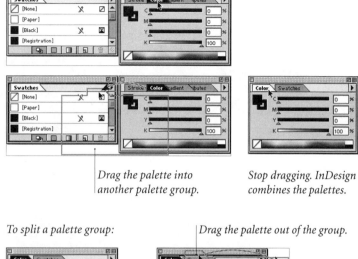

*Drag the palette into
another palette group.*

*Stop dragging. InDesign
combines the palettes.*

To split a palette group:

Drag the palette out of the group.

*Position the cursor
over a palette tab.*

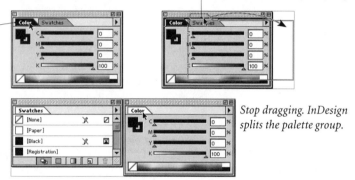

*Stop dragging. InDesign
splits the palette group.*

To dock one palette to another, drag the tab of a palette into the area at the bottom of another palette. As you drag, InDesign highlights the bottom of the target palette. Stop dragging and release the mouse button, and InDesign joins the palettes (see Figure 1-13).

Palette navigation. To move from one field in a palette to the next, press Tab. To move from one field to the previous field, press Shift-Tab. If you've made any changes in the field, InDesign applies the changes.

To "jump" back to the palette field you used most recently, press Command-` (accent grave; it's just to the left of the number 1 at the upper-left corner of your keyboard)/Ctrl-`.

When you display a palette using the corresponding menu option or keyboard shortcut, InDesign selects the first field in the palette.

FIGURE 1-13

Docking palettes

*Drag the tab of one
palette into the bottom
of another palette.*

*InDesign displays a
highlight when the
palettes are ready to
dock.*

*Stop dragging and release
the mouse button. InDesign
docks the two palettes.*

Small Palette Rows. To reduce the height of each item in any of the "list" palettes (i.e., the Swatches, Swatch Color Library, Paragraph Styles, Character Styles, Links, and Layers palettes), choose Small Palette Rows from the palette's pop-up menu. InDesign reduces the height of the items in the list (see Figure 1-14).

FIGURE 1-14

Small palette rows

*Choose Small Palette Rows
from a list palette menu...*

*...and InDesign reduces the
height of each list entry.*

Overriding Units of Measurement. Being able to switch from one measurement system to another is great, but what do you do when you want to enter a value in a measurement system other than the one currently selected? Do you have to go to the Units & Increments Preferences dialog box and switch to another measurement system? No—all you need to do add a "measurement override" when you enter the value. Want to enter 115.3 points in a field that's currently showing decimal inches? It's easy: enter "115.3 pt," or even "0p115.3" in the field, and InDesign will take care of the conversion for you.

You can use these shortcuts in any numeric field in any InDesign palette or dialog box. Table 1-2 shows you how to enter measurement overrides.

TABLE 1-2
Measurement overrides

When you want:	Enter:	Example:
points	pt	136 pt
points	0p	0p136
picas	p	1p
picas and points	p	1p6
inches	i*	1.56i
centimeters	mm	2.45mm
ciceros	c	3c
ciceros and didots	c	3c4

* or "in" if you feel the need to type the extra character.

Doing Arithmetic in Fields. You can add, subtract, multiply, or divide in any numeric field in any InDesign palette or dialog box. Want an object to be half its current width? Type "/2" after the value in the W (width) field in the Transform palette and press Enter. Want an object to move two picas to the right? Enter "+2p" (yes, all of the measurement unit overrides shown above work with these operations) after the value shown in the X field in the Transform palette. Enter "*" to multiply, or "-" to subtract. You get the idea.

A Quick Tour of the Palettes

Here's a quick description of the palettes you'll see as you work with InDesign. Most of the rest of the book is taken up by descriptions of how you use the palettes—this section is your formal introduction to the palettes and to the gadgets they contain.

Align palette. Use the Align Palette to arrange objects relative to other objects. To display the Align Palette, press F8 (see Figure 1-15). To align two or more objects, select them and then click the alignment button corresponding to the alignment you want.

Note that the Align palette's distribution options do not include the ability to space objects a specific distance apart (as the alignment features in both QuarkXPress and PageMaker do). For more on working with the Align palette, see Chapter 8, "Transforming."

The tiny, but useful, Attributes palette.

Attributes palette. Have you been looking for the object-level overprinting options in the Stroke palette or the Color palette? You won't find them there, because they're in the Attributes palette. I'm not sure why. Choose Attributes from the Window menu to display the Attributes palette.

FIGURE 1-15
Align palette

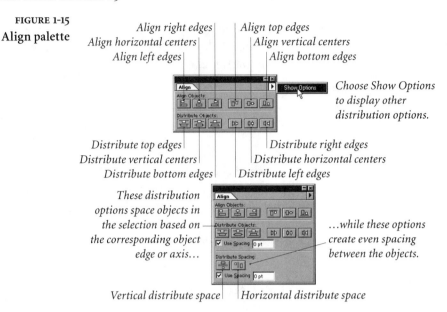

Align right edges
Align horizontal centers
Align left edges

Align top edges
Align vertical centers
Align bottom edges

Choose Show Options to display other distribution options.

Distribute top edges
Distribute vertical centers
Distribute bottom edges

Distribute right edges
Distribute horizontal centers
Distribute left edges

These distribution options space objects in the selection based on the corresponding object edge or axis...

...while these options create even spacing between the objects.

Vertical distribute space | Horizontal distribute space

Character palette. You'll find InDesign's character formatting commands in the Character palette (see Figure 1-16). If you've grouped the Transform palette and the Character palette, InDesign will display the Character palette when you click the text tool in a text frame. Press Command-T/Ctrl-T to display the Character palette.

The Character palette menu contains a number of important typesetting commands, controlling features such as ligature replacement, small caps, superscript, and subscript.

FIGURE 1-16
Character palette

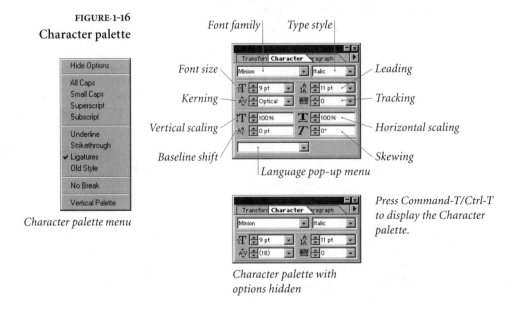

Font family | *Type style*

Font size
Kerning
Vertical scaling
Baseline shift

Leading
Tracking
Horizontal scaling
Skewing

Language pop-up menu

Character palette menu

Press Command-T/Ctrl-T to display the Character palette.

Character palette with options hidden

You can display the Character palette in a horizontal mode (an arrangement similar to PageMaker's Control palette or the Measurements palette found in QuarkXPress), or you can switch the palette to a vertical configuration (which is similar to the Character palette in Illustrator). To change the palette's display mode, choose Horizontal or Vertical from the palette's pop-up menu.

You can also choose to show or hide several Character palette options: the Horizontal Scale and Vertical Scale fields, the Baseline Shift field, the Skew field, and the Language pop-up menu. To hide these controls, choose Hide Options from the Character palette's pop-up menu. To show these options again, choose Show Options.

Character Styles palette. You use the Character Styles palette to create, edit, and apply InDesign's character styles (see Figure 1-17).

To create a character style, select text that has the formatting attributes you want and choose New Style from the Character palette menu (or click the Create New Style button at the bottom of the palette). InDesign displays the New Character Style dialog box. At this point, you can enter a new name for the style, or otherwise tinker with the style's definition. When you close the dialog box, note that InDesign does not apply the style to the selected text.

FIGURE 1-17
Character Styles palette

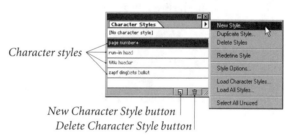

Character styles

New Character Style button
Delete Character Style button

To edit a style, hold down Command-Option-Shift/Ctrl-Alt-Shift and double-click the style name. This opens the style for editing, but does not apply it to the selected text. You can also double-click the style name to edit the style, but that this applies the style to the selected text (if you have text selected) or to the document default.

To delete a character style, select the style (which applies the style to any selected text—you might want to deselect the text before you select the style) and choose Delete Style from the palette's pop-up menu. InDesign removes the style.

For more on character styles, see Chapter 4, "Type."

Check Spelling palette. As you'd expect from its name, you use this palette to check the spelling of the text in a publication (see Figure 1-18). To display this palette, press Command-I/Ctrl-I (or choose Check Spelling from the Edit menu).

For more on the Check Spelling palette, see Chapter 3, "Text."

InDesign displays a list of spelling alternatives in the Suggested Corrections list.

Color palette. Use the Color palette to define and apply colors (see Figure 1-19). To display the Color palette, press F6 (or choose Color from the Windows menu). You won't find colors from standard color libraries—such as Pantone or TruMatch—here. They're in swatch libraries (see Swatch Library palette, later in this chapter) or in the Swatches palette.

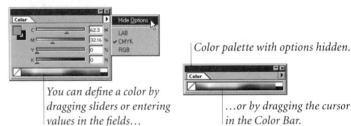

Color palette with options hidden.

You can define a color by dragging sliders or entering values in the fields...

...or by dragging the cursor in the Color Bar.

To define a color, choose the color model you want to work with from the Color palette's menu, then adjust the color parameters in the Color palette.

The Color palette interacts with the Swatches palette. When you select a color swatch in the Swatches palette, InDesign loads the Colors palette with the color definition of the swatch. The Swatches palette returns the favor: when you choose New Swatch from the Swatches palette menu, or click the New Swatch button at the bottom of the Swatches palette, InDesign creates a new swatch with the color definition currently in the Color palette.

For more on defining, editing, and applying colors, see Chapter 9, "Color."

Edit Dictionary palette. InDesign's hyphenation and spelling features depend on dictionaries. When a word isn't in a dictionary, InDesign has no idea how to spell the word, and has to make guesses about where the word should be hyphenated. With the Edit Dictionary palette, we can help InDesign learn new words, or change the way that it treats words it already knows (see Figure 1-20).

FIGURE 1-20
Edit Dictionary palette

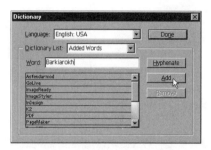

Find/Change palette. As you'll see in Chapter 3, "Text," InDesign's ability to search for, find, and change text is an extremely powerful word processing and formatting tool. The key to using this feature is yet another palette: the Find/Change palette (see Figure 1-21). Press Command-F/Ctrl-F to display the Find/Change palette (or choose Find/Change from the Edit menu).

Gradient palette. InDesign's ability to apply gradients to the fill and stroke of paths and text characters is one of the program's signature features, and the Gradient palette is the way you create, edit, and apply gradients (see Figure 1-22).

Layers palette. Layers give you a way to control the stacking order of objects in your publication, and also help you control the speed with which InDesign draws and redraws your publication's pages. Layers can be hidden, or locked. To work with layers, you use the Layers palette (see Figure 1-23). To display the Layers palette, press F7 (or choose Layers from the Window menu).

The following are quick descriptions of each control in the Layers palette.

◆ Show/Hide button. If you see an "eye" icon on this button, the layer is visible. Click the icon to hide the layer. To show the layer again, click the button.

◆ Lock/Unlock button. To lock a layer, click this button. When a layer is locked, a pencil with a red slash through it (as in the

FIGURE 1-20

Find/Change palette

The pop-up menus associated with the Find What and Change To fields make searching for special characters easy.

Enter the text you want to search for in the Find What field...

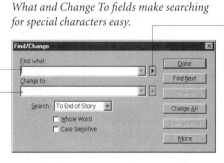

...then enter the text you want to replace it with in the Change To field (if necessary).

The "alert" icons tell you that formatting attributes have been set.

In this example, I've entered text in the fields, specified a search range (the current Story), and specified formatting (click the More button to display the Find Style Settings and Change Style Settings options).

To set formatting attributes you want to search for (or replace with), click the Format button. You can find and change any formatting InDesign can apply.

FIGURE 1-21

Gradient palette

| Gradient preview | Gradient stop | Midpoint |

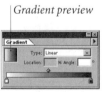

Gradient palette with options shown (Linear gradient).

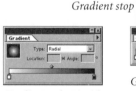

Gradient palette with options shown (Radial gradient).

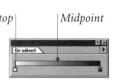

Gradient palette with options hidden.

international "prohibited" symbol) appears on this button. To unlock the layer, click the button again.

◆ Layer color swatch. The color shown on this button determines the color of the selection handles of objects assigned to this layer.

FIGURE 1-22
Layers palette

Layer names

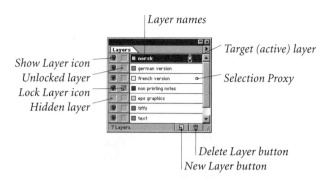

Show Layer icon
Unlocked layer
Lock Layer icon
Hidden layer

Target (active) layer

Selection Proxy

Delete Layer button
New Layer button

◆ Target layer icon. This icons shows you which layer is active. Any new objects you create, objects you paste into the publication, or groups you create will appear on this layer.

◆ Layer name. The name of the layer.

◆ Selection Proxy. The Selection Proxy represents the items you've selected. If the selection contains objects from more than one layer, you'll see more than one Selection Proxy in the Layers palette. Note that clicking on a layer does not move the selection to that layer, as it would in some other programs (notably FreeHand). Instead, you move objects from layer to layer by dragging the Selection Proxy up or down in the list of layers in the Layers palette. This makes it harder for you to accidentally send objects to a layer.

◆ New Layer button. Click this button to create a new layer. The new layer appears at the top of the list of layers.

◆ Delete Layer button. Click this button to delete the selected layer. If, somewhere in your publication, objects are assigned to the layer, InDesign will display a dialog box that asks if you want to delete the layer. If you do, click the Yes button—InDesign will delete the layer and any objects assigned to the layer. If you don't want to delete the objects, click No.

◆ Resize handle. Drag this icon to change the width and height of the Layers palette.

Double-click a layer to display the Layer Options dialog box, where you can change the layer color, layer name, and other layer options.

For more on working with layers, see Chapter 2, "Page Layout."

Library palette. Use the Library palette (or palettes, as you can have multiple libraries open at once) to store and retrieve commonly-used items (see Figure 1-23). Does your company or client have a logo they like to plaster all over every publication you lay out? Put it in a library.

FIGURE 1-23
Library palette

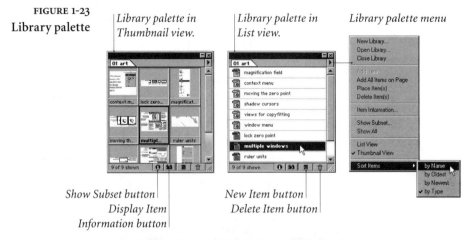

Library palette in Thumbnail view.

Library palette in List view.

Library palette menu

Show Subset button
Display Item
Information button

New Item button
Delete Item button

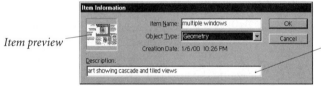

Item preview

You can use this field to add notes to the library item—this can help a great deal when you're searching for an item.

When you click the Display Item Information button, InDesign displays the Item Information dialog box.

When you click the Show Subset button, InDesign displays the Subset dialog box. Specify the parameters you want and click the OK button, and InDesign displays the library items that match.

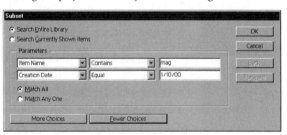

Navigator palette. This palette gives you another way to get around in your publication—it's a kind of alternative to scrolling and zooming. When you display the Navigator palette, you'll see in it a thumbnail view of your page or page spread (see Figure 1-24).

Around the spread, you'll see a red rectangle (by default—you can change the color if you want). This rectangle is the View box, and represents the area of the publication visible on your screen. You can drag the View box in the Navigator palette to change your view of the publication. As you drag, InDesign scrolls your view of the publication to match the area shown in the View box.

FIGURE 1-24
Navigator palette

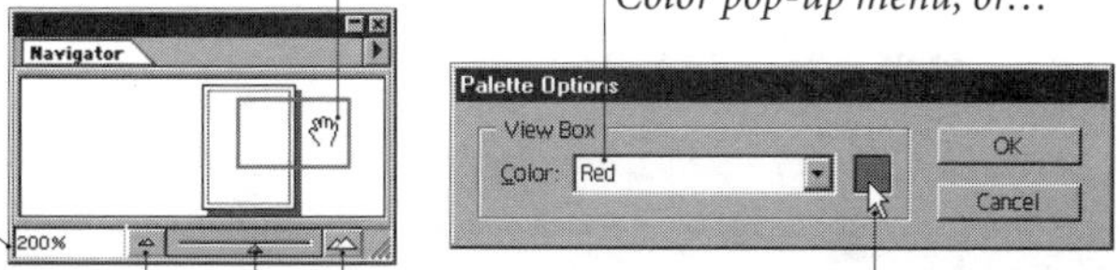

Drag the View box to scroll your view of the publication.

To change the color used to display the View Box, choose Palette Options from the palette menu. Choose a color from the Color pop-up menu, or…

The View Box represents the area of your screen.

Enter a magnification percentage in the Magnification field, or …

…click this button to zoom to the next lower magnification preset (e.g., from 200% to 100%), or …

…drag the Zoom slider to change the magnification percentage (as you drag, the View Box will change size), or …

…click this button to zoom to the next higher magnification preset (e.g., from 100% to 200%).

…double-click to display a color picker.

If you don't use the Navigator palette, turn it off—you'll get faster screen redraw.

You can also zoom using the Navigator palette. Click the Zoom buttons to zoom in or out to the next "standard" magnification, or enter a new magnification in the palette's Magnification field (or choose a magnification from the pop-up menu associated with the field). Or drag the Zoom slider.

I use the Zoom tool, Hand tool, Pages palette, and keyboard shortcuts to move from place to place in my publications, rather than the Navigator palette, but you should give the palette a try—you might like it better than I do.

If you don't use the Navigator palette, turn it off to get faster screen redraw. It takes InDesign time to draw the little page preview in the palette.

Pages palette. The Pages palette is for creating, deleting, and rearranging pages and master pages (see Figure 1-25). It's also a great way to navigate from one page to another, and it's where you apply master pages to document pages. The following are brief descriptions of the controls found in the Pages palette.

◆ Spread and page icons. These icons represent the document pages and master pages in your publication. You can drag these pages around in the Pages palette to change the page order. You can also apply a master page to a document page (or to another master page) by dragging the master page's page icon onto the page icon of the target page. You can also create a new master page by dragging document pages into the master page area of the palette.

◆ New page button. Click this button to create a new document page.

FIGURE 1-25
Pages palette

Pages display the prefix ("B" or "C," in this example) of the master page applied to them.

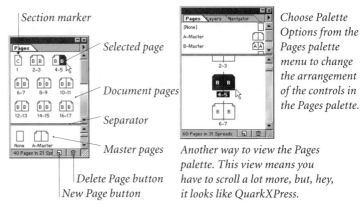

Section marker

Selected page

Document pages

Separator

Master pages

Delete Page button

New Page button

Choose Palette Options from the Pages palette menu to change the arrangement of the controls in the Pages palette.

Another way to view the Pages palette. This view means you have to scroll a lot more, but, hey, it looks like QuarkXPress.

Pages palette menu

◆ Delete page button. Click this button to delete the selected page or pages.

◆ Master/Document page separator. This bar separates the master pages in your publication (at the bottom of the palette) from the "normal" publication pages (at the top). You can drag the separator up or down to change the size of these areas.

◆ Resize box. Drag this icon to resize the Pages palette.

Paragraph palette. You use the controls in the Paragraph palette to specify paragraph formatting. To display the Paragraph palette, press Command-M/Ctrl-M (see Figure 1-26).

When you choose Hide Options from the Paragraph palette menu, InDesign hides the Paragraph Space Above, Paragraph Space

FIGURE 1-26
Paragraph palette

Press Command-M/Ctrl-M to display the Paragraph palette.

Paragraph palette menu

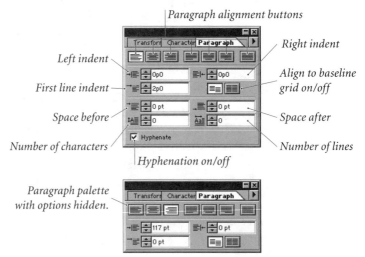

Paragraph alignment buttons

Left indent

First line indent

Space before

Number of characters

Right indent

Align to baseline grid on/off

Space after

Number of lines

Hyphenation on/off

Paragraph palette with options hidden.

Below, Drop Cap Characters, and Drop Cap Lines fields, and the Hyphenate checkbox and shrinks the palette to a smaller size. To display these options again, choose Show Options from the menu.

For more on working with paragraph specifications, see Chapter 4, "Type."

Paragraph Styles palette. InDesign's paragraph styles are the most powerful text formatting feature in the program, and the Paragraph Styles palette is the way you work with them (see Figure 1-27).

◆ New Paragraph Style button. Click this button to create a new paragraph style. If you have text selected, the new paragraph style will have the formatting attributes of the first paragraph in the selection.

◆ Delete Paragraph Style button. Click this button to delete the selected paragraph style (or styles).

◆ Resize box. Drag this icon to resize the Paragraph Styles dialog box.

FIGURE 1-27
Paragraph Styles palette

Paragraph styles

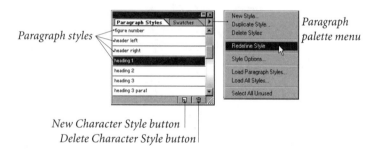

Paragraph palette menu

New Character Style button
Delete Character Style button

Story palette. You've heard that InDesign features hanging punctuation (which, in InDesign, goes by the name "Optical Margin Alignment"), but you haven't been able to find the control for it? Relax—it's in the Story palette (see Figure 1-28). Actually, there's nothing else in the Story palette (I'm pretty sure there will be more in the near future). To display the Story palette, choose Story from the Type menu.

For more on the Story palette, see Chapter 4, "Type."

FIGURE 1-28
Story palette

Stroke palette. A stroke is the outline of a path; the Stroke palette controls the formatting of that outline (see Figure 1-29).

The basic Stroke palette is minimalist: there's only the Weight option to play with. Choose Show Options, however, and InDesign expands the Stroke palette to include options controlling the line cap, miter limit, line join, stroke type, and arrowhead properties of a path. What most of these options really mean is discussed more fully in Chapter 5, "Drawing."

FIGURE 1-29

Stroke palette

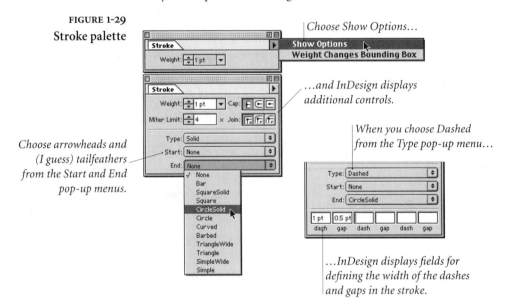

Choose Show Options...

...and InDesign displays additional controls.

When you choose Dashed from the Type pop-up menu...

Choose arrowheads and (I guess) tailfeathers from the Start and End pop-up menus.

...InDesign displays fields for defining the width of the dashes and gaps in the stroke.

Swatch Library palette. The Swatch Library palettes (there's more than one) contain various color libraries (see Figure 1-30).

Swatch Libraries are actually Illustrator files, and can be opened and edited using that program.

Swatches palette. Swatches can be colors, tints of colors, or gradients. They're a way of storing the values in the Color palette or the Gradient palette for future use. The Swatches palette gives you a way to organize, edit, and apply swatches in your publications (see Figure 1-31). To display the Swatches palette, press F5 (or choose Swatches from the Window menu).

While you can get by without the Swatches palette—by using the Color palette and the Gradient palette to apply fill and stroke attributes—I don't recommend it. Here's why: When you apply a fill or stroke using the Swatches palette, you create a relationship between the object's formatting and the swatch. If you later find you need to

FIGURE 1-30
Swatch Library palettes

Opening the Trumatch swatch library also opens the HKS E library. I'm not sure why.

Hold down Command-Option/Ctrl-Alt and click in the list to activate the list. Once you've done this, the list "has focus" (thick border appears around the selected list), and you can select a swatch by typing its name or number. This makes selecting a specific Pantone color much easier.

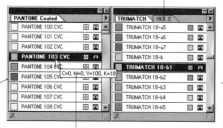

Double-click a swatch to add it to the Swatches palette, or select a series of swatches and choose Add to Swatches from the Swatch Library palette menu. Once you've added the swatches you need, you can close the Swatch Library .

InDesign displays the color values of the swatch (using the color model assigned to the swatch). Don't let this fool you—these are still Pantone spot colors, not CMYK simulations.

FIGURE 1-31
Swatches palette

The icons in this column show you the color model of the swatch.

Use the default "None" swatch to remove the fill or stroke (or both).

The default "Registration" swatch prints on all separations.

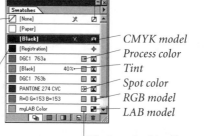

CMYK model
Process color
Tint
Spot color
RGB model
LAB model

The icons in this column tell you whether a swatch is a spot or a process color.

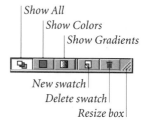

Show All
Show Colors
Show Gradients

New swatch
Delete swatch
Resize box

change the definition of the swatch, the appearance of any objects formatted using the swatch will change. Swatches, like paragraph and character styles, are a feature that can really save your sanity when your client/boss/whatever changes their mind about a color scheme an hour before your publication deadline.

◆ Show All button. Click this button to display all of the swatches in the publication.

◆ Show Colors button. Click this button to display all of the color and tint swatches in the publication (and hide any gradient swatches).

◆ Show Gradients button. Click this button to display all of the gradient swatches in the publication (and hide any color or tint swatches).

◆ New Swatch button. Click this button to create a new swatch.

◆ Delete Swatch button. Click this button to delete the selected swatch or swatches.

◆ Resize box. Drag this icon to resize the Swatches palette.

For more on working with color swatches, see Chapter 9, "Color." For more on gradient swatches, see Chapter 5, "Drawing."

Tabs palette. Use InDesign's Tabs palette to set tab stops and paragraph indents (see Figure 1-32). To display the Tabs palette, press Command-Shift-T/Ctrl-Shift-T.

◆ Tab Alignment buttons. Set the alignment of the selected tab stop (or set the default tab stop alignment).

◆ Tab stop icons. These mark the positions of the tab stops in the selected paragraph.

◆ Tab Ruler. To add a tab stop, delete a tab stop, or to change the position of a tab stop, drag a tab stop icon on the Tab Ruler.

◆ Tab Position field. Enter a value in this field when you know exactly where you want to position a tab stop.

◆ Tab Leader field. Enter up to two characters in this field to apply a tab leader to the selected tab stop.

◆ Snap Palette button. Click this button to align the Tab Ruler's zero point at the left edge of the text frame.

For more on the Tabs palette, see Chapter 4, "Type."

FIGURE 1-32
Tabs palette

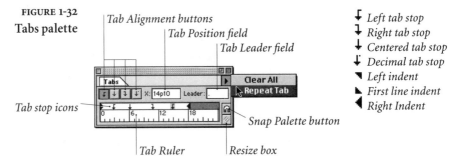

Tab Alignment buttons
Tab Position field
Tab Leader field

↧ *Left tab stop*
↧ *Right tab stop*
↧ *Centered tab stop*
↧ *Decimal tab stop*
◥ *Left indent*
◣ *First line indent*
◀ *Right Indent*

Tab stop icons

Snap Palette button

Tab Ruler   *Resize box*

Transform palette. Look. In two dimensional page layout and illustration programs, there's just no escape from basic geometry. So you might as well just learn to like working with numbers. Sometimes, they're the best way to get the job done. And it's not difficult—especially with InDesign's Transform palette to help out (see Figure 1-33).

The Transform palette shows you with horizontal (X) and vertical (Y) location of the selected object (or the cursor). The coordinates that appear in the X and Y fields are shown in the current units of measurement, and are relative to the current location of the zero point. The W (for width) and H (for height) fields show you the size of the selection. The Vertical and Horizontal scaling fields show you any scaling applied to the object, the Rotation field shows you the current rotation angle, and the Shear field shows you the skewing angle applied to the object. Not only do these fields give you information on the selection, they can also be used to change its location, size, rotation angle, or skewing angle.

FIGURE 1-33

Transform palette

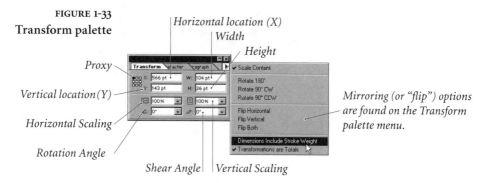

Horizontal location (X)
Width
Height

Proxy

Vertical location(Y)

Horizontal Scaling

Rotation Angle

Mirroring (or "flip") options are found on the Transform palette menu.

Shear Angle   *Vertical Scaling*

As an object moves to the right, relative to the horizontal zero point, the object's X coordinate increases. As an object moves *down* on the page, the value of its Y coordinate increases. Note that this means that the vertical (Y) axis of InDesign's coordinate system is upside down compared to the graphs you created in junior high school (see Figure 1-34).

A "proxy" represents something or someone—the Proxy in InDesign's Transform palette represents the selection (see Figure 1-35). The squares at the edges and in the center of the Proxy represent the corners, sides, top, and center of the selection's bounding box, and control the way that changes in the Transform palette affect the selected object or objects.

While the X and Y fields display the current cursor position when you move the Selection tool or the Direct Selection tool, they don't change when you're using any other tool. So you can't use the X and Y fields for positioning information as you draw a path with the Pen tool, or create a text frame with the Text tool.

FIGURE 1-34
InDesign's
coordinate system

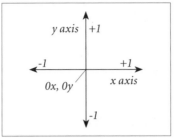

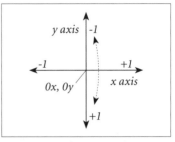

"Classical" geometric coordinates: y values increase as you go up the vertical axis.

InDesign coordinates: y values increase as you go down the vertical axis.

FIGURE 1-35
The Proxy

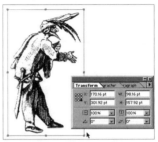

The Transform palette's Proxy "stands in" for the selection.

Select a point on the Proxy, and InDesign displays the location of the point of the selection (the upper-left corner, in this example).

Select a different point on the Proxy, and you'll see different values in the X and Y fields (in this example, I've selected the lower-right corner).

Note for PageMaker users: Unlike PageMaker's Control palette, whose Proxy features both "move" and "stretch" modes, InDesign's Proxy is always in "move" mode. Entering a new X coordinate for a side handle, for example, will always move the handle to that location without resizing the selected object. You'll have to simulate the effect of "stretch" mode using the W(idth) or H(eight) fields, or the Scaling fields.

Using the toolbox

If the publication window is the layout board where you collect the galleys of type, illustrations, and photographs you want to use in your publication, the toolbox is where you keep your waxer, X-Acto knife, T-square, and bandages. (Note to youngsters: these are tools used by the Classical Greeks in the early days of page layout. You don't have to understand how they work to use the corresponding tools in InDesign. But it helps.)

Some of the following descriptions of the tool functions aren't going to make any sense unless you understand how InDesign's points and paths work, and that discussion falls in Chapter 5, "Drawing." You can flip ahead and read that section, or you can plow through this section, get momentarily confused, and then become enlightened when you reach the descriptions of points and paths. Or you can flip ahead to Chapter 5, "Drawing" for even more on points and paths. It's your choice, and either method works. This is precisely the sort of nonlinear information gathering that hypertext gurus say can't be done in books.

You can break InDesign's toolbox into six conceptual sections (as shown in Figure 1-35).

◆ Selection tools (the Selection and Direct Selection tools)

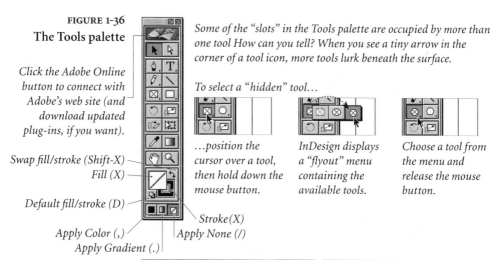

FIGURE 1-36

The Tools palette

Click the Adobe Online button to connect with Adobe's web site (and download updated plug-ins, if you want).

Swap fill/stroke (Shift-X)

Fill (X)

Default fill/stroke (D)

Apply Color (,)

Apply Gradient (.)

Stroke (X)

Apply None (/)

Some of the "slots" in the Tools palette are occupied by more than one tool How can you tell? When you see a tiny arrow in the corner of a tool icon, more tools lurk beneath the surface.

To select a "hidden" tool...

...position the cursor over a tool, then hold down the mouse button.

InDesign displays a "flyout" menu containing the available tools.

Choose a tool from the menu and release the mouse button.

	Tool name	Shortcut		Tool name	Shortcut
	Selection	V*		Ellipse	L
	Direct Selection	A		Elliptical Frame	Shift-L
	Pen	P		Rectangle	M
	Add Point	+		Rectangular Frame	Shift-M
	Delete Point	-		Polygon	N
	Convert Point			Polygonal Frame	Shift-N
	Scissors	C		Rotate	R
	Text	T		Free Transform	E
	Path Text	Shift-T		Scale	S
	Pencil	N		Shear	Shift-S
	Smooth	Shift-N		Gradient	G
	Eraser	Shift-N		Eyedropper	I
	Line	E		Hand	H**
				Zoom	Z

* Hold down Command/Ctrl to switch to the Selection tool temporarily.

** Hold down Spacebar and drag to switch to the Hand tool temporarily; hold down Option/Alt if the cursor is in a text frame.

◆ Tools for drawing basic shapes (the Rectangle, Polygon, Oval, and Line tools) and their equivalent frames (Rectangular Frame, Polygonal Frame, and Oval Frame tools)

◆ Path-drawing and editing tools (the Pen, Add Point, Delete Point, Convert Point, Gradient, Pencil, Eraser, Smooth, and Scissors tools)

◆ Transformation tools (the Rotate, Reflect, Shear, Scale, and Free Transform tools)

◆ The Text tool and Path Text tool

◆ Navigation tools (the Zoom and Hand tools).

You use the Selection tool and the Direct Selection tool to select objects you want to change in some way. You can do different things with the objects depending on the selection tool you've used. The basic shape tools draw complete paths containing specific numbers of points in specific positions on the path, while the path-drawing tools draw paths point by point (or, in the case of the Scissors tool, delete points or split paths). The transformation tools change the rotation angle, size, and skewing angle of objects on your pages, you use the Text tool to enter and edit text, and the navigation tools help you move around in your publication.

The tool descriptions in the following section are brief and are only intended to give you a feeling for what the different tools are and what they do. To learn more about entering text with the Text tool, see Chapter 3, "Text." For more on drawing objects with the drawing tools, see Chapter 5, "Drawing." For more on working with the Transformation tools, see Chapter 8, "Transforming."

Talking about InDesign's tools and their use can get a little confusing. When you select a tool in the Tools palette (or press the keyboard shortcut to select a tool), what does the cursor become? In this book, I'll sometimes use phrases like "select a tool and drag," or "drag the tool on the page." I hope this is clear—from my point of view, the cursor *is* the tool.

Hiding the Tools palette. Or Not. Sometimes, I want to hide all of the palettes except the Tools palette. To do that, make sure that the cursor isn't in a text frame, and then press Shift-Tab. InDesign hides all open palettes, but leaves the Tools palette open. If you've hidden all of the palettes including the Tools palette, you can display it by choosing Tools from the Window menu. Note that there isn't a way to hide the Tools palette other than hiding all palettes.

Tools palette Keyboard Shortcuts. You can choose most of the tools in the toolbox through keyboard shortcuts. This is usually faster than going back across the screen to the toolbox.

Hidden Tools/Tool Variants. To save some of your precious screen real estate, some of the slots in the Tools palette contain more than a single tool. You can tell by looking at the tool icon—when you see a tiny triangle on a tool icon, you know that other tools are lurking beneath it. In general, tools are grouped by their function. The Rectangular Frame tool, for example, shares a slot with the Rectangle tool. To use one of the "hidden" tools, position the cursor over a tool icon and hold down the mouse button (the left mouse button, for Windows users). InDesign displays a short pop-up menu, or "flyout," containing the available tools. Choose one of the tool icons, and that tool will be displayed in the Tools palette.

For each of the basic shape tools, InDesign offers a corresponding frame drawing tool. There's really very little difference between the path drawn by the Rectangle tool and a frame drawn by the Rectangular Frame tool, and paths can be converted to frames— and frames to paths—very easily. There's no penalty for drawing a path one way or another, as there is in some other programs.

For any of the hidden tools, pressing Shift plus the tool shortcut ("p" for the Pen tool, for example) selects the next tool. Pressing Shift plus the shortcut multiple times selects each hidden tool in turn. As you press the shortcut, you'll see the tool icon in the Tools palette change.

Adobe Online   When you click the button at the top of the Tools palette, InDesign displays the Adobe Online window (see Figure 1-36). You can connect to Adobe's web site to obtain technical support or download new plug-ins. You'll also find columns, articles, and white papers on various topics related to InDesign.

Selection Tool   You use the Selection tool to select and transform objects. Press V to select the Selection tool (when the cursor is not in text). To temporarily switch to the Selection tool, hold down Command/Ctrl when any other tool is selected. If you press Tab while you're holding down Command/Ctrl, you'll switch to the Direct Selection tool. To switch back to the Selection tool, press Tab again. When you release Command/Ctrl, the cursor turns back into whatever tool you were using before you summoned the Selection/Direct Selection tool.

FIGURE 1-36
Adobe Online

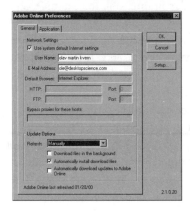

Click the Refresh button to check for the presence of new Adobe Online components.

Click the Preferences button to display the Adobe Online Preferences dialog box. The controls in the panels of this dialog box control the way that Adobe Online interacts with your system. I prefer to keep fairly strict control over what gets downloaded and installed, so I've set my preferences accordingly.

Direct Selection Tool

How many selection tools does a page layout application really need? I don't know, but InDesign has two—one for everyday selection; another for selecting objects on Sundays and holidays. No, seriously, the Direct Selection tool is for selecting objects that are inside other objects, such as the following.

◆ Individual points on paths. For more on editing the shape of a path, see Chapter 5, "Drawing."

◆ Component paths of compound paths. For more on working with compound paths, see Chapter 5, "Drawing."

◆ Objects inside groups. For more on selecting objects inside groups, see Chapter 2, "Page Layout."

◆ Objects pasted inside other objects. For more on working with path contents, see Chapter 8, "Transforming."

To select the Direct Selection tool, press A. To temporarily switch to the Direct Selection tool when you have any other tool selected, hold down Command/Ctrl (to switch to the Selection tool), then press Tab.

Pen Tool

You use the Pen tool to draw paths containing both straight and curved line segments (that is, paths containing both curve and corner points). Illustrator users will recognize the Pen tool immediately, because it's pretty much identical to Illustrator's Pen tool (maybe there's something to all this "cross-product" talk, after all). Click the Pen tool to create a corner point; drag to create a curve point. Press P to select the Pen tool.

Under the Pen tool, you'll find the following tools:

◆ Add Point tool (press + to switch to this tool). When you click the Add Point tool on a selected path, InDesign adds a point at that location on the path.

◆ Delete Point tool (press – to switch to this tool). When you click the Delete Point tool on a point on a selected path, InDesign deletes the point.

◆ Convert Point tool. When you click the Convert Point tool on a point on a selected path, InDesign converts the point to the other kind of point—if the point you click is a corner point, InDesign converts it to a curve point; if it's a curve point, InDesign converts it to a corner point. You can also use the Convert Point tool to adjust the direction handles of a point.

◆ Scissors tool. The Scissors tool cuts paths or points. Select a path, choose the Scissors tool from the Tools palette (or press C), and then click the path (see Figure 1-37). InDesign splits the path at the point at which you clicked.

For more (much more) on working with the Pen tool (and its variants) to draw and edit paths, see Chapter 5, "Drawing."

FIGURE 1-37
Scissors tool

As you move the Scissors tool close to a point, the cursor changes to show you you're about to split the point.

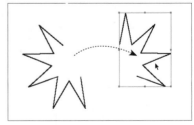

Select a path and point at the line segment or point you want to cut…

…and then click the Scissors tool on the path. Once you've cut a path, you can drag it apart (I've cut the path at two points in this example).

Text Tool You enter and edit text using the Text tool. To create a text block, select the Text tool and drag the tool in the publication window; a text block appears with a flashing text-insertion point (or text cursor) in its first line. To edit text, select the Text tool and click in a text block. For more on entering, editing, and formatting text, see Chapter 3, "Text." To select the Text tool, press T.

Path Text Tool Use the Path Text tool to enter and edit text on a path. To add text to a path, select the Path Text tool and click the tool on a path. A flashing text insertion point (or text cursor) appears on the path. At this point, text you enter will flow along the path. See Chapter 6, "Where Text Meets Graphics" To select the Path Text tool, press Shift-T.

Pencil Tool If you're one of the millions of computer users who find the Pen tool—and the whole process of drawing by manipulating points, line segments, and control handles—confusing, give the Pencil tool a try. With the Pencil tool, you can sketch freeform paths. As you drag the tool, InDesign creates a path that follows the cursor, automatically placing points and adjusting curve handles as it does so.

  If you don't like something about a path you've drawn using the Pencil tool, you can adjust it using any of InDesign's other drawing tools (including that scary Pen tool). You might want to start with the other tools that share the same space in the Tools palette: the Smooth tool and the Eraser tool (see below).

Smooth Tool I'm a guy, and so, naturally, I like power tools. A good belt sander, for example, can reduce just about anything to a smooth, rounded blob in mere seconds. The Smooth tool (press Shift-N) is something like that. Select a path—any path—and drag the Smooth tool over it. It'll get smoother. Not smooth enough yet? Drag again.

  As you drag the Smooth tool, InDesign adjusts the points and control handles that define the path to create a smoother transition from one line segment to another. InDesign often removes points during this process. If you continue to repeat the smoothing process, I think you'll eventually end up with a simple curve between two points.

Eraser Tool The Eraser tool (press Shift-N until the Eraser tool appears) erases line segments and points. To use the Eraser tool, select a path, then drag the eraser tool over part of the path. InDesign splits the path and removes the line segments and points where you dragged the Eraser tool.

Line Tool   Use the Line tool to draw straight lines—paths containing two corner points. If you hold down Shift as you drag the Line tool, the lines you draw will be constrained to 0-, 45-, and 90-degree angles. Press E to select the Line tool.

Ellipse Tool   Use the Ellipse tool to draw ellipses and circles. Hold down Shift as you drag the Ellipse tool, and InDesign draws circles. Press L to select the Ellipse tool.

Rectangle Tool   Use the Rectangle tool to draw rectangles. If you hold down Shift as you draw a rectangle, you draw squares. Press M to select the Rectangle tool.

If you need a rectangle with rounded corners, draw the rectangle using the Rectangle tool, then choose Corner Effects from the Object menu to display the Corner Effects dialog box (you can also get to this dialog box via the context menu, or by pressing Command-Option-R/Ctrl-Alt-R). Choose Rounded Corners from the Effect pop-up menu and enter a distance in the Size field to set the corner radius you want to use for the corners of the rectangle (see Figure 1-39).

If you draw a rectangle with square corners and then decide that you'd rather its corners were rounded, use the Corner Effects dialog box. The Corner Effects dialog box can provide a variety of other corner shapes, as discussed in Chapter 5, "Drawing."

FIGURE 1-39

Applying Corner Effects

There's no special tool for drawing a rectangle with rounded corners. Instead, you use corner effects.

Select a rectangle...

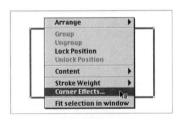

...choose Corner Effects from the Context menu (or press Command-Option-R/Ctrl-Alt-R).

InDesign displays the Corner Effects dialog box.

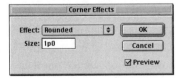

Choose a corner effect from the Effect pop-up menu. Enter a corner radius in the Size field.

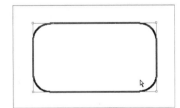

InDesign applies the corner effect.

Polygon Tool   The Polygon tool makes it easy to draw equilateral polygons, such as pentagons, hexagons, and dodecagons. (Polygons are closed geometric objects that have at least three sides; they're equilateral if all sides are the same length.) You can also use the Polygon tool to draw stars. Press N to select the Polygon tool. Under the Polygon tool, you'll find the Polygonal Frame tool.

To change which polygon the Polygon tool draws, double-click the tool in the Tools palette. InDesign displays the Polygon Settings dialog box (see Figure 1-40). Enter the number of sides you want in the Number of Sides field. If you want the polygon to be a star polygon, enter a percentage (from 0 to 99 percent) in the Star Inset field. If you don't want the polygon to be a star polygon, enter 100 percent in the Star Inset field.

FIGURE 1-40
Polygon Settings

Rotate Tool   To rotate the selection, select the Rotate tool from the toolbox and then drag the tool on your page. When you select the Rotate tool, InDesign displays the transformation center point icon on or around the selected object. The center point icon sets the center of rotation (the point you'll be rotating around), and corresponds to the selected point on the Transform palette's Proxy. Drag the transformation center point icon to a new location (or click one of the points in the Proxy) to change the center of rotation.

Hold down Shift as you drag the Rotate tool to constrain rotation to 45-degree increments (that is, as you drag the Rotate tool, InDesign snaps the selection to 0, 45, 90, 135, 180, 225, 270, and 315 degree angles).

Scale Tool   To scale (or resize) an object, select the object, select the Scale tool, and then drag the tool in the publication window. When you select the Scale tool, InDesign displays the transformation center point icon on or around the selected object. The location of the center point icon sets the center of the scaling transformation, and corresponds to the selected point on the Transform palette's Proxy. Drag the transformation center point icon to a new location (or click one of the points in the Proxy) to change the point you're scaling around.

Hold down Shift as you drag a corner handle to retain the object's proportions as you scale it.

Shear Tool

To put the Shear tool to work, press Shift-S (see Figure 1-41). InDesign switches to the Shear tool, and hides the Scale tool (you can bring the Scale tool back again by pressing Shift-S once again).

Shearing, or skewing, an object, alters the angle of the vertical or horizontal axes of the object. This makes it appear that the plane containing the object has been slanted relative to the plane of the publication window. To shear an object, drag the Shear tool in the publication window. As you drag, InDesign shears the object.

When you shear an object, InDesign distorts the stroke weights of the paths in the selection.

FIGURE 1-41
Shear tool

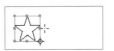

Set the position of the center of transformation (if necessary)...

...and drag the Shear tool. As you drag, InDesign displays a preview of the transformed bounding box.

When you stop dragging, InDesign skews the object.

Center of transformation icon.

Free Transform Tool

The Free Transform (press E) tool is a combination of the Scale and Rotate tools, plus some aspects of the Selection tool, all bundled into a single tool. What the tool does depends on the position of the cursor-when it's over one of an object's selection handles, it acts as the Scale tool-drag the Free Transform tool, and you scale the object around its center point. When the tool is just outside one of the selection handles, it behaves as if it were the Rotate tool-drag the tool to rotate the object around its geometric center. When the Free Transform tool is inside the bounds of the selection, it acts as a "move" tool-drag the tool to move the object.

This last feature is of particular interest when you need to move a graphic that's inside a clipping path that you've pasted inside another object. As you've probably discovered, it's way too easy to move the graphic without moving the clipping path, or to move the clipping path without moving the graphic. The Free Transform tool is the key to keeping the clipping path and the graphic together, as shown in Figure 1-42.

For more on working with the Free Transform tool, see Chapter 8, "Transforming."

Eyedropper Tool

The Eyedropper tool can pick up formatting attributes (from the fill and stroke of a path to the character and paragraph formatting of text) and apply them to other objects. You can also use the Eyedropper tool to sample a color in an object on an InDesign page-including imported graphics-and add it to your Swatches palette.

FIGURE 1-42

Selecting objects inside other objects

In this example, I've pasted a graphic with a clipping path inside a frame. Now I want to move the graphic inside the frame.

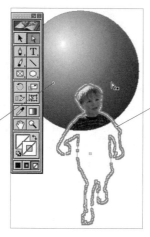

When I click the Direct Selection tool inside the frame to select its contents, InDesign selects the clipping path.

If I drag the clipping path, InDesign moves the path, but leaves the graphic behind.

If I select the graphic using the Direct Selection tool and then drag, InDesign moves the graphic, but doesn't move the clipping path. Argh!

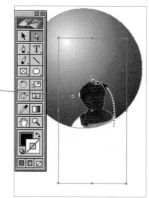

The solution? Select the path with the Direct Selection tool, then press V to switch to the Selection tool, and then press E to switch to the Free Transform tool.

Move, rotate, or scale the graphic using the Free Transform tool, and InDesign transforms the graphic and its clipping path as a unit.

To "load" the Eyedropper tool, click the tool on an object (the object doesn't have to be selected) if you have an item selected when you click, InDesign applies the attributes of the item under the cursor to the selected item. Click the loaded Eyedropper tool on an object to apply the formatting (see Figure 1-43). To apply the formatting to text, select the text, then click the Eyedropper tool on an object bearing the formatting you want.

Double-click the Eyedropper tool to display the Eyedropper Options dialog box. Use the settings in the three panels of this dialog box to define the attributes sampled and affected by the Eyedropper tool (see Figure 1-44).

Gradient Tool   Use the Gradient tool to apply gradients, or to adjust gradients you've applied. When you drag the Gradient tool, you're setting the location of the beginning and ending points of an existing gradient (see Figure 1-45).

FIGURE 1-43

Eyedropper tool

Select an object or a series of objects and then choose the Eyedropper tool from the Tools palette.

Position the Eyedropper tool over an object that has the formatting you want to apply.

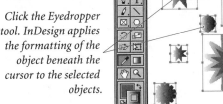

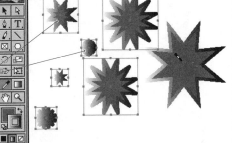

To format text using the Eyedropper tool, select the text using the Text tool.

Click the Eyedropper tool. InDesign applies the formatting of the object beneath the cursor to the selected objects.

Here's another method.

Select the Eyedropper tool from the Tools palette.

Position the cursor over an object and click. InDesign loads the Eyedropper tool with the formatting attributes of the object.

Click another object (it doesn't have to be selected. InDesign applies the formatting attributes to the object.

Zoom Tool

Use the Zoom tool to change the magnification in a publication window. To switch to the Zoom tool, press Z (obviously, this shortcut will work a lot better if you're not editing text). To switch to the Zoom tool temporarily, hold down Command-Spacebar/Ctrl-Spacebar (when you're done using the tool, InDesign will select the tool you were using before you switched to the Zoom tool).

Once you've switched to the Zoom tool (regardless of the method you've used), click the tool on the area you want to magnify, or drag a selection rectangle around it. To zoom out, hold down Option/Alt—you'll see that the plus ("+") inside the Zoom tool changes to minus ("-")—and then click or drag to zoom out.

For more on using the Zoom tool, see "Zooming," later in this chapter.

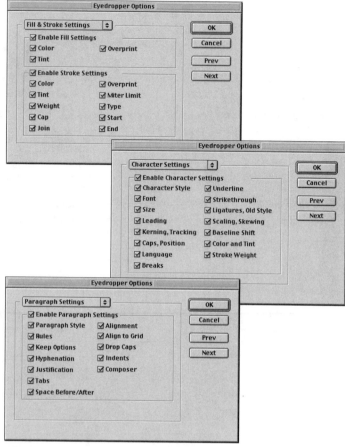

FIGURE 1-44
Eyedropper tool options

FIGURE 1-45
Gradient toolfigure

The Gradient tool affects the formatting of either the fill or stroke, depending on the state of the Fill or Stroke buttons.

Once you've applied a gradient to a path, you can use the Gradient tool to change the gradient.

To edit a gradient, select an object and drag the Gradient tool.

When you stop dragging, InDesign changes the appearance of the gradient.

Fill and Stroke

The Fill and Stroke buttons, or "selectors," near the bottom of the Tools palette control what part (the fill or the stroke) of the selected path or text is affected when you apply a color. To make a selector active, click it. InDesign brings the active selector to the front. Here are two very useful shortcuts:

◆ To swap colors—apply the color assigned to the fill to the stroke, or vice versa—click the swap fill and stroke icon (or press Shift-X).

◆ Press X (when you're not editing text) to switch between the Fill selector and the Stroke selector.

At the very bottom of the Tools palette, you'll find three more buttons—they're shortcuts for applying colors or gradients, or for removing a fill or stroke from an object. Click the Apply Color button to apply the current color (in the Color palette or Swatches palette) to the fill or stroke of the selected object. The state of the Fill and Stroke selector determines which part of the object is affected. Click the Apply Gradient button to apply the current gradient (in the Swatches palette or the Gradient palette), and click the Apply None button to remove the fill or stroke from the selected object.

As you'd expect, InDesign has shortcuts for these buttons, too.

◆ To apply the most recently used color to the current fill or stroke (which attribute is affected depends on which selector is active), press , (comma—again, this won't work when you have text selected).

◆ Press . (period) to apply the current gradient.

◆ Press / (slash) to remove the fill or stroke from the selected object or objects.

For more on applying colors, see Chapter 9, "Color."

Context Menus

Context menus are menus that pop up at the location of the cursor, and change according to the location of the cursor and the object you have selected (see Figure 1-46). On the Macintosh, you summon a context menu by holding down Control as you click the mouse button. In Windows, click the right mouse button to display the context menu.

Context menus give you a great way to do a lot of things—from changing the formatting of the selected objects to changing your magnification. Let's face it—your attention is where the cursor is, and there's a limited amount of it. Dragging the cursor across the screen to reach a menu or button is distracting, time-consuming, and tiring. The only thing wrong with InDesign's context menus is that you can't add more commands to them.

In addition, some commands—such as Fit Selection In Window—appear only on the context menus.

FIGURE 1-46

Context menus

Hold down Control and click to display the Context menu on the Macintosh; in Windows, press the right mouse button.

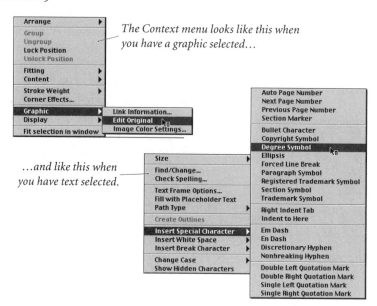

The Context menu looks like this when you have a graphic selected...

...and like this when you have text selected.

Keyboard Shortcuts

I hate it when software manufacturers change the keyboard shortcuts I know and love. Especially when they change an easy-to-reach, frequently-used shortcut to one that's difficult to use (PageMaker users, you know exactly what I'm talking about). InDesign gives me something I think should be in every application—I can make the program's keyboard shortcuts work the way I think they ought to.

For the most part, the keyboard shortcuts you can redefine are those that correspond to menu commands—you can't redefine some of the keyboard shortcuts that modify mouse actions. If you hate having Spacebar as the shortcut for the Hand tool, you're out of luck—at least this time around.

To define or redefine a keyboard shortcut, follow these steps (see Figure 1-47).

1. Choose Edit Shortcuts from the File menu (or press Command-Option-Shift-K/Ctrl-Alt-Shift-K). InDesign displays the Edit Shortcuts dialog box.

2. To create a new shortcut set, click the New Set button. To use an existing set, choose the set's name from the Set pop-up menu (if that's all you want to do, you can skip to Step 7). To delete a set, choose the set's name from the Set pop-up menu and then click the Delete button.

FIGURE 1-47

Editing keyboard shortcuts

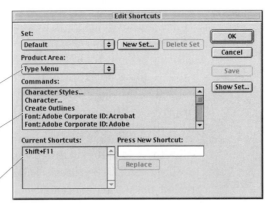

When you select an option from this pop-up menu…

…InDesign displays a list of the available commands.

When you select a command, InDesign displays the short-cut in this field.

Press Command-Option-Shift-K/ Ctrl-Alt-Shift-K to display the Edit Shortcuts dialog box.

Click the New Set button, or choose the QuarkXPress 4.0 shortcut set from the Set pop-up menu.

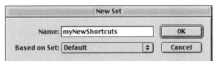

If you loaded the Quark XPress 4.0 set, and don't want to edit any shortcuts, click the Save button, then close the dialog box.

If you're creating a new set, InDesign displays the New Set dialog box. Enter a name for your set and click the OK button.

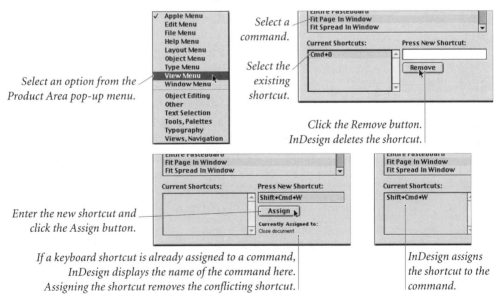

Select an option from the Product Area pop-up menu.

Select a command.

Select the existing shortcut.

Click the Remove button. InDesign deletes the shortcut.

Enter the new shortcut and click the Assign button.

If a keyboard shortcut is already assigned to a command, InDesign displays the name of the command here. Assigning the shortcut removes the conflicting shortcut.

InDesign assigns the shortcut to the command.

3. Choose an option from the Product Area pop-up menu. InDesign fills the Commands list with the available commands for the corresponding area of the program.

4. Select a command from the list. InDesign displays the current shortcut (or shortcuts) assigned to the command.

5. To remove a selected shortcut, click the Remove button. To assign a shortcut to a command, or to replace an existing shortcut, move the cursor to the Press New Shortcut field and press the keys you want to use for the shortcut. If the shortcut you've entered has already been assigned to a command, InDesign displays the Replace button (even if the current command has no keyboard shortcut).

6. Click the Add button to assign a shortcut to the command, or (if you had a shortcut selected) click the Replace button to replace the selected shortcut. Note that a single command can have multiple shortcuts assigned to it. If you want, you can save your changes without closing the dialog box by pressing the Save button.

7. Once you've changed all of the shortcuts you want to change, click the OK button to close the dialog box and save the set.

Keyboard shortcut sets are saved in the Short Sets folder in your InDesign folder. Want to take your keyboard shortcuts with you to another machine? Take the shortcuts file from your machine and copy it into the Short Sets folder of the copy of InDesign you'll be using. Open the Edit Shortcuts dialog box and choose your shortcut set from the Sets pop-up menu.

To return to InDesign's default keyboard shortcuts, all you need to do is choose the Default set from the Sets pop-up menu.

To view or print a complete listing of the shortcuts in a set, select the set from the Sets pop-up menu, then click the Show Set button. InDesign creates a text file containing a list of the shortcuts in the set and then opens it using the default text editor on your system (SimpleText on the Macintosh, Notepad in Windows). You can print or save this file for your reference.

A few thoughts on making up your own shortcuts. There are two approaches to making up your own keyboard shortcuts. The first is assign shortcuts using a key that has something to do with the name of the command—like "P" for "Print." Usually, these shortcuts are easy to remember. Another, and, in my opinion, better, approach is to analyze the way you work with commands, and then take the commands you use most often and assign them shortcuts that are easy to reach with one hand (usually the left hand, given that the shortcuts for copy, cut, and paste are all located on the left side of the keyboard).

What's the most frequently used keyboard shortcut? For me, it's got to be Fit Page In Window, because I navigate by zooming in with the Zoom tool, then I zoom out to the Fit Page In Window view, and then I zoom in on another part of the spread. The default shortcut for the Fit Page In Window view, Command-0/Ctrl 0 doesn't work for me. It's a long reach for the left hand, and 0 (zero) is a difficult key to hit without looking at the keyboard. I use Command-Shift-W/Ctrl-Shift-W to make this shortcut the same as it is in FreeHand—it's an easy, one-handed reach.

Setting Preferences

Why do applications have Preferences dialog boxes? I've heard more than one computer user complain about this ubiquitous feature of today's applications. It's simple: there's often more than one "right" way to do something. Rather than dictatorially decide to limit users, InDesign gives you a choice. Preferences are one way you can control the appearance and behavior of the program (defaults are the other—see "Setting Defaults," later in this chapter). They're a place where you can customize the program to better fit your work habits and personality.

To display InDesign's Preferences dialog box, choose General from the Preferences submenu of the File menu, or press Command-K/Ctrl-K. The Preferences dialog box contains a number of panels. Once you've opened the Preferences dialog box, you can move to the next panel by pressing the Next button, or display the previous panel by pressing the Previous button. Better yet, you can press Command-Down Arrow/Ctrl-Down Arrow to go to the next panel, or Command-Up Arrow/Ctrl-Up Arrow to display the previous panel.

You can also reach any panel of the Preferences dialog box directly, using the corresponding item of the Preferences submenu of the File menu.

I refer to each panel in the Preferences dialog as a separate dialog box—for example, I'll say "the General Preferences dialog box" rather than "the General panel of the Preferences dialog box." It's a little shorter, and the panels do function as if they were separate dialog boxes.

The settings in the Preferences dialog box affect the active publication—or, if no publication is open, control the preferences settings for any new publications you create. Changes you make to the preferences of one publication do not affect other publications.

General Preferences   The General Preferences dialog box (see Figure 1-48) is the "kitchen sink" of the dialog box universe—it contains the things that didn't fit anywhere else.

FIGURE 1-48
General Preferences
dialog box

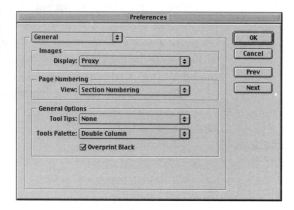

Images. The options in this section control the way that InDesign displays imported graphics (not just bitmap images, as you'd expect from the wording) on your screen (see Figure 1-49). This setting has no effect on the way the images print.

When you choose Full Resolution Images from the Display menu, InDesign gets its information about how to render an image (a TIFF, usually) from the original file that's linked to your publication, which means that InDesign renders the best possible display of the image for the current magnification.

Choose Proxy Images to have InDesign construct a low-resolution screen version of the imported graphic and use that image for display at all magnification levels.

Choose Gray Out Images to draw every image as a gray box.

You can change the display resolution of individual imported graphics using the options on the Display submenu of the Context menu. These settings override the option selected from the Display pop-up menu in the General Preferences dialog box.

FIGURE 1-49
Image display

Full Resolution Images setting

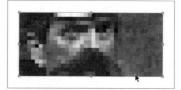

Proxy Images setting

Gray Out Images displays imported graphics as gray boxes.

Page Numbering. The options on the View pop-up menu change the way InDesign displays page numbers in the Pages palette. When you choose Absolute Numbering, InDesign numbers the pages sequentially, staring with page one, and pays no attention to the page numbering options of any of the sections in the publication. Choose Section Numbering to have InDesign display page numbers based on the page numbering options you've set up in the Section Options dialog box for each section. For more on setting up sections and numbering pages, see Chapter 2, "Page Layout."

Show Tool Tips. If you're having trouble remembering the names of the tools in InDesign's palettes, turn on the Show Tool Tips option. When you do, InDesign displays a small window containing a tool's name when your cursor passes over the tool (see Figure 1-50). Tool tips do not work for every tool or gadget in every palette. Once you're familiar with InDesign, turn this option off—showing tool tips does slow down the application.

FIGURE 1-50
Tool tips

When the Show Tool Tips option is on...

...InDesign displays information about the user interface item beneath the cursor.

Overprint Black. If you always want black ink to overprint, turn on the Overprint Black option. This setting overrides any changes you might make in the Print dialog box.

Tools Palette. You can choose to display the Tools palette in one of three arrangements: Single Row, Double row, or singlc column. Choose the option you like best.

Text Preferences   The Text Preferences dialog box (see Figure 1-51) contains preferences that affect the way that InDesign formats and displays text in your publications.

Character Settings. When you apply Superscript or Subscript to text, InDesign scales the selected characters and shifts their baseline position. How can you control the amount of scaling and baseline shift? That's where the options in this section come in. The Size fields are percentages of the size of the selected characters (you can enter from 1 to 200 percent); the Position fields are percentages of

FIGURE 1-51

Text Preferences
dialog box

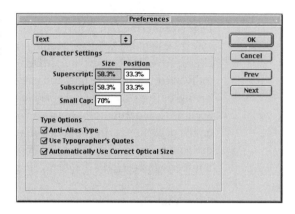

the leading (you can enter from −500 to 500 percent). When you apply Small Caps formatting to text, InDesign scales the selected characters by the percentage you enter in the Small Cap Size field (from one to 200 percent).

Note that these settings affect all superscript, subscript, and small caps formatting you've applied in the current document (like QuarkXPress, but unlike PageMaker, where superscript, subscript, and small caps formatting options are set at the character level).

For more on working with superscript, subscript, and small caps, see Chapter 4, "Type."

Anti-Alias Type. InDesign has its own built-in font rasterization capabilities, and can load and display fonts placed in its Fonts folder (inside your InDesign application folder), you can get by without Adobe Type Manager.

If you're already using Adobe Type Manager to anti-alias type on your screen, leave this option turned off. If you're not using Adobe Type Manager, turn it on (see Figure 1-52).

FIGURE 1-52

Anti-aliasing type

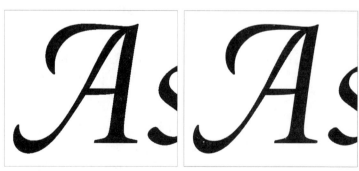

Anti-Alias Type option off   *Anti-Alias Type option on*

Use Typographer's Quotes. Using "typewriter" quotation marks and apostrophes (" and ') instead of their "typographic" (", ", ', and ') equivalents is one of the hallmarks of amateur desktop publishing design. On the Macintosh, it's sometimes difficult to remember what keys to press to get the preferred marks (press Option-Shift-] to produce an apostrophe), and on Windows systems it's downright painful (Alt-0144 will give you an apostrophe, for example). When you turn on the Use Typographer's Quotes option, InDesign enters the correct quotation marks for you as you type.

Automatically Use Correct Optical Size. This setting only comes into play when you're working with multiple master fonts—and then only with those fonts that have a defined optical size axis (not all multiple master fonts do).

If the multiple master font (or fonts) you're working with do include an optical size axis, turning this option on forces the font to use an optical size axis that matches the point size of the text, regardless of the optical size axis setting of the instance of the font. When this option is off, InDesign uses the optical size axis setting of the font instance.

Composition Preferences

Composition is the process of making type fit in the columns and pages in your publication. The options in the Composition Preferences dialog box (see Figure 1-53) give you some control over InDesign's excellent Multi-line Composer, and also help you catch composition problems. To really understand how these settings affect composition, you'll have to learn more about how the Multi-line composer does its work. See Chapter 4, "Type."

Adobe Multi-line Composer. The options in this section control InDesign's Multi-line Composer, and affect all paragraphs that use

FIGURE 1-53
Composition Preferences dialog box

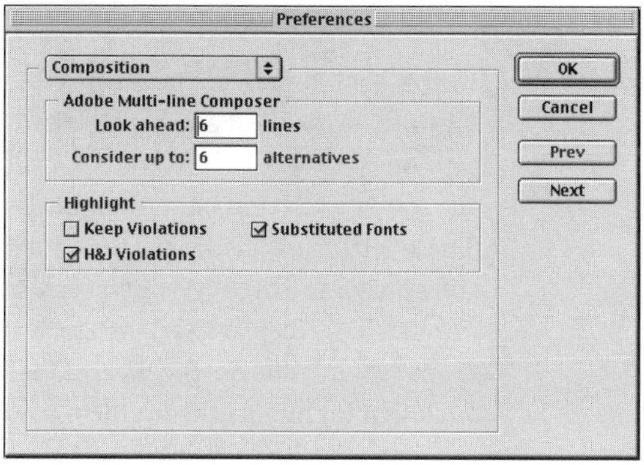

that composer. These settings have no effect on any paragraphs composed using the Single-line Composer.

Look Ahead. The value (from 3 to 30) you enter in this field sets the number of lines ahead (of the line currently being composed) the Multi-line Composer scans as it searches for alternative line break positions. The only reason to think about increasing this value is if the majority of your paragraphs are longer than six lines long.

Consider Up to N Alternatives. The value (from 3 to 30) you enter in this field sets the number of possible alternative line breaks considered by the Multi-line composer. Increasing this value can slow composition without too much improvement; decreasing it misses the point of the Multi-line Composer.

Highlight. The options in the Highlight section help you spot composition problems before they become printed mistakes. All three options work the same way: when they spot a composition problem (a place where InDesign has had to break your rules to lay out a publication, or where InDesign lacks the font to properly compose a piece of text), they "highlight" the text by drawing a colored bar behind it (see Figure 1-54)

FIGURE 1-54
Highlighting
composition problems

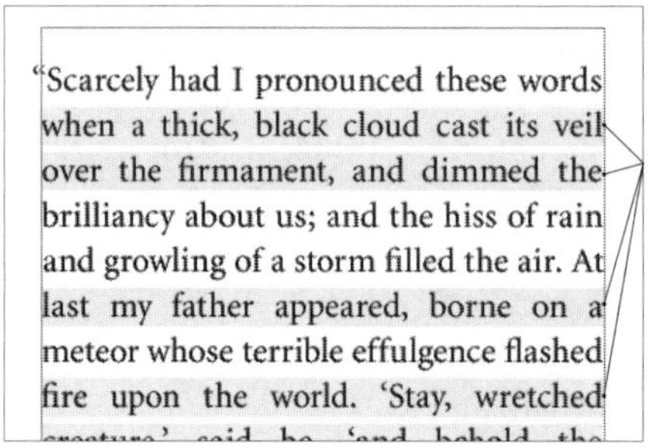

"Scarcely had I pronounced these words when a thick, black cloud cast its veil over the firmament, and dimmed the brilliancy about us; and the hiss of rain and growling of a storm filled the air. At last my father appeared, borne on a meteor whose terrible effulgence flashed fire upon the world. 'Stay, wretched

When you turn on the H&J Violations option in the Highlight section of the Text Preferences dialog box, InDesign highlights lines of text that break the spacing rules you entered in the Justification dialog box.

Keeps Violations. In the Keep Options dialog box (choose Keep Options from the Paragraph palette's menu, or press Command-Option-K/Ctrl-Alt-K), you'll see a variety of settings that determine the way the selected paragraph deals with column and page breaks. These settings, collectively, are called "keeps." InDesign will sometimes have to disobey your keeps settings in order to compose a publication. Keeps violations are very rare, but you can easily spot them by turning on the Keeps Violations option. When you do, InDesign highlights the problem paragraphs.

H&J Violations. When InDesign composes the text in your publications, it tries to follow the guidelines you've laid out for each paragraph (using the Justification dialog box), but, sometimes, it just can't. In those cases, InDesign applies word spacing that's looser or tighter than the minimum or maximum you've specified. This is known as an "H&J violation." When you turn on the H&J Violations option, InDesign highlights the problem lines by displaying a yellow bar behind the text. The intensity of the tint used to draw the bar gives you a rough indication of the severity of the "violation"—darker tints equal greater variation from your settings.

Substituted fonts. When you turn on the Substituted Fonts option, InDesign highlights text formatted using fonts you do not currently have loaded. This makes it very easy to spot that space character you accidentally formatted using Hobo before you left your office. The highlight color is pink.

Units & Increments Preferences

We've all got favorite units of measure—I'm partial to furlongs and stone, myself—so we should be able to choose what/which measurement system we use to lay out our pages. That's what the Units & Increments Preferences dialog box is for (see Figure 1-55).

FIGURE 1-55
Units & Increments
Preferences dialog box

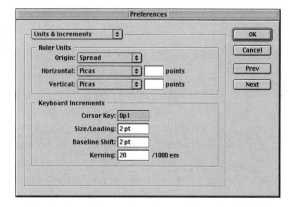

Ruler Units. The Origin pop-up menu sets the default location of the ruler zero point. choose Spread to have InDesign position the zero point at the upper-left corner of the spread. Choose Page, and InDesign locates the zero point at the upper-left corner of the page. Choose Spine, and the ruler zero point will appear at the top of the spine (regardless of the number of pages in the spread).

Use the Horizontal and Vertical pop-up menus to select the measurement units (inches, inches decimal, picas, points, millimeters, and ciceros) you want to use for the horizontal and vertical rulers.

In addition to the standard measurement systems, you can choose to use custom increments for either or both rulers. When you choose Custom, you can enter a distance in the field attached to the pop-up menu.

As you set up a publication's measurement units, there are two things you should keep in mind (they'll save you trips back to this dialog box):

◆ You can use the Context menu to change ruler units—Control-click (Macintosh) or Right-click on the ruler, and InDesign displays a Context menu containing the same options as you see in the Units & Increments Preferences dialog box.

◆ You can always override units of measurement in any field in any palette or dialog box in InDesign. For more on entering measurement unit overrides, see "Overriding Units of Measurement," earlier in this chapter.

Keyboard Increments. What happens when you push an arrow key? That depends on the settings you've entered in the following fields.

Cursor Key. When you have an object selected using the Selection tool, you can move it by pressing the arrow keys. How far do you want it to move with each key press? Enter that value in this field.

Size/Leading. When you have text selected (using the Text tool), you can increase or decrease the size and/or leading of the text by pressing keyboard shortcuts (by default, you press Command-Shift->/Ctrl-Shift-> to increase the size of the text; Command-Shift-</Ctrl-Shift-< to decrease the size; Option-Up arrow/Alt-Up arrow to increase the leading; or Option-Down arrow to decrease the leading). How much larger or smaller should the point size or leading get with each key press? Enter the amount you want in this field.

Baseline Shift. When you have selected text using the Text tool, you can increase baseline shift by pressing (by default) Option-Shift-Up Arrow/Alt-Shift-Up Arrow, or decrease baseline shift by pressing Option-Shift-Down Arrow/Alt-Shift-Down Arrow. How much baseline shift should each key press apply? Enter the amount you want in this field.

Kerning. When the text cursor is between two characters, you can apply kerning by pressing Option-Left Arrow/Alt-Left Arrow or Option-Right Arrow/Alt-Right Arrow. When a range of text is selected with the text tool, pressing this shortcut applies tracking. Enter the kerning amount you want to apply (in thousandths of an em) in this field.

Grids Preferences   InDesign can display two different types of grid: baseline and document. You control various aspects of their appearance using the options in this dialog box (see Figure 1-56). Both grids are very similar to the guides (ruler guides, margin guides, and column guides), and have a similar effect on items on your pages.

Baseline grid. The baseline grid is an array of horizontal guides that mark off the page in units equal to a specified leading amount (note that the baseline grid isn't really a grid, as it has no vertical lines).

FIGURE 1-56
Grids Preferences
dialog box

Choose one of InDesign's preset colors from the pop-up menu, or...

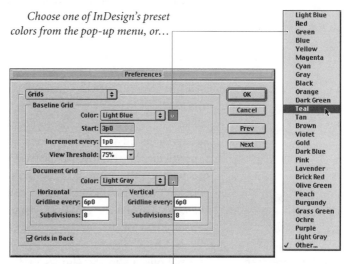

...double-click the color swatch to display a dialog box where you can define a custom color.

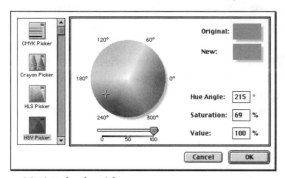

Macintosh color picker

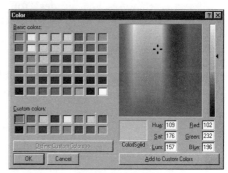

Windows color picker

Color. Choose a color for the baseline grid using the Color pop-up menu, or double-click the color well to display a color picker.

Start. Enter a value in the Start field to set the distance from the top of the page at which you want the baseline grid to begin.

Increment Every. Enter a distance—in general, the leading value of your publication's body text—in the Increment Every field.

View Threshold. Set the magnification at which the grid becomes visible in the View Threshold field.

Document grid. The document grid is a network of horizontal and vertical guidelines spaced a specified distance apart.

Color. Choose a color for the baseline grid using the Color pop-up menu, or double-click the color well to display a color picker.

Gridline Every. Enter the distance you want between grid lines in this field.

Subdivisions. Just as the document grid divides the page, subdivisions divide the grid into smaller sections. The number you enter in this field sets the number of subdivisions between each grid line. If you don't want to subdivide the document grid, enter 1 in this field. InDesign displays the grid subdivision lines using a tint of the color you specified for the document grid.

Guides Preferences

Use the options in the Guides Preferences dialog box (see Figure 1-57) to set the color you want to use to display margin and column guides. Why isn't there an option for setting the color of ruler guides? You don't have to use the same color for all of your ruler guides—you specify the color using the Ruler Guides dialog box.

Snap to Zone. Use this option to set the distance, in screen pixels, at which guides begin to exert their mysterious pull on objects you're drawing or dragging.

Guides in Back. Turn on this option to make the guides fall to the bottom of the stacking order of the layer they're on.

Dictionary Preferences

Choose a language from the dictionary pop-up menu to set the default dictionary used by the paragraphs in the publication (see

FIGURE 1-57
Guides Preferences
dialog box

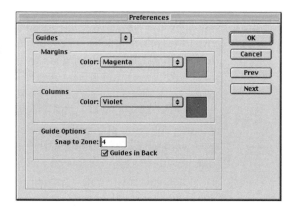

Figure 1-58). Any selection you make using the Language pop-up menu in the Paragraph palette overrides this setting. Some dictionaries might offer more than one option for hyphenation vendor and spelling vendor—if you're working with one that does, you'll see more than one choice on the corresponding pop-up menus. I've only ever seen the Proximity dictionaries.

For more languages and spelling, see Chapter 3, "Text."

FIGURE 1-58
Dictionary Preferences
dialog box

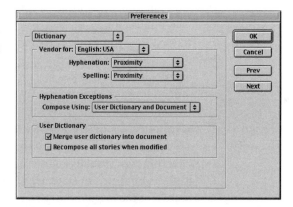

Reverting to Indesign's Original Preferences

InDesign's preferences are stored with the application's defaults (see "Setting Defaults," below) in the file InDesign Defaults. This file exists in different places on different systems; the best way to find it is to search for its file name. Delete this file, and InDesign will return to its original preferences.

Setting Defaults

"Defaults" are the settings you begin with when you start InDesign. InDesign's defaults control page size, fill type and stroke color, available styles, type specifications, and other details. InDesign has two kinds of defaults—application defaults and document defaults. Application defaults determine the appearance and behavior of all new publications; document defaults control the specifications of objects you create in a particular publication.

Neither document defaults nor application defaults change any existing objects or publications—you can change the defaults at any time without fear that you'll harm publications you've already laid out.

When you create a new InDesign publication, do you immediately add a set of colors to the Colors palette, change the default line weight, display the rulers, or add styles to the Style palette? If you do, you probably get tired of making those changes over and over again. Wouldn't it be great if you could tell InDesign to create new documents using those settings?

You can. To set InDesign's application defaults, close all publications (without closing InDesign), then, with no publication open (what I like to call the "no pub state," or, as my friend Steve Broback would say, "Utah"), add or remove styles and colors, set type specifications, and otherwise make the changes you've been making in each new publication.

The next time you create a new InDesign publication, it'll appear with the settings you specified.

Some document properties cannot be set as application defaults— you cannot, for example, create a new layer or add master pages.

Reverting to InDesign's Original Defaults

If you've gotten hopelessly away from InDesign's original defaults and want to go back to them, quit InDesign and then throw away two files: InDesign Defaults and InDesign SavedData (they're in different places on different systems, so the easiest way to find them is to search for the file names). When you restart InDesign, the program will regenerate the files using its original "factory" settings.

Publication Navigation

InDesign offers three ways to change your view of the publication: zooming, scrolling, and moving from page to page. Zooming changes the magnification of the area inside the publication window. Scrolling changes the view of the publication in the publication window without changing the magnification. Moving from page to page can be thought of as either automated scrolling or zooming, but I'm not sure which.

Zooming   Most of the time, I use zooming (that is, changing magnifications of the view of the publication) rather than scrolling (that is, changing the view of the publication without changing magnification) to move from one area of the page or pasteboard to another.

Zooming with the View menu. The View menu offers InDesign's "standard" magnifications, or views, and provides keyboard shortcuts for most of them (see Table 1-3).

To zoom to this view:	Press:
Actual size (100%)	Command-1/Ctrl-1
200%	Command-2/Ctrl-2
400%	Command-4/Ctrl-4
50%	Command-5/Ctrl-5
Fit Page in Window	Command-0/Ctrl-0
Fit Spread in Window	Command-Option-0/Ctrl-Alt-0
Zoom in	Command-+/Ctrl-+
Zoom out	Command-- (minus)/Ctrl--(minus)

All of these commands except Fit to Page center the object you've selected in the publication window. If you don't have an object selected, these shortcuts zoom in or out based on the center of the current view. Fit Page In Window centers the current page in a publication window. This makes Fit Page In Window the perfect "zoom-out" shortcut.

Fit Selection In Window. Another view command I use all of the time is Fit Selection In Window. Don't bother looking for it on the View menu—it's not there. Instead, it appears on the context menu when you have an object selected. It does just what it says—zooms (in or out) on the current selection and centers it in the publication window (see Figure 1-59). Press Command-Option-=/Ctrl-Alt-= to zoom to the Fit Selection In Window view.

Zooming with the Zoom tool. Another zooming method: choose the Zoom tool, point at an area in your publication, and click. InDesign zooms to the next larger view size (based on your current view—from 100% to 200%; for example), centering the area you clicked on in the publication window. Hold down Option/Alt and the plus ("+") in the Zoom tool changes to a minus ("-"). Click the Zoom tool to zoom out.

FIGURE 1-59
Fit selection in window

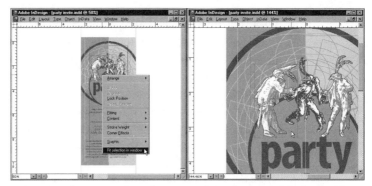

It doesn't really matter where the selection is hiding...

... "Fit Selection in Window" will find it and make it more visible.

Switching to the Zoom Tool. Press Command-Spacebar/Ctrl-Spacebar to temporarily change any tool into the Zoom tool to zoom in; or hold down Command-Option-Spacebar/Ctrl-Alt-Spacebar to change any tool into the Reducing Glass to zoom out.

The Best Way to Zoom. To zoom in, press Command/Ctrl and hold down Spacebar to turn the current tool (whatever it is) into the Zoom tool, then drag the Zoom tool in the publication window. As you drag, a rectangle (like a selection rectangle) appears. Drag the rectangle around the area you want to zoom in on, and release the mouse button. InDesign zooms in on the area, magnifying it to the a magnification that fits in the publication window (see Figure 1-60).

FIGURE 1-60
Drag magnification

Hold down Command-Spacebar/ Ctrl-Spacebar to switch to the Zoom tool.

Drag the Zoom tool around the area you want to magnify.

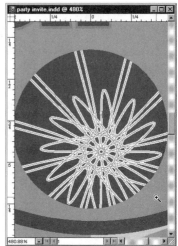

InDesign zooms in on the area you defined by dragging.

To zoom out, use one of the keyboard shortcuts—Command-0/Ctrl-0, for Fit Page In Window, is especially handy (it's even better if you redefine the shortcut to make it easier to reach with one hand—why take your hand off of the mouse if you don't need to?).

Entering a magnification percentage. To zoom to a specific magnification percentage, enter the percentage in the Magnification field and press Return/Enter. To "jump" into the Magnification field, press Command-Option-5/Ctrl-Alt-5. InDesign zooms to the percentage you specified (centering the selection, if any, as it does so).

Scrolling

As I said earlier in this chapter, I rarely use the scroll bars to scroll. So how do I change my view of my publication? I use the Hand tool (also known as the "Grabber Hand"), or I let InDesign do the scrolling for me as I move objects.

Scrolling with the Grabber Hand. So how do *you* use the Hand tool? Sure, you can always click on the Hand tool in the Tools palette, or press the keyboard shortcut to switch to the Hand tool, but there's a better way. Provided you're not editing text, holding down the Spacebar turns the cursor into the Hand tool. Avoid this shortcut if you are editing text—you'll enter spaces. Instead, hold down Option/Alt to switch to the Hand tool. Drag the Hand tool, and InDesign scrolls in the direction you're dragging (see Figure 1-61). When you stop dragging, InDesign switches back to the tool you were using before you used the Hand tool.

FIGURE 1-61
Using the Hand tool

If the cursor is in a text frame, or if text is selected, hold down Option/Alt instead of Spacebar.

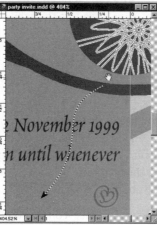

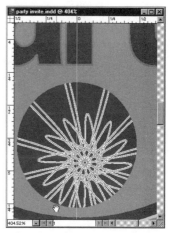

Hold down Spacebar to switch to the Hand tool, then drag the Hand tool to scroll.

When the publication window looks the way you want it to, stop dragging.

Scrolling as you drag objects. Don't forget that you can change your view by dragging objects off the screen. If you know an object should be moved to some point outside your current view, select the object and do one of the following things:

◆ To scroll down, drag the cursor into the scroll bar at bottom of the publication window. Don't drag the cursor off the bottom of the screen—InDesign won't scroll if you do this (for some unknown reason).

◆ To scroll to the right, move the cursor into the vertical scroll bar, or drag the cursor off of the left edge of the screen.

◆ To scroll to a point above your current view, drag the cursor into the horizontal ruler.

◆ To scroll to the left, drag the cursor into the vertical ruler (or off the screen, if the ruler is not visible).

The window scrolls as long as the mouse button is down. Sometimes it's the best way to get something into position.

InDesign won't let you drag objects to an area in the publication window that is behind a palette. If you drag the cursor into any palette other than the Library palette, InDesign displays the "prohibited" symbol. When you drop objects you're dragging into an area covered by a palette, InDesign bounces the objects back to their original locations. I guess it's trying to tell you that you can't drop objects into any palette other than the Library palette, but it can be a nuisance. You can't hide palettes while you're dragging objects, so you might want to get into the habit of hiding the palettes before you begin dragging.

Place Icons

When you place (that is, import) a file InDesign changes the cursor into an icon called a "place icon," or "place gun" (see Figure 1-62). You can click the place icon to specify the position of the upper-left corner of the incoming file, or you can drag the place icon to define the width and height of the file.

◆ To "unload" a place icon without placing the file, click the place icon on any of the tools in the toolbox.

◆ If you had a path or frame selected when you started the place operation, InDesign places the file in that object. This is, in

FIGURE 1-62
Place icon

Text place icon (manual flow)
Text place icon (semi-automatic flow)
Text place icon (autoflow)
Graphic place icon
Image place icon
Text place icon (in frame)
Text place icon (autoflow, in frame)
Image place icon (in frame)
Graphic place icon (in frame)

general, a very useful feature, but it can sometimes mean that imported files end up in frames you didn't want to fill with the file. When this happens to you, press Command-Z/Ctrl-Z (or choose Undo from the Edit menu), and InDesign will display the loaded place icon. Now you can click or drag the place icon to place the file.

I'll talk more about place icons in next chapter, and in Chapter 7, "Importing and Exporting."

Mangaging InDesign's Plug-ins

Everything you see in InDesign is provided by a plug-in. The "application" itself is little more than a plug-in manager. The functions we traditionally think of as being central to a page layout application—things like text composition, text editing, or basic drawing tools—they're all plug-ins. I'm not kidding.

This means that you can turn plug-ins on and off to customize InDesign to the way that you work and the publications you work with. Specifically, you can turn off the plug-ins you don't use.

To define the set of plug-ins InDesign will load the next time you start the program, choose Configure Plug-ins from the Apple menu on the Mac OS, or from the Help menu in Windows. InDesign dsiplays the Configure Plug-ins dialog box (see Figure 1-63).

Why would you want to turn plug-ins off? Simple—to reduce the amount of memory taken up by InDesign and to increase the speed of the application (slightly).

Some plug-ins are required by InDesign—they're the ones with the little padlock next to them. But all of the other plug-ins are fair game. Never use the Navigator palette? Turn it off!

My favorite candidate for shutdown is Adobe Online. Yes, it's cool to be able to go to adobe.com and download new plug-ins. But *how often do you really need to do that?* Once a month? Never?

FIGURE 1-63

Configure Plug-ins
Dialog box

FIGURE 1-63

Configure Plug-ins
Dialog box

*If you're not using a partic-
ular plug-in, click the check
mark to the left of the plug-
in's name to turn it off.*

*The next time you start
InDesign, the plug-in will
not be loaded.*

Getting Help

If you installed InDesign's online help system, you can display information on the meaning and use of specific InDesign features (see
Figure 1-64). Press Help/F1 to display the Help system.

FIGURE 1-64

Help system

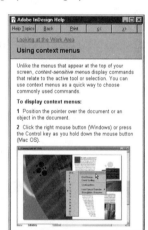

On with the Tour

At this point in the InDesign tour, we've seen most of the sights.
Don't worry if you're a little confused—it's hard to take it all in at
once. In the following chapters, I'll help you put the tools in context—so far, we've just talked about what the tools *are*. In the rest of
the book, I'll talk about that you can do with them.

2

Page Layout

Now that you know what's what, and what's where, in InDesign, it's time to create an InDesign publication and set up some pages. As you work your way through the process of defining the page size, margins, column layout, and master pages for your new publication, think ahead. How will the publication be printed? How will it be bound? Will you need to create a different version of the publication for a different paper size (such as switching from US Letter to A4 for an international edition)? Will you need to create a different version of the publication for online distribution?

I know, I know—having to think about these things and make design decisions early in the process can be boring. And InDesign makes it relatively easy to make changes to your layout late in the production process. Easy, but not without a certain amount of trouble. How high is your threshold of pain? Will it decrease as your deadline approaches? You decide.

Creating a New Publication

When you choose New from the File menu, InDesign displays the New Document dialog box (see Figure 2-1). You use the controls in this dialog box to set up the basic layout of the pages in your publication. Don't worry—you're not locked into anything; you can change these settings at any time, or override any of them for any page or page spread in your publication. Getting them right at this point, however, might save you a little time and trouble later on.

FIGURE 2-1

The New Document dialog box

Note: To enter the starting page number, you use section options (in the Pages palette).

Choose a page size from this pop-up menu...

...or enter a custom page size using these fields.

Enter page margin settings in the fields in this section. Note that the margin settings of individual master pages override these settings.

If you turn off the Facing Pages option, the "Inside" and "Outside" fields change to read "Right" and "Left."

Enter the number of pages you want.

Should InDesign create a text frame on the master page? If so, turn this option on. The width and height of this "automatic" text frame are defined by the area inside the page margins; its column settings correspond to the column settings for the page.

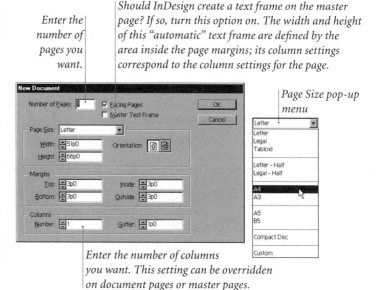

Page Size pop-up menu

Enter the number of columns you want. This setting can be overridden on document pages or master pages.

Inside margin

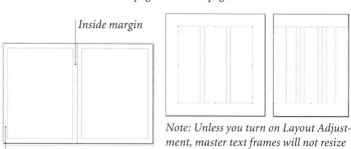

Outside margin

Note: Unless you turn on Layout Adjustment, master text frames will not resize when you change page size, margin, or column settings.

Setting New Document Defaults

Do you find that you frequently have to change the settings in the New Document dialog box? If you're in the United States and work with a magazine printed on A4 paper, for example, you'll rapidly tire of the New Document dialog box—because you'll have to choose the A4 paper size from the Page Size pop-up menu for each new publication you create. But you can't change the defaults in the New Document dialog box, because doing so simply creates another new publication. The following steps tell you how to change the defaults used by the New Document dialog box.

1. Open the Document Setup dialog box (press Command-Option-P/Ctrl-Alt-P or choose Document Setup from the File menu). Change the options in the dialog box to match the basic page layout you most commonly use. Press OK to close the dialog box when you're done.

2. Open the Margins and Columns dialog box (choose Margins and Columns from the Layout menu) and adjust the settings in the dialog box to match your typical publication. Click the OK button to close the dialog box.

The next time you display the New Document dialog box, you'll see that it contains the settings you specified.

Opening Publications

You know, I've been asked why I bother writing about the process of opening documents. Doesn't everyone know the drill by now? Nevertheless, I'll cover it because some readers might be new to computing altogether, and because InDesign offers a couple of slightly unusual options.

Choose Open from the File menu, or press Command-O/Ctrl-O, and InDesign displays the Open a File dialog box (see Figure 2-2). Locate and select the InDesign publication you want to open, then click the Open button and InDesign opens the selected publication in a new publication window.

The "twist" InDesign adds to the standard process of opening a publication has mainly to do with publications you've saved as templates (also known as "stationery" on the Macintosh), or publications you want to treat as templates (later in the chapter, I'll describe templates). To open a copy of the file, turn on the Open Copy option. InDesign opens an untitled copy of the file you selected. To open a template file for editing, turn on the Open Original option.

InDesign can also open PageMaker 6.5 or QuarkXPress 4.0 files. To do this on the Macintosh, choose All Documents from the Show pop-up menu in the Open dialog box; in Windows, choose the file type you want to open from the Files of Type pop-up menu, or choose All Documents. Select the file you want to convert, and then

FIGURE 2-2
The Open a File
dialog box

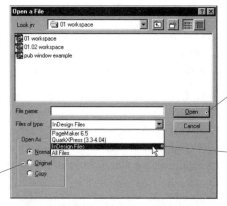

Locate and select a file using the file listing.

Click the Open button to open the publication.

Choose Normal to open the publication; choose Original to open and edit a file you've saved as an InDesign template file; and choose Copy to open a file as an untitled publication.

The option you choose from the Files of Type menu determines which files you see in the file list.

The Macintosh version of InDesign can display a preview of InDesign publications. To do this, click the Show Preview button. You can't view a preview of a Windows InDesign publication until you've saved it using the Macintosh version of the program.

click the Open button. InDesign converts the file and opens it as a new, untitled InDesign publication.

How well does this conversion process work? That depends on the publication you're trying to open, but you should never expect the conversion process to be perfect. There are simply too many differences in the capabilities of the different products.

InDesign will usually manage to capture the basic geometry of a publication, the position of imported graphics, and the content of text frames. InDesign will also do a good job of converting text formatting, though line endings may change due to InDesign's superior composition features (the Adobe Multi-line Composer is applied by default by the conversion process). The following sections provide more detail on what you can expect to see when you convert publications from other page layout programs.

QuarkXPress Files   Watch for the following changes:

◆ **Text on a path.** InDesign 1.0 does not support text on a path. When you open a QuarkXPress document containing text on a path, InDesign places that text in a standard text frame.

◆ **Dashed strokes and "fancy" borders.** InDesign converts strokes formatted using the QuarkXPress "Solid," "Dotted," "Dotted 2," "Dash Dot," stroke types but does not convert the "All Dots" stroke type, the multi-line stroke types ("Double," for example), or any of the border styles ("Yearbook," for example). Paths formatted using the unsupported stroke types are converted to paths formatted using the Solid stroke type.

◆ **Index and table of contents.** InDesign imports any index or table of contents stories in the QuarkXPress document as normal text, and does not convert any index entries or table of contents attributes of the text in the publication.

◆ **Leading.** InDesign and QuarkXPress use different methods to calculate the position of the first baseline of text in a text frame, so you can expect to see the position of the text in converted text frames move up or down on the page (depending on the settings in the First Baseline section of the Text tab of the Modify dialog box in QuarkXPress and the First Baseline section of the Text Frame Options dialog box in InDesign).

◆ **Keyboard shortcuts for styles.** QuarkXPress allows a wider range of keyboard shortcuts for paragraph and character styles than InDesign does. Any keyboard shortcuts in the QuarkX-Press document outside the range of shortcuts supported by InDesign (keys on the numeric keypad plus Command/Ctrl or Option/Alt) are not assigned to the styles in the converted publication.

◆ **Non-printing objects.** If you've turned on the Suppress Printout option in the Modify dialog box for any objects in the QuarkXPress document, InDesign places those objects on a separate, non-printing layer (named "Non-printing items") in the converted publication.

◆ **Special characters.** InDesign converts all em spaces in the QuarkXPress publication to standard em spaces (versions of QuarkXPress prior to 4.0 use the composed width of two zeros to set the width of an em space; version 4.0 and higher use this value as the default width of an em). QuarkXPress "flex space" characters convert to standard word spaces. Uppercase characters with accents display and print differently in InDesign than they do in QuarkXPress.

◆ **"Colorized" images.** InDesign can apply colors to bilevel (black-and-white) and grayscale TIFF images; QuarkXPress can apply color to other image file formats. When, during the conversion process, InDesign encounters a "colorized" image in one of the other formats, it converts the image, but does not apply the color.

◆ **Gradients.** InDesign can distinguish properly between linear and radial gradients, but the gradients applied to the resulting InDesign objects will contain only two gradient stops, regardless of the gradient's definition in the QuarkXPress document.

◆ **Guides.** Ruler guides can shift slightly on the page or pasteboard during the conversion process. In general, the amount of the shift depends on the measurement system you're using. If you're using points, or picas and points, InDesign rounds guide positions to the nearest whole point. If you're using inches, you can count on InDesign correctly positioning a guide when the guide's position uses two decimal places (e.g., .25), or when the guide's position falls on an "even" location (such as .125 or .625), but not when the position is less common (.306, for example, is usually changed to .3056).

PageMaker files   As you convert, or prepare to convert, publications from PageMaker to InDesign, keep the following in mind.

◆ **Pasteboard items.** Any objects on the pasteboard in a PageMaker publication are placed on the pasteboard of the first spread in the converted publication.

◆ **Master page items.** All master page items are assigned to a layer named "Master."

◆ **Ruler guides.** All ruler guides in the PageMaker publication are converted and are placed on a new layer named "Guides."

◆ **Non-printing objects.** If you've suppressed the printing of an object in PageMaker (to do this, you select the object and choose Non-Printing from the Element menu), InDesign moves those objects to a new layer named "Non-printing items," and then makes that layer a non-printing layer.

◆ **Book list.** InDesign has no corresponding feature, so the book list of the PageMaker publication is not copied to the InDesign version of the publication.

◆ **Composition.** InDesign applies the Adobe Multi-line Composer to all of the paragraphs in the converted publication. Because this composition method is very different from (and better than) the composition system found in PageMaker, many of the line endings and column depths in the publication will change. The Adobe Single Line Composer is similar to PageMaker's composition system, and you can apply it to the paragraphs in the publication if you like. If you do this, the resulting line endings might be more similar to those of the original PageMaker publication (then again, they might not, as the composition system and hyphenation settings differ).

◆ **Leading.** PageMaker has three leading methods: Top of Caps, Proportional, and Baseline. InDesign's leading method is most similar to PageMaker's Baseline leading method. When you convert a PageMaker publication, you can expect text in paragraphs using the other PageMaker leading methods to shift up or down on the page (usually down).

In addition, the position of the first baseline of text in a text frame is determined by the Offset pop-up menu in the First Baseline section of the Text Frame Options dialog box. By default, InDesign applies the Ascent option—which can make text in converted PageMaker publications shift vertically. If you've been using the Baseline leading method in your PageMaker publications (as I think you should), choose Leading from the Offset pop-up menu to restore the position of your text baselines to their original position.

◆ **Text position.** In PageMaker, you can choose to position the text in a text frame at the top, bottom, or middle of the frame (to do this, you use the options on the Vertical Alignment pop-up menu in the Frame Options dialog box). InDesign lacks these options, and positions text at the top of the frame.

◆ **Font and type style conversion.** When, during the process of converting a PageMaker publication, InDesign encounters a font change or type style change, it tries to map the PageMaker formatting into its InDesign equivalent. This isn't always possible. When you apply the font "Minion" and type style "Bold" to text in a PageMaker publication, PageMaker applies Minion Semibold—and that's what InDesign applies. When you apply the type style "Bold" to Minion Bold or Minion Black however, InDesign displays an error message (see Figure 2-3) and applies Minion Bold. The conversion is actually better than

FIGURE 2-3
Fonts not found during
conversion

I'd expected, given the differences in specifying fonts in the
two programs—but you'll have to closely check converted
publications against your original PageMaker versions.

InDesign does not support the PageMaker type style
Shadow, and formats any text using that type style as plain text.
InDesign converts text formatted using the Outline type style
to text formatted with a hairline (.25 point) stroke and a fill
of the color "Paper." You'll also notice that the position and
thickness of the bar in text using the Underline or Strikethrough type styles changes slightly in the InDesign version
of the publication.

◆ **Tracking.** InDesign removes all kerning applied by PageMaker's
Expert Tracking command (the tracks "Very Loose," "Loose,"
"Normal," "Tight," and "Very Tight"). InDesign's "tracking" is
the same as PageMaker's Range Kerning feature, not PageMaker's Expert Tracking feature.

◆ **Colors.** Colors defined using the HLS and Hexachrome color
models are converted to RGB colors. Tints are converted to new
colors in the Swatches palette (tints based on colors defined
using the HLS or RGB model will become new RGB colors; tints
based on process colors will become new process colors).

◆ **Image control settings.** InDesign doesn't have a set of features
corresponding to those found in PageMaker's Image Control
dialog box, and any settings you've applied to images using
these controls will be removed from the images in the converted
version of the publication. Note that InDesign doesn't have a
way to apply halftone screen settings to individual images.

◆ **Masks and masked objects.** If you've used an object to mask
other objects in a PageMaker publication, those objects will be
pasted into the masking object in the InDesign publication (you
can select them using the Direct Selection tool).

◆ **Fill patterns.** PageMaker features a variety of goofy fill patterns
(making possible what Edward Tufte dubbed "chartjunk") that

date from the early Stone Age of desktop publishing. InDesign doesn't have a similar feature, so these anachronisms are converted to solid fills during the conversion process.

◆ **Imported graphics.** Even if an image is embedded in a Page-Maker publication, InDesign requires an up-to-date link to the original version of the graphic. If InDesign can't find the original graphic, it uses the screen preview image in the PageMaker publication (if any such image exists).

   If you've placed a PDF in the PageMaker publication you're converting, InDesign will always place the first page of that PDF in the InDesign version of the publication—regardless of the page you selected to place in PageMaker.

   Finally, any graphics you've placed in a PageMaker publication using OLE (Object Linking and Embedding) methods (usually the Insert Object command in the Windows version of PageMaker) will not be converted.

◆ **Table of contents and index.** InDesign converts any indexes or table of contents in the PageMaker publication to plain text (that is, the text appears in the InDesign publication, but it's lost its "magic" properties. Any index entry markers in the text are ignored by InDesign. The Include in Table of Contents attribute of paragraphs in the PageMaker publication is also ignored as InDesign converts the paragraphs.

Saving Publications

To save a publication, choose Save from the File menu (or press Command-S/Ctrl-S). To save a publication under a different name, choose Save As (or press Command-Shift-S/Ctrl-Shift-S), and InDesign will display the Save File As dialog box. Use this dialog box to set a location for the new file, assign a file name, and decide whether the file should be saved as a publication file or as a template.

If you're trying to save the file in a format other than an InDesign file, the command you want is not save but export. For more on exporting publications or parts of publications in file formats other than InDesign's native format, see Chapter 7, "Importing and Exporting."

Saving as a Template   Here's a process I've gone through several times. Stop me if you've heard this one before. I need to base a new publication on the design of a publication I've already laid out. I want to open the older publication, then save it under a new name, and then change its content. I open the publication, replace a few elements and delete others, and edit and format text. Then I save the file.

And only then do I realize that I haven't renamed the publication, and that *I've just written over a publication I probably wanted to keep.* You can undo many stupid actions in InDesign—but an inadvertent "Save" isn't one of them.

Has this ever happened to you? If not, please accept my hearty congratulations. If so, you should know that the ability to save or open a file as a template is something that was developed for marginally competent people like you and me. When you try to open a file that was saved as a template, InDesign automatically opens a copy of the file (though it doesn't select the Copy option in the Open dialog box). If, at that point, you try to save the file, InDesign will display the Save As dialog box. Which means you can proceed with your plan to save the publication under a new name. Remember? Your plan?

To save an InDesign publication as a template in Windows, choose Save As from the File menu. InDesign displays the Save As dialog box. Enter a name for the template file and then Choose InDesign Template from the Save As Type pop-up menu. Click the Save button to save the template file.

On the Macintosh, choose Save As from the File menu to display the Save As dialog box. Choose Stationery Option from the Format pop-up menu. InDesign Displays the Stationery Option dialog box. Turn on the Stationery option, then click OK to close the dialog box. Click the Save button in the Save As dialog box to save your publication.

You can also choose to open any publication as a template by turning on the Open Copy option in the Open a File dialog box. InDesign will open a new, untitled publication with the contents of the file you selected.

Crash Recovery

It will happen. At some point, your computer will suddenly stop working. A wandering child, dog, or co-worker will trip over the power cord, or accidentally press the reset switch. A lightning storm will leave your area without electrical power. Or the software we jokingly refer to as the "operating system" will fail for some unknown reason.

At this point, it's natural to assume you've lost work—and maybe that you've lost the file forever. That is, after all, the way things work in most other programs.

But it's not true for InDesign. InDesign keeps track of the changes you've made to a document—even for an untitled document you haven't yet saved. When you restart InDesign after a system failure, the program reads from a file named InDesign SavedData. This file is saved in different places on different operating systems, so the best way to find it is to use your operating system's Search utility (Sherlock on most Macintosh systems; Find Files or Folders on the Start menu in most Windows systems) to find the file. InDesign uses this file to reconstruct the publication or publications that were open when your system crashed. Because InDesign uses the Saved-Data file to keep a record of your actions—which is how you get the "Undo" feature—you'll be right back where you left the program.

If you don't want to recover the most recent changes you made to a publication before a crash (which you might want to do if you felt that your changes caused the crash), delete this file. You should also delete this file if InDesign is crashing on startup as it tries to read the file. In this case, the file has been damaged and cannot be opened—you'll have to rebuild the publication from a previous version (or from scratch, if you hadn't saved the file). You should also delete the files in the InDesign Recovery folder (which you'll find in the same folder as the InDesign SavedData file).

Setting Basic Layout Options

As I said earlier, you can always change the margins, columns, page size, and page orientation of a publication. You change the margin and column settings using the Margins and Columns dialog box, and you can apply these changes to any page, page spread, or master page in a publication.

Changing Page Size and Orientation

Page size and page orientation affect the entire document (you can't mix page sizes and page orientations in a file), and you use the Document Setup dialog box (press Command-Option-P/Ctrl-Alt-P to display this dialog box, or choose Document Setup from the File menu) to change these settings. To change the page size, choose a new page size for the publication from the Page Size pop-up menu (or enter values in the Width and Height fields); to change the page orientation, click the orientation button corresponding to the page orientation you want.

If you've turned on InDesign's layout adjustment feature, InDesign might move objects and guides on your pages when you change the page size or page orientation. See "Adjusting Layouts," later in this chapter, for more on this topic.

Specifying Margins and Columns

You aren't stuck with the margin and column setup you specified in the New Document dialog box—you can change margin and column settings for any page, at any time. To change new margin and column settings, select the page or pages you want to change, and then choose Margins and Columns from the Layout menu (see Figure 2-4). Click the OK button to close the dialog box, and InDesign applies the new margin and column settings to the selected pages. To reset the fields in the dialog box to the publication's default margin and column settings, hold down Option/Alt. InDesign changes the Cancel button into the Reset button. Click the Reset button to return the fields to their default state.

To create columns of unequal width, drag the column guides on the page (see "Adjusting Column Guides," later in this chapter).

FIGURE 2-4
Margins and Columns dialog box

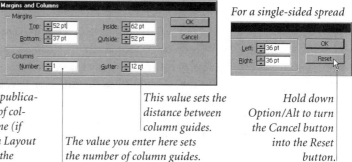

For a single-sided spread

Changing column settings for the publication does not change the number of columns in the master page text frame (if any exist) unless you've turned on Layout Adjustment, and has no effect on the number of columns in other text frames.

This value sets the distance between column guides.

The value you enter here sets the number of column guides.

Hold down Option/Alt to turn the Cancel button into the Reset button.

What happens to the objects on a page when you change the margin and column settings for that page? Do they reposition themselves relative to the new margins? Or do they stay put? That depends on the settings in the Layout Adjustment dialog box. See "Adjusting Layouts," later in this chapter, for more on adjusting layouts.

Guides

InDesign can display three types of guide: margin guides, column guides, and ruler guides. Guides are nonprinting guidelines you can use for positioning objects on the pages and pasteboard of an InDesign publication. Margin guides appear inside the page margins for a particular page. Column guides are actually pairs of guides that move as a unit. The space between the two guides making up the column guide is the gutter, or column spacing. This built-in spacing makes these guides good for—you guessed it—setting up columns. A ruler guide is a horizontal or vertical guideline you can use as an aid to aligning or positioning page items.

You use guides to mark a position on the page or pasteboard. The most important thing about guides is not just that they give you a visual reference for aligning objects to a specific location, but that they can exert a "pull" on objects you're moving or creating. To turn on that "pull," choose Snap to Guides from the View menu. When this option is on, and you drag an object within a certain distance of a guide, InDesign snaps the object to the guide.

This is one of my favorite psychocybernetic illusions—as an object snaps to a guide, your nervous system tells you that your hand can feel the "snap" as you drag the mouse. Turning on Snap to Guides can't physically affect the movement of your mouse, of course, but the illusion is very useful.

When you want to drag an object freely, without having it snap to any guides it encounters on its path across the publication window, turn Snap to Guides off. Do not try to align an object to a guide while Snap to Guides is turned off, however—there aren't enough pixels available on your screen to allow you to do a good job of this at any but the highest magnifications (see Figure 2-5).

Objects do not snap to guides when guides are hidden. This includes guides that are on a hidden layer.

FIGURE 2-5
Don't trust your screen

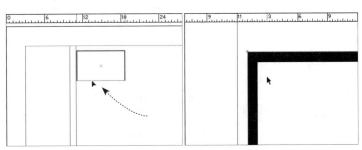

When InDesign's Snap to Guides feature is turned off, it's easy to think that you've gotten an object into perfect alignment with a guide...

...but zooming in will often show you that you've missed the guide. Turning on Snap to Guides can help.

Hiding and Displaying Guides

Tired of looking at all of the guides? To hide all guides, choose Hide Guides from the View menu (press Command-;/Ctrl-;). To display the guides again, choose Show Guides (press Command-;/Ctrl-; again).

To hide only the document grid, choose Hide Document Grid from the View menu, or press Command-'/Ctrl-'. Choose Show Document Grid, or press the keyboard shortcut again to show the document grid.

To hide only the baseline grid, choose Hide Baseline Grid from the View menu or press Command-Option-'/Ctrl-Alt-'. Choose Show Baseline Grid or press the keyboard shortcut again to show the baseline grid.

Note that you can also make guides disappear by changing the view threshold associated with the guides (see Figure 2-6). For the document grid, baseline grid, margin guides, and column guides, you set the view threshold using the Preferences dialog box (see Chapter 1, "Orientation."). For individual ruler guides, use the View Threshold field in the Ruler Guides dialog box (select a guide and choose Ruler Guides from the Layout menu or the context menu).

FIGURE 2-6
Guide view threshold

The View Threshold of these ruler guides is set to 100%...

...the View Threshold of these ruler guides is set to 5%.

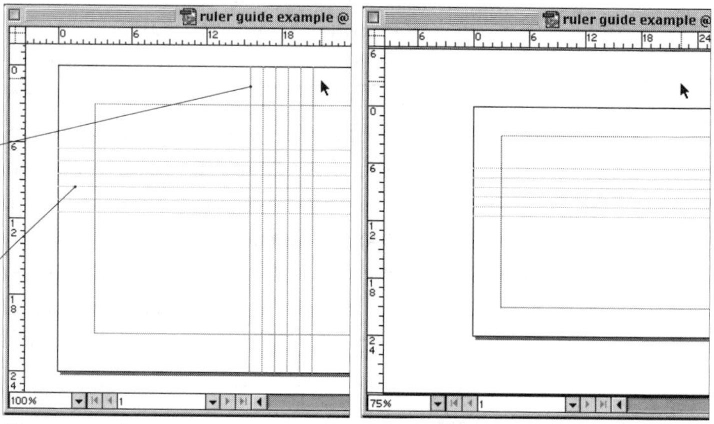

Now you see 'em...   *...now you don't.*

Adjusting Column Guides

The method you use to adjust the position of column guides depends on what you're trying to do. If you're trying to divide the area inside the page margins into equal columns, select the page and enter a new value in the Number field in the Columns section of the Margins and Columns dialog box.

If, on the other hand, you're trying to get columns of unequal width, you can adjust the column guides by dragging them on the page (see Figure 2-7).

You can't adjust the distance inside the column guides by dragging—you'll have to go to the Margins and Columns dialog box. To change the distance inside the column guides, enter a new value in the Gutter field (see Figure 2-8).

When you open the Margins and Columns dialog box after you've set up a custom column guide arrangement, InDesign enters

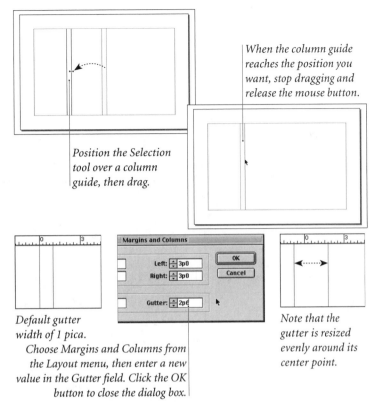

FIGURE 2-7

Creating columns of unequal width

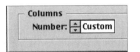

When you create columns of unequal width, InDesign displays "Custom" in the Number field of the Margins and Columns dialog box.

When the column guide reaches the position you want, stop dragging and release the mouse button.

Position the Selection tool over a column guide, then drag.

FIGURE 2-8

Adjusting gutter width

Default gutter width of 1 pica.

Choose Margins and Columns from the Layout menu, then enter a new value in the Gutter field. Click the OK button to close the dialog box.

Note that the gutter is resized evenly around its center point.

"Custom" in the Number field. Do not enter a number in this field, or InDesign will move your column guides so that they evenly divide the space between the margins. If you change the gutter width without touching the Number field, InDesign leaves your column guides in their original positions, but changes the space inside each guide.

You should also bear in mind that text frames can, by themselves, contain multiple columns of equal width. For more on this topic, see Chapter 3, "Text." Sometimes it's easier to work with a single multi-column text frame than with multiple single-column text frames.

Creating a New Ruler Guide

To create a new ruler guide, position the cursor over one of the rulers (for a horizontal ruler guide, move the cursor to the vertical ruler; for a vertical ruler guide, use the horizontal ruler) and then drag. As you drag, InDesign creates a new ruler guide at the position of the cursor. When you've positioned the ruler guide where you want it, stop dragging. InDesign adds a ruler guide (see Figure 2-9).

To create a horizontal ruler guide that crosses the current spread, including the pasteboard (rather than the current page), hold down Command/Ctrl as you drag the guide. To adjust this type of ruler

FIGURE 2-9
Creating a ruler guide

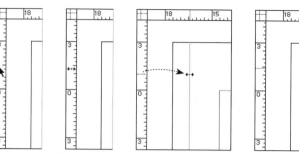

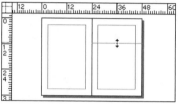
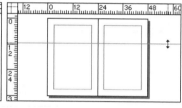

*Position the cursor over a
ruler, then hold down the
mouse button...*

*...and drag. As you
drag, a ruler guide
follows the cursor.*

*When the ruler
guide reaches the
position you want,
stop dragging.*

*Drag a ruler guide on a page to limit
the guide to that page...*

*...or drag the cursor outside the
spread to create a guide that crosses
pages in the spread.*

guide, drag the guide on the pasteboard—if you drag it on a page,
InDesign will limit the guide to that page.

When you drag a ruler guide into the pasteboard, it automatically extends to the width (for a horizontal ruler guide) or height
(for a vertical guide) of the pasteboard. If you want, you can use
guides on the pasteboard to align objects before dragging the objects
onto a page.

You can also double-click a ruler to create a new ruler guide—
InDesign creates a guide at the point at which you clicked.

**Adding Ruler Guides
around an Object**

InDesign doesn't have the ability to automatically position a ruler
guide at the top, left, right, bottom, or center of a selected object.
Luckily, one of the scripting examples on the InDesign CD can do
this for you (I know it can—I wrote it). The script is named Add
Guides, and you'll find it in the Scripting folder inside the Adobe
Technical Information folder. Run the script, and InDesign adds
guides around the selected object or objects. If you're using Windows, the script will display a dialog box you can use to set the positions of the ruler guides (see Figure 2-10).

This script is especially useful when you're setting up a publication for use with InDesign's layout adjustment features.

FIGURE 2-10
Add Guides script

Select an object.

Run the script. Choose the locations of the guides you want to add and click the Add Guides button.

InDesign adds guides at the locations you specified.

Selecting Ruler Guides

To select a ruler guide, click on the guide using one of the selection tools, or drag a selection rectangle over the guide. This differs from PageMaker and QuarkXPress, where you cannot select a ruler guide as you would any other object. You can select multiple ruler guides at once by dragging a selection rectangle over them. If the selection rectangle touches an object, InDesign selects the object, in preference to any ruler guides touching the selection rectangle—you cannot select both ruler guides and objects in the same selection. When a ruler guide is selected, it displays in the layer color of the layer you assigned it to.

Editing Ruler Guides

To change the location of a ruler guide, do one of the following.

◆ Drag the guide (using the Selection or Direct Selection tool).

◆ Select the ruler guide and then enter a new position in the X field (for a vertical guide) or in the Y field (for a horizontal guide) of the Transform palette.

◆ Select the guide and press an arrow key to "nudge" the guide one direction or another.

You can also select a series of ruler guides and drag them, as a unit, to a new location (see Figure 2-11).

Moving a Ruler Guide to a Specific Layer

You can assign a ruler guide to a layer as you would any other selected object—drag the Proxy that appears in the Layers palette up or down, then drop it on the layer to which you want to send the guide (see Figure 2-12).

The guide will appear on top of other objects on that layer if you turned off the Guides in Back option in the Guides Preferences dialog box, or behind them (if you turned the option on).

FIGURE 2-11
Moving multiple guides

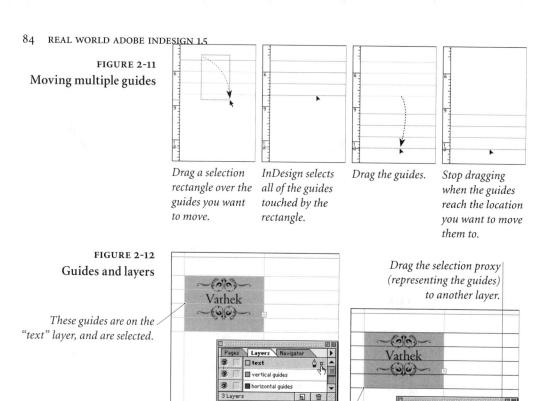

Drag a selection rectangle over the guides you want to move.

InDesign selects all of the guides touched by the rectangle.

Drag the guides.

Stop dragging when the guides reach the location you want to move them to.

FIGURE 2-12
Guides and layers

These guides are on the "text" layer, and are selected.

Drag the selection proxy (representing the guides) to another layer.

At this point, the guides appear to be in front of the text—guides always come to the front when selected.

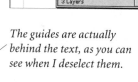

The guides are actually behind the text, as you can see when I deselect them.

Setting Guide Options

When you create a ruler guide, InDesign applies the default guide color (which you specified in the Guides Preferences dialog box) and a default view threshold (usually 5%) to the guide, but you can change these options if you want (see Figure 2-13).

1. Select the ruler guide (or guides).

2. Choose Ruler Guides from the context menu (or choose Ruler Guides from the Layout menu). InDesign displays the Ruler Guides dialog box.

3. Choose one of InDesign's preset colors from the Color pop-up menu, or create a custom guide color by double-clicking the color well to the right of the pop-up menu. When you do this, InDesign displays the Color dialog box. Specify a color using

the controls in this dialog box, then click the OK button to close the dialog box.

4. Click the OK button to close the Ruler Guides dialog box. InDesign displays the guide (or guides) in the color you chose.

5. You can also change the view threshold of the selected ruler guide by entering a new value in the View Threshold field of the Ruler Guides dialog box. The percentage you enter is the percentage magnification at and above which you want the ruler guide to appear. Enter 5% to make the guide visible at all magnifications.

FIGURE 2-13
Setting guide options

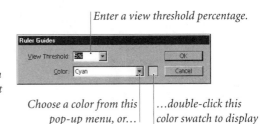

Enter a view threshold percentage.

Select a guide, then display the Context menu and choose Ruler Guides.

Choose a color from this pop-up menu, or...

...double-click this color swatch to display the Color dialog box.

Why would you want to assign different colors to guides? Guides are such useful tools that I find I use *lots* of them. Color coding guides that I use for different tasks makes it easier for me to see what's going on. One set of guides, for example, might be used for aligning captions in one illustration; another set might be used in a different illustration. Applying colors, changing view thresholds, and assigning guides to layers helps control the way that InDesign draws the guides in the publication window.

Note that guides always take on the layer selection color of their layer when they're selected.

Locking Ruler Guides

To lock the position of a ruler guide, choose Lock Position from the Object menu (or press Command-L/Ctrl-L), or display the Context menu and choose Lock Position (see Figure 2-14). Once you've locked the position of a ruler guide, you can change the color of the guide, move the guide to another layer, or change its view threshold, or copy the guide, but you can't change its position.

To unlock the guide, select the guide and choose Unlock Position from the Object menu, or choose Unlock Position from the Context menu.

You can lock all ruler guides by pressing Command-Option-;/ Ctrl-Alt-; (or by choosing Lock Guides from the View menu or the context menu).

FIGURE 2-14
Locking ruler guides

To lock the position of a ruler guide, select the guide and choose Lock Position from the Context menu.

To unlock a locked ruler guide, select the guide and choose Unlock Position from the Context menu.

You can also lock the position of guides by locking the layer containing the guides.

Finally, you can lock all guides by choosing Lock Guides from the View menu (or the Context menu). When you do this, you're locking more than guide position—you won't be able to select a guide until you choose Unlock Guides (from the View menu or the Context menu).

Deleting Ruler Guides

To delete a ruler guide (or guides), select the guide (or guides) and press the Delete key. Trying to drag the guide onto a ruler or out of the publication window (the technique used in PageMaker and QuarkXPress) simply scrolls your view of the publication window, so don't bother.

Copying Ruler Guides

You can also copy selected ruler guides and paste them into other spreads or publications. When you paste, the guides appear in the positions they occupied in the original spread (that is, they're not pasted into the center of the publication window as page objects are), provided the page sizes are the same (see Figure 2-15). If the page sizes are not the same, InDesign gets as close to the original positions as it can.

FIGURE 2-15
Copying ruler guides

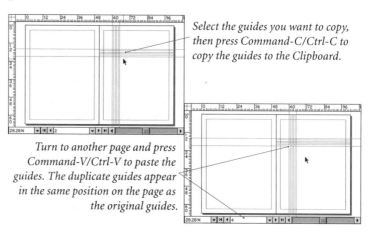

Select the guides you want to copy, then press Command-C/Ctrl-C to copy the guides to the Clipboard.

Turn to another page and press Command-V/Ctrl-V to paste the guides. The duplicate guides appear in the same position on the page as the original guides.

But wait! It gets better! You can use InDesign's Step and Repeat feature to duplicate ruler guides (see Figure 2-16). For more on Step and Repeat, see Chapter 8, "Transforming."

FIGURE 2-16
Duplicating ruler guides

Select the guides you want to duplicate, then press Command-Shift-V/Ctrl-Shift-V to display the Step and Repeat dialog box.

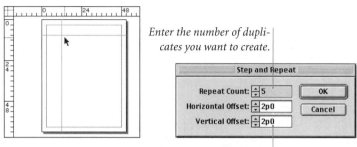

Enter the number of dupli-cates you want to create.

Enter the horizontal and vertical offset distances for each duplicate guide.

Click the OK button, and InDesign duplicates the guides.

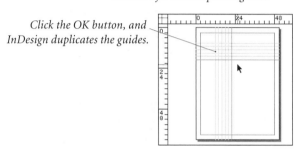

Grids

InDesign can display two different grids: the document grid and the baseline grid. Both grids are arrangements of guidelines spaced a specified distance apart. (Note that the baseline grid is not truly a grid, as it has no vertical guidelines.)

You set up both grids using the Grids Preferences dialog box, as described in Chapter 1, "Orientation."

To display a grid, choose the corresponding option (Show Document Grid or Show Baseline Grid) from the View menu, or from the Context menu (when nothing is selected, and when a tool other than the Text tool is active). If the magnification of the current publication window is below the view threshold of the baseline grid (again, this setting is in the Grids Preferences dialog box), you'll have to zoom in to see the grid (see Figure 2-17).

If you've turned on the Snap to Guides option (from the View menu), objects you're moving will snap to the baseline grid. If you've turned on Snap to Document Grid (on the View menu), they'll snap to the document grid. As I said earlier, the grids aren't very useful without the relevant "snap."

FIGURE 2-17

Setting the view
threshold of the
baseline grid

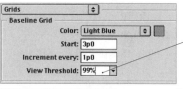

You can set the magnification at (and above) which the baseline grid becomes visible using the View Threshold field in the Grids Preferences dialog box.

If you've chosen Show Baseline Grid from the View menu, and yet the baseline grid has not appeared…

…it's because you haven't zoomed in enough to cross the view threshold. Once you do, you'll see the grid.

When you turn on the Snap to Document Grid option, objects snap to the document grid even when the grid is not visible. When you hide the baseline grid, on the other hand, objects will not snap to it even if you've turned on the Snap to Guides option.

You can also have the baselines of lines of text in a paragraph snap to the underlying baseline grid—a very useful typesetting feature. For more on working with leading grids and the baseline grid, see Chapter 4, "Type."

Pages and Spreads

I considered naming this section "Pages Palette Workout," because that's what it is. You won't get far in InDesign without mastering the Pages Palette, the fundamental tool for creating, arranging, deleting pages, and applying master pages (see Figure 2-18). It's also a great way to move around in your publication.

Selecting Pages and Spreads

To work with pages or spreads in the Pages palette, you've got to select them. InDesign makes different options available depending on the method you've used to select the objects (see Figure 2-19).

To select a page, click the page icon in the Pages palette. To select a spread, click the spread name—the text beneath the page icons. You can also select one page in the spread, then hold down Shift and select the other page or pages, but it's slower. Note that you must select all of the pages in a spread in order to use the Spread Options option on the Pages palette menu—InDesign does not make it available when you select a single page of the spread.

FIGURE 2-18
Pages palette

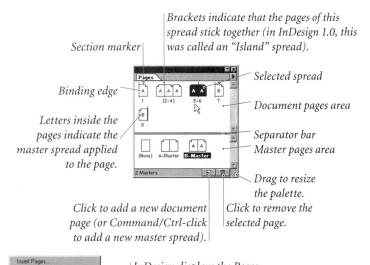

Brackets indicate that the pages of this spread stick together (in InDesign 1.0, this was called an "Island" spread).

Section marker

Binding edge

Selected spread

Document pages area

Letters inside the pages indicate the master spread applied to the page.

Separator bar
Master pages area

Drag to resize the palette.

Click to add a new document page (or Command/Ctrl-click to add a new master spread).

Click to remove the selected page.

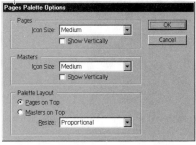

Choose Palette Options to change the appearance of the Pages palette.

Pages palette menu

InDesign displays the Pages Palette Options dialog box.

This set of palette options makes the palette resemble the Pages palette in InDesign 1.0 (as shown above).

These settings make your Pages palette look something like the Pages palette in QuarkXPress.

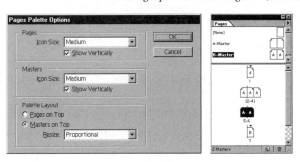

To select more than one spread at a time, select the first spread, then hold down Shift as you select the other spreads.

Double-click a page icon to scroll to that page and display it in the publication window (see Figure 2-20). Hold down Option/Alt as you double-click the page icon, and InDesign will change the page view to the Fit Page in Window view.

FIGURE 2-19
Selecting pages and spreads
Click a page icon to select the page.

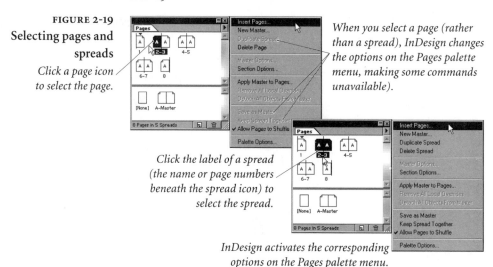

When you select a page (rather than a spread), InDesign changes the options on the Pages palette menu, making some commands unavailable).

Click the label of a spread (the name or page numbers beneath the spread icon) to select the spread.

InDesign activates the corresponding options on the Pages palette menu.

FIGURE 2-20
Navigating with the Pages palette

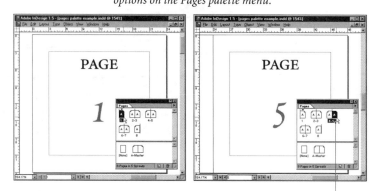

Double-click a page icon to scroll to that page; hold down Option/Alt as you double-click to display the page at Fit Page in Window view.

Adding Pages

To add a page, do any of the following.

Click the Add Page button. InDesign adds a page to the publication and displays the new page in the publication window (see Figure 2-21). At the same time, InDesign applies the most recently applied master page to the new page. If you hold down Option/Alt as you click the Add Page button, InDesign displays the Insert Pages dialog box (see below). If you press Command/Ctrl as you click the Add Page button, InDesign adds a new master page.

Choose Insert Pages from the Pages palette menu. InDesign displays the Insert Pages dialog box (see Figure 2-22). Enter the number of pages you want to add in the Pages field. Use the Insert pop-up

FIGURE 2-21

The Add Page button

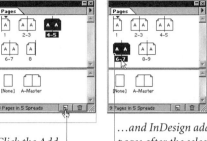

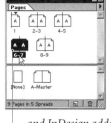

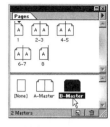

*Click the Add
Page button...*

*...and InDesign adds
pages after the selected
page or spread.*

*Hold down Command/
Ctrl as you click to add a
new master spread.*

FIGURE 2-22

Using the Insert Pages
dialog box

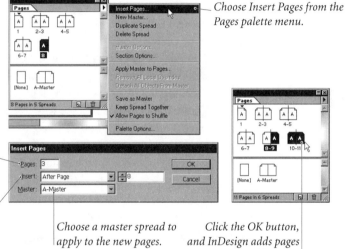

*Choose Insert Pages from the
Pages palette menu.*

*Enter the number of pages
you want to add.*

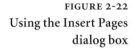

*Use these controls to tell
InDesign where you want
to add the pages.*

*Choose a master spread to
apply to the new pages.*

*Click the OK button,
and InDesign adds pages
to your publication.*

menu to select the position at which you want the inserted pages to
appear. If your publication has more than one section, you can also
enter the section to which you want to add the pages in the Section
field (if your publication contains only a single section, this field will
be unavailable). If you want to apply a master page or spread to the
pages, choose that master page from the Master Page pop-up menu.
Click the OK button to add the pages. If you hold down Option/Alt,
InDesign turns the Cancel button into the Reset button. Click the
Reset button, and the controls will be set back to the state they were
in when you opened the dialog box.

**Drag a master spread icon into the document pages area of the
Pages palette.** This creates a new document page or page spread and
applies the master page to it (see Figure 2-23). Note that you can't
drag a single page from a spread (if you try to do this, InDesign displays the "prohibited" symbol); you must drag the entire spread. To

FIGURE 2-23
Drag a master spread
into the document
pages area

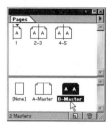 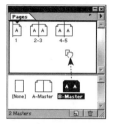 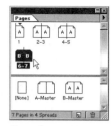

*Select a master
spread icon.*

*Drag the master spread
out of the masters area
and into the document
pages area.*

*Drop the master
spread icon in the
document pages area.
InDesign adds a new
spread.*

create a page without applying a master page to it, drag and drop the
None master page.

Hold down Option/Alt as you drag a page or page spread icon. You
can drag document pages or master pages. When you drop the page
icon, InDesign will create a duplicate of the page or spread (see
Figure 2-24). You can't use this technique to duplicate individual
pages of a multi-page spread.

Choose Duplicate Spread from the Pages palette's menu. This duplicates the selected spread (including any page objects on the spread's
pages) and adds it to the current section (see Figure 2-25). Note that
this option is not available unless you have a spread selected.

FIGURE 2-24
Drag and drop
duplication

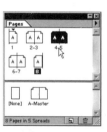 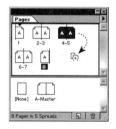 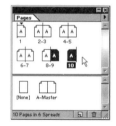

*Select a page or
spread icon.*

*Hold down Option/
Alt and drag.*

*Drop the icon where
you want to add the
page (or spread).*

FIGURE 2-25
Duplicating a spread

*Select a spread icon (not an
individual page icon) and
choose Duplicate Spread
from the Pages palette menu.*

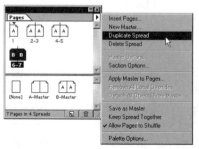 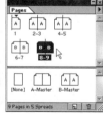

InDesign duplicates the spread.

Arranging Pages

Ordinarily, the pages in your publication are arranged into spreads according to the state of the Facing Pages option in the New Document and Document Setup dialog boxes. If you've turned the Facing Pages option on, InDesign arranges the majority of pages into two-page spreads (if the first page in a section is odd, or if the last page in a section is even, InDesign will set that page as a single page spread). If the Facing Pages option is off, InDesign makes each page in the publication into a single page spread.

But you're not limited to these arrangements of pages and spreads. At any point, in any section of your publication, you can create a spread containing anything from one to ten pages. InDesign 1.0 called these custom arrangements of pages "island" spreads. I don't know what makes one of these an island, and not a peninsula or an isthmus, but—for once—I'll stick with InDesign's terminology (because I can't think of anything better, myself).

An island spread pays no attention to the default arrangement of pages, but follows its own whim. It doesn't matter what you do—you can add or remove page that precede the island spread in a section, and the island spread will remain unchanged.

To create an island spread, select a spread and then choose Keep Spread Together from the Pages palette menu. InDesign displays brackets around the name of the spread to indicate that it's an island spread (see Figure 2-26). Selecting more than a single spread before you choose Set As Island Spread converts all of the spreads to separate island spreads; it does not join them into a single island spread.

When you drag a page or spread into an island spread, InDesign adds the pages of the spread to the island spread. When you drag a page out of an island spread, InDesign does not set the page as an island spread (that is, the pages of the island spread do not inherit the spread's "island" quality).

Defining Sections

Sections are ranges of pages that have unique page numbering properties. By using sections, you can combine front matter numbered using lowercase roman numerals starting with page one (or i) and regular pages numbered using Arabic numerals and beginning with page one. Another example would be a magazine layout containing a special advertising section that has a page numbering system that differs from that used in the rest of the magazine. With sections,

FIGURE 2-26
Creating an island
spread

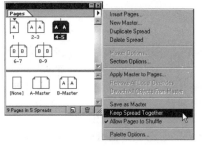
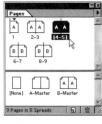

Select a spread and choose Keep Spread Together from the Pages palette menu.

InDesign converts the spread to an island spread (brackets around the spread's label indicate an island spread).

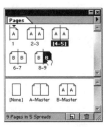
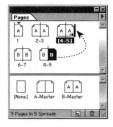
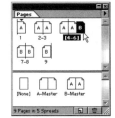

To add a page to an island spread, select a page icon...

...and drag it into or adjacent to the island spread.

InDesign adds the page to the island spread.

setting up this sort of page numbering variation inside a single publication is easy. You can have multiple sections in an InDesign publication, and each section can have its own starting page number, page numbering system, and page numbering prefix.

To define a section, follow these steps (see Figure 2-27).

1. Select the page icon in the Pages palette that represents the first spread in the section.

2. Choose Section Options from the palette's menu. InDesign displays the Section Options dialog box.

3. Use the controls in the Section Options dialog box to specify the page numbering options of your new section.

Section Prefix. When you turn to a page in your publication, InDesign displays the section prefix before the page number in the Page field. If you want, you can enter a label for the section in this field (you can enter up to five characters). InDesign does not display or print the section prefix on the page (if that's what you're trying to do, see "Section Marker," below).

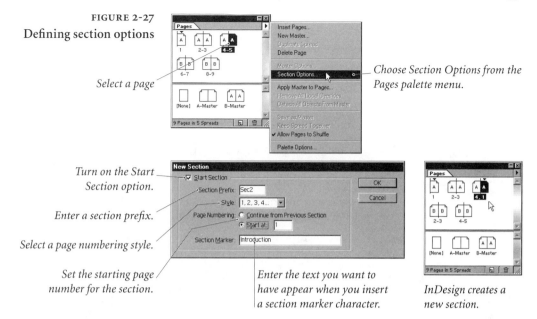

FIGURE 2-27
Defining section options

Select a page

Choose Section Options from the Pages palette menu.

Turn on the Start Section option.

Enter a section prefix.

Select a page numbering style.

Set the starting page number for the section.

Enter the text you want to have appear when you insert a section marker character.

InDesign creates a new section.

Style. Choose the page numbering style you want from the Style pop-up menu.

Page Numbering. If you want InDesign to continue the page numbering from the previous section, choose the Continue from Previous Section option. Otherwise, turn on the Start At option and enter a starting page number in the associated field.

Section Marker. If you want InDesign to automatically enter text on some or all of the pages of the section, enter that text in this field. Most of the time, this field will be used to enter the name of the section itself—but you can enter anything you want (up to around 100 characters).

Numbering Pages

While you can always type the page number of a page into a text frame, there's an easier way to number a page. By entering a page number marker, you can have InDesign automatically number the page for you. If you move the page, or change the page numbering for the section containing the page, InDesign will update the page number.

To enter a page number marker, click the Text tool in a text frame and do one of the following:

♦ Display the Context menu (press Control and hold down the mouse button on the Macintosh; click the right mouse button in Windows), then choose Page Number Marker from the Insert Special Character submenu.

♦ Choose Insert Page Number from the Layout menu.

♦ Press Command-Option-N/Ctrl-Alt-N.

InDesign inserts a page number marker. If you're on a master page, you'll see the master page prefix (if you're on master page "A," for example, you'll see an "A"); if you're on a document page, you'll see the page number itself (see Figure 2-28).

FIGURE 2-28
Inserting page numbers

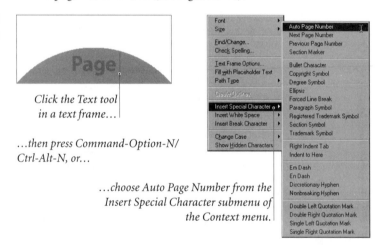

Click the Text tool in a text frame…

…then press Command-Option-N/ Ctrl-Alt-N, or…

…choose Auto Page Number from the Insert Special Character submenu of the Context menu.

InDesign inserts a page number marker at the location of the text cursor.

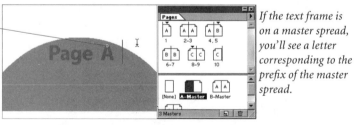

If the text frame is on a master spread, you'll see a letter corresponding to the prefix of the master spread.

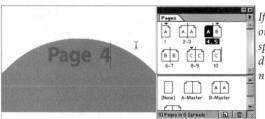

If the text frame is on a document spread, InDesign displays the page number.

Adding Section Marker Text

If you want to have InDesign automatically enter the section marker text in a story, click the Text tool in a text frame and do one of the following:

◆ Choose Section Marker from the Insert Special Characters submenu of the Context menu.

◆ Press Command-Option-Shift-N/Ctrl-Alt-Shift-N.

InDesign inserts the text you entered in the Section Marker field of the Section Options dialog box (see Figure 2-29). If you change the contents of the Section Marker field, InDesign changes the text entered by the section marker character.

Most of the time, you'll probably want to enter automatic page number and section marker characters in text frames on master pages—but you can also enter them on document pages.

FIGURE 2-29
Inserting section marker text

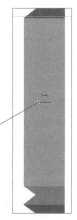

Click the Text tool in a text frame. (In this example, I'm adding a section marker to a tab at the edge of the page; I've rotated the text frame 90 degrees.)

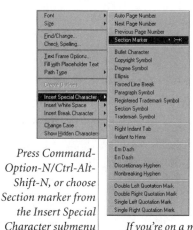

Press Command-Option-N/Ctrl-Alt-Shift-N, or choose Section marker from the Insert Special Character submenu of the Context menu.

If you're on a master page, you'll see the word "Section" where you entered the section marker.

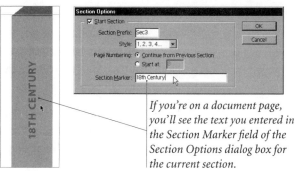

If you're on a document page, you'll see the text you entered in the Section Marker field of the Section Options dialog box for the current section.

Working with Master Spreads

Master spreads are the background on which you lay out your publication's pages. When you assign a master spread to a document page, InDesign applies the margin and column settings of the master spread to the page. Any page items on the master spread also appear on the document page, on the layers they occupy on the master spread. Master page items cannot be edited on document pages unless you choose to override (that is, copy) the items from the master pages (see "Overriding Master Page Items," below).

You lay out master spreads using the same techniques you use to lay out document pages. Repeating page elements, such as page numbers, headers and footers, and background images, are all great candidates for master spread page items. In addition, empty text frames can be placed on a master spread to provide a text layout template for document pages.

Creating Master Spreads

To create a new master spread, use any of the following techniques:

◆ Hold down Command/Ctrl as you click the Add Page button at the bottom of the Pages palette. InDesign adds a new master spread to the publication (see Figure 2-30). If you've turned on the Facing Pages option in the New Document or Document Setup dialog boxes, the new master spread will be a two page spread, if the option is off, InDesign creates a one page spread.

◆ Choose New Master from the Pages palette menu. InDesign displays the Master Page Options dialog box (see Figure 2-31).

◆ Drag a spread from the document pages section of the Pages palette into the master pages section (see Figure 2-32). If you've already laid out a document page using the layout you'd like to use as a master page, this is the easiest way to transfer that layout to a master page. This is called "creating a master spread by example." When you do this, InDesign creates a new master page with the margins, column guides, ruler guides, and content of the document page. The new master spread is based on the master spread applied to the example document pages. Note that this does not remove the spread from the document pages area.

◆ Hold down Option/Alt as you drag and drop an existing master spread icon in the master pages area of the Pages palette. InDesign creates a copy of the master spread (see Figure 2-33).

FIGURE 2-30
Command/Ctrl-click the Add Page button to create a master spread

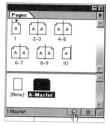

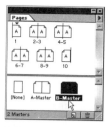

Hold down Command/Ctrl and click the Add Page button.

InDesign adds a new master spread. This new master spread is not based on the selected master spread.

FIGURE 2-31
Choose New Master to create a master spread

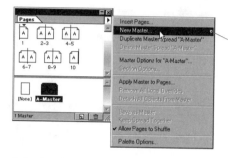

Choose New Master from the Pages palette menu.

InDesign displays the New Master dialog box

Enter a name for the master spread, if you want.

Enter a prefix for the master spread.

Choose an existing master spread from this pop-up menu to base the new master spread on that spread.

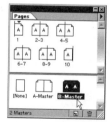

Enter the number of pages in the master spread.

Click the OK button, and InDesign creates a new master spread.

FIGURE 2-32
Basing a master spread on a document spread

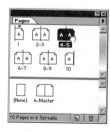

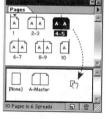

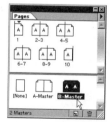

Position the cursor over a page spread.

Drag the page spread into the master spreads area of the Pages palette.

InDesign creates a new master spread with the same margins, guides, and page objects.

◆ Choose Duplicate Master Spread from the Pages palette menu. This has the same effect as the above method (see Figure 2-34).

FIGURE 2-33

One way to duplicate a
master spread

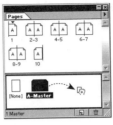

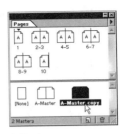

*Note that you press Option/
Alt after you start dragging
the master spread; pressing
the key before you drag will
result in an error message.*

*Tap the Option/Alt key as you
drag a master spread in the master
spreads area of the Pages palette.*

*InDesign creates a copy of
the master spread.*

FIGURE 2-34

Another way to duplicate
a master spread

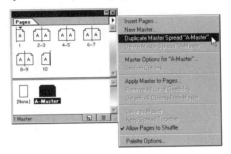

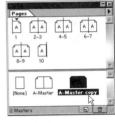

*Select a master spread and then choose Duplicate
Master Spread from the Pages palette menu.*

*InDesign creates a new
master spread with the
margins, guides, and
objects of the selected
master spread.*

Applying Master Pages and Master Spreads

To apply a master page or master spread, do one of the following.

◆ Drag and drop the master page spread icon or master page icon
on a page icon or a page spread (see Figure 2-35). Or drag and
drop the master spread icon on a document spread.

Note that you can apply individual pages from a master
spread to individual document or master pages, or you can
apply a master spread to any page spread. You can also apply
a single page from a master spread to all of the pages in a
spread. To do this, drag the page icon onto the document page
spread name. InDesign displays a rectangle around the page
spread icon. Drop the master page icon, and InDesign applies
the master page to all of the pages in the spread.

◆ Choose Apply Master to Pages from the Pages palette menu.
InDesign displays the Apply Master dialog box (see Figure
2-36). InDesign sets the Apply Master field to the selected
master spread. Enter the page, or pages, you want to apply
the master spread to in the To Pages field. You can enter non-
contiguous pages by separating the page numbers by commas

FIGURE 2-35
Applying master spreads
with drag and drop

FIGURE 2-35
Applying master spreads
with drag and drop

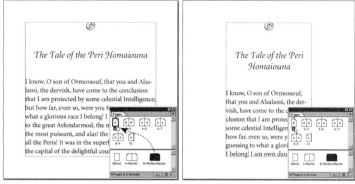

Drag a master spread icon out of
the master spreads area of the Pages
palette and drop it on a document
page or spread.

InDesign applies the margins and columns of the master spread to the document spread.

FIGURE 2-36
Applying master spreads
using the Apply Master
to Pages option

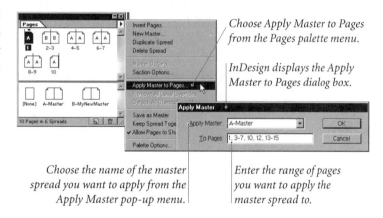

Choose Apply Master to Pages
from the Pages palette menu.

InDesign displays the Apply
Master to Pages dialog box.

Choose the name of the master
spread you want to apply from the
Apply Master pop-up menu.

Enter the range of pages
you want to apply the
master spread to.

("1, 3, 10, 12, 22), or enter page ranges ("55-73"), or mix ranges
and individual pages ("1, 3, 7-13, 44").

Editing Master Spreads

To edit a master spread, display the master spread (the easiest way to
do this is to double-click the master spread's label in the Pages palette. Select and edit the master spread's margins and ruler guides,
and any page items on the master spread just as you would any items
and attributes of a document spread. Turn on the Enable Layout
Adjustment option in the Layout Adjustment dialog box (choose
Layout Adjustment from the Layout menu to display the Layout
Adjustment dialog box) to apply any changes you've made to the
master spread to any pages in the document to which you've applied
the master spread.

Deleting Master Spreads

To remove a master spread from a publication, choose the master spread in the Pages palette, then choose Delete Master Spread from the Pages palette menu. InDesign removes the selected master spread from the publication.

Basing one Master Spread on Another

Imagine that you produce a catalog, and that, over the course of a year, you produce seasonal issues of the catalog. The basic design elements—the section, margins, columns, and page numbering—remain the same throughout the year, but the colors used, and the page footers change with each issue. Do you have to create a new set of master spreads for each issue? Not when you have InDesign's ability to base a master spread on another master spread, you don't.

When you base a new master spread on an existing master spread, the new master *inherits* the properties of the existing master spread. This is part of the reason that we refer to the relationship between the original style and the new style a "parent/child" relationship. Once you've applied a master spread to another master spread, you can work with (override) page elements on the pages of the "child" spread, just as you can from any document page (see "Overriding Master Page Items," below).

Here's how inheritance works: When the attributes between a "child" spread and its "parent" spread *differ*, those attributes are controlled by the definition found in the "child" spread. When you change any of the attributes defined by the "parent" spread, those changes appear in the "child" spread. Take a look at the (somewhat overwrought) example Figure 2-37, and you'll see what I mean.

Overriding Master Items

Want to modify or delete a master page item from a document page, but leave all of the other master pages items alone? Wait! Don't cover the master page item with a white box! There's a better way. InDesign calls it "overriding" a master page item.

To override a master page item, hold down Command-Shift/Ctrl-Shift and click the master page item (or, if you're using the Text tool, click inside the master page item). InDesign copies the master page item to the document page, where you can select it, format it, or delete it as you would any other page item (see Figure 2-38).

Once you've overridden a master page item, InDesign won't display or print the original master page item until you remove the overrides applied to the document page. This isn't the same thing as

FIGURE 2-37

Basing one master spread on another

TimeTravelTickets is a (fictional) company offering time travel to the great artistic performances of all time. Their catalog is divided into sections based on the century of the performance, and each section is divided into the categories "Theatre," "Music," and "Dance." I've set up master spreads to reflect the organization of the catalog.

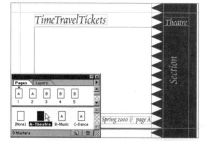

All master spreads are based on master spread "A" (which I'll apply to all of the pages in the "Theatre" category).

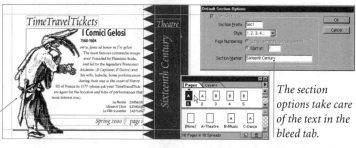

Master spread "A" applied to a document page.

The section options take care of the text in the bleed tab.

Master spread "B" uses a different color scheme and replaces the word "Theatre" with "Music", but is otherwise identical to master spread "A."

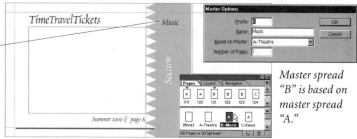

Master spread "B" is based on master spread "A."

Here's an example of master spread "B" in another section (note the differing section text).

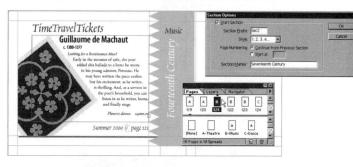

Ready to update the catalog? Enter a new season in the page footer of the "parent" master spread...

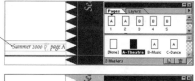

...and that change will be reflected in all of the "child" master spreads.

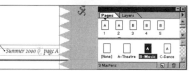

See how easy it was to update all of the catalog's master spreads for a new season? While a layout like this takes time to set up initially, it can save you lots of time and trouble in the long run.

deleting the overridden items, however. To remove all master page overrides, choose Remove All Local Overrides from the Page palette menu. To remove a specific local override (or a series of overrides), select the object (or objects) and choose Remove Selected Local Overrides from the Page palette menu (see Figure 2-39).

FIGURE 2-38
Overriding a master item

If you click on the master spread item you want to change, nothing happens. This is probably a good thing, as it prevents me from accidentally changing master items.

In this example, I want to create a new master spread based on the "A-Theatre" master spread. In the new spread, I want to change the word "Theatre" to "Music."

Instead of using copy and paste to move the master page item from the original master page, hold down Command-Shift/Ctrl-Shift…

…and click the object. InDesign copies the object to the current page and marks it as a "local override."

Now you can edit, transform, or format, the text.

FIGURE 2-39
Removing local overrides

To remove a local override, select the object…

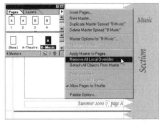

…and choose Remove Selected Local Override from the Pages palette menu.

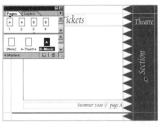

InDesign removes the object from the current spread and displays the original master spread object.

To remove all of the local overrides on a spread, press Command-Shift-A/Ctrl-Shift-A to deselect any selected objects…

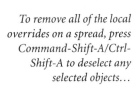

…then choose Remove all Local Overrides from the Pages palette menu.

InDesign removes all of the local overrides on the current spread.

To restore the overridden master page object while retaining the copy of it that's on the document page, reapply the master page to the document page. At this point, the copy is no longer considered a local override—it's a page item. Removing local overrides from this document page will have no effect on the object.

Overridden items are not entirely free of the influence of their master page counterpart. Changes to the fill and stroke of the original path (though not to its contents, including text characters) will be reflected in the fill and stroke of the overridden version of the object, provided you haven't changed the object's fill or stroke. If you have changed the overridden object's fill and stroke, changes made to the corresponding attributes of the original master page item will not be applied to the overridden object. Other modifications to the original master page item have no effect on the overridden object.

When you reapply the master page to a document page containing overridden items, the original master page items reappear on the document page, but the overridden page items are not deleted. This isn't usually a good thing—it's easy to end up with stacks of duplicated objects (which is probably not what you want).

Layers and Master Pages

In PageMaker and QuarkXPress, objects on master pages are always displayed behind document page objects. In PageMaker, this is true in spite of the layer you've assigned to the master page items. This means that page numbers often end up being hidden by items on your document pages, and that you have to copy the master page item to your document page to get it to display or print.

In InDesign, objects on master pages are arranged according to the layer they're on. This means that you can put page numbers on the uppermost layer in a publication without worrying about them being obscured by images or other page items on the document pages (see Figure 2-40).

Adjusting Layouts

What happens when you change the margins of a page, or apply a different master page? Should the items on the affected pages move or resize to match the new page geometry? Or should they stay as they are? You decide. Choose Layout Adjustment from the Layout

FIGURE 2-40
**Using layers to control
the stacking order of
master spread items**

*With only a single
layer...*

*Master page text hidden
behind the background
image.*

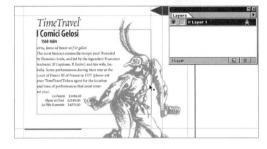

*...master spread
objects (in this
example, the tab,
page header, and
page footer) appear
behind document
page objects.*

*Master page text appears in
front of the background
image.*

*To avoid this prob-
lem, put your master
spread items on at
least one layer. If you
do this, you'll be able
to control their stack-
ing order.*

menu. InDesign displays the Layout Adjustment dialog box. What
do the controls in the dialog box do? Here's a quick walk-through
(see Figure 2-41).

Enable Layout Adjustment. Turn this option on, and InDesign
adjusts the position and size of the objects on the affected pages
according to the other settings in this dialog box. When this option
is off, InDesign does not change the object positions or sizes when
you apply master pages, change page size, or otherwise change page
geometry.

Snap Zone. How close to a guide does an object have to be to be
affected by layout adjustment? That's what you're telling InDesign
by the value you enter in this field. Objects within the specified distance will move or resize; objects outside that range won't.

FIGURE 2-41

Adjusting layouts

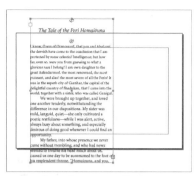

When the Enable Layout Adjustment option is off, InDesign does not change the position or size of page objects when you change the geometry of the page…

…even for a change as radical as changing page orientation

Turn on the Enable Layout Adjustment option, and InDesign changes the position and size of page objects in response to changes in page size, orientation, column setup, or margins.

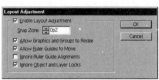

The options in the Layout Adjustment dialog box give you a way to "fine tune" the automated adjustment process.

Here's the layout, as adjusted by InDesign.

Ruler guide positions are very important to the layout adjustment feature. In this example, changing the page size changes the shape and position of the graphics—all because of their relationship to the ruler guides that surround them.

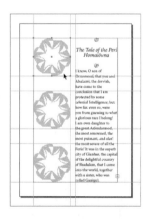

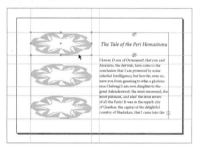

As the ruler guides move, InDesign resizes the graphics you've "stuck" to the ruler guides.

Allow Graphics and Groups to Resize. When this option is off, InDesign will not resize objects while adjusting layouts. When it's on, InDesign will resize objects to match the new page layout.

Allow Ruler Guides to Move. Should ruler guides move when you change the layout of the page or spread? If you'd like the ruler guides to move, turn this option on; if not, turn it off.

Ignore Ruler Guide Alignments. When this option is off, InDesign moves and resizes objects to match the positions of ruler guides in the new page layout. When it's on, InDesign does not consider the locations of ruler guides when resizing or moving objects—only the location of margin guides and page edges. The effect of this option also depends on the state of the Allow Ruler Guides to Move option (described above).

Ignore Object and Layer Locks. What should InDesign do while adjusting your layout when it encounters a locked object, or an object on a locked layer? When you turn this option on, InDesign will treat the objects as if they were unlocked. To leave locked objects alone, turn this option off.

The key thing to remember is that InDesign bases all layout adjustment decisions on the positions of margin guides, ruler guides, column guides, and page edges. InDesign cannot know that you want an object to change its size or position unless you somehow associate the object with a guide or a page edge.

Selecting and Deselecting

Before you can act on an object, you have to select it (see Figure 2-42). You select objects using the Selection tool by clicking them, dragging a selection rectangle over them, or by Shift-selecting (select one object using the Selection tool, hold down Shift, and select another object).

When you select an object using the Selection tool, InDesign displays the object's selection handles and the object's bounding box—the smallest rectangular area capable of enclosing the selection.

The selection handles also correspond to the points on the proxy in the Transform palette.

When you select an object using the Direct Selection tool, InDesign displays the points on the object's path.

Note that you do not have to entirely surround an object with a selection rectangle to select it—if the selection rectangle touches any part of the object, InDesign will select it. Choose Select All from the Edit menu to select everything on the current spread.

To deselect all selected objects, click an uninhabited area of the page or pasteboard, or, better yet, press Command-Shift-A/Ctrl-Shift-A.

FIGURE 2-42
Selecting objects

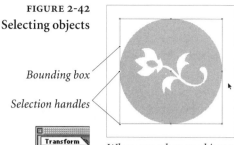

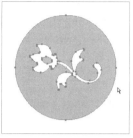

Bounding box

Selection handles

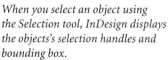

Proxy

The proxy in the Transform palette represents the selection handles of the selected object.

When you select an object using the Selection tool, InDesign displays the object's's selection handles and bounding box.

When you select an object using the Direct Selection tool, InDesign displays the points on the object's path.

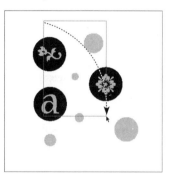

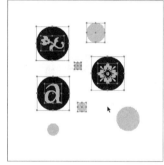

When you drag a selection rectangle around an object or objects...

...InDesign selects all of the objects that the selection rectangle touched.

Selecting Through Objects

Sometimes, you have to select an object that's behind another object. You might, for example, need to select and edit a background graphic behind a text frame. What can you do? Do you need to drag the text frame out of the way? Or hide the layer containing the text frame? There's a better way. Try this: click the Selection tool on the object on top of the stack, then press Command/Ctrl and click again. InDesign selects the next object in the stack. Each successive click selects the next object down in the stack (see Figure 2-43).

You can accomplish the same end using a keyboard shortcut. To select the object behind the currently selected object in a stack of objects, press Command-Option-[/Ctrl-Alt-[.

Once you reach the bottom of a stack of objects, InDesign stops. Pressing the keyboard shortcut again does nothing.

To select the object above the currently selected object in a stack of objects, press Command-Option-]/Ctrl-Alt-].

When overlapping objects are exactly or nearly the same size, it can be difficult to see which object in a stack is selected. Don't start dragging objects out of the way—look for clues. The color of the selection handles, the state of the Fill and Stroke buttons in the

FIGURE 2-43
Selecting through objects

Want to select an object that's behind other objects? You don't need to drag objects out of the way. Instead, hold down Command/Ctrl and click the Selection tool above the object you want to select.

Text frame selected   *Background graphic selected*

The first click selects the object on top of the stack of objects…   *…but each subsequent click selects the next object in the stack.*

Toolbox, and the Stroke palette all provide information that can help you determine which object is selected.

Subselecting Objects

Sometimes, you need to select an object that you've pasted inside another object, or to select an object inside a group. The Direct Selection tool, as you might expect, is the tool you'll use to do this, and the process is called "subselection" (and when you select an object that's inside another object, I say the object is "subselected").

Selecting objects inside groups. You don't have to ungroup a group of objects to edit the objects in the group—you can select them and work with them just as if they were outside the group. To do this, select the Direct Selection tool and click the element that you want to edit. InDesign selects the object. Once the object is selected, you can change its attributes, text, shape, or position. When you deselect the subselected item, it goes back to being part of the group (see Figure 2-44).

FIGURE 2-44
Subselecting objects inside groups

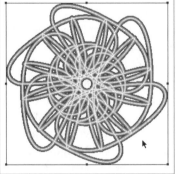

Click the group with the Selection tool to select the group, or…   *…click one of the objects in the group with the Direct Selection tool.*

Selecting path contents. One of the trickiest things to master in InDesign is the process of selecting and working with objects you've pasted inside other objects. When you click the Direct Selection tool inside a path, InDesign selects the path's contents, if any (see Figure 2-45). Note that this is true even when the area you clicked is not inside any of the objects you've pasted into the path. When you click the Direct Selection tool on the path's stroke (or the outline of the path, for a path with no stroke), InDesign selects the path.

For more on working with path contents, see Chapter 8, "Transforming."

FIGURE 2-45
Selecting path contents

Click the Direct Selection tool inside a path to select its contents.

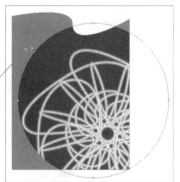

In this example, I've pasted a circle containing a group of more complex shapes inside the path. When I click inside the first path, InDesign selects the circle.

When I click inside the first circle, InDesign selects the group that's pasted inside the circle.

When I click the Direct Selection tool on one of the paths inside the group, InDesign selects the path.

When you've selected an object using the Direct Selection tool, switching to the Selection tool (by pressing V or, in Windows, Ctrl-Tab) will display the object's selection handles. At this point, you can scale the object by dragging one of its selection handles.

If you're trying to select an object in a group that's behind other objects, you can use the keyboard shortcut for selecting objects behind/in front of other objects that I mentioned earlier (Command-Option-[/Ctrl-Alt-[and Command-Option-]/Ctrl-Alt-]).

Stacking Objects

Page items on an InDesign page can be arranged in front of or behind each other. You can imagine that every object exists on an invisible plane that it cannot share with other objects, if you like. These planes can be shuffled to place one object above another, or behind another.

Simple stacking isn't the only way to control the front-to-back order of objects on a page—layers are another, and usually better, method. Arranging objects on a single layer, however, is very similar to tasks we perform every day as we stack and sort physical objects (my life, for example, seems to revolve around stacks of pieces of paper).

To move an object to the front, or send an object to the back of the layer it occupies, select the object and do one of the following (see Figure 2-46).

To bring an object to the front:

◆ Press Command-Shift-]/Ctrl-Shift-]

◆ Choose Bring to Front from the Arrange submenu of the Object menu.

◆ Display the context menu and choose Bring to Front from the Arrange submenu.

To send an object to the back:

◆ Press Command-Shift-[/Ctrl-shift-[

◆ Choose Send to Back from the Arrange submenu of the Object menu.

◆ Display the Context menu and choose Send to Back from the Arrange submenu.

You can also choose to bring objects closer to the front or send them farther to the back in the stacking order of objects on a layer. To do this, select the object and then do one of the following (see Figure 2-47).

To bring an object closer to the front:

◆ Press Command-]/Ctrl-]

FIGURE 2-46
Bring to front and send to back

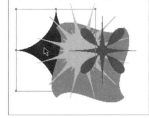

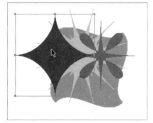

Note that bringing an object to the front or sending it to the back only changes its position of the stacking order of the current layer. Objects on other layers can still appear in front of objects brought to the front; objects on layers behind the current layer will still appear behind objects sent to the back.

To bring an object to the front, select the object…

…and then press Command-Shift-]/Ctrl-Shift-]. InDesign brings the selected object to the front of the current layer.

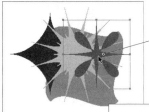

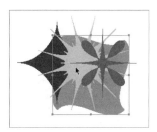

To send an object to the back of the current layer, select the object…

…and then press Command-Shift-[/Ctrl-Shift-[.

FIGURE 2-47
Bring forward and send backward

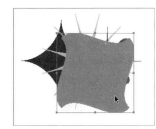

Select an object.

Press Command-[/Ctrl-[to send the object backward.

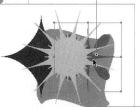

You can also press Command-]/Ctrl-] to move the object forward.

Note that the stacking order includes all of the objects on the layer containing the object you're moving. If the next object in the stacking order does not intersect the object you're moving, you won't see any change on your screen.

Press the shortcut again to move the object farther back in the layer's stacking order.

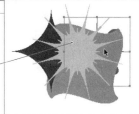

◆ Choose Bring Forward from the Arrange submenu of the Object menu.

◆ Display the Context menu and choose Bring Forward from the Arrange submenu.

To send an object backward:

◆ Press Command-[/Ctrl-[

◆ Choose Send Backward from the Arrange submenu of the Object menu.

Layers

InDesign's layers are transparent planes on which you place page items. You've probably heard that layers are a way to organize your publication (that's what all the marketing materials say, after all). But there's far more to InDesign's layers than just organization—layers give you control over what parts of your publication display and print, and whether they can be edited or not.

Layers Basics   In the old days (before personal computers and desktop publishing), our page layouts sometimes consisted of a number of overlapping sheets of transparent mylar and tracing paper, each sheet bearing galleys of type, photographs, printing instructions, and scalpel-cut windows of rubylith or amberlith (these last were sticky films you'd use to indicate the position of an image).

The different layers of material told our commercial printers how to create printing plates from the layout. The layers organized the way that our pages would be photographed for printing.

InDesign's layers have a few characteristics you should understand before you start using them. First, layers affect an entire document—not individual pages or page spreads. Next, layers created in one document do not affect layers in another document.

As far as I can tell, there's no technical limit to the number of layers you can have in a publication; it's possible to make hundreds or more of them if you have enough RAM. But just because you can do that doesn't mean that you should. Too many layers can make a publication difficult to manage.

Layers are especially useful when you're working with pages containing slow-drawing graphics, when your publication features complicated stacks of objects, or when you want to add a nonprinting layer of comments or instructions to a publication. Layers are also helpful when you want to create "conditional" layers containing differing text or graphics (you could create multiple versions of the publication in different languages, for example, and store all of the versions in a single publication).

The Layers Palette

You use the Layers palette to create, edit, rearrange, and delete layers (see figure 2-48). To display the Layers palette, choose Layers from the Window menu (or press F7). If you're familiar with the Layers palettes found in Illustrator and PageMaker (and, to a more limited extent, Photoshop), you'll be right at home with the InDesign Layers palette.

FIGURE 2-48
Layers palette

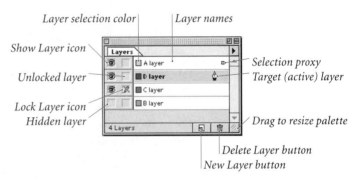

Layer selection color | *Layer names*

Show Layer icon — *Selection proxy*
Unlocked layer — *Target (active) layer*
Lock Layer icon
Hidden layer — *Drag to resize palette*

Delete Layer button
New Layer button

To reduce the amount of vertical space taken up by the Layers palette...

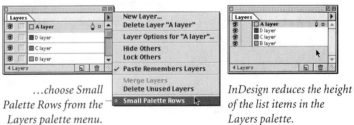

...choose Small Palette Rows from the Layers palette menu.

InDesign reduces the height of the list items in the Layers palette.

What do you see when you look at the Layers palette?

Show/hide column. When you see an "eye" icon in this column, the layer is visible. When there's no icon in this column, all of the objects on the layer are hidden (invisible). Click in this column to change from one state to another. You can't select or edit objects on hidden layers, and objects on hidden layers don't print.

When you want to hide all of the layers in a publication except the selected layers, hold down Option/Alt as you click anywhere in the show/hide column (or choose Hide Others from the Layers palette menu). Clicking again in the column while holding down

Option/Alt will show all layers (which is equivalent to choosing Show All Layers from the Layers palette menu). See Figure 2-49.

FIGURE 2-49
Showing and hiding other layers

To hide all but one layer, follow these steps.

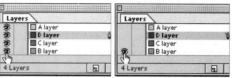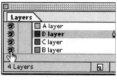

Point at the layer's Visibility icon, hold down Option/Alt...

...and click. InDesign hides all of the other layers.

Press Option/Alt and click again to make the layers visible.

Lock/unlock icon. Click in the column to the right of the show/hide column to lock a layer. InDesign displays the "lock" icon (a pencil with a red line through it) in that column. To unlock the layer (and remove the icon), click on it (see Figure 2-50).

You can't select objects on locked layers (so you can't move or format them, either), and you can't assign objects to locked layers. When you want to lock all of the layers in a publication except the currently-selected layer (or layers), hold down Option/Alt and click in the lock/unlock column (or choose Lock Others from the Layers palette menu). To unlock any locked layers, hold down Option/Alt and click the lock/unlock column (this is the same as choosing Unlock All Layers from the Layers palette menu).

FIGURE 2-50
Locking and unlocking other layers

To lock all but one layer, follow these steps.

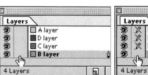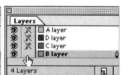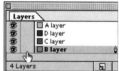

Point at the layer's Lock/Unlock icon, hold down Option/Alt...

...and click. InDesign locks all of the other layers.

Press Option/Alt and click again to unlock the layers.

Layer selection color. Each layer has its own "selection color" that helps you see which objects are on which layers; when you select an object, its selection handles appear in the selection color of that layer. You set the selection color of a layer when you create the layer, but you can change the color at any time. To do this, either double-click a layer in the Layers palette, or select a layer and choose Layer Options from the Layers palette menu. Either method will display the Layer options dialog box, where you can assign a new selection color.

Layer name. When you create a layer, you can assign a name to it—or you can let InDesign name the layer for you. You can change the layer name at any time using the Layer Options dialog box.

Target layer icon. This icon shows you which layer is the "target layer"—the layer on which InDesign will place any objects you create, import, or paste. You can also see this information in the lower-left corner of the Layers palette. Making a layer the target layer does not assign the current selection to that layer.

Selection Proxy. When you select an object, InDesign highlights the name of the layer containing the object. In addition, InDesign displays a small square to the right of the layer name. This square is the Selection Proxy, which represents the layer or layers containing the selected objects (just as the proxy in the Transform palette "stands in" for the bounding box of the selection). To move objects from one layer to another, drag the Selection Proxy to another layer.

New Layer icon. Click this icon to create a new layer. InDesign displays the New Layer dialog box.

Delete Layer icon. Click this icon to delete the selected layer or layers (to select more than one layer, hold down Shift/Ctrl as you click the layer names). If the selected layers contain objects, InDesign will ask if you want to delete the objects with the layer.

Paste Remembers Layers. This option takes care of a question: "If I copy objects from several layers and then paste, where should the pasted objects end up?" Should they be placed on the target layer (in a stack corresponding to their layer order)? Or should they be placed on the layers they originally came from.?

I think you'll turn this option on and leave it on. If you do this, you'll be able to copy layers between publications. To do this, select objects on different layers in one publication, then copy them, and then switch to another publication and paste. When you paste, the layers will appear in the publication's Layers palette.

If layers with the same names already exist in the publication, InDesign moves the incoming objects to the corresponding layers, which is why you might want to turn the Paste Remembers Layers option off. If you don't, and if the layer stacking order is not the same as it was in the publication you copied the objects out of, the appearance of the pasted objects might change.

Delete Unused Layers. To get rid of layers you're not using, choose Delete Unused Layers from the Layers palette menu.

Merge Layers. Want to combine two or more layers into a single layer? Select the layers, then choose Merge Layers from the Layers palette menu. InDesign merges the two layers (the name of the "merged" layer will be that of the layer you selected first). InDesign arranges the objects on the layers according to the stacking order of the layers.

Creating a New Layer   To create a new layer, follow these steps (see Figure 2-51).

1. Choose New Layer from the Layers palette (or click the New Layer icon at the bottom of the Layers palette). InDesign adds a new layer to the top of the Layers palette. To add the layer at the bottom of the layers list, hold down Command-Option/Ctrl-Alt as you click the New Layer icon.

2. If you want to change the layer's attributes (its name, selection color, visibility, guide behavior, and locked/unlocked status) choose Layer Options from the Layers palette menu, or double-click the layer name. InDesign displays the Layer Options dialog box.

Name. Enter a name for the layer in this field. InDesign assigns a default name to each layer you create, but I think it's better to enter a layer name that means something in the context of your publication. It's far easier to remember that the enormous, slow drawing image of grazing Herefords is on the layer you've named "Big Slow Cows" than it is to remember what it is you've placed the image on the layer named "Layer 51."

Color. If you like, you can change the selection color of the layer. You can do this by either choosing one of InDesign's default layer colors from this pop-up menu or by double-clicking the associated color swatch. When you take the latter approach, InDesign displays a color picker where you can choose a custom selection color. I have never felt the need to change a layer's selection color in an actual project, but it's nice to know that you can.

Show Layer. Should the layer be visible, or hidden? This option performs the same task as the show/hide column in the Layers palette.

FIGURE 2-51
Creating a layer

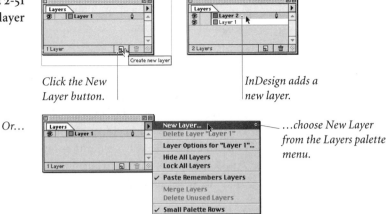

Click the New Layer button.

InDesign adds a new layer.

Or...

...choose New Layer from the Layers palette menu.

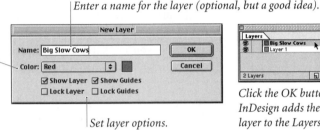

InDesign displays the New Layer Dialog box.

Choose a layer color from the pop-up menu, or double-click the color swatch.

Enter a name for the layer (optional, but a good idea).

Set layer options.

Click the OK button, and InDesign adds the new layer to the Layers palette.

Lock Layer. Should the layer be locked or unlocked? This option performs the same task as the lock/unlock icons.

Show Guides. Should the ruler guides on the layer be visible or hidden? Turn this option on to show the guides.

Lock Guides. Should the ruler guides on this layer be locked or unlocked? Turn this option on to lock the guides.

Editing Layer Properties

To edit the properties of a layer, double-click the layer name in the Layers palette (or choose Layer Options from the Layers palette menu). InDesign displays the Layer Options dialog box for the layer.

Deleting Layers

To delete a layer, select the layer and choose Delete Layer from the Layers palette menu. If there are any objects on the layer, InDesign will display a message asking if you want to remove the layer. To delete all of the unused layers (layers that have no objects assigned to them) in a publication, choose Delete Unused Layers from the Layers palette menu.

Assigning Objects to Layers

To move objects from one layer to another, drag the selection proxy from one layer and drop it on another layer (see Figure 2-52.

While this method of moving objects from one layer to another makes it difficult to accidentally move objects, it also makes it difficult to move objects from multiple layers to a single layer. To accomplish this, you'll have to make multiple trips up and down the Layers palette, selecting and moving the selection proxy for each layer in the selection.

To copy objects from one layer to another, hold down Option/Alt as you drag the selection proxy.

To move objects to a locked or hidden layer, hold down Command /Ctrl as you drag the selection proxy to the layer. To copy objects as you move them to a hidden or locked layer, hold down Command-Option/Ctrl-Alt as you drag.

Changing Layer Stacking Order

To change the stacking order of layers, drag the layer up (to bring the layer closer to the front) or down (to send the layer farther to the back) in the Layers palette. As you drag, InDesign displays a horizontal bar showing the position of the layer. When the layer reaches the point at which you want it to appear, stop dragging. InDesign moves the layer (and all the objects on it) to a new location (see Figure 2-53).

Merging Layers

To combine a series of layers into a single layer, select the layers and choose Merge Layers from the Layers palette menu. InDesign merges the layers into a single layer—the first layer you selected (see Figure 2-54). Note that merging layers sometimes changes the stacking order of objects on the merged layers.

Moving Layers from One Publication to Another

To move a layer from one publication into another publication, make sure you've turned on the Paste Remembers Layers option (on the Layers palette menu), then copy an object from that layer and paste it into the publication that lacks that layer. When you paste, InDesign adds the layer to the list of layers.

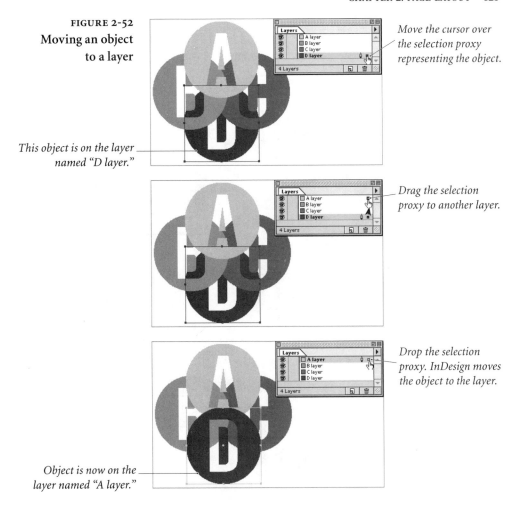

FIGURE 2-52

Moving an object to a layer

Move the cursor over the selection proxy representing the object.

This object is on the layer named "D layer."

Drag the selection proxy to another layer.

Drop the selection proxy. InDesign moves the object to the layer.

Object is now on the layer named "A layer."

Grouping Objects

What does it mean to "group" objects in a page layout program? When you group objects, you're telling the application to treat the objects as a single object. The objects in the group move and transform (scale, skew, and rotate) as a unit.

To group the objects in a selection, press Command-G/Ctrl-G (or choose Group from the Context menu, or choose Group from the Object menu). When you group a series of objects, the group moves to the topmost layer of the selection (see Figure 2-55). To ungroup a selected group, press Command-Shift-G/Ctrl-Shift-G (or choose Ungroup from the Context menu or the Object menu).

To select (or "subselect") an object inside a group, click the object using the Direct Selection tool.

FIGURE 2-53
**Changing layer
stacking order**

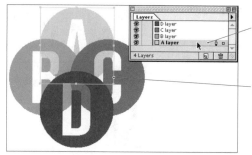

*Move the cursor over
the layer you want to
move.*

*The selected object is
on the layer named "A
layer."*

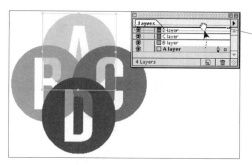

*Drag the layer to a new
position in the Layers
palette.*

*The layer named "A layer"
is now the layer closest
to the front.*

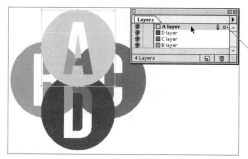

*When the layer
reaches the location
you want, stop drag-
ging. InDesign changes
the layer stacking
order.*

FIGURE 2-54
Merging layers

*Select a series of layers and
choose Merge Layers from the
Layers palette menu.*

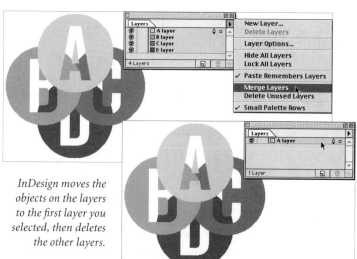

*InDesign moves the
objects on the layers
to the first layer you
selected, then deletes
the other layers.*

FIGURE 2-55
Grouping and
ungrouping objects

Groups can come in handy
when you've created an
assemblage of objects you
want to treat as a single
object. In addition, grouping
objects speeds up screen
redraw—InDesign draws
selection handles for one
object, rather than for all of
the objects in the group.

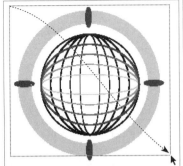

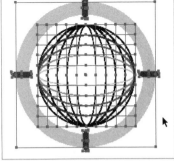

Select the objects you want to group.

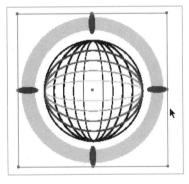

Press Command-G/Ctrl-G. InDesign groups the objects. You can
move, scale, shear, or rotate the
group as you do any other single
object. To select an object inside the
group, switch to the Direct Selection
tool and click the object.

To ungroup, select a group and press
Command-Shift-G/Ctrl-Shift-G.

Locking Object Positions

When you want to keep from changing the location of an object, you
can lock it. To do this, select the object and then press Command-
L/Ctrl-L (or choose Lock Position from the Context menu or the
Object menu). When an object is locked, you can select it, but you
can't change its position on the page or pasteboard. You can, however, move the object to another layer, or change its position in the
stacking order using the commands on the Arrange submenu of the
object menu. When you try to drag a locked object, the cursor will
turn into a "padlock" icon (see Figure 2-56).

FIGURE 2-56
Locking and
unlocking objects

Select an object and press
Command-L/Ctrl-L or
choose Lock Position from the
context menu.

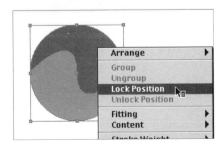

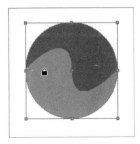

If what you're looking for is a way to keep from selecting and formatting objects, lock the layer that contains the object (see "Layers," earlier in this chapter).

A Good Foundation

I admit that I am not a spectacularly organized person. In general, I respond to an event when something or someone catches fire, whacks me up the side of the head, files a lien on my house, or threatens legal action.

I've found, however, that being methodical every now and then can save me a lot of trouble later. Setting up master pages, defining layers, creating layout grids, and positioning ruler guides are not the most glamorous parts of InDesign, but they're a good place to expend a little organizational energy.

Far from cramping your creative style, taking care of basic layout options—at the very beginning of the production process, if possible—provides a stage on which you produce and direct the play of your page layout.

3

Text

Text is the stream of characters that inhabit the text frames of your publication. Text is not about what those characters look like (that's "type")—it's about the characters themselves, and the text frames that hold them.

There are areas of overlap between these definitions, of course. Changing the number of columns in a text frame, for example, definitely changes the appearance of the text, but I've put it in this chapter because it's an organizational change, not one that changes the appearance of individual characters.

The text in an InDesign publication is contained inside text frames (see Figure 3-1). Text frames are similar to the text "boxes" found in QuarkXPress, and they're also similar to the "text blocks" found in PageMaker (and, yes, text blocks are text frames—they just hide the frame from your view). In my opinion, InDesign's text frames present a "best of both worlds" approach—you get the flexibility and fluidity of PageMaker's text blocks combined with the precision of QuarkXPress' text boxes.

FIGURE 3-1
Text blocks

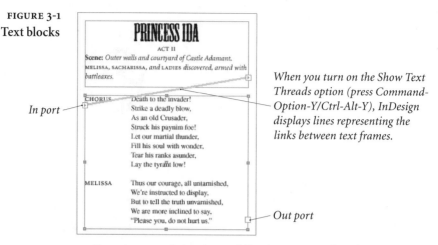

When you turn on the Show Text Threads option (press Command-Option-Y/Ctrl-Alt-Y), InDesign displays lines representing the links between text frames.

In port

Out port

Text, in a word, is what publications are really all about. A picture might be worth a thousand words, but they're not very specific words. When you create a poster for a concert, for example, the text is what tells you where the concert will be presented, at what time, and on which day. The point of using an image, color, or a stylish layout in publication is to get people to *read the text*.

This chapter is all about how to get text into your InDesign publications: how to create and edit text frames, enter text, edit text, and import text files. It's also about checking the spelling of the text in your publication; and about finding and changing text. I'll even go a little bit off the deep end with a description of InDesign's tagged text import and export format.

Creating Text Frames

Before you can add text to your InDesign publication, you've got to have something to put it in: a text frame. To create a text frame, you can use any of the following methods.

◆ Draw a frame using one of the frame drawing tools (the Rectangular Frame, Oval Frame, or Polygonal Frame tools). To convert the frame to a text frame, choose Text from the Content submenu of the Object menu, or click inside the frame using the Text tool (see Figure 3-2).

◆ Draw a frame using the Rectangle, Oval, or Polygon tools, and then convert it to a text frame by choosing Text from the Content submenu of the object menu (or click the Text tool inside the frame). See Figure 3-3.

FIGURE 3-2

Converting a graphic frame to a text frame

Select a frame drawing tool

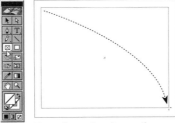

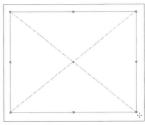

Drag the tool to draw a frame.

InDesign sets the content type of the new frame to "Graphic."

Click the Text tool inside the frame, or...

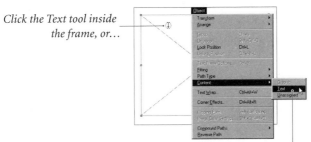

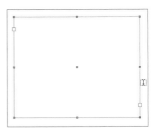

...select Text from the Content submenu of the object menu.

InDesign converts the graphic frame to a text frame.

FIGURE 3-3

Converting a basic shape to a text frame

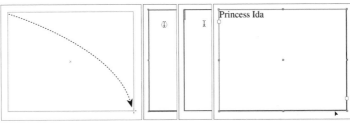

Draw a path. InDesign creates a frame with a content type of "Unassigned."

Click the Text tool inside the frame...

...and InDesign converts the basic shape to a text frame.

◆ Click the Text tool inside any empty frame. If the frame is a graphic frame, clicking it with the Text tool converts it to a text frame (see Figure 3-4).

◆ Drag the Text tool to create a frame whose height and width are defined by the area you specified by dragging (see Figure 3-5).

◆ Drag a text place icon. The text place icon appears whenever you import a text file, or when you click the in port or out port of a text frame (for more on text place icons, and the in port and out port of a text frame, see "Importing text" later in this chapter). See Figure 3-6.

FIGURE 3-4

Click a frame with the Text tool

You've probably figured this out already, given the previous illustrations, but what the heck.

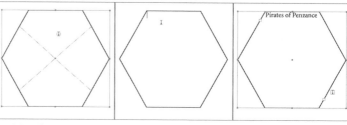

Position the Text tool over any empty frame (the frame does not have to be selected).

Click the Text tool inside the frame. InDesign converts the frame to a text frame.

Enter or place text.

FIGURE 3-5

Drag the Text tool

Select the Text tool

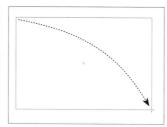

Drag the Text tool.

InDesign creates a text frame that's the width and height you specified by dragging.

FIGURE 3-6

Drag a text place icon

You "load" a text place icon by placing a text file or by clicking the in port or out port of a text frame.

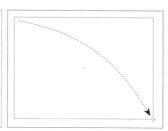

Drag the text place icon…

…to create a text frame that's the width and height you specified by dragging.

◆ Deselect all (Command-Shift-A/Ctrl-Shift-A) and then paste text into the publication (or drag it out of another application and drop it into the publication, which accomplishes the same thing). InDesign creates a text frame containing the text (see Figure 3-7).

◆ Drag a text file (or series of text files) out of your operating system's file browser (the Finder on the Macintosh, or the Windows Explorer in Windows) and drop them into an InDesign publication (see Figure 3-8).

FIGURE 3-7
Paste text

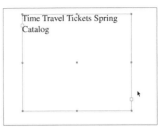

Copy text out of another application...

...and paste it into InDesign.

FIGURE 3-8
Drag and drop text files

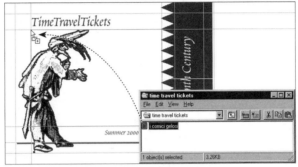

Drag a text file (or files) out of a Finder window (on the Macintosh) or Explorer window (in Windows) into the InDesign publication window.

Drop the file. InDesign places the file in your publication.

Note that InDesign does not require you to create a text frame *before* you add text, as (for example) QuarkXPress does. Most of the text frame creation methods described above dynamically create a text frame as you enter, import, or paste text.

Once you've created a text frame, you can change its size, shape, and rotation angle just as you would any other object you've created (see Chapter 6, "Drawing" and Chapter 8, "Transforming"). You can also change the shape of the text frame using InDesign's drawing and path editing tools (see Chapter 6, "Drawing").

Text can also appear *on* a path—for more on this topic, see Chapter 5, "Where Text Meets Graphics."

Setting Text Frame Options

Text frames have attributes that are not shared with graphics frames or with frames whose content is set to "Unassigned." You can view and edit these attributes by choosing Text Frame Options from the Type menu (or by pressing Command-B/Ctrl-B). InDesign displays the Text Frame Options dialog box (see Figure 3-9). The controls in this dialog box set the number of columns, inset distances, and first baseline calculation method for the text frame.

FIGURE 3-9
Text frame options

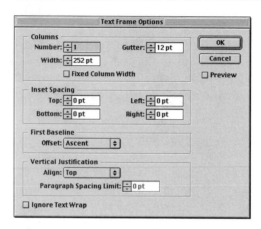

How Many Columns?   InDesign text frames can contain up to 40 columns—enter the number of columns you want in the Number field. To define the distance between columns, or "gutter," enter a value in the Gutter field.

Measure for Measure   When I think of the typesetting specifications for a block of text, I think first of the typeface, then the point size, the leading, and the measure, or column width. When I see a line of type, my thoughts go something like this: "That's Bodoni Book, eleven-on-fifteen, on a fourteen pica measure." The length of the lines of text is roughly as important as the character shapes, their size, and their leading.

InDesign recognizes the importance of column width in typesetting by giving you the ability to determine the width of a text frame by the width of its columns—and not the other way around (though you can do that, too). When you turn on the Fixed Column Width option, InDesign forces all of the columns in the selected text frame to be the width you've entered in the Width field. InDesign will increase or decrease the width of the selected text frame to accommodate the columns. As you resize the text frame, you'll notice that it snaps to widths determined by the fixed widths of the columns (and gutters) it contains (see Figure 3-10).

FIGURE 3-10
Fixed column width

When you turn on the Fixed Column Width option…

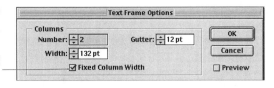

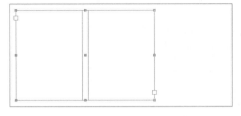

…InDesign resizes the text frame based on the column width you entered (rather than evenly dividing the width of the text frame into columns of equal width).

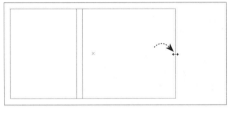

If you resize a text frame that has a fixed column width…

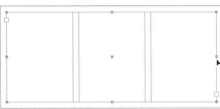

…InDesign will "snap" the frame widths based on that column width. No matter how narrow you make the frame, it will always contain at least one column of that width.

Setting Text Frame Insets

The values you enter in the Inset Spacing section of the Text Frame Options dialog box control the distances InDesign will push text from the edges of the text frame. You can enter an inset distance from 0 to 720 picas or 120 inches. (Note that you can't enter negative values to make the text hang out of the text frame.)

Inset distances work in conjunction with (and in addition to) the margins of the paragraphs in a text frame (see Figure 3-11). In general, I prefer to work with the text inset values set to zero, and use the left and right indent values of individual paragraphs to control the distance from the edges of the text to the edges of the text column.

Setting First Baseline Position

The Offset pop-up menu in the First Line Leading section of the Text Frame Options dialog box offers three methods for calculating the position of the first baseline of text in a text frame: Ascent, Cap Height, and Leading (see Figure 3-12).

FIGURE 3-11

Text frame insets

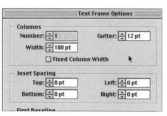

By default, InDesign applies no inset—note that this differs from QuarkXPress, which applies a one point inset by default.

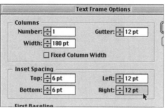

Enter inset distances in the fields in the Inset Spacing section of the dialog box to push text away from the edges of the text frame.

When you select the text frame with the Selection tool, InDesign displays the text inset boundary.

Paragraph indents are applied in addition to the text frame inset distances.

FIGURE 3-12

First baseline position

Example leading is 24 points.

Distance from the top of the text frame to the first baseline:
18 points.
(We got lucky this time.)

Distance from the top of the text frame to the first baseline:
15.5997991562 points.
(Approximately.)

Distance from the top of the text frame to the first baseline:
24 points.
(Isn't it better to know?)

If you use either the Ascent or Cap Height method, the tops of characters in your text frames will touch (or come close to touching) the top of the text frame (provided, of course, that the top frame inset is zero). This comes at a price, however: it's almost impossible to calculate the distance from the top of the frame to the baseline of the first line of text in the frame.

In addition, using these methods means that InDesign will vary the leading of the first line when you enter characters from different fonts in the line, or change the size of characters, or when you embed inline graphics in the line.

Is that bad? It is, if you care about type.

It's important that you know exactly where the first baseline of text in a text frame will appear, relative to the top of text frame. Why? Because if you know the position of the first baseline, you can snap the top of the text frame to your leading grid—and rest secure in the knowledge that the first baseline will fall neatly on the next baseline.

To control the location of the first baseline of text in a text frame, choose Leading from the Offset menu in the First Baseline section. When you do this, the first baseline appears one leading increment from the top of the text frame—regardless of the size of the characters (or the height of inline graphics) in the line.

For more on leading, see Chapter 4, "Type."

Ignoring Text Wrap

In a typical magazine spread, some text wraps around graphics; some text doesn't. Imagine that you want the body text of an article to wrap around an image—but you want to place a headline on top of the same image. To keep text in a text frame from obeying a text wrap, select the frame, display the Text Frame Options dialog box, and then turn on the Ignore Text Wrap option (see Figure 3-13).

FIGURE 3-13
Ignoring text wrap

When you try to place a text frame inside a text wrap, InDesign hides the text.

Unless, that is, you display the Text Frame Options dialog box (select the text frame and press Command-B/Ctrl-B) and turn on the Ignore Text Wrap option.

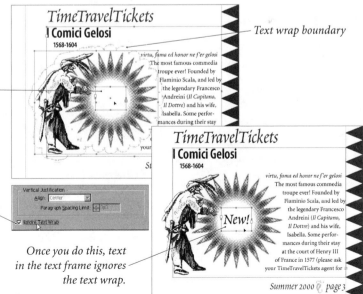

Text wrap boundary

Once you do this, text in the text frame ignores the text wrap.

Vertical Justification   Just as the alignment of a paragraph controls the horizontal position of the paragraph in a column, vertical justification controls the vertical position of the text in a text frame (see Figure 3-14). To set the vertical justification method used for a text frame, select the text frame, display the Text Frame Options dialog box, and then choose a method from the Align pop-up menu.

- ◆ **Top.** Aligns the text to the top of the text frame, positioning the first baseline of text in the frame according to the method you've selected from the Offset pop-up menu (see above).

- ◆ **Center.** Vertically centers the text in the text frame. When you choose this method, the method you've chosen from the Offset pop-up menu has no effect.

FIGURE 3-14
Vertical justification

When you choose Center from the Align pop-up menu, you might want to choose the Cap Height or Ascent option from the Offset pop-up menu (in this case, choosing Leading is not a good idea, as it pushes the text away from the visual center of the text frame).

When you choose Justify from the Align pop-up menu, InDesign adds space to force the text to fill the height of the frame. The method InDesign uses is based on the value you enter in the Paragraph Spacing Limit field (you can enter values from 0 to 8640 points).

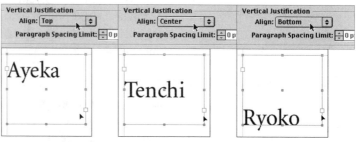

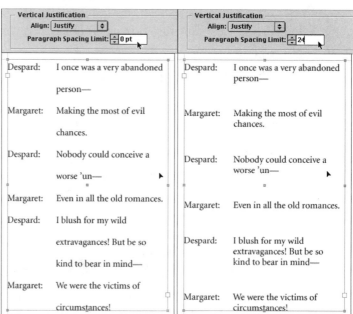

When you enter zero, InDesign applies leading to make the text fill the height of the text frame.

When you enter a value, InDesign applies paragraph spacing up to that amount before changing the leading.

◆ **Bottom.** Aligns the baseline of the last line of text in the text frame to the bottom of the frame. When you choose this method, the method you've chosen from the Offset pop-up menu has no effect.

◆ **Justify.** Adds vertical space to the text in the text frame (using paragraph spacing and/or leading to add this space) to fill the text frame with the text. Note that using the Justify method will not pull overset text into the text frame.

Paragraph Spacing Limit. When you choose Justify from the Align pop-up menu, InDesign activates this control. The value you enter in this field sets the maximum amount of space you'll allow InDesign to add between paragraphs in the text frame. Once the space between paragraphs reaches this value, InDesign adjusts the leading of each line in the text frame, rather than adding more space between paragraphs. To keep InDesign from changing the distance between lines of a paragraph, enter a large value (up to 8640 points) in this field. To force InDesign to apply vertical justification by changing leading values (rather than by changing paragraph spacing), enter zero in this field.

Linking and Unlinking Text Frames

You can link one text frame to another to make the text continue—or flow—from frame to frame. In InDesign, the controls for linking and unlinking text frames are the in port and out port icons on the text frames themselves. This means that the process of linking text frames in InDesign is similar to working with the "window-shade handles" on PageMaker text blocks, and should feel familiar to PageMaker users. There's no need to go to the Toolbox to get a "linking" tool, as there is in QuarkXPress.

Text frames come with their own special and somewhat obscure terminology. Any continuous series of text characters is a *story.* A story can be as small as a single, unlinked text frame, or as large as a series of hundreds of text frames containing tens of thousands of words and spanning dozens of pages. When you link text frames together, you're *threading* stories through the text frames. When you place text to create a series of linked text frames, you're *flowing* text.

The text in a story has a direction—it has a beginning, a middle, and an end. When I speak, in this section, of a particular text frame appearing before or after another, I'm talking about its position in the story, not relative to its position on the page.

The way that InDesign displays the in port and out port of a text frame tells you about the text frame and its position in a story (see Figure 3-15).

◆ When the in port or out port is empty, no other text frame is linked to that port. When both ports are empty, the text you see in the text frame is the entire story.

◆ When you see a plus sign (+) in the out port, it means that not all of the text in the story has been placed. The remaining (or "overset") text is stored in the text frame, but is not displayed.

◆ When you see a triangle in the in port or the out port (or both), InDesign is telling you that the text frame is linked to other text frames.

FIGURE 3-15
In ports and out ports

This text frame is at the start of a story, because the in port is empty.

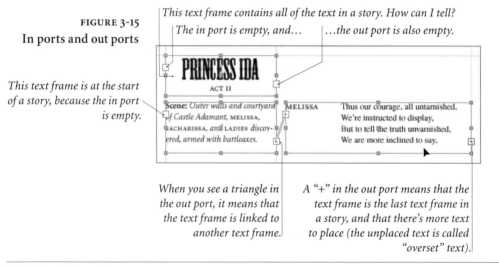

This text frame contains all of the text in a story. How can I tell?

The in port is empty, and…   *…the out port is also empty.*

When you see a triangle in the out port, it means that the text frame is linked to another text frame.   *A "+" in the out port means that the text frame is the last text frame in a story, and that there's more text to place (the unplaced text is called "overset" text).*

Linking Text Frames

To link one text frame to another, click either the in port or the out port of a text frame. InDesign displays the text place icon. Point at another frame (when you do this, InDesign displays the text link icon) and then click. InDesign links the two frames (see Figure 3-16). That sounds pretty simple, but there are a number of details you should keep in mind:

◆ Unlike QuarkXPress, InDesign can link two text frames when both frames contain text. When you do this, the stories in the text frames are merged into a single story. If the text in the first

FIGURE 3-16
Linking text frames

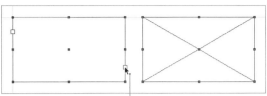

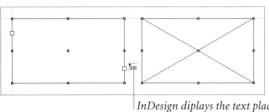

Select a text frame and click its out port.

At this point, you can also create a new text frame by dragging the text place icon. The new frame will be linked to the text frame you clicked.

You can aslo click the in port to load the text place icon.

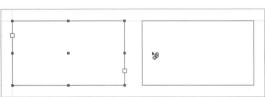

InDesign diplays the text place icon.

Position the text place icon over a frame.

InDesign changes the text place icon to the link icon.

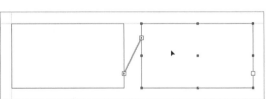

If you've turned on the Show Text Threads option (on the View menu), InDesign will display a line linking the out port of one text frame with the in port of another.

Click the link icon on the frame. InDesign links the two frames.

text frame did not end with a carriage return, InDesign will run the text in the second text frame into the last paragraph of the first text frame (see Figure 3-16).

◆ Unlike PageMaker's text blocks, InDesign frames can be linked when they're empty. This means you can easily set up text layouts without having the copy to hand and without resorting to a "dummy text" placeholder.

◆ Where you click (the in port or the out port) sets the position of the link in the sequence of linked text frames making up the story. If you click the out port, the text frame you link to will come after the current text frame; click the in port to link to a text frame earlier in the story (see Figure 3-17).

◆ When you click the out port of a text frame that contains more text than it can display (that is, an out port that displays the "+" symbol), the additional text will flow into the next text frame in the story (see Figure 3-18).

FIGURE 3-17
Linking stories

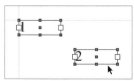

Two unlinked text frames.

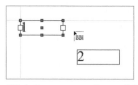

Click the out port of one of the frames to load the text place icon.

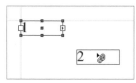

Click the text place icon on the other frame.

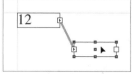

InDesign links the two frames. If the first frame did not end with a carriage return, InDesign runs the text from the first paragraph of the second frame into the last paragraph of the first frame.

FIGRUE 3-18
Controlling the order of text frames in a story

Two unlinked text frames.   *When you load the text place icon by clicking the out port…*   *…and link to another text frame…*   *…that frame becomes the next frame in the story.*

If, on the other hand, you load the text place icon by clicking on an in port…   *…the frame you link to becomes the previous text frame in the story.*

FIGURE 3-19
Placing overset text

This text frame contains overset text. When you link it to another text frame…   *…InDesign places the overset text in the following text frame (in this example, all of the text in the story has been placed).*

◆ You don't have to link to another text frame—you can also create a link to a graphic frame or a frame whose content type has been set to "None." When you link a text frame to a graphic frame, InDesign discards any previous content of the graphic frame.

◆ To create a new text frame that's linked to an existing text frame, click the in port or out port of the existing frame and then drag the text place icon.

Link icon   *Unlink icon*

◆ As you link and unlink text, InDesign changes the appearance of the cursor to give you a clue (or, as a more formal author would say, a "visual indication") about what you're doing or are about to do.

◆ What if you have a "loaded" text place cursor and then realize that you need to scroll, or turn to another page? Do you need to "unload" the text place cursor (see below) before issuing other commands? Probably not—you can scroll, zoom, turn pages, create or modify ruler guides, and create new pages while InDesign displays the text place cursor.

◆ To "unload" the text place cursor, click on any tool in the Toolbox.

◆ To view the links between text frames, choose Show Text Threads from the View menu. InDesign displays lines connecting text frames in the selection (see Figure 3-19).

FIGURE 3-19
Viewing text threads

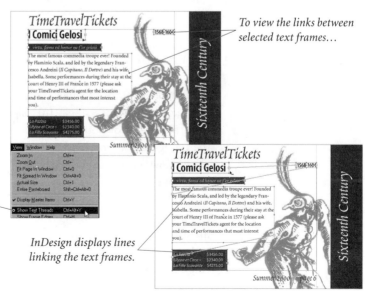

To view the links between selected text frames...

...choose Show Text Threads from the View menu.

InDesign displays lines linking the text frames.

Unlinking Text Frames

To break a link between text frames, double-click the in port or out port on either side of the link (see Figure 3-20). When you break a link between text frames that have text content, the text flows back into the text frame before (again, this is in terms of the story) the broken link. This usually means that the text becomes overset text stored in the last text frame in the story.

Alternatively, you can click the out port of one frame and then click the next frame in the thread (see Figure 3-21). When you move the text place icon over the next frame, InDesign will display the Unlink Text icon. When you click the Unlink Text icon on the frame, InDesign breaks the link. This method is slower and involves more mouse movement than double-clicking, but some people like it better.

FIGURE 3-20
Unlinking text frames

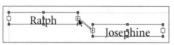

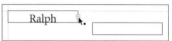

Select a text frame and double-click the out port (or in port).

InDesign breaks the link at the point at which you clicked.

FIGURE 3-22
Another method

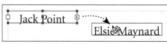

Select a text frame then click the out port (or in port). InDesign displays a text place icon.

Move the text place icon over the next (or previous, if you clicked an in port) text frame. InDesign displays the unlink icon.

InDesign breaks the link between the two text frames.

Cutting and Pasting Text Frames

What happens to links when you cut a linked text frame or series of linked text frames? First, InDesign does not delete the text in the frame—the only time it'll do that is when you select all of the frames in the story and delete them. Otherwise, InDesign will always flow the text contained by the frames you've deleted into the remaining frames in the story. If you want to delete text, you have to select it using the Text tool first—simply deleting the text frame it's in will not—necessarily—make it go away. For more on selecting text, see "Editing Text," later in this chapter.

When you cut or copy a series of linked text frames, then paste, you'll see that InDesign maintains the links between the duplicated frames—but not between the duplicates and the original frames or any other frames in the publication (see Figure 3-22). The copies of the frames contain the same text as the originals.

An interesting side effect of this behavior is that you can copy text frames from a story that are not linked to each other, and, when you paste, the text frames will be linked. This can come in handy in certain circumstances, as shown in Figure 3-23.

FIGURE 3-23
Cutting and pasting
linked frames.

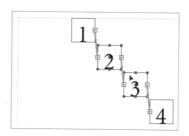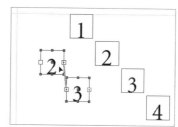

FIGURE 3-24
More about copying
and pasting

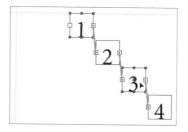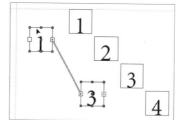

Adding a New Frame to a Story

Here's something that's difficult to do in other programs, but easy to do in InDesign—adding a text frame in the middle of a sequence of linked text frames. Follow these steps (see Figure 3-24).

1. Click the out port at the point in the story at which you want to add the new frame.

2. Drag the text place icon to create a new text frame, or click an existing unlinked frame (InDesign will only let you link to another chain of linked text frames when you're linking them to the end of a thread). InDesign threads the frame into the existing story.

FIGURE 3-25
Adding a new frame
to a story

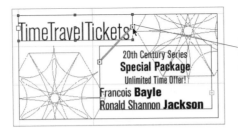

Click the out port of a text frame at the point at which you want to add the new frame (or click the in port of the following frame).

InDesign displays the text place icon.

Drag the text place icon.

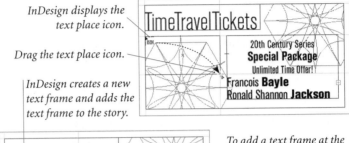

InDesign creates a new text frame and adds the text frame to the story.

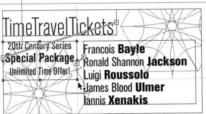

To add a text frame at the beginning of the story, click the in port of the first text frame in the story.

Flowing Text

When you place a text file, or click the in port or out port of a text frame that contains text with the Selection tool, InDesign displays the text place icon. Drag the text place icon to create a text frame of the size and shape you specify by dragging, or you can place text in an existing frame by clicking the frame with the text place icon. Flowing text is all about the care, maintenance, and feeding of the text place icon (see Table 3-1 for more on text place icons).

Once you've "loaded" the text place icon, you can use one of three text flow methods: Manual text flow, Semi-automatic text flow, or Autoflow. These determine what happens when you click or drag the text place icon. Here's the lowdown.

◆ Manual text flow. By default, InDesign uses the manual text flow method. When you click the text place icon in a column, or drag the text place icon, InDesign creates a new text frame and flows the text into it (see Figure 3-25). When you click the text place icon in a column, the width of the text frame is determined by the width of the column you clicked in; the height of the frame is the distance from the point at which you clicked the text place icon to the bottom of the column (see Figure 3-26). InDesign then flows the text into the new text frame. When you click the text place icon on an existing text frame or series of linked text frames, InDesign flows the text into the frame or frames (see Figure 3-27). In either case, once InDesign is done flowing the text, the text place icon disappears and you're back to whatever tool you had selected before you loaded the text place icon. To continue placing text, you'll need to click to reload the text place icon.

◆   Semi-automatic text flow. Semi-automatic text flow is almost exactly like manual text flow—the difference is that InDesign

FIGURE 3-26
Manual text flow

Load the text place icon (by placing a text file or clicking the in port or out port of any text frame).

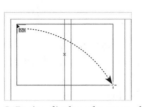

InDesign displays the manual text flow icon. Drag the icon.

InDesign flows text into the area you defined by dragging.

FIGURE 3-27
Manual text flow and column guides

Load the text place icon. InDesign displays the manual text flow icon.

Click the manual text flow icon in a column.

InDesign flows the text into the column. Click the out port to reload the text place icon.

Click the the manual text flow icon in the next column. InDesign creates a new text frame and links it to the previous text frame.

Repeat this process until you've placed all of the text you want to place.

FIGURE 3-28
Manual text flow and existing text frames

Load the text place icon.

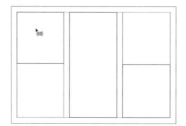

When you position the manual text flow icon over an existing frame, InDesign changes the icon to indicate that clicking will flow text into the frame beneath the cursor.

Click the place icon, and InDesign flows the text into the frame (and into any other frames linked to the frame). When you use manual text flow, InDesign does not create new frames, and stores any additional text as overset text.

reloads the text place icon after you've placed some text. The advantage? You don't have to click the out port of a text frame to reload the text place icon. To turn on semi-automatic text flow, hold down Option/Alt when the Text Place is visible. InDesign displays the semi-automatic text place icon when you do this (see Figure 3-28).

◆ Autoflow. When you hold down Shift, the text place icon turns into the autoflow icon. When you click the autoflow icon, InDesign will place all of the text into the publication's pages, creating new pages as necessary (see Figure 3-29). When you click the autoflow icon in a text frame or series of linked text frames, InDesign duplicates that frame (or frames) on any new pages it creates and will place the text in the duplicated frames. When you click the autoflow icon in a column, InDesign creates a new text frame in the column, and will go on creating new text frames and new pages until it has placed all of the text.

TABLE 3-1
Text flow icons

Icon:	What it means:
	Manual text flow icon. Click to flow text into a frame; click in a column to create a frame that's the width of the column, or drag to create a frame.
	Semi-automatic text flow icon. InDesign will "reload" the text flow icon after each click or drag.
	Autoflow text flow icon. Click to place all of the text in the story.
	The text flow icon is above a guide or grid "snap" point.
	The text flow icon is above a frame; clicking will place the text in the frame.

FIGURE 2-29
Semi-automatic text flow

*Load the text place icon.
InDesign displays the
manual text flow icon.*

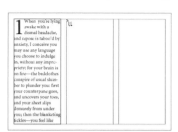

*Hold down Option/Alt to switch to
the semiautomatic text flow icon,
then click the icon in a column.*

*InDesign flows the text into the
column, then automatically reloads
the text place icon.*

*Click the the semiautomatic text flow
icon in the next column. InDesign
creates a new text frame and links it
to the previous text frame.*

*Repeat this process until you've
placed all of the columns of text you
want to place.*

FIGURE 3-30
Autoflow

*Load the text place icon.
InDesign displays the
manual text flow icon.*

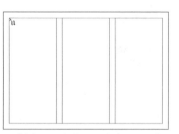

*Hold down Shift to switch to autflow
text flow icon, then click the icon in
a column.*

*InDesign flows the text into the
available columns or text frames,
and continues adding new text
frames and pages until there's no
more text left to place.*

Entering Text

The simplest way to get text into the text frames in your InDesign
publications is to type it. To do this, create a text by dragging the
Text tool, or select the Text tool and click in a frame (again, it
doesn't have to be a text frame). Either method places a blinking
text cursor (or "text insertion point") inside the text frame. Type,
and the characters you type will appear in the text frame.

Inserting Special Characters

I don't know about you, but I'm not getting any younger, and have trouble remembering exactly which keys to press to produce certain special characters. Quotation marks, bullets and registered trademark symbols I know, but I'm sometimes stumped when it's time to type a dagger (†) or a circumflex (^). And I often spend time hunting through KeyCaps (on the Macintosh) or Character Map (in Windows) looking for the right character in a symbol font (such as Zapf Dingbats).

If you also have this problem, you'll like InDesign's Insert Character feature. To use this feature, choose Insert Character from the Type menu as you're entering text (see Figure 3-31). InDesign displays the Insert Character dialog box. Choose the font, if necessary, then select a character from the list of characters in the font. Click the Insert button to enter the character at the location of the cursor.

FIGURE 3-31
Inserting characters

Click the Text tool in a text frame.

Choose Insert Character from the Type menu (if you have text selected, this menu item changes to "Replace Character").

Select a font family and type style...   *...select a character...*

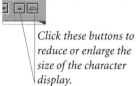

Click these buttons to reduce or enlarge the size of the character display.

...and then click the Insert button. InDesign inserts the character.

If you've selected an OpenType font, you can choose alternate character glyphs from the pop-up menus associated with each character.

Now here's the cool part: If a character can be found inside a font, you can use it—even if the character is outside the range of characters supported by your system. This seems like a silly feature—after all, why would fonts contain characters that would be inaccessible to any other program? I don't know, mate, but they do. Characters such as "fi" and "fl" ligatures, which aren't part of the Windows character set, suddenly become available (without switching to an "expert" font). It's well worth your time to trawl through your fonts with the Insert Character dialog box, just to see if there's anything you can use that you haven't been using.

Better yet, many special characters appear on InDesign's Context menu. As you're entering text, press the right mouse button (in Windows) or hold down Control and click the mouse button (on the Macintosh). InDesign displays the Context menu. Choose a special character from the Insert Special Character submenu, and InDesign enters it for you (see Figure 3-30).

If you'd rather type the special characters (and sometimes I would), use the keystrokes shown in Table 3-2.

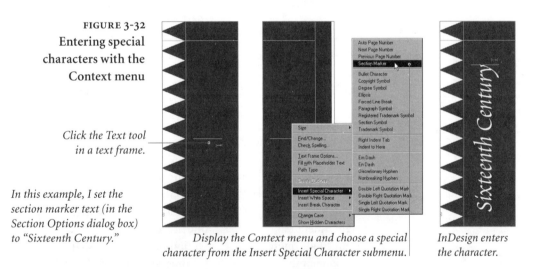

FIGURE 3-32
Entering special characters with the Context menu

Click the Text tool in a text frame.

In this example, I set the section marker text (in the Section Options dialog box) to "Sixteenth Century."

Display the Context menu and choose a special character from the Insert Special Character submenu.

InDesign enters the character.

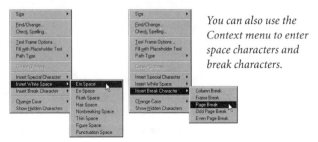

You can also use the Context menu to enter space characters and break characters.

TABLE 3-2
Entering special
characters

Special character:	What you press:
bullet (•)	Option-8/Alt-8
column break	Keypad Enter
copyright symbol (©)	Option-G/Alt-G
discretionary hyphen	Command-Shift--/Ctrl-Shift--
ellipsis (…)	Option-;/Alt-;
em dash (—)	Option-Shift--/Alt-Shift--
em space	Command-Shift-M/Ctrl-Shift-M
en dash (–)	Option--/Alt--
en space	undefined*
even page break	undefined*
figure space	Command-Shift=8/Ctrl-Shift-Alt-8
flush space	Command-Option-J/Chrl-ShiftAlt-J
frame break	Shift-Keypad Enter
hair space	Command-shift-I/Ctrl-Shift-Alt-I
indent to here	Command-\Ctrl-\
left double quote (")	Option-[/Alt-[
left single quote (')	Option-]/Alt-]
next page number	Command-Option-Shift-] Ctrl-Alt-Shift-]
non-breaking hyphen	Command-Option--/Ctrl-Alt--
non-breaking space	Command-Option-X/Ctrl-Alt-X
odd page break	undefined*
page break	Command-Keypad Enter Ctrl-Keypad Enter
paragraph symbol (¶)	Option-7/Alt-7
previous page number	Command-Option-Shift-[Ctrl-Alt-Shift-[
punctuation space	undefined*
registered trademark (™)	Option-2/Alt-2
right double quote (")	Option-Shift-[/Alt-Shift-[
right indent tab	undefined*
right single quote (')	Option-Shift-]/Shift-Alt-]
section name	Command-Option-Shift-N Ctrl-Alt-Shift-N
section symbol (§)	Option-6/Alt-6
thin space	Command0Option-Shift-M Ctrl-Alt-Shift-M
trademark (®)	Option-RAlt-R

* By default this special character has no keyboard shortcut, but
you can add a shortcut using the Edit Shortcuts dialog box—the
special characters are in the Other section.

Dummy Text   The client wants to see the new layout. But the writer won't give you the text. You're stuck—a layout looks, so, well, *incomplete* without text. And the client, a singularly humorless individual, cannot be appeased by whatever snatches of text from Gilbert & Sullivan, Brecht, or Edgar Rice Burroughs come easily to mind. What you need is something that *looks* like text, but isn't really text at all.

Graphic artists have been prepared for this eventuality for *centuries* (rumor has it that even *Gutenburg's* writers couldn't deliver text in time for an important meeting)—we use something called "dummy text." Dummy text is a meaningless stream of fake Latin text that *looks* very much like real text (it's so realistic that it's used to fill the pages of a bestselling series of yellow books and a major national newspaper). It's just the thing you need to survive your meeting and get that approval your business depends on.

InDesign makes it easy to add dummy text to a text frame—select the text frame using the Selection tool, or click the Text tool in a text frame and choose Fill with Placeholder Text from the Context menu (or from the Type menu). InDesign fills the text frame with dummy text (see Figure 3-33).

FIGURE 3-33
Filling a frame with dummy text

Select a text frame with the Selection tool, or click the Text tool in a text frame.

Choose Fill with Placeholder Text from the Context menu (or from the Type menu…

…and InDesign fills the selected frame with dummy text.

Importing Text

Most of the time, the text you work with in a page layout program isn't originally written using that program—it's written using a word processing program (such as Microsoft Word) and text editors (such as BBEdit on the Macintosh). To get the text into InDesign, you must import (or "place") the text files. InDesign can import text in a variety of formats, including Microsoft Word (97-98), Microsoft Excel (97-98), text-only (ASCII), Rich Text Format (RTF), and InDesign tagged text.

You can view the complete list of available import filters in the Files of Type pop-up menu in the Place Document dialog box in

Windows, or in the Component Information dialog box (for either platform—see "Component Information" in Chapter 1, "Basics").

If you don't see your word processor or text editor listed as one of the available import filters, don't despair. InDesign can import text in common "interchange" formats, such as text-only and RTF, and chances are good that your word processor or text editor can save text in one of those formats.

In addition, InDesign's tagged text filter can import formatted text from any application that can write a text-only file. The tagged text format is something like RTF—it's a text-only format that uses special codes to define the typesetting of the text in the file.

To place a text file, follow these steps (see Figure 3-31).

1. Choose Place from the File menu (or press Command-D/Ctrl-D). InDesign displays the Place dialog box.

2. Locate and select the text file you want to import. On the Macintosh, you can click the Show Preview button to view a preview of the file if you want–this will display the first few lines of the file in a preview window. Turning this option on can make it take longer to browse through lists of files, as InDesign must create a preview for each file you select.

3. Set up the import options you want.

   ◆ **Convert Quotes.** Turn on the Convert Quotes option to convert any straight quotes (i.e., foot and inch marks) to proper typographic quotation marks and apostrophes.

   ◆ **Retain Format.** Turn on the Retain Format option to keep the formatting specified in the text file (if any).

     What does "Retain Format" really mean? In general, InDesign imports any character or paragraph formatting attributes specified in the text file (this is mainly true for files from Microsoft Word or saved as RTF), but does not import any page layout information, such as headers and footers, or page margins. When the Retain Format option is off, InDesign strips the formatting out of the text file (including paragraph styles), and places the text using the current default formatting.

   ◆ **Show Import Options.** Turn on the Show Import Options option to display another dialog box containing more import options for the specific type of file you're placing. This dialog box appears *after* you click the OK button to import the text file.

FIGURE 3-34
Placing a text file

Select an unlinked frame (optional).

Press Command-D/Ctrl-D to display the Place dialog box.

Macintosh only: Click this button…

…to display a preview of the selected file.

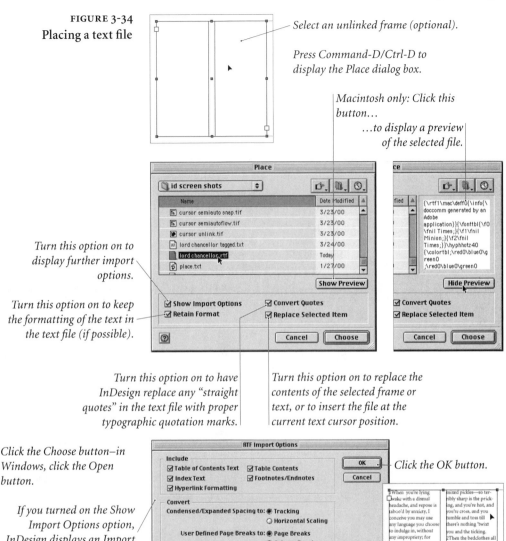

Turn this option on to display further import options.

Turn this option on to keep the formatting of the text in the text file (if possible).

Turn this option on to have InDesign replace any "straight quotes" in the text file with proper typographic quotation marks.

Turn this option on to replace the contents of the selected frame or text, or to insert the file at the current text cursor position.

Click the Choose button–in Windows, click the Open button.

If you turned on the Show Import Options option, InDesign displays an Import Options dialog box.

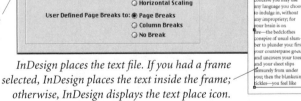

InDesign places the text file. If you had a frame selected, InDesign places the text inside the frame; otherwise, InDesign displays the text place icon.

◆ **Replace Selected Item.** If you had a frame selected before you displayed the Place dialog box, InDesign makes the Replace Selected Item option available. Turn this option on to replace the contents of the frame (if any) with the text file. If you had text selected, or if you had clicked the Text tool in a text frame, turning the Replace Selected Item option on inserts the text from the file into the text frame.

Note to PageMaker users: If you've looked, in vain, for an option similar to the Read Tags option in PageMaker's Place Document dialog box, you can give up. InDesign cannot read paragraph style tags. Instead, you'll have to learn how to accomplish the same thing using InDesign's tagged text format (see that section, later in this chapter).

4. Click the Choose/Open Button. If you turned on the Show Import Options option, InDesign displays a dialog box containing options for importing the type of file you selected (see Figure 3-32). Make any changes in this dialog box that you want, and then click the OK button. InDesign displays the Text Place cursor.

5. Drag the Text Place icon on the page, or click an existing frame (for more on flowing text using the Text Place icon, see "Flowing Text, above). InDesign imports the text file. If the incoming text file contains fonts that aren't currently loaded, InDesign warns you of their presence.

Show Options Shortcut: Hold down Shift and double-click a text file in the Place dialog box. Or hold down Shift as you click the Choose/Open button. InDesign displays the Import Options dialog box for the type of file you're importing.

Word and RTF Import   In general, InDesign imports the text formatting in Word and RTF text files, and does not import any page layout information saved in the file. This means, for example, that InDesign imports paragraph indents, but does not import page margins.

For a more complete list of the formatting imported by the Word and RTF import filters, see the Filters ReadMe file (you'll find it in your InDesign folder).

When you turn on the Show Import Options option and place a Word or RTF file, InDesign displays the corresponding Import Options dialog box (see Figure 3-35).

FIGURE 3-35
Word/RTF
import options

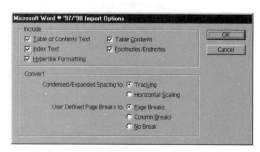

Table of Contents Text. Turn this option on to import the table of contents text (if any) in the Word file. The table of contents entries lose their special qualities. The page numbers appear as they were in the Word or RTF document the last time the file was saved, and do not change as you place the text on the pages of your InDesign publication. The table of contents also loses its navigational (i.e., hyperlink) properties. To InDesign, it's just text.

Index Text. Turn this option on to import an index (or indices) you've inserted in the Word/RTF document. Note that this does not import individual index entries-only the index itself.

Hyperlink Formatting. Turn on this option to import the formatting Word applies to text marked as a hyperlink. By default, that's underlined text that has a fill of the color "Blue." The imported text loses all hyperlinking capabilities.

Table Contents. When you turn this option on, InDesign imports the text in any tables in the incoming document as tab-delimited text. Leave this option turned off to omit the tables.

Footnotes/Endnotes. When you turn on this option, InDesign places any footnotes or endnotes at the end of the story. Leave this option off to omit any footnote or endnote text.

Condensed/Expanded Spacing. You can format text in a Word file using "expanded" or "condensed" spacing (using the options on the Spacing pop-up menu in the Character Spacing tab of Word's Font dialog box)—this option defines the method InDesign uses to apply this formatting. Choose Tracking to have InDesign apply kerning to the text, or choose Horizontal Scaling to have InDesign stretch or squash the characters of the text.

User Defined Page Breaks. What should InDesign do when it encounters a paragraph containing a page break setting (in Word, you'll find this option in the Line and Page Breaks tab of the Paragraph dialog box)? InDesign applies page and column break settings using the Start Paragraph pop-up menu in the Keep Options dialog box. To choose In Next Column, choose Column Breaks; to choose On Next Page, choose the Page Breaks option; or, to choose Anywhere, choose the No Break option. Manually-entered page breaks (press Command-Enter/Ctrl-Enter in Word) are ignored.

Beware the Fast Save. It's so seductive. It's hard to resist the natural impulse to turn on the Allow Fast Saves option in Word's Options dialog box (see Figure 3-36). It sounds like such a good idea. Faster saves mean you spend less time waiting for Word to save files—and saving time is good, right?

Not in this case, it isn't. The Word file format is very complicated, and using this option sometimes produces files that import filters can't read. Heck, when you turn this option on, Word sometimes writes files that *Word* can't read.

And, if you're having trouble importing a Word file, open the file in Word (if you can) and save it under another file name—it's very likely the person who gave you the file had forgotten to turn off the Allow Fast Saves option.

FIGURE 3-36
Word's Allow Fast
Saves option

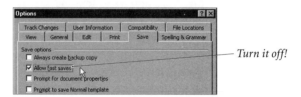

Turn it off!

**Text-Only
Import Options**

Text-only files often arrive full of extra characters—usually spaces and carriage returns added to change the appearance of text on screen. Text prepared for online viewing, for example, often contains a carriage return at the end of each line, as well as carriage returns bewteen paragraphs. The options in the Text Only Import Options dialog box give you a way to have the import filter do some of the clean-up for you (see Figure 3-37).

Character Set. If you're seeing odd characters in the text files you import, it might be that the character set of the computer used to create the files is not the same character set as the one in use by your copy of InDesign. As you import a text file, you can choose a character set that matches the character set of the text file.

Platform. Windows and the Macintosh use different character sets, and also use different ways of ending a paragraph. If you're using Windows, and know that the text file you're placing came from a Macintosh—or vice versa—choose the appropriate platform from this pop-up menu.

Set Dictionary To. Use this pop-up menu to apply a default spelling and hyphenation dictionary to the incoming text.

FIIGURE 3-37
Text Only
import options

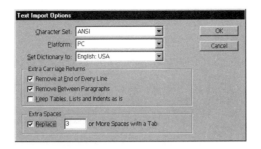

Extra Carriage Returns. The people who prepare the text files for you want to help. They really do. That's why they entered all of those carriage returns (to force a page break). Why they entered all of those spaces (to center the headline). They are trying to do some of the formatting so that you don't have to. The only trouble, of course, is that they usually make a mess that you're left to fix. InDesign's Text Import filter can solve many of the problems your helpful co-workers create. The options in the Extra Carriage Returns section of the Text Import Options dialog box help you clean up the extraneous carriage return characters.

Extra Spaces. Why do people enter extra spaces in text? Usually, they're trying to indicate to you, their trusted typesetter, that they want to enter some amount of horizontal space. In other words, a tab. InDesign can replace some number of spaces in the incoming text file with tabs—just enter a value for the number of contiguous space characters you want replaced. Note that this approach often enters multiple tab characters in the story, but that that problem is easily cleaned up using Find and Change.

Excel Import Options   Use the options in the Excel Import Options dialog box to specify the range of cells you want to import and the formatting applied to those cells (see Figure 3-39).

View, Sheet, and **Cell Range**. Use these options to define which custom view, worksheeet, and range of cells you want to import. By default, the Cell Range field selects the filled cells of the worksheet you've selected.

Apply Default Spreadsheet Style. If you want to apply Excel's default formatting (the General settings in Excel's Format Cells dialog box) to the incoming text, turn this option on (if you do, you won't be able to use the Cell Alignment and Decimal Places options).

FIGURE 3-38
Excel import options

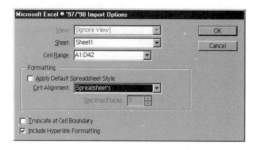

Cell Alignment. How do you want InDesign to align the text from the cells you're importing?

Decimal Places. How many decimal places do you want to use in the imported spreadsheet cells?

Truncate at Cell Boundary. Do you want InDesign to cut off any cell contents that extend beyond cell boundary (that is, the size of the cell as it appears in the selected spreadsheet)?

Include Hyperlink Formatting. Turn on this option to import the formatting Excel applies to text marked as a hyperlink. This imports only the formatting—the text loses its hyperlinking capabilities.

Tagged Text Import Options

InDesign's Tagged Text import filter, as I said earlier, gives you a great way to get formatted text from any applicaton that can create a text-only file. You can use FileMaker Pro, vi on a UNIX workstation, or even the original Quark word processor for the Apple II (dongle-equipped, of course) to enter tags in a text file that specify InDesign formatting. For more on creating tagged text files, see "Working with InDesign Tagged Text," later in this chapter. When you import a tagged text file, you can set some import options (see Figure 3-30).

FIGURE 3-39
Tagged Text
import options

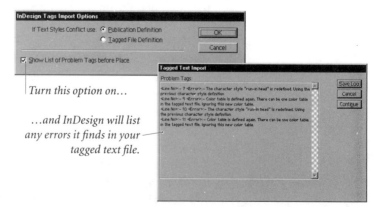

Turn this option on...

...and InDesign will list any errors it finds in your tagged text file.

If Style Conflicts Use. If the name of an incoming style (character or paragraph) matches a style that already exists in the publication, which style definition should InDesign use? Choose the Publication Definition option to apply the formatting defined by the existing style, or Tagged File Definition to import the style defined in the tagged text file. When you choose the latter method, InDesign adds the style to the publication and appends the word "copy" to the style's name. This does not affect the formatting of any text in the publication tagged with the original style.

Show List of Problem Tags Before Place. If you're not getting the formatting you expect from your tagged text files, turn this option on to have InDesign display a list of errors. If InDesign does find errors, you can choose to place the file, or to cancel the place operation. You can write the error list to a text file by clicking the Save Log button.

Text Files and File Linking

When you import a text file, InDesign maintains a link to the text file itself, and adds the link to the Links palette (to display the Links palette, choose Links from the File menu, or press Command-Shift-D/Ctrl-Shift-D). You can embed the text file, or update the link to a text file (if you do this, however, any formatting you've applied in InDesign will be lost). For more on working with links, see Chapter 2, "Page Layout").

Exporting Text

When you need to get your text back out of an InDesign publication and back into a some other program—a text editor, word processor, or database—you can export the text in a variety of text formats. To export a story, follow these steps (see Figure 3-33).

1. Select the story you want to export (click the Text tool in the story) and choose Text from the Export submenu of the File menu. InDesign displays the Export dialog box.

2. Choose an export format for the text from the Format pop-up menu.

3. Specify a name and location for the file.

4. Click the Save button to export the story.

FIGURE 3-40

Exporting text

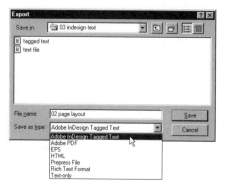

Editing text

Once you've entered or imported text, chances are good you're going to have to change it. InDesign includes most common word processing features, such as the ability to move the cursor through text using keyboard shortcuts, check the spelling of text, or find and change text and formatting.

Moving the Cursor Through Text

When I'm entering text, one of the last things I want to do is take my hands away from the keyboard. I don't want to have to use the mouse to move the text cursor or select text. That's why I like to use keyboard shortcuts to move the cursor and select text—they keep my hands where they belong: on the keyboard.

InDesign comes with a fairly complete set of keyboard shortcuts, as shown in Table 3-3. Note that some of the shortcuts have several keys associated with them—pick the combination that works best for you. I like the shortcuts on the numeric keypad, even though it takes my right hand away from the "home row." To use the keypad shortcuts, turn Num Lock off. The keypad shortcuts do not seem to work on the Macintosh.

Showing and Hiding "Invisibles"

Sometimes, the best tools are the simple ones. When you're handed another person's file to clean up, choose Show Hidden Characters from the Type menu. InDesign displays the carriage returns, tabs, spaces, and other invisible characters in the text (see Figure 3-34).

Checking Spelling

Toward the end of a project, I fall prey to the delusion that everything, every last word, on all of my pages, is misspelled. I find myself staring blearily at relatively simple words. Is "dog" really spelled

TABLE 3-3
Moving the cursor
through text

To move the cursor:	Press
Right one character	Right arrow, Keypad 6
Left one character	Left arrow, Keypad 4
Right one word.	Command-Right arrow
	Ctrl-Right arrow, Ctrl-Keypad 6
Left one word	Command-Left arrow
	Ctrl-Left arrow, Ctrl-Keypad-4
Up one line	Up arrow, Keypad 8
Down one line	Down arrow, Keypad 1
Up one paragraph	Command-Down arrow
	Ctrl-Down arrow, Ctrl-Keypad 8
Down one paragraph	Command-Down arrow
	Ctrl-Down arrow, Ctrl-Keypad 1
End of line	End, Keypad 1
Start of line	Home, Keypad 7
Start of story	Command-Home/Ctrl-Home, Keypad 7
End of story	Command-End/Ctrl-End, Keypad 1

Hold down Shift as you press
these shortcuts to select text
as you move the cursor.

FIGURE 3-41
Showing hidden
characters

Space ... *End of story*

Em space — *Tab* —

Carriage return

Line end

"D-O-G?" In my typical pre-deadline panic, I don't know. Everything looks wrong.

I don't know what I'd do without psychotherapy—and, of course, the spelling checkers in the page layout and word processing programs I use.

InDesign can check the spelling of any text in an InDesign text frame, and can also catch duplicated words ("the the") and possible capitalization errors. InDesign uses the dictionary or dictionaries associated with your text to perform the spelling check.

To check spelling, follow these steps (see Figure 3-35).

1. Press Command-I/Ctrl-I (or choose Check Spelling from the Edit menu) to display the Check Spelling palette (note that this isn't a dialog box, even though it looks like one).

FIGURE 3-42

Checking spelling

InDesign scrolls to display any suspect words it finds while checking spelling.

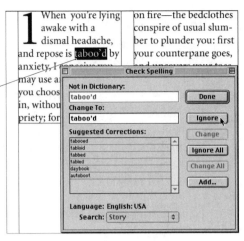

2. Define the scope of the spelling check using the Search pop-up menu at the bottom of the palette. Note that InDesign can check the spelling of all of the open publications, if you want, or you can restrict the spell check to the selected story only.

3. Click the Start button to start checking the spelling of text in the range you've chosen. When InDesign finds a potential mis-spelled word, the word appears in the Not In Dictionary field, and a number of possible corrections appear in the Suggested Corrections list. At this point, you can:

   ◆ Skip the word without making any change. To do this, click the Ignore button. InDesign continues with the spell check. To have InDesign ignore every occurrence of the word, click the Ignore All button.

   ◆ Replace the word with one of the suggestions. Select the suggestion, and InDesign enters the suggested word in the Change To field. Click the Change button to replace the selected word with the suggestion. Click the Change All button to replace every instance of the selected text with the text in the Change To field.

   ◆ Enter replacement text in the Change To field. Click the Change button to replace the selected word with the text you've entered, or click the Change All button to replace every instance of the selected text.

   ◆ Add the word to the user dictionary. This is a good thing to do with technical terms and names that appear frequently in your publications. For more on entering words in the user dictionary, see "Adding words to the user dictionary," below.

After you've taken any of the above actions, InDesign continues with the spelling check.

4. When you've finished checking the spelling of the publication (or publications), you can click the Done button to close the Check Spelling palette.

Adding Words to the User Dictionary

We use lots of words in our publications that aren't found in InDesign's dictionary. Even quite common, household words such as "Kvern" will provoke an angry query from the spelling checker. You can allay InDesign's fears by entering these words in a separate dictionary, the "user dictionary." When InDesign can't find a word in its dictionary, it consults the user dictionary before questioning the spelling of the word. If a word appears in both the standard dictionary (which can't be edited) and the user dictionary, InDesign favors the word in the user dictionary.

To add a word to the user dictionary, follow these steps (see Figure 3-43).

1. Display the Check Spelling palette (press Command-I/Ctrl-I) and click the Add button. InDesign displays the Dictionary dialog box.

2. Enter the word you want to add in the Word field, if necessary (if you're in the middle of a spelling check, InDesign enters the word displayed in the Not in Dictionary field for you).

FIGURE 3-43
Adding a word to the user dictionary

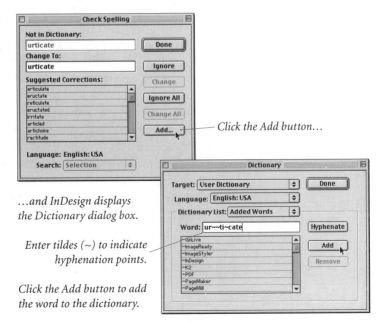

Click the Add button...

...and InDesign displays the Dictionary dialog box.

Enter tildes (~) to indicate hyphenation points.

Click the Add button to add the word to the dictionary.

3. Click the Hyphenate button when you want to view the word's hyphenation points (for more on hyphenation, see Chapter 4, "Type"). InDesign displays the hyphenation points (or, if the word is not in the dictionary, the proposed hyphenation points) in the word.

   Hyphenation points are ranked—the best hyphenation point is indicated by a single tilde ("~"), the next best point is indicated by two tildes ("~~"), and, at the least good hyphenation points, you'll see three tildes ("~~~"). You can enter hyphenation points in words you're adding to the user dictionary, or change the hyphenation points of words already in the user dictionary.

   If you do not want InDesign to hyphenate the word, enter a tilde before the first character of the word.

4. Click the Add button to add the word to the user dictionary.

To remove a word from the user dictionary, select the word from the list and then click the Remove button.

Find and Change

Economists and productivity experts keep telling me that personal computers have not lived up to their promise of increased productivity. Workers, they say, are no more productive than they were before the microcomputer revolution.

They are, of course, wrong—or maybe they've never worked as typists or typesetters. Since the advent of word processing and desktop publishing software, we "text workers" have been enjoying a productivity increase that is nothing short of mind boggling. Although I'm not sure "enjoying" is quite the right word.

One of the key innovations made possible by the text processing renaissance is the ability to find text in a document and, if necessary, to change it to something else—and all in an automated fashion. It doesn't matter what you call it—"find and change" or "search and replace," it's a kind of text-manipulation tool we haven't had before.

Find and change is all about pattern recognition. Most of what we do in InDesign (or in life, for that matter) is repetitive. We work our way through text, selecting each occurrence of "ffi" and changing it to "ffi" (the ligature). Or we select each bullet character we've typed, and replace it with a character from Zapf Dingbats. In each case, we're searching for one pattern in our text and replacing it with another.

Finding and changing text is all about working with strings. A string is any range of text—a single character, a word, or a phrase. Strings can also contain special, nonprinting characters, such as tab characters, em spaces, or carriage returns.

There are at least four different ways to perform a search-and-replace mission.

◆ Search for a text string and replace it with a different text string.

◆ Search for formatting and replace that formatting with other formatting.

◆ Search for a text string and apply formatting to it (after you find it).

◆ Search for formatting, and replace it with a string.

Finding Text   If you need to find some text, follow these steps (see Figure 3-44).

1. Open the Find/Change dialog box (press Command-F/Ctrl-F).

2. Enter the string you want to find in the Find What field.

3. Choose one of the options on the Search pop-up menu to set the scope of the search. Turn on Whole Word if you want to find only exact matches for the text you entered in the Find What field (if you've entered "dog" and want to find only that word, and not "dogged" or "underdog"). Turn on the case sensitive option to find only text with the same capitalization as the word you entered (this way, you'll find "dog," but not "Dog").

4. Click the Find Next button. InDesign finds an occurrence of the string you entered in the Find What field and displays it in the publication window, turning pages and scrolling to display the text, if necessary. You can continue clicking the Find Next button to find the next occurrence of the text in the specified search range until, eventually, you'll return to the first instance InDesign found.

About metacharacters. You can't enter nonprinting characters—such as tab characters, line-end characters, or carriage returns—in the Find What or Change To fields. To get around this, you enter codes—known as "metacharacters"—representing those characters (see Table 3-4). InDesign makes the process of entering metacharacters easy—they're on the pop-up menus attached to the Find What and Change To fields.

TABLE 3-4
Metacharacters

To search for this character:	Enter:#
Automatic page number	^x
Bullet	^8
Caret	^^
Copyright	^2
Carriage return	^p
Line end	^n
Inline graphic	^g
Paragraph	^7
Registered trademark	^r
Section	^6
Tab	^t
Right indent tab	^y
Indent to here	^i
Em dash	^_
Em space	^m
En dash	^=
En space	^>
Flush space	^f
Hair space	^|
Nonbreaking space	^s
Thin space	^<
White space	^w
Discretionary hyphen	^-
Nonbreaking hyphen	^~
Double left quotation mark	^{
Double right quotation mark	^}
Single left quotation mark	^[
Single right quotation mark	^]
Any character	^?
Any digit	^9
Any letter	^$

To enter a metacharacter in the Find What or Change To fields, you can either enter it directly (if you know the code) or choose it from the pop-up menus associated with the fields.

Wildcard Metacharacters

Imagine that you need to find all of the part numbers in a publication. Your part numbers start with the string "IN" and are always followed by four letters, a dash, and four numbers. How can you find all of the strings?

You can use InDesign's "wildcard" metacharacters—these give you a way to find patterns containing unspecified characters. To

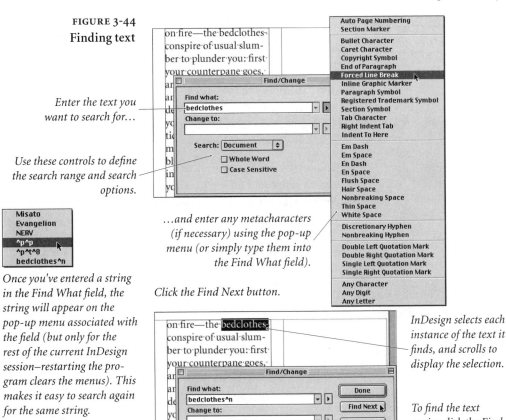

FIGURE 3-44
Finding text

Enter the text you want to search for...

Use these controls to define the search range and search options.

Once you've entered a string in the Find What field, the string will appear on the pop-up menu associated with the field (but only for the rest of the current InDesign session–restarting the program clears the menus). This makes it easy to search again for the same string.

If InDesign finds the text in overset text, the phrase "Overset Text" appears above the Find What field.

...and enter any metacharacters (if necessary) using the pop-up menu (or simply type them into the Find What field).

Click the Find Next button.

InDesign selects each instance of the text it finds, and scrolls to display the selection.

To find the text again, click the Find Next button again.

match any single, unspecified character, type "^?" in the Find What field. Enter "^9" to find any single digit, or "^$" to find any single letter.

To find all of the part numbers in the example, you'd enter "IN^$^$^$-^9^9^9^9" in the Find What field. Note that using wildcard metacharacters also helps you avoid finding the strings you don't want to find—if, in our example, we'd used the wildcard-laden string "IN^?^?^?^?^?^?^?^?^?" we'd run the risk of finding the word "INdubitable," which appears in our imaginary catalog many times, rather than the part numbers.

Be careful—entering these wildcard characters in the Change To field will result in text being replaced by the metacharacter codes themselves. That's why the wildcards don't appear on the Change To field's pop-up menu.

Replacing Text

To replace one text string with another, you enter text in both the Find What and Change To fields of the Find/Change dialog box (see Figure 3-40). Once you've done this, you have two choices:

◆ You can choose to have InDesign replace all instances of the string in the Find What field with the string you entered in the Change To field throughout the search range by clicking the Change All button.

◆ You can find each occurrence of the string in the specified search range and decide to replace it or not. To do this, click the Find Next button, view the found text, and then click either the Find Next button (to move on to the next instance of the string without making any changes) or the Change button (which replaces the selected text with the contents of the Change To field).

FIGURE 3-45
Replacing text

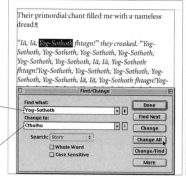 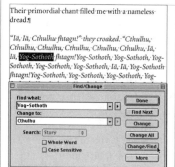

Enter the text you want to find in the Find What field.

Enter the replacement text in the Change To field.

Click the Find Next button to find the first instance of the text.

Click the Change button to replace the selection with the text in the Change To field, or click the Change All button to change all occurrences of the text in the Find What field…

…or click the Change/Find button to make each change yourself.

Finding and Changing Formatting Attributes

What do you do when you want to find all of the occurrences of the word InDesign formatted as 10-point Helvetica bold? And, for that matter, change the word's formatting to 12-point Adobe Caslon italic? It's easy—use the Find Style Settings and Change Style settings controls at the bottom of the Find/Change dialog box (if you can't see these settings, it's because you need to expand your Find/Change dialog box—click the More button, and InDesign will display these options).

To choose the formatting attributes you want to find, click the Format button in the Find Style Settings field. InDesign displays the Find Format Settings dialog box (see Figure 3-46). This dialog

FIGURE 3-46
Find and change
formatting attributes

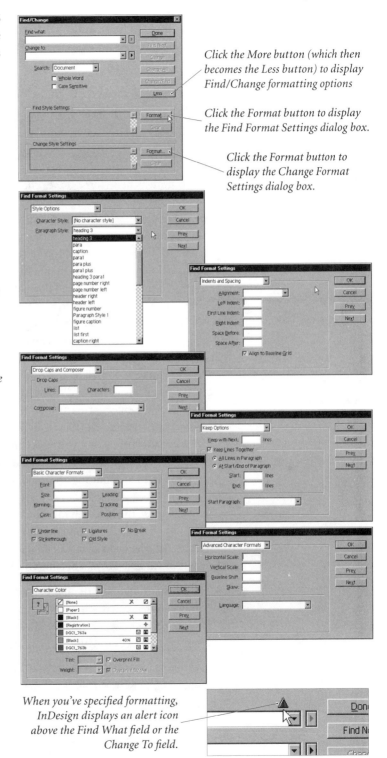

Click the More button (which then becomes the Less button) to display Find/Change formatting options

Click the Format button to display the Find Format Settings dialog box.

Click the Format button to display the Change Format Settings dialog box.

Use the panels of the Find Format Settings dialog box to specify the formatting you want to find. Or use the Change Format Settings dialog box to set up the formatting you want to apply to any text you find.

To get from one panel to another without using the pop-up menu, hold down Command/Ctrl and press the up or down arrow keys.

When you've specified formatting, InDesign displays an alert icon above the Find What field or the Change To field.

box is another of those multi-panel extravaganzas InDesign will no doubt be famous for. And, as in the other dialog boxes, the best way to get through it is to hold down Command/Ctrl as you press the up or down arrow key (this is the same as pressing the Prev or Next buttons to display the previous or next panel).

The eight panels of the Find Style Settings dialog box give you the ability to specify any formatting that can be applied to text in InDesign. Navigate through the panels until you find the formatting options you want, then use them to specify the formatting you want to find. When you're done, click the OK button to return to the Find/Change dialog box. InDesign displays a list of the options you've chosen in the field in the Find Style Settings section.

To set up the formatting options you want to apply to any text you find, click the Format button in the Change Style Settings field. This displays the Change Format Settings dialog box, which is identical in all but name to the Find Format Settings dialog box. Use the Change Format Settings dialog box to specify the formatting you want to apply, then return to the Find/Change dialog box. InDesign displays the formatting you've chosen in the field in the Change Style section.

When you've specified formatting in the Find Style Settings section, InDesign displays a red "alert" triangle below the Find What field. When you enter formatting in the Change Style Settings field, InDesign displays the red triangle below the Change To field.

To clear the formatting you've set in either the Find Format Settings or the Change Format Settings dialog boxes, click the Clear button in the corresponding section of the Find/Change dialog box.

Once you've specified the formatting you want to find and/or change, you use the Find/Change dialog box in the same manner as you would when finding/changing text strings.

Note that when you have specified formatting in the Find Format Settings or Change Format Settings dialog boxes, you can:

◆ Leave the contents of the Find What and Change To fields empty. When you do this, InDesign searches for instances of the formatting you've specified in the Find Format Settings dialog box, and replaces it with the formatting you've entered in the Change Format Settings dialog box.

◆ Enter text in both the Find What and Change To fields. In this case, InDesign searches for an instance of the string you entered in the Find What field that has the formatting specified in the Find Style Settings section, and replaces the text it finds with the string you entered in the Change To field. InDesign applies the formatting from the Change Style Settings section to the replacement text.

♦ Enter text in only the Find What field and leave the Change To field blank. When you do this, InDesign searches for the string you entered in the Find What field (and any formatting you've specified in the Find Style Settings section), and changes the formatting of the found text to the formatting specified in the Change Style Settings section.

♦ Enter text only in the Change To field and leave the Find What field blank. In this case, InDesign searches for the formatting you entered in the Find Style Settings area (InDesign won't start a search in which the Find What field is empty and no formatting is specified in the Find Style Settings section), and replaces any text it finds with the string you entered in the Change To field (plus any formatting you've specified in the Change Style settings Section). While you aren't very likely to use this find/change method (it's pretty obscure), it's nice to know it's available.

Automating Run-In Headings

If you've been in this business for a while, you've probably encountered that bane of the desktop publisher's existence—a run-in heading. What's a run-in heading? It's a heading that starts a paragraph of body text. The text of the heading "runs into" the body text. You'll often see them used for paragraphs starting with "Note:" or "Warning:" or "Tip:" or the like.

The trouble is, writers and editors usually want to keep the heading as a separate paragraph so that they can view it as a heading level in the outline mode of their word processing program (Microsoft Word, for example). It's only when the text reaches you for layout that it needs to be formatted using run-in headings.

Luckily, in InDesign, you can use Find and Change to make this change. The technique I'm about to show involves a two-step process—first, you find and format the text of the headings; next, you make the headings "run in" to the body text paragraphs following them. In the following example, the paragraph style applied to the run-in headings is called "heading 2," the paragraph style of the body text is "para1," and the character style we want to apply to the new run-in headings is "run-in heading." Ready? See Figure 3-47.

1. Press Command-F/Ctrl-F to display the Find/Change dialog box.

FIGURE 3-47
Formatting run-in headings with find and change

This text contains heading paragraphs (in this example, they've been formatted using the paragraph style "heading 2"). To convert these paragraphs into run-in headings...

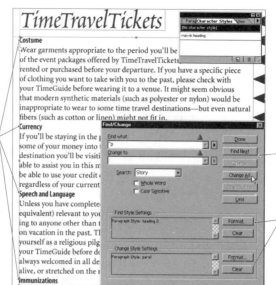

...display the Find/Change dialog box...

...set up the Find Style and Change Style settings as shown...

...and then click the Change All button. InDesign applies the character style to all of the characters in the heading paragraphs (and sets the paragraph style to that of the body text paragraph following the heading.

Display the Find/Change dialog box again, and search for all carriage returns formatted using the heading paragraph style—and replace them with a separator character (a colon, in this example) followed by a space.

Click the Change All button again.

InDesign runs the headings into the text.

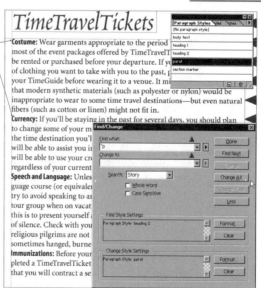

2. Clear any formatting in the Find Style Settings or Change Style Settings sections (click the Clear button in each section), if necessary. Set the scope of the find/change operation by choosing one of the options on the Search pop-up menu.

3. Click the Format button in the Find Style Settings section. InDesign displays the Find Format Settings dialog box. Display the Style Options panel, if it's not already visible. Choose the name of the paragraph style containing the headings ("heading 2") from the Paragraph Style pop-up menu. Click the OK button to close the Find Style Settings dialog box.

4. Click the Format button in the Change Style settings section. InDesign displays the Change Format Settings dialog box. Display the Style Options panel and choose the character style you want to use for the run-in headings ("run-in heading"). Choose the paragraph style of the paragraph following the headings ("para1") from the Paragraph Style pop-up menu. Click the OK button to return to the Find/Change dialog box.

5. Because you are completely fearless (and because you know InDesign can undo this action), click the Change All button. InDesign applies the character style ("run-in heading") and paragraph style ("para1") to all of the headings. Do not close the Find/Change dialog box.

6. Enter a carriage return metacharacter ("^p") in the Find What field. Enter the separator (usually a period or colon, followed by a space) you want to use for the run-in heading in the Change To field.

7. Click the Clear buttons in both the Find Style Settings and Change Style Settings areas. Click the Format button in the Find Style Settings section. InDesign displays the Find Format Settings dialog box. Display the Style Options panel, if it's not already visible. Choose the character style you're using for the run-in heading ("run-in heading") from the Character style pop-up menu, then close the dialog box.

8. Click the Change All button. InDesign runs all of the headings into the paragraphs following them, creating run-in headings out of the heading paragraphs.

Goodbye, Paragraph! I frequently work with publications containing notes written to me by other people—you know, things like, "Ole, this section still needs work." I don't want to see that paragraph in the printed version of the piece (and I have, believe me!), so I tag these paragraphs with a paragraph style named "Comment."

When I'm laying out the publication, I remove all of the paragraphs tagged with this style name. Do I hunt through the text, laboriously selecting each paragraph and pressing the Delete key? No way—I use an unexpected and probably unintended feature of InDesign's Find/Change dialog box. Here's the easy way to delete paragraphs tagged with a particular style (see Figure 3-41).

1. Press Command-F/Ctrl-F to display the Find/Change dialog box.

2. Leave the Find What and Change To fields empty. Choose a search range from the Search pop-up menu to define the scope of the find/change operation.

3. Click the Clear buttons in both the Find Style Settings and Change Style Settings areas, if necessary. Click the Format button in the Find Style Settings section. InDesign displays the Find Format Settings dialog box.

4. Display the Style Options panel, if it's not already visible. Choose the paragraph style you want to annihilate from the paragraph style pop-up menu, then close the Find Format Settings dialog box.

5. Click the Change All button. InDesign deletes every paragraph tagged with the paragraph style from the search range.

Working with InDesign Tagged Text

It's been pointed out to me that I live on another planet. This planet, everyone agrees, is one very much like Earth. In fact, almost everything is the same—right down to the existence of a desktop publishing program named "InDesign." At that point, however, things get different. Disturbingly, subtly different.

The most recent reason for the "Kvern is an alien weirdo" talk around my office is that one of the features that excites me most about InDesign is rarely mentioned in the marketing materials. Or on the back of the box. It's not the typesetting features, nor it it the ability to place native Photoshop and Illustrator files. And it's not the fact that the program can export PDF without the aid of the Acrobat Distiller. I think those are great features, but they're not it.

FIGURE 3-48

Removing all paragraphs tagged with a specific paragraph style

This text contains paragraphs tagged with the style "editorial comment"— they're left over from the writing process. To remove them all, display the Find/Change dialog box…

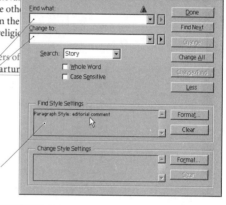

…make sure that the Find What and Change to fields are empty…

…choose the style name from the Paragraph Style pop-up menu in the Style Options panel of the Find Format Settings dialog box…

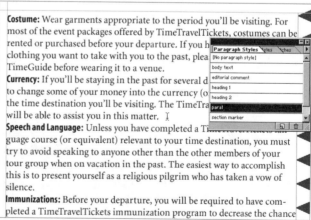

…and click the Change All button. InDesign removes all paragraphs tagged with the paragraph style you selected.

What is this mystery feature? It's two features, really—the tagged text import and export filters. To explain why these filters are important, I've got to explain a little bit about what tags are.

The Land That WYSIWYG Forgot

Tags have been around for a long time. Before desktop publishing appeared, the world of typesetting was ruled by dedicated typesetting systems. As we set type on these machines, we didn't see anything that looked like the type we were setting. Instead, we saw the text of our newspapers, books, and magazines surrounded (and sometimes obscured) by cryptic symbols: typesetting tags and codes. To see what these symbols meant, we had to print the file. Only then would we see our type with its formatting applied.

Then came the Macintosh, PageMaker, the LaserWriter, and WYSIWYG (What you See Is What You Get) publishing. This revolution made it easier for more people to set type—in part because it freed us from having to learn and use the obscure codes and tags of the dedicated typesetting systems. These days, modern desktop publishing programs are better typesetting systems than anything we had in the old days—and you can see what you're doing.

Why Bother with Tags?

So why should you mess with tags in this day and age? They can make some jobs easier, and sometimes they can make it possible to do things that wouldn't be practical to do using menus, dialog boxes, and the Character and Paragraph palettes.

The tagged text import filter reads tags—strings of text you've entered in the text file—and turns them into InDesign formatting. The tagged text export filter takes InDesign formatting and turns it into tags in a text file. There's a key point to make here: InDesign's tagged text export filter is the only text export filter that doesn't change the appearance of the text you're exporting.

Here are some of the reasons I want to use tags:

◆ I like using text editors (such as BBEdit on the Macintosh)—they're small , fast, and can do lots of things word processors cannot. The trouble is that I need to be able to indicate simple formatting changes—such as bold or italic—as well as paragraph styles—in the text files I prepare for import into InDesign. It would be nice if I could specify some font changes, as well. In short, I want to be able to take advantage of all of InDesign's text formatting features, but create and manage my text using a program that speaks nothing but ASCII (text only) format.

◆ Any application that can save files in text-only format can be used to create formatted text for use in InDesign. This means that your catalog clients can use their FileMaker database to mark up their text—Visual Basic, Microsoft Excel, and Microsoft Access are other obvious choices. It might even help your old uncle who lives in a cave and uses nothing but EDLIN.

◆ You can place text that's been marked up using XPress tags or PageMaker tags.

◆ You can store frequently-used formatted text as tagged text files. It's far quicker to place a tagged text file than it is to open another InDesign publication and copy/paste the text you want. In addition, the tagged text file takes up far less disk space than an InDesign publication or InDesign library file.

Getting Started with Tagged Text

To learn how tags work, the best thing you can do is to export formatted text from InDesign and then use a word processor or text editor to look a the file (you can't, unfortunately, place a tagged text file in InDesign without converting the tags to formatting).

The "official word" on tagged text is the Tagged Text.pdf file, which you'll find inside the Adobe Technical Info folder on your InDesign installation CD. This guide includes basic instructions and a list of all of the tags you can use.

What Tags Can Contain

InDesign's tags can specify character formatting (such as font, point size, color, or baseline shift), paragraph formatting (such as indents, tabs, and paragraph space before and after), and styles (both paragraph styles and character styles).

Tag Structure

InDesign tags are always surrounded by open (<) and close (>) "angle brackets" (which most of us also know as "greater than" and "less than" symbols). The first characters in a tagged text file must state the character encoding (ASCII, ANSI, UNICODE, BIG5, or SJIS), followed by the platform (MAC or WIN). So the typical Windows tagged text file begins with <ASCII-WIN>, and the Macintosh verison begins with <ASCII-MAC>. If InDesign doesn't see one of these tags at the start of the file, InDesign will not interpret the tags in the file—all of the tags will appear as text. Here are a few more details about tagging conventions.

◆ When you need to refer to a font, style, or color name inside a tag, you must surround the name with straight quotes—not typographic ("curly") quotation marks. For example:

```
<FONT "Zapf Dingbats">
```

◆ Any characters you enter outside a tag will appear as characters in the imported text.

♦ Enter an empty tag to return the formatting affected by the tag to its default state. For example:

```
Baseline <cBaselineShift:3>Shift<cBaselineShift:> text following
should be back to normal.
```

Paragraph Style Tags   If you're a long-time PageMaker user, you've probably worked with PageMaker's style tags to apply paragraph formatting to text files. InDesign's tagged text format is something different, but we can create a "minimalist" tagged text file that's almost as easy to work with as PageMaker's paragraph style tags. Here's the header for an example tagged text file:

```
<ASCII-WIN>
<DefineParaStyle:heading=<Nextstyle:para1>>
<DefineParaStyle:para1=<Nextstyle:para>>
<DefineParaStyle:para=<Nextstyle:para>>
<ColorTable:=<Black:COLOR:CMYK:Process:0,0,0,1>>
<ParaStyle:heading>This is a heading
<ParaStyle:para1>This is the first paragraph of body text.
<ParaStyle:para><pLeftIndent:3p6>This the basic body text format.
```

Note that the paragraph style definitions do not contain any formatting—my assumption is that you'll set up corresponding paragraph styles in your publication. Then all you need to do is paste the appropriate header at the top of a text file, and then enter the paragraph style tags for each paragraph. If, when preparing a file for import into PageMaker, you entered "<heading>," enter "<ParaStyle:heading>" for InDesign.

After words

In academic circles, debate continues on whether we're born with the ability to understand language, or whether it's something we're taught. I don't know the answer, and, most of the time, I don't even know which side of the argument I'm on. What I do know is that language is the most important technology humans have developed.

In this chapter, I've shown how to get words into InDesign, how to organize them in your publications, and how to get them out again. Next stop—typesetting with InDesign!

4

Type

Late night. The pale glow from the monochrome monitor of my Compugraphic phototypesetter. The smell of the office standard "French Vanilla" coffee—warming, now, for several hours and resembling nothing so much as battery acid. The gentle snoring of one of the staff writers, who is curled up in the warmth of the unit that holds the spinning filmstrips containing the fonts I'm using to set his story.

These are the things I think of when I hear the word "typesetting"—they're memories from my job at Seattle's free rock and roll newspaper *The Rocket*, circa 1982. Desktop publishing didn't exist yet, and digital (as opposed to photo) typesetting systems—with their WYSIWYG displays—were rare. The code and characters I saw on my screen wouldn't look anything like type until they were printed, one character at a time, on a strip of photographic film and developed. I could set just about any kind of type using that machine, provided the characters would fit on a piece of film not more than seven inches wide, and provided I didn't need to use characters from more than six fonts.

When desktop publishing systems appeared, I found that they couldn't do everything I could do with my Compugraphic—but that being able to see what my type would look like *before I printed it* more than made up for any deficiencies in precision, automation, and flexibility. These days, page layout programs are far more capable than my trusty EditWriter. Does that mean, however, that there's no more room for improvement? For surprising new features? Is typesetting "done?"

Not a chance—but InDesign offers a number of improvements and surprises in the area of typesetting. It's an evolutionary product—not a "revolutionary" one, but, on its release, InDesign became the best desktop typesetting program available, and raised the bar for its competition.

In this chapter, I'll walk through InDesign's typesetting features. I'll start with character formatting (font, point size, kerning, and baseline shift are examples of character formatting), move on to paragraph formatting (indents, tabs, space above and below, and composition), and then dive into formatting using character and paragraph styles. Along the way, there may be a joke or two.

Character Formatting

Character formatting is all about controlling the appearance of the individual letters characters in your publication. Font, type size, color, and leading are all aspects of character formatting.

I refer to all formatting that can be applied to a selected range of text as "character" formatting, and refer to formatting that InDesign applies at the paragraph level as "paragraph" formatting. Tab settings, indents, paragraph rules, space above, and space after are examples of paragraph formatting. There are areas of overlap in these definitions. Leading, for example, is really a property that applies to an entire *line* of text (InDesign uses only the largest leading value in a line to set the leading for that line), but I'll call it "character" formatting, nonetheless, because you can apply it to individual characters.

In addition to these distinctions, InDesign's paragraph styles can include character formatting, but apply to entire paragraphs. See "Styles," later in this chapter.

Character Palette   The key to character formatting in InDesign is—you guessed it—the Character palette (see Figure 4-1). To display the Character palette, press Command-T/Ctrl-T.

FIGURE 4-1
Character palette

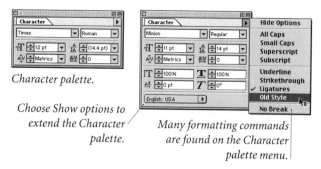

Character palette.

Choose Show options to extend the Character palette.

Many formatting commands are found on the Character palette menu.

Font Family and Font

Selecting a font in InDesign is a little bit different than selecting a font in most other page layout programs. To InDesign, fonts are categorized as font "families," and each family is made up of one or more type styles. A font family is a set of typefaces designed to have a common "look." A "font," then is specified by its font family and type style. In this book, I've used the font family Minion, and the type style Regular for the body text—so the font of the body text is "Minion Regular."

InDesign's user interfaces for selecting fonts mirror this approach. When you choose a font from the Font submenu of the Type menu, you must select both the font family and a specific type style (that is, you can't simply select the font family).

Using the Character palette to select a font is a two-part process. First, you choose the name of a font family from the Font Family pop-up menu. Next, you specify a member of that family using the Type Style pop-up menu. Note that InDesign does not have "type styles" in the same way that other programs do—it makes no assumption that the selected font family has a "bold" or "italic" member, and will never *generate* a fake bold or italic version of a font. The names that appear on the Type Style pop-up menu are all taken from the fonts themselves—if you don't have a font for a particular type style, you won't see it listed in the Type Styles menu (see Figure 4-2).

FIGURE 4-2
Selecting a font

Select a font family...

...and then select a type style. InDesign will not generate bold or italic type styles.

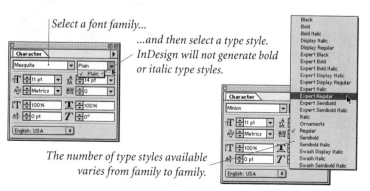

The number of type styles available varies from family to family.

To select a font family or type style in the Character palette, you can type into the appropriate field—you don't have to use the menu. As you type the name of a font family or type style, InDesign will display the available font or fonts that match the characters you typed.

Font selection keyboard shortcuts. You can also define a keyboard shortcut to select a specific font. If you frequently switch from one font to another, this can really save you a lot of time and trouble. To do this, follow these steps (see Figure 4-3).

1. Choose Edit Shortcuts from the File menu. InDesign displays the Edit Shortcuts dialog box.

2. Choose Type from the Product Area menu. InDesign adds a list of type commands to the Commands list. In this list, you'll see a number of commands beginning with the word "Font." These are the commands for selecting any of the currently-loaded fonts.

3. Locate and select the font you want to apply.

4. Click the text cursor in the Press New Shortcut field and press the new shortcut. InDesign will warn you (by placing a tiny caption below the Press New Shortcut field) if the keyboard shortcut is already in use.

5. Click OK to close the Edit Shortcuts dialog box and save your new shortcut.

FIGURE 4-3
Defining a keyboard shortcut for a font

Select a font, then...

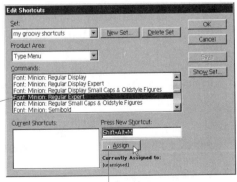

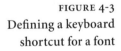

...enter a shortcut, and click the Assign button.

There's always a catch. The trouble with defining a keyboard shortcut for a font is that if you add or remove fonts, the font applied by the shortcut might change (the shortcut selects a font by its position on the Font menu, not by its name).

Size   Enter the point size you want in the Size field of the Character palette, or choose a point size from the attached pop-up menu (see Figure 4-4). If you enter the size, you can specify it in .001-point increments. After you've entered the size you want, apply the change by pressing Enter or by pressing Tab to move to another field.

FIGURE 4-4
Point size

*Click the "nudge"
buttons, or...*

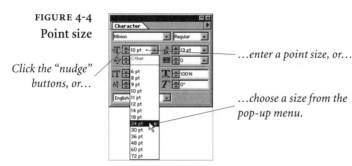

...enter a point size, or...

*...choose a size from the
pop-up menu.*

Size adjustment keyboard shortcuts. You can increase the size of selected type by pressing Command-Shift->/Ctrl-Shift->, or decrease the size by pressing Command-Shift-</Ctrl-Shift-<. The amount that InDesign increases or decreases the point size when you use these shortcuts depends on the value in the Size/Leading field in the Units and Increments Preferences dialog box.

To increase the size of the selected text by five times the value entered in the Size/Leading field, press Command-Option-Shift->/ Ctrl-Alt-Shift->; to decrease the point size by the same amount, press Command-Option-Shift-</Ctrl-Alt-Shift-<.

Leading   Text characters—usually—sit on an imaginary line, which we call the baseline. Leading (pronounced "ledding") is the vertical distance from the baseline of one line of text to the next text baseline. In InDesign, leading is measured from the baseline of the current line of text to the baseline of the line of text above (see Figure 4-5). When you increase the leading in a line of text, you push that line farther from the line above it, and farther down from the top of the text block.

FIGURE 4-5
Leading

*Leading is the distance from
the baseline of one line to the
baseline of the line above it.*

*You set the leading of selected
characters by entering a value
in the Leading field (or you can
choose Auto to base the leading
on the point size of the text).*

In InDesign, leading is an attribute of individual characters, but the largest leading value in a line predominates (see Figure 4-6). This differs from QuarkXPress, where leading is a paragraph attribute (well, really, it's a line attribute—if you're using the Relative leading mode, the largest leading in a line predominates).

For those of us who came to desktop publishing from typesetting, the idea of leading being a character attribute seems more natural than QuarkXPress' method of setting it at the paragraph level. At the same time, having the largest leading in a line set the leading for an entire line seems peculiar. In pre-DTP typesetting, leading was a character attribute, and applied to every character. To raise or lower the baseline of a character in a line of type, we would decrease or increase the leading applied to the character. In most desktop publishing programs, you use baseline shift to accomplish this.

In InDesign, you can vary the leading of lines in a paragraph—something you sometimes have to do to optically balance display copy.

FIGURE 4-6
The largest leading in a line wins

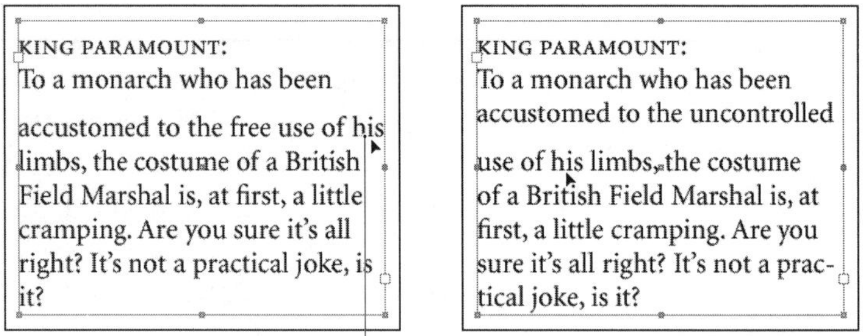

KING PARAMOUNT:
To a monarch who has been

accustomed to the free use of his limbs, the costume of a British Field Marshal is, at first, a little cramping. Are you sure it's all right? It's not a practical joke, is it?

This word has a larger leading value than the other characters in the line.

KING PARAMOUNT:
To a monarch who has been accustomed to the uncontrolled

use of his limbs, the costume of a British Field Marshal is, at first, a little cramping. Are you sure it's all right? It's not a practical joke, is it?

When the word moves to another line (due, in this example, to a change in the text), the larger leading is applied to that line.

How to Avoid Wacky Leading

The disadvantage of making leading a character attribute is that it requires a bit more vigilance on your part than the "leading-as-a-paragraph-attribute" approach taken by QuarkXPress and most word processors. Most of the time, leading values should be the same for all of the characters in the paragraph. If, as you apply leading amounts, you fail to select all of the characters in a paragraph, you'll get leading that varies from line to line—which, most of the time, is a typesetting mistake.

If you've seen paragraphs where the leading of the last line of the paragraph is clearly different from that of the lines above it, you know exactly what I'm talking about (see Figure 4-7). Why does this happen?

FIGURE 4-7

That crazy
carriage return

In this example, the carriage return character carries an Auto leading value and point size left over from previous paragraph formatting (the leading of the rest of the text in the paragraph is 13 points). The large leading value applied to the carriage return distorts the leading of the last line of text.

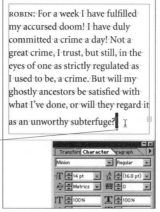

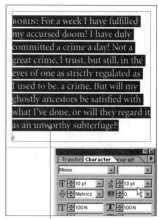

To avoid this problem, triple-click to select the entire paragraph before applying character formatting—this selects the carriage return character. Or, better yet, apply a paragraph style, which applies the same leading to all characters in the paragraph.

It's simple—the carriage return, that sneaky invisible character, has a different leading value that the other lines in the paragraph. When the person formatting the text selected the paragraph, they failed to select the carriage return. You can avoid this by triple-clicking a paragraph to select it, rather than dragging the text cursor through the text. Or you can apply a paragraph style—when you apply a paragraph style, InDesign applies the character formatting specified in the style to every character in the paragraph.

Leading Shortcuts

You can increase the leading of selected type by pressing Option-Up arrow/Alt-Up arrow or decrease the size by pressing Option-Down arrow/Alt-Down arrow. The amount that InDesign increases or decreases the leading depends on the value you entered in the Size/Leading field in the Units and Increments Preferences dialog box (see "Units and Increments Preferences" in Chapter 1, "Basics").

To increase the leading of the selected text by five times the value in the Size/Leading field, press Command-Option-Up arrow/Ctrl-Alt-Up arrow. To decrease the leading by the same amount, press Command-Option-Down arrow/Ctrl-Alt-Down arrow.

Kerning

The goal of kerning—the adjustment of the space between characters—is to achieve even spacing. As you'd expect from a new page layout program, InDesign offers both pair kerning (the adjustment of the space between adjacent characters) and tracking (or "range kerning")—the adjustment of all of the inter-character spaces in a series of characters.

For any space between any pair of characters in a publication, InDesign applies the total of the pair kerning and tracking values.

InDesign adjusts kerning using percentages of an em (an em is equal in width to the size of the type), and can kern in increments as fine as one one-thousandth of an em. The numbers shown in the Kerning field of the Character palette are thousandths of an em, and you can enter values from –1000 (minus one em) to 10000 (plus 10 ems) in the field.

Manual Kerning

To adjust the spacing between a pair of characters, move the text insertion point between the characters and apply manual kerning (see Figure 4-8). To apply kerning:

◆ Enter a value in the Kerning field of the Character palette. If the kerning field already contains a value entered by one of the automatic kerning methods (see below), you can replace the value by typing over it, or add to or subtract from it (by typing a "+" or "-" between the value and the amount you want to add or subtract).

◆ Click one of the arrow buttons attached to the kerning field in the Character palette. Click the up arrow button to increase the kerning amount by the value you entered in the Kerning field in the Units and Increments Preferences dialog box, or click the down arrow button to decrease kerning by the same amount.

◆ Press a keyboard shortcut (see Table 4-1).

To remove all kerning and tracking from the selected text, press Command-Shift-Q/Ctrl-Shift-Q.

TABLE 4-1
Kerning keyboard
shortcuts

To change kerning by:	Press:
+20/1000 em*	Option-Right arrow/Alt-Right arrow
-20/1000 em*	Option-Left arrow/Alt-Left arrow
+100/1000 em**	Command-Option-Right arrow Ctrl-Alt-Right arrow
-100/1000 em**	Command-Option-Left arrow Ctrl-Alt-Left arrow

* This is the default value in the Kerning field of the Units and Increments Preferences dialog box.

** Or five times the default kerning amount.

FIGURE 4-8
Kerning text

Click the Text tool between the characters you want to kern.

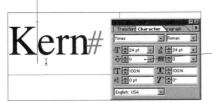

Enter values in the Kerning field, choose them from the associated pop-up menu, click the kerning buttons, or press a kerning keyboard shortcut.

InDesign adjusts the spacing between the characters.

You can't apply pair kerning when you have a range of text selected—if you try, InDesign displays an error message. When you want to apply a kerning value to a range of text, use Tracking.

Automatic Kerning

InDesign offers two automatic kerning methods: pair kerning based on kerning pairs found in the font itself (choose Metrics from the Kerning pop-up menu), and kerning based on the outlines of the characters (choose Optical). What's the difference between the two methods (see Figure 4-9)?

Metrics. When you turn on the Metrics automatic kerning method, InDesign reads the kerning pairs built into the font by the font's designer (or publisher). These kerning pairs cover—or attempt to cover—the most common letter combinations (in English, anyway), and there are usually about 128 pairs defined in a typical font.

You'd think that using the kerning pairs defined in the font would be the perfect way to apply automatic kerning to your text.

FIGURE 4-9
**Automatic
kerning methods**

*Choose Optical or Metrics
from the Kerning pop-up
menu.*

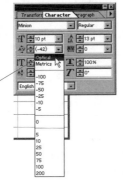

Automatic kerning using the Metric method

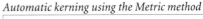

Automatic kerning using the Optical method

Who, after all, knows the spacing peculiarities of a given font better than its designer? Would that that were true! In reality, very few fonts contain well-thought-out kerning pairs (often, pair kerning tables are simply *copied* from one font to another), and the number of kerning pairs defined per font is inadequate (even for English, let alone a language where character combinations differ significantly from those found in English).

We really need a better method—a method that can adjust the spacing between *every* character pair, while taking into account the peculiarities of the character shapes for a particular font. We also need a kerning method that can automatically adjust the spacing between characters of different fonts. With InDesign's Optical kerning method, we get both.

Optical. What's new and different about kerning text in InDesign is the Optical kerning method, which considers the composed shapes of the characters and applies kerning to even out spacing differences between characters.

If you've ever worked with PageMaker's Expert Kerning dialog box, you'll understand the basic technology behind Optical Kerning, but you'll be surprised by the speed with which InDesign automatically kerns your type.

In general, the kerning applied by InDesign when you use the Optical kerning method looks looser than that applied by the Metrics kerning method. That's okay—once you've accomplished even spacing, you can always track the text to tighten or loosen its overall appearance. Because tracking applies the same kerning value to all of the text in the selection, in addition to any pair kerning, the even spacing applied by the Optical kerning method is maintained.

Viewing automatic kerning amounts. As you move your cursor through the text, you'll be able to see the kerning values applied to the text. Kerning values entered by either of InDesign's automatic kerning methods are surrounded by parentheses; manual kerning values you've entered are not (see Figure 4-10).

InDesign displays automatic kerning amounts in parentheses.

Tracking Tracking, in InDesign, applies the same kerning value to every character in a selected range of text (see Figure 4-11). InDesign applies tracking in addition to kerning values you've entered using pair

FIGURE 4-11
Tracking

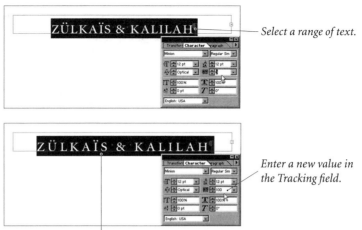

Select a range of text.

*Enter a new value in
the Tracking field.*

InDesign changes the spacing of the selected text.

kerning (regardless of the method—manual or automatic—used to enter the pair kerning). Note that this is the same as one of the definitions of "tracking" used by QuarkXPress, and different from the definition used by PageMaker. In PageMaker, "tracking" also applies kerning, but the amount of kerning applied varies depending on the point size of the selected text and the tracking table in use. In PageMaker, InDesign's "tracking" would be called "range kerning."

Just as you cannot apply kerning using the Kerning field when you have multiple characters selected, you can't apply kerning using the Tracking field when the text insertion point is between two characters.

**Horizontal and
Vertical Scaling**
Enter a value in the Horizontal Scaling or Vertical Scaling fields (or both) to change the size of the selected text (see Figure 4-12). When the values you enter in these fields are not equal, you're creating fake "expanded" or "condensed" type. I say "fake" because true expanded or condensed characters must be drawn by a type designer—when you simply scale the type, the thick and thin strokes of the characters become distorted.

Note that entering values in these fields does not affect the point size of the type.

Baseline Shift
Sometimes, you need to raise the baseline of a character or characters above the baseline of the surrounding text. You can't do this by changing the leading setting of the characters (remember, the largest leading in the line predominates). Instead, you use the Baseline Shift field in the Character palette (see Figure 4-13).

FIGURE 4-12
Squashing and
stretching type

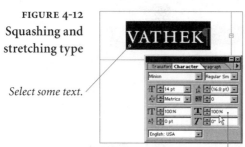

Select some text.

Enter a scaling value in the Horizontal Scaling field (and/or Vertical Scaling field).

InDesign squashes and stretches the characters of the selected text.

FIGURE 4-13
Baseline shift

Select the character or characters you want to shift...

...then enter a baseline shift distance in the Baseline Shift field (positive values move the baseline up; negative values move it down).

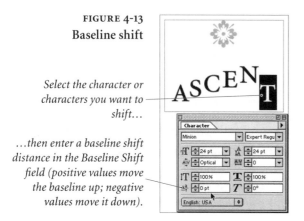

InDesign shifts the baseline of the selected character or characters.

Enter an amount in the Baseline shift field to shift the baseline of the selected text by that amount. As you'd guess, positive values move the selected text up from the baseline; negative values move the selected text down from the baseline.

Baseline Shift Keyboard Shortcuts. You can apply baseline shift using your keyboard. To do this, select some text and press Option-Shift-Up Arrow/Alt-Shift-Up Arrow to move the baseline of the text up two points—or whatever value you've entered in the Baseline Shift field of the Units and Increments Preferences dialog box, or Option-Shift-Down Arrow/Alt-Shift-Down Arrow to shift the baseline down by the same distance.

To shift the baseline of the selected text *up* by a distance equal to five times the value you entered in the Baseline Shift field of the Units and Increments Preferences dialog box, press Command-Option-Shift-Up Arrow/Ctrl-Alt-Shift-Up Arrow. To shift the baseline down by the same amount, press Command-Shift-Down Arrow/Ctrl-Alt-Shift-Down Arrow.

Skewing   When you apply skewing to a range of characters in an InDesign text frame, InDesign slants the vertical axis of the type by the angle you enter here (see Figure 4-14). You can enter from -85 degrees to 85 degrees. Positive skew values slant the type to the right; negative values slant it to the left.

This might be useful as a special text effect, but you shouldn't count on it to provide an "italic" version of a font family that lacks a true italic type style. Why? Because there's more to an italic font than simple slanting of the characters (see Figure 4-15).

FIGURE 4-14
Skewing text

Select some text.

*Enter a value
in the Skew field.*

*InDesign skews the characters
of the selected text.*

FIGURE 4-15
**Real and fake
italic characters**

*Note the differences in
character shapes.*

$$AaBbCcDdEeFf$$

Real: Minion Italic

$$AaBbCcDdEeFf$$

*Fake: Minion Regular
with -10 degree skewing.*

Language   The language you choose for a range of text determines the dictionary InDesign uses to hyphenate and check the spelling of the text (see Figure 4-16). Because language is a character-level attribute, you can apply a specific language to individual words—which means you can tell InDesign to stop flagging "frisson" or "gemütlichkeit" as misspelled words, if you want.

Case Options   If Chapter 3, "Text," was all about entering text, why didn't I put the case conversion options there? Because they don't enter text, of course. When you apply the All Caps text effect, or the Small Caps text effect, InDesign changes the appearance of the characters in the selected range of text, but does not retype the characters themselves. This means that to InDesign's spelling checker, or to the Find and

FIGURE 4-16
Assigning a language

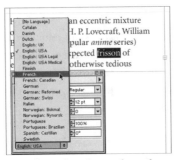

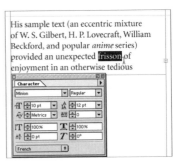

Select a word or phrase, then select a language from the Language pop-up menu.

InDesign will use the language you selected when composing text or checking spelling.

Change features, the text is exactly as it was entered—not the way it appears on your screen.

When you choose All Caps from the Character palette menu, InDesign changes the appearance of the selected text to all caps (see Figure 4-17).

When you choose Small Caps from the Character palette menu, InDesign examines the font used to format the selected text. If the font is an Open Type font, and if the font contains a set of true small caps characters, InDesign makes the selected text look like the corresponding small caps character. If the font is not an Open Type font, or does not contain small caps characters, InDesign changes the appearance of the characters to all caps and scales the uppercase characters according to the values you entered in the Small Cap field in the Text Preferences dialog box (see "Text Preferences" in Chapter 1, "Basics"). See Figure 4-18.

FIGURE 4-17
All caps

Select the text you want to capitalize, then choose All Caps from the Character palette menu.

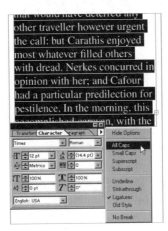

InDesign displays (and prints) the selected text in all caps.

FIGURE 4-18
Small caps

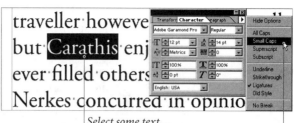

Select some text...

...then choose Small Caps from
the Character palette menu

If you're using an OpenType
font (as in this example,
InDesign displays the small
caps version of the selected
characters (if the OpenType
font contains small caps
alternate characters).

If you're using a PostScript Type 1 or TrueType font, InDesign
displays scaled, capitalized versions of the selected characters.

If you're using a PostScript
Type 1 font, don't use the
Small Caps character for-
matting option; instead,
change the font of the text to
an "expert set."

Adobe Garamond Pro (Open Type)

THESE ARE TRUE SMALL CAPS

Adobe Garamond (PostScript Type 1)

THESE ARE NOT TRUE SMALL CAPS

Changing Case If Chapter 3, "Text," was all about entering text, why didn't I put the Change Case command there? Because, frankly, that chapter is already laid out and I don't want to upset my indexer.

In addition to being able to temporarily change the case of characters using the case options, you can have InDesign change the case of the characters by typing new characters for you using the Chnage Case command (which you'll find on the Type menu and on the context menu when text is selected).

To change the case of selected characters, choose an option (Uppercase, Lowercase, Title Case, or Sentence Case) from the Change Case submenu of the Type menu (or, better yet, use the context menu). Note that Sentence Case is very simpleminded—rather than applying any title case capitalization rules (which would leave prepositions and articles lowercase), it capitalizes the first character of each word in the selection (see Figure 4-19).

Underline When you choose Underline from the Character palette menu, InDesign applies an underline to the selected text (see Figure 4-20). To remove the Underline text effect, select the text and choose Under-

FIGURE 4-19
Changing case

Select some text.

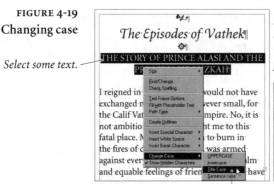

InDesign's Title Case command capitalizes the first character of each word (you'll have to fix articles and prepositions yourself).

Choose a case conversion option from the Change Case submenu (on the Type menu or the Context menu).

InDesign converts the case of the selected text. This conversion, unlike the All Caps and Small Caps formatting options, actually enters new characters in the text.

FIGURE 4-20
Underline

Underline stroke weights vary, because they're based on the size of the text.

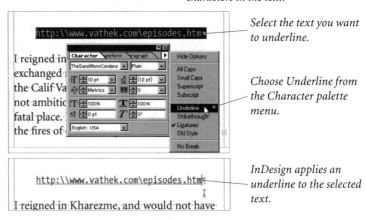

Select the text you want to underline.

Choose Underline from the Character palette menu.

InDesign applies an underline to the selected text.

line from the Character palette menu (when you have text containing the Underline effect selected, InDesign displays a check mark next to the Underline menu item). The stroke weight of the underline varies depending on the size of the text.

InDesign's underline includes any spaces in the selection—if you want to remove the underline from the spaces, you can select the spaces and remove the Underline type effect. You can also use the Find/Change dialog box to search for a space with the Underline text effect applied.

Strikethrough   When you choose Strikethrough from the Character palette menu, InDesign applies the strikethrough text effect to the selected text (see Figure 4-21). To remove the Strikethrough text effect, select the text and choose Strikethrough from the Character palette menu (when you have text containing the Strikethrough effect selected,

FIGURE 4-21
Strikethrough

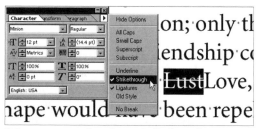

The stroke weight of the Strikethrough effect is always the same weight, regardless of the size of the text.

Select some text, then choose Strikethrough from the Character palette menu.

InDesign displays a check mark next to the Strikethrough menu item). The stroke weight of the strikethrough is set to one half point.

Ligatures

Some character combinations are just trouble—from a typesetting standpoint, at least. In particular, when you combine the lowercase "f" character with "f," "i," or "l," the tops of the characters run into each other. To compensate for these problems, type designers provide ligatures—special characters "tied" ("ligature" means "tie") together.

When you choose Ligatures from the Character Palette's menu, InDesign replaces some of the character combinations in the selected range of text with the corresponding ligatures (see Figure 4-22).

If the font you've selected is not an Open Type font, InDesign replaces only the "fl" and "fi" character combinations. In Windows, InDesign uses these ligature characters if they're available in the font (and they are, for most PostScript Type 1 fonts), even though they are not part of the Windows character set. If the font you've selected is an OpenType font, InDesign makes whatever ligature substitutions are suggested by the font.

FIGURE 4-22
Ligatures

Select some text and then choose Ligatures from the Character palette menu.

If you're using an OpenType font, InDesign uses additional ligatures defined in the font. In this example, InDesign applies the "ffi" and "ffl" ligatures.

Ligatures off
Adobe Garamond Pro (OpenType)
file difficult reflect affliction

Adobe Garamond (PostScript Type 1)
file difficult reflect affliction

Ligatures on
Adobe Garamond Pro (OpenType)
file difficult reflect affliction

Adobe Garamond (PostScript Type 1)
file difficult reflect affliction

Superscript and Subscript

While you can always create superscript or subscript characters (for use in fractions or exponential notation) by changing the point size and baseline shift of selected characters, InDesign provides a shortcut: the Superscript and Subscript text effects (see Figure 4-23).

When you select Superscript or Subscript from the Character palette menu, InDesign scales the selected text and shifts its baseline. InDesign calculates the scaling applied to the text by multiplying the percentage found in the Size fields (Superscript or Subscript) in the Text Preferences dialog box (see "Text Preferences" in Chapter 1, "Basics") by the current point size. InDesign calculates the baseline shift by multiplying the current leading value by the percentages in the Superscript Position and Subscript Position fields.

InDesign does not display the effective point size or baseline shift values in the corresponding fields of the Character palette when you select the text.

FIGURE 4-23
Superscript and subscript

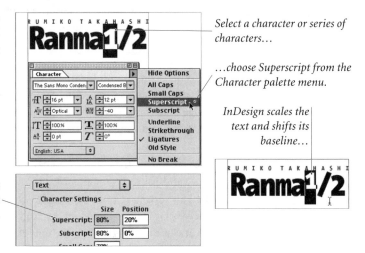

Select a character or series of characters...

...choose Superscript from the Character palette menu.

InDesign scales the text and shifts its baseline...

...according to the values you entered in the Text Preferences dialog box.

Old Style

I like "old style" numerals (you know, 1234567890) better than "lining figures" (1234567890), and I've always gotten them by selecting the characters and changing their font to an "expert" version of whatever font I was using. So I was very happy to see that InDesign included an "Old Style" text effect.

Until, that is, I read the fine print—this text effect only works with OpenType fonts. A new font format I haven't really incorporated into my everyday life (okay, truth to tell, I have *three* Open-Type fonts I've used to test parts of this book).

So, if you have an OpenType font, and if that font contains old style figures, InDesign will replace any numerals in the selected text with those characters when you choose Old Style from the Character palette menu (see Figure 4-24).

FIGURE 4-24
Old style

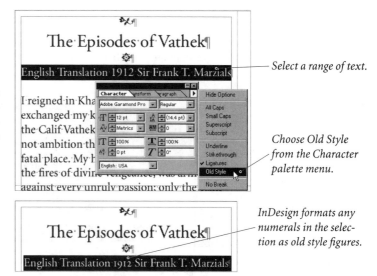

The Old Style character format does not work with PostScript Type 1 or TrueType fonts—only OpenType fonts.

Select a range of text.

Choose Old Style from the Character palette menu.

InDesign formats any numerals in the selection as old style figures.

No Break   To prevent a range of text from breaking across lines, select the text and turn on the No Break option (see Figure 4-25).

FIGURE 4-25
No break

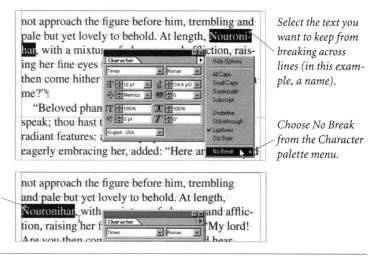

Select the text you want to keep from breaking across lines (in this example, a name).

Choose No Break from the Character palette menu.

InDesign will not break the text when it falls at the end of a line.

Filling and Stroking Characters

Most page layout programs—at least on the Macintosh—give you the ability to apply an "outline" type style to text. When you do this, you get a stroke around the text that varies in size depending on the point size of the text. But what if you want to apply a stroke of a particular width to the text? What if you want to apply a fill of a different color?

With InDesign, you can fill or stroke text as you would any other path—the only difference is that you have to select the text using the Text tool. Once you've done this, you can set the fill color, or the stroke color and stroke weight (see Figure 4-26). You can even apply gradients to the fill and stroke of the type—without converting the type to outlines.

FIGURE 4-26
Character fill and stroke

Select characters using the Text tool, then apply a fill and/or stroke to the text using the controls you use to apply a fill and stroke to any path.

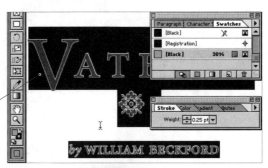

Character without a fill quickly becomes unreadable as you increase the stroke weight.

Note that the fill retains the shape of the character as you increase stroke weight.

Paragraph Formatting

What makes a paragraph a paragraph? InDesign's definition is simple—a paragraph is any string of characters that ends with a carriage return. When you apply paragraph formatting, the formatting applies to all of the characters in the paragraph. Paragraph alignment, indents, tabs, spacing, and hyphenation settings are all examples of paragraph formatting.

You don't have to select all of the text in a paragraph to apply paragraph formatting—all you need to do is click the Text tool in the paragraph. To select more than one paragraph, drag the cursor through the paragraphs you want format. The selection doesn't have to include all of the text in the paragraphs, it only has to *touch* each paragraph.

If what you're trying to do, however, is apply character formatting to all of the characters in the paragraph, you should triple-click the paragraph with the Text tool—that way, you'll select all of the characters, including the invisible carriage return character.

Alignment   Click the paragraph alignment buttons in the Paragraph palette (press Command-M/Ctrl-M to display the palette if it's not already visible) to set the alignment of the selected paragraphs (see Figure 4-27).

InDesign supports the usual set of paragraph alignments—right (also known as "rag left"), left (also known as "rag right"), centered, justified, and force-justified, but also adds a couple of variations on the justified alignment you might not be familiar with:

In addition to the standard "justified" alignment, which treats the last line of the paragraph as if it were left aligned, InDesign offers the "right justified" and "center justified" alignments. These treat the last line of the paragraph as right aligned and center aligned, respectively. In the old days of typesetting, these alignments were known as "quad right" and "quad center."

FIGURE 4-27
Paragraph alignment

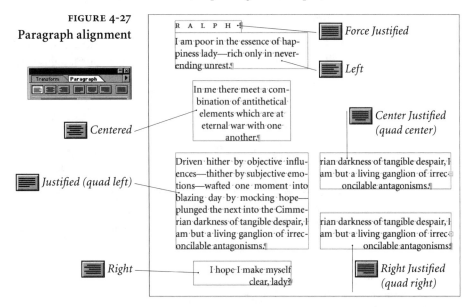

Indents InDesign paragraphs can be indented from the left and right sides of the column using the Left Indent and Right Indent fields in the Paragraph palette (see Figure 4-28). You can enter values from zero (0) to 720 picas in these fields, but you can't enter negative numbers to make the edges of the paragraph "hang" outside the edges of the column or text frame.

FIGURE 4-28
Paragraph indents

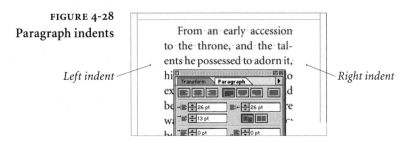

You can set indents using either the controls in the Paragraph palette or those found in the Tabs palette—whichever you prefer.

There's also a special indent, First, that applies to the first line of the paragraph alone. The value you enter in the First field sets the distance between the first line indent and the left indent. The first line indent may be positive or negative, but cannot be a negative number greater than the left indent (see Figure 4-29).

To change an indent value, select a paragraph and then do one of the following things:

◆ Display the Tabs palette (press Command-Shift-T/Ctrl-Shift-T), and drag one of the indent icons (see Figure 4-30).

◆ Display the Paragraph palette, then enter a value in the First Line Indent, Left Indent, and/or the Right Indent fields (see Figure 4-31).

FIGURE 4-29
First line indent

Don't use tab characters to apply a first line indent...

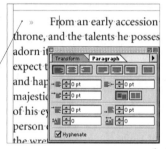
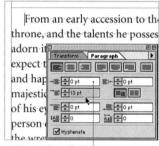

...use the First Line Indent field.

FIGURE 4-30
Indents on the Tabs palette

Left indent   *Right indent*

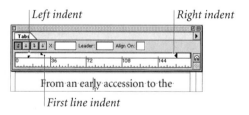

First line indent

FIGURE 4-31
Setting an indent

Click the Text tool in the paragraph you want to format.

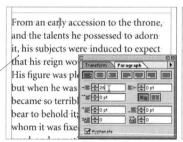

Enter values in the Left, Right, or First fields.

InDesign applies the indents you've specified.

**Creating a
Hanging Indent**

If you learn nothing else from this chapter, I'd like you to come out of it knowing how to set a hanging indent—a paragraph format you use for numbered lists, bullet lists, or any of several other situations. Use hanging indents, rather than breaking and indenting each line using carriage returns and tabs—you'll thank yourself for it later, when you need to edit the text.

To create a hanging indent that adapts when you change the width of a text block, edit copy, or change formatting in other ways, follow these steps (see Figure 4-32).

1. At the beginning of the paragraph, type a bullet, or whatever, followed by a tab (if you haven't already done this).

2. Click the Text tool in the paragraph, and then press Command-Shift-T/Ctrl-Shift-T to display the Tabs palette. Hold down Shift and drag the left indent to the right—leaving the first-line indent marker in position.

3. Insert a left tab marker at exactly the same position as the left indent marker (this step is optional).

FIGURE 4-32
Setting a hanging indent

Click the Text tool in a paragraph, then press Command-Shift-T/Ctrl-Shift-T to display the Tabs palette.

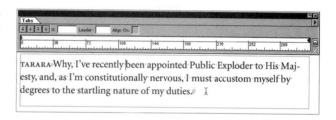

Hold down Shift and drag the Left indent icon to the right of the First Line indent marker.

As you drag, InDesign displays a vertical guide that follows the location of the Left indent icon.

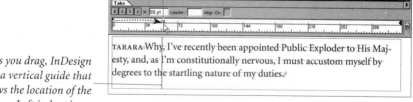

Stop dragging, and InDesign applies a hanging indent to the selected paragraph.

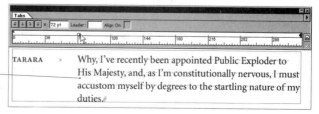

You can also set a hanging indent numerically in the Paragraph Specifications dialog box or the Control palette—to do this, enter a positive left indent and a negative first-line indent. You'll still have to go to the Tabs palette to set the tab.

Tabs

Whiz! Clunk. Whiz! Clunk. Ding! My father brought home a large, black typewriter—a machine so antiquated that even his school district (he was a high school math teacher) didn't want it anymore. It was a behemoth, a leviathan among typewriters. I couldn't lift it, and typing a letter took the entire strength of my seven-year-old arm.

My brother and I were fascinated by the movement of the carriage. For one thing, the spring that pulled it was massive—probably capable of launching a small aircraft—so pressing the Tab key was, by itself, pretty exciting. But what really caught our attention were the tabs themselves: thick slabs of metal you "set" by pushing them into the teeth of a bar set below the carriage. With each press of the Tab key, the carriage would leap to the right—then a protruding part would slam into one of the tabs. Bam! Unstoppable force meets immovable object. The rear of the typewriter would jump half an inch to the right. This was cool.

Tabs, Mice, and History

Tabs come to desktop typesetting from typewriters, by way of word processing (with a stopover along the way at the Linotype machine). They solve a problem that didn't exist in hand-set metal type—namely, how do you position characters at precise locations in a line of type when you can't simply slide them into place with your finger?

There are two methods of controlling the horizontal position of text in a line. First, you can use space characters—word spaces, thin spaces, en spaces, and em spaces. This method places characters at *relative* positions in the line—where they appear depends on the width of the spaces and of the other characters in the line. Tabs, by contrast, provide *absolute* position on the line—a tab stop set at 6 picas will remain at that position, regardless of the text content of the line.

Before I go any farther, I'd better make sure we're using the same terminology. *Tab stops* are formatting attributes of paragraphs. *Tab characters* are what InDesign enters in a line of text when you press the Tab key. Tab characters push text around in a line; tab stops determine the effect of the tab characters. Each tab stop has a position (relative to the left edge of the text container), an alignment (which specifies the composition of the text following a tab character), and, potentially, a leader (a tab leader is a series of repeated characters spanning the distance from beginning of the tab character to the beginning of the following text). Put tab stops and tab characters together, and you get *tabs*, the feature.

A Little Tab Dogma

Look. I try to be reasonable. I try not to insist that everyone work the way that I do, or that my way of doing things is necessarily the best way (in fact, I sometimes know it's not). But tabs are different—if you don't do it my way, you'll be causing yourself needless pain. You probably already know the following rules, but let's review, just in case:

◆ Use tabs, not spaces, to move text to a specific position in a line of text.

◆ Use a first line indent, not a tab, when you want to indent the first line of a paragraph.

◆ Do not force lines to break by entering tab characters (or multiple tab characters) at the end of a line! If you do, you'll find tab characters creeping back into the text as editing changes force text recomposition. To break a line without entering a carriage return, use the "soft return" character (it's Shift-Return/Shift-Enter).

◆ Don't use multiple tab characters when you can use a single tab character and an appropriately positioned tab stop. There are some cases, of course, in complex tables, where you'll have to break this rule.

Types of Tab Stops

InDesign features five types of tab stop (see Figure 4-33).

Left, Right, and Centered tab stops. InDesign's left, right, and centered tab stops are the same as the basic tab stops you'll find in any word processor.

◆ Left tab stops push text following a tab character to a specific horizontal location in a column, and then align the text to the left of the tab stop position.

◆ Right tab stops push text to a location and then align the text to the right of the tab stop position.

◆ Centered tab stops center a line of text at the point at which you've set the tab stop.

FIGURE 4-33

Tab stop alignment

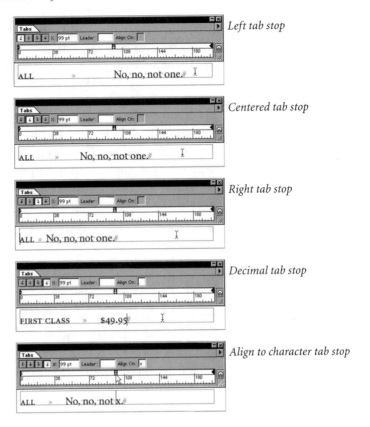

Left tab stop

Centered tab stop

Right tab stop

Decimal tab stop

Align to character tab stop

Decimal tab stops. Decimal tab stops push text following a tab character so that any decimal point you've entered in the text aligns with the point at which you set the tab stop. If there's no decimal in the text, FreeHand treats the decimal tab stop as a right tab stop.

Align to character tab stops. Align to character tab stops are just like decimal tab stops, but align to a character you specify (rather than a decimal point). If the character is not found in the text, FreeHand treats the tab stop as a right tab stop.

Setting Tab Stops   To set a tab stop, follow these steps (see Figure 4-34).

1. If you haven't already entered tab characters in the text, enter them.

2. Select the text you want to format.

3. Display the Tabs palette (press Command-Shift-T/Ctrl-Shift-T), then click the Magnet button to snap the Tabs palette into position at the top of the text frame (if possible).

FIGURE 4-34

Setting a tab stop

Click a tab stop button

Drag the tab stop into position on the tab ruler.

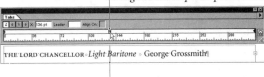

As you drag, InDesign displays a vertical guide that follows the location of the tab stop icon.

When the tab stop icon is in position, stop dragging.

4. Click one of the tab stop alignment buttons, then click in the tab ruler and drag. As you drag, the X field shows you the position of the tab icon (relative to the left edge of the text frame).

    If you want to add a tab leader, enter one or two leader characters in the Leader field in the Tabs palette (if you can't see this field, you'll need to increase the width of the palette).

5. When the tab stop icon reaches the position at which you want to set the tab stop, drop it onto the ruler.

You can also add a tab stop at a specific location on the tab ruler. To do this, enter the position you want in the X field in the Tabs palette and then press Enter. InDesign adds the tab stop. The new tab stop uses the current tab stop alignment.

Removing tab stops. To remove a tab stop, drag the tab stop icon off the tab ruler and drop it on the page or pasteboard (see Figure 4-35). Note that this doesn't remove any tab characters you've typed in your text, though it does make them behave differently.

Editing tab stops. To change a tab stop's position, drag the tab stop on the tab ruler (see Figure 4-36). Alternatively, you can select the tab stop (click on it), then enter a new value in the X field.

    To change a tab stop's alignment, select the tab stop on the tab ruler and then click the tab stop button corresponding to the alignment you want.

FIGURE 4-35
Removing a tab stop

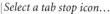

Select a tab stop icon…

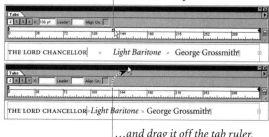

…and drag it off the tab ruler.

FIGURE 4-36
Editing a tab stop

To change the position of a tab stop, drag the tab stop icon on the tab ruler.

To change the alignment of a tab stop, select the tab stop icon…

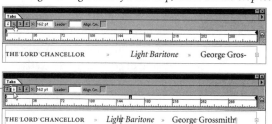

…and click one of the tab stop alignment buttons

Repeating tab stops. To create a series of tab stops spaced an equal distance apart, select a tab stop on the tab ruler and choose Repeat Tab from the Tabs palette menu (see Figure 4-37). InDesign repeats the tab across the width of the current column. The distance between the new tab stops is equal to the distance between the tab stop you selected and the previous tab stop (or indent) in the column.

Working with tab leaders. A tab leader is a series of repeated characters that fill the area taken up by the tab character (see Figure 4-38). The most common tab leader character is a period—think of all of the "dot" leaders you've seen in tables of contents.

Characters in a tab leader are not spaced in the same fashion as other characters—if they were, the characters in tab leaders on successive lines would not align with each other. That would be ugly. Instead, characters in a tab leader are monospaced—positioned as if on an invisible grid. This means you'll see different amounts of space between the last character of text preceding a tab leader and the first tab leader. It's a small price to pay.

FIGURE 4-37
Repeating a tab stop

FIGURE 4-37
Repeating a tab stop

*Select the tab stop icon you
want to repeat...*

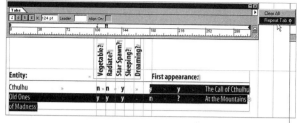

...and choose Repeat Tab from the Tabs palette menu.

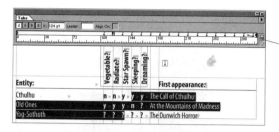

*InDesign repeats
the tab stop across
the width of the
tab ruler.*

FIGURE 4-38
Applying a tab leader

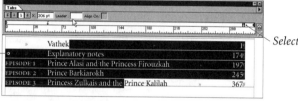

Select a tab stop.

Select some text.

*Enter the character or characters you want to use for the tab
leader in the Leader field. Press Enter...*

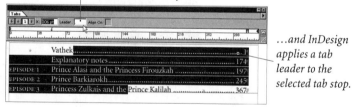

*...and InDesign
applies a tab
leader to the
selected tab stop.*

In InDesign, you can format the characters in a tab leader by
selecting the tab character and applying formatting, just as you
would any other character.

**Adding Space Before
and After Paragraphs**

When you want to add extra space between paragraphs, don't use
carriage returns (not even one). If do, you're certain to end up
with unwanted carriage returns at the tops of text frames when text
recomposes due to editing or formatting changes. Instead of carriage returns, use the Space Before and Space After fields in the Paragraph palette. When you add space using these controls, InDesign
removes the space when the paragraph falls at the top of a text frame
(see Figure 4-39).

FIGURE 4-39
Space before
and space after

If you try to use carriage
returns to add vertical
space...

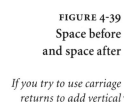

...you'll often
end up with
carriage
returns at the
top of a text
column.

To avoid this problem, use
paragraph space before (or
after).

Select some paragraphs...

...then enter a
value in the
Space Above
(or Space
Below) field.

If a paragraph falls at the
top of a text frame, InDesign
does not apply the paragraph
space above.

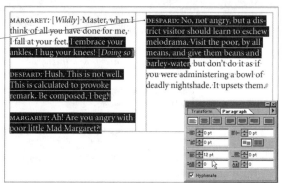

In addition, adding an exact amount of space is easier when you use the Paragraph palette—want to add four picas of vertical space above the paragraph? Enter it in the Space Above field. There's no need to guess how many carriage returns it would take to make up that vertical distance.

Align to Grid   In most page designs, you'll find elements that have to have leading values that differ from the leading applied to the body text. Inline graphics, paragraph rules, and headings are all examples of the sort of elements I'm talking about. When one of these elements appears in a column of text, the leading of the lines in that column gets thrown off.

You need a way to compensate for leading variations inside a column of text. "Leading creep," the misalignment of baselines in adjacent text columns, is one of the hallmarks of amateur typesetting, so you want to avoid it.

While you could adjust the space above and below such intrusions to compensate, there's an easier way: use InDesign's Align to Baseline Grid command. Select a paragraph and click the Align to Baseline Grid button in the Paragraph palette, and InDesign forces the baselines of the lines in the paragraph onto the baseline grid (see Figure 4-40).

FIGURE 4-40
Align to grid

This is all very pretty...

...but it throws the leading of the following paragraph off of the leading grid.

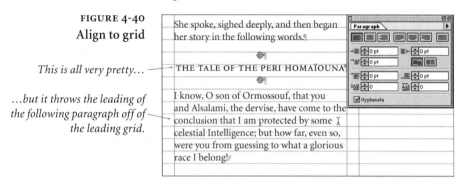

To fix this problem, select the paragraph and click the Align to grid button.

InDesign snaps the baselines of the text in the paragraph to the baseline grid.

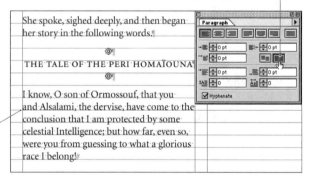

Drop Caps   Drop caps are a paragraph-level attribute in InDesign (just as they are in QuarkXPress). To apply a drop cap to a paragraph, enter a value in the Number of Lines field of the Paragraph palette (this sets both the baseline shift and the point size of the drop cap). To make InDesign apply the drop cap formatting to more than one character, enter a number in the Number of Characters field. InDesign enlarges the characters you specified and shifts their baseline down according to the value you entered in the Number of Lines field (see Figure 4-41).

FIGURE 4-41
Drop caps

Select a paragraph.

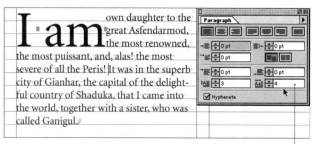

*Enter the number of lines you want to
"drop" the initial character(s).*

*Enter the number of characters you want to
apply the drop cap format to, if necessary.*

Multi-line Composition

Composition—the method our desktop publishing program uses to fit text into a line—isn't glamorous. It's not going to be the focus of any glossy magazine advertisement. In fact, the effect of this feature might be hard to see in a printed publication. On the other hand, it's easy to see the lack of a multi-line composition system in the poorly-spaced columns of type that no human has had the time or inclination to adjust.

If you're serious about type, you already know that a large part of your typesetting time is spent fixing bad line breaks and lines with poor word and letter spacing. In my experience, fully one third of my typesetting and production time is spent "walking the lines"—fixing bad line breaks and spacing problems.

Every other desktop publishing program uses a "single line composer" to compose lines of text in a text column. As the program arranges the characters on each line, it's only considering the spacing of that line. This means that the next line might have dramatically different spacing—and wide spacing variation between lines can make a text hard to read (as well as unappealing to look at). InDesign's multi-line composer can examine up to 30 lines ahead of the current line, and evaluate up to 30 possible different ways of composing the text (the default settings are for five lines ahead and five composition alternatives).

How does it work? The multi-line composer creates a list of possible line break points in the lines it examines. It then ranks the different sets of possible break points, considering the effect of each break point on spacing and hyphenation. Finally, it chooses the best of the alternatives. You'd think that this would take a lot of time—but it doesn't. When you use the default settings, you get composition speed that's equal to that of a single-line composition system, and you get better-looking text.

Multi-line composition takes some getting used to, however, because characters *preceding* the cursor will sometimes *move* as you enter text—something you won't see in most page layout, word processing, or illustration programs. You really can't be certain of the position of the line breaks in a paragraph until you've entered the last word in the paragraph. Luckily, it doesn't take long to adjust to this behavior—especially when the results are so much better than what you're used to (see Figure 4-42).

FIGURE 4-42
Multi-line composition

Note the extreme variation in word and letter spacing from line to line in the text composed using the Single-line composer.

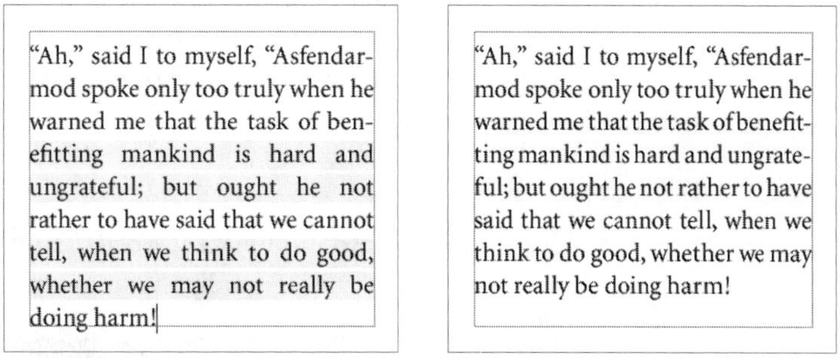

"Ah," said I to myself, "Asfendar-mod spoke only too truly when he warned me that the task of ben-efitting mankind is hard and ungrateful; but ought he not rather to have said that we cannot tell, when we think to do good, whether we may not really be doing harm!|

Single-line composition.

"Ah," said I to myself, "Asfendar-mod spoke only too truly when he warned me that the task of benefit-ting mankind is hard and ungrate-ful; but ought he not rather to have said that we cannot tell, when we think to do good, whether we may not really be doing harm!

Multi-line composition.

In some cases you might want or need to turn multi-line composition off and exercise manual control over the line breaks in a paragraph. Multi-line composition is on by default; to use the single-line composition method, select a paragraph and choose Adobe Single-line Composer from the Paragraph palette menu. To turn multi-line composition back on again for the paragraph, choose Adobe Multi-line Composer.

To set options for the Multi-line Composer, use the controls in the Composition Preferences dialog box (see "Composition Preferences" in Chapter 1, "Basics").

Hyphenation Controls

If you're tired of having your favorite page layout program hyphenate the word "image" after the "m," you'll like InDesign's hyphenation controls. To set the hyphenation options for a paragraph, choose Hyphenation from the Paragraph palette's pop-up menu. InDesign displays the Hyphenation dialog box (see Figure 4-43).

First of all, you can turn hyphenation on or off for the selected paragraph or paragraphs using the Hyphenation option.

Words Longer Than. You can direct InDesign's hyphenation system to leave short words alone using the Words Longer Than option.

After First. The value you enter here sets the minimum size, in characters, of the word fragment preceding a hyphen.

Before Last. The value you enter here sets the minimum size, in characters, of the word fragment following a hyphen.

Hyphen Limit. You can limit the number of consecutive hyphens you'll allow to appear at the left edge of a column of text using the Ladder Limit field. Enter a value greater than zero to allow consecutive hyphens.

Hyphenation Zone. Enter a value in this field to set the distance from the end of a line at which you'll allow InDesign to break the line. Use this setting to control the shape of the paragraph for non-justified type. This setting is only applied to paragraphs using the Single-line composer.

Hyphenate Capitalized Words. To prevent capitalized words (i.e., proper names) from hyphenating, turn off this option.

FIGURE 4-43
Hyphenation dialog box

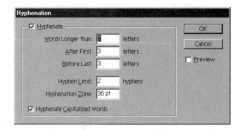

Controlling Word and Letter Spacing

When InDesign composes the text in your publications, it does so by following the spacing rules you've laid down using the controls in the Justification dialog box (choose Justification from the Paragraph palette menu to display the dialog box). See Figure 4-44.

FIGURE 4-44
Justification dialog box

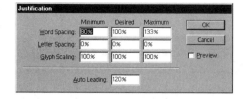

What do the values in the fields refer to? In InDesign, the values in the word spacing fields are *percentages of* the standard word space in a font (the width of the space is defined by the font's designer, and is stored in the font—inside the screen font on the Macintosh, or in the .PFM file in Windows). For letter spacing, the percentages shown represent the *amount of variation* from a standard spacing unit—the "spaceband" defined in the font.

You will never find a set of spacing values that will work for all fonts, point sizes, and line lengths. You'll have to experiment to discover the settings that work best for you and your publications. InDesign's default settings give you a reasonable starting point, these spacing values encourage wide word spacing over narrow word spacing, and attempt to discourage letter spacing.

Glyph scaling. InDesign's controls for letterspacing and word spacing (choose Justification from the Paragraph palette's pop-up menu) look very similar to those found in PageMaker's Spacing dialog box—you can set the minimum, optimum, and maximum spacing amounts you want the program to use while composing text. The Glyph Scaling option, however, is something new, different, and, potentially, more than a little strange.

When you enter anything other than 100% in any of the Glyph Scaling fields, you give InDesign permission to horizontally scale the characters in the paragraph to make them fit. I am always opposed to distorting character shapes (my opposition doesn't extend to Multiple Master typefaces, which are designed to be squashed and stretched), but I have to admit that, used in very small doses (1-2% variation from 100%), this feature could come in handy. You can also enter larger values to use Glyph Scaling as a wacky design effect, but you'll have to endure the scowls of typesetting purists (see Figure 4-45).

Highlighting Typographic Problems

Like PageMaker, InDesign can "flag" text composition problems— cases where the program has had to break your rules for composing text, or where substituted fonts appear in your publication. Choose Composition from the Preferences submenu of the Edit menu, then turn on the options in the Highlight section of the Composition

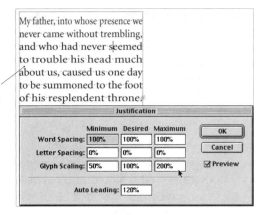

FIGURE 4-45

Glyph scaling

Watch out—abuse of the Glyph Scaling option can result in obvious differences in the shape of characters from line to line.

Now...you'd never really do this...would you?

Preferences dialog box. Lines in which InDesign has had to violate composition rules you've established (using the controls in the Justification and Keep Options dialog boxes) are highlighted in yellow; substituted fonts are highlighted in pink (see Figure 4-46).

FIGURE 4-46

Highlighting loose and tight lines

When you turn on the H&J Violations option...

InDesign uses three shades of yellow to highlight loose or tight lines—darker shades indicate more severe spacing problems.

...InDesign highlights lines that break the spacing ranges you set in the Justification dialog box.

"Scarcely had I pronounced these words when a thick, black cloud cast its veil over the firmament, and dimmed the brilliancy about us; and the hiss of rain and growling of a storm filled the air. At last my father appeared, borne on a meteor whose terrible effulgence flashed fire upon the world. 'Stay, wretched

Styles

When you think about the text in your publication, chances are good you're thinking of each paragraph as being a representative of a particular kind of text. You're thinking, "That's a headline, that's a subhead, and that's a photo caption." Chances are also good that you're thinking of those paragraphs as having certain formatting attributes: font, size, color, and leading.

That's what text styles do—they bundle all those attributes together so you can apply them to text with a single click. But there's more—if you then change your mind about the formatting, you can edit the style, and all the text with that style applied to it (that is, "tagged" with the style) is reformatted automatically.

Once you've created a text style for a specific kind of text, you'll never have to claw your way through the Character palette or Paragraph palette again to format that text. Unless, of course, you want to apply a local formatting override to your styled text, which you're always free to do.

Global versus Local Formatting. I just mentioned "local" formatting. What am I talking about? The key to understanding text styles is understanding the difference between style-based formatting and local formatting.

Local formatting is what you get when you select text and apply formatting directly, using the Character palette or the choices on the Type menu. When you apply formatting using text styles, on the other hand, you're applying "global" formatting (that is, formatting specified by the selected style).

You can tell if there's local formatting applied to a styled paragraph by looking at the Paragraph Styles palette. Click the text tool in a styled paragraph, and you'll see a "+" before the style name if the paragraph contains local formatting (see Figure 4-47).

FIGURE 4-47
Styles and local overrides

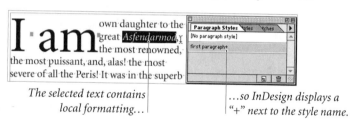

The selected text contains local formatting...

...so InDesign displays a "+" next to the style name.

Plus what? When you see that the text you've selected in a styled paragraph contains a local override, how can you tell what that local override is? It's easy—choose New Style from the Paragraph Styles palette menu, and InDesign displays the New Style palette. Look at the listing of attributes in the Style Settings list at the bottom of the palette—it'll say "<stylename> + next: Same Style +" (where "<stylename>" is the name of the style applied to the paragraph) and a list of formatting. The items in the list are the local formatting (see Figure 4-48).

FIGURE 4-48
Local formatting?
What local formatting?

InDesign lists the formatting that varies from the formatting applied by the style.

What does the "+" mean? To find out, choose New Style from the Paragraph Styles palette menu.

Styles Are More than Formatting. When you apply a style to a paragraph (which I call "tagging" a paragraph with a style), you're doing more than just applying the formatting defined by the style. You're telling FreeHand what the paragraph is—not just what it looks like, but what role it has to play in your publication. Is the paragraph important? Is it an insignificant legal notice in type that's intentionally too small to read? The style says it all.

The most important thing to remember when you're creating and applying styles is that tagging a paragraph with a style creates a link between the paragraph and all other paragraphs tagged with that style, and between the paragraph and the definition of the style. Change the style's definition, and watch the formatting and behavior of the paragraphs tagged with that style change to match.

Character Styles

By now, most of us are used to the idea of paragraph styles, which give us a way to apply multiple paragraph formatting attributes to an entire paragraph with a single action. Character styles are just like paragraph styles, except that they can be applied to ranges of text smaller than an entire paragraph (and, obviously, they lack paragraph formatting features, such as alignment). Applying a character style to a text selection establishes a link between that text and the definition of the style—edit the style, and the formatting of the text will change.

Use character styles for any character formatting you use over and over again. Run-in headings, drop caps, and special ornamental characters are all good candidates for character styles. Each time you use a character styles, you're saving yourself several seconds you would have spent fiddling with settings in the Character palette or the Type menu. It might not seem like much, but saving a few seconds several hundred times a day can add up.

Creating character styles. The easiest way to create a character style is to follow these steps (see Figure 4-49).

1. Select some text that has the formatting you want.

2. Click the New Style button at the bottom of the Character Styles palette. InDesign displays the New Character Style dialog box.

3. At this point, you can enter a name for the character style, or choose another character style from the Based On pop-up menu (this creates a relationship between the two styles—see "Creating Parent-Child Style Relationships," later in this chapter). You can also assign a keyboard shortcut to the character style—the

FIGURE 4-49
**Creating a
character style**

*To create a new character
style, select some text that
has the formatting you
want...*

*...Choose
New Style
from the
Character
Styles pal-
ette menu
(or click the
New Style
button).*

*InDesign defines a new
character style based on
the formatting of the
selected text.*

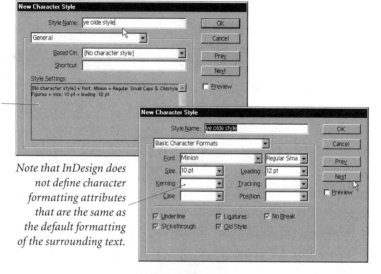

*Note that InDesign does
not define character
formatting attributes
that are the same as
the default formatting
of the surrounding text.*

*InDesign adds the new
character style to the list of
character styles.*

key used must use a modifier key (Command, Ctrl, or Shift and
a number key from the numeric keypad (NumLock must be on
to define the shortcut).

InDesign creates a character style that contains the character formatting attributes of the selected text that *differ* from the default
character formatting of the surrounding text. This means that if the
paragraph style applied to the paragraph containing the text uses
the font Minion Italic, and the text you've selected uses the same
font, the font attribute of the character style will not be defined.

This is actually a good thing—it means you can create character
styles that affect some, but not all, of the attributes of a selection

when you apply them. But it's different from the way that every other application defines character styles. If you want to define every attribute of a character style based on the selection, use the CreateCharacterStyle script—it's on your InDesign installation CD, inside the Scripting folder in the Adobe Technical Information folder.

When you apply a character style, the attributes in the text that correspond to the undefined attributes in the character style are left unchanged. This means that you can create a character style that applies only the underline type style and color (for example)—leaving all other character formatting as is (see Figure 4-50).

If you want to "undefine" an attribute in a character style, simply select and delete the current value (see Figure 4-51).

FIGURE 4-50
Character styles affect only defined attributes

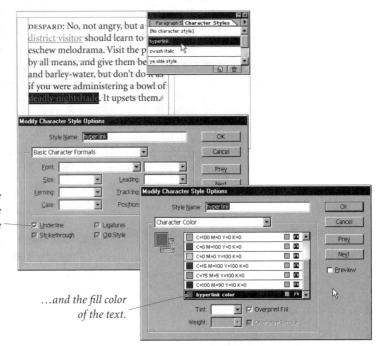

The character style "hyperlink" in this example affects only the Underline character format...

...and the fill color of the text.

FIGURE 4-51
Undefining attributes

To prevent a character style from affecting a formatting attribute, select the attribute...

...and press Delete. When you apply the style, InDesign will leave this attribute unchanged.

Applying character styles. To apply a character style, select some text and click the character style name in the Character Styles palette, or press the keyboard shortcut you assigned to the character style (see Figure 4-52).

To remove a character style from a text selection, click No Character Style in the Character Styles palette. Note that this does not change the formatting of the selected text—it simply applies the formatting applied by the character style as local formatting.

To remove a character style and reset the formatting to the publication's default formatting, hold down Option/Alt as you click No Character Style in the Character Styles palette.

FIGURE 4-52

Applying a character style

Select the text you want to format.

InDesign applies the character style to the text.

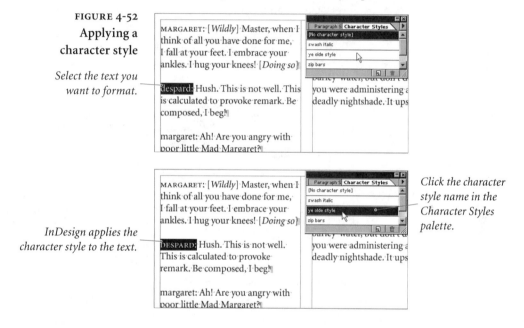

Click the character style name in the Character Styles palette.

Editing character styles. To edit a character style, hold down Command-Option-Shift/Ctrl-Alt-Shift and double-click the character style name in the Character Styles palette. InDesign will display the Edit Character Style palette.

All of the other methods for editing the character style—double-clicking the character style name, or selecting the character style and choosing "Edit Style" from the Character Styles palette menu—apply the style. This means that the only time you can use these methods safely (i.e., without applying the character style) is when you have text selected, and when all of the text in the selection has been formatted using the character style.

Remember—clicking a character style in the Character Styles palette when you have no text selected sets the publication default—the next time you create a text frame, the text in the text frame will be formatted using that character style.

So get used to using the keyboard shortcut. It's safer.

Redefining character styles. If you've formatted some text with a character style, and then have applied local formatting to the text (which means that a "+" will appear next to the character style name in the Character Styles palette), you can redefine the character style based on the formatting of the text. To do this, select the text and press Command-Option-Shift-C/Ctrl-Alt-Shift-C. InDesign redefines the character style based on the selected text (see Figure 4-53).

Alternatively, you can select the text and choose Redefine Style from the Character Style palette menu. But the keyboard shortcut is more fun.

FIGURE 4-53
Redefining a character style

Apply local formatting to an instance of the character style you want to redefine. Select a character or characters...

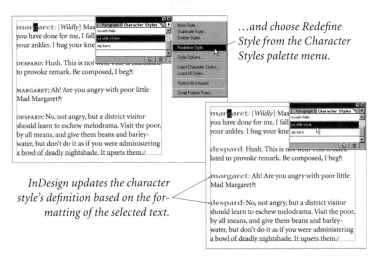

...and choose Redefine Style from the Character Styles palette menu.

InDesign updates the character style's definition based on the formatting of the selected text.

Deleting character styles. To remove a character style, press Command-Shift-A/Ctrl-Shift-A to deselect everything (do this so that you don't accidentally apply the character style to text), then select the character style and choose Delete Styles from the Character Styles palette menu. InDesign deletes the character style.

Note that the formatting you applied using the character style does not change, but becomes local formatting.

Paragraph Styles   Paragraph styles encapsulate all text formatting—both paragraph formatting and character formatting.

Creating paragraph styles. The easiest way (in my opinion) to create a text style is to use local formatting to format a paragraph, then create a new style based on that paragraph (see Figure 4-54).

1. Select a formatted paragraph.

2. Display the Paragraph Styles palette, if it's not already visible (press F11).

3. Choose "New Style" from the Paragraph Styles palette menu (or click the New Style button, or press the keyboard shortcut you've defined using the Define Paragraph Style command in the Typography section of the Edit Shortcuts dialog box—this is a great use for a keyboard shortcut). InDesign displays the New Paragraph Style dialog box.

4. Enter a name for the style in the Style Name field, or leave the name set to the default. I think it's better to enter a descriptive name—I think "heading 1" is quite a bit easier to remember than "Paragraph Style 6."

    You can also assign a keyboard shortcut to the style—the shortcut must use a modifier key (Shift, Command/Ctrl, Option/Alt, or some combination of the above) and a number key from the numeric keypad (NumLock must be on to define the shortcut).

5. Click the OK button.

InDesign adds a new paragraph style to the list of available styles in the Paragraph Styles palette. This style includes all the character and paragraph formatting applied to the selected text. If there are multiple formats in the selection, InDesign uses the formatting of the first character in the selection.

That's all there is to it—you've created a paragraph style. InDesign does not apply the style to the selected paragraph, so you'll probably want to do that now (see "Applying Styles," below).

If you prefer, you can create a style by using the style definition dialog boxes, rather than basing your style on an example.

1. Choose "New Style" from the Styles palette menu. InDesign displays the New Style dialog box.

2. Work your way through the dialog box, setting the options as you want them for your new style. When everything looks the way you want it to, press Return to close the dialog box.

FIGURE 4-54

Defining a
paragraph style

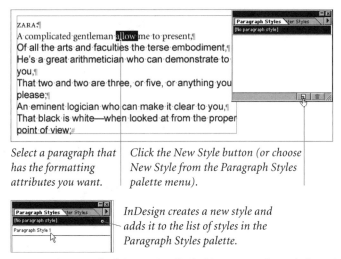

Select a paragraph that
has the formatting
attributes you want.

Click the New Style button (or choose
New Style from the Paragraph Styles
palette menu).

InDesign creates a new style and
adds it to the list of styles in the
Paragraph Styles palette.

Creating a style this way is a little bit more awkward than simply
basing a style on an example paragraph, but some people prefer it.
I've met at least one person who likes setting tabs "without all that
pesky text in the way."

Applying Paragraph Styles. To apply a paragraph style, select a paragraph or series of paragraphs (remember, you don't have to select
the entire paragraph to apply paragraph formatting—for a single
paragraph, simply clicking the Text tool in the paragraph will do)
and click a style name in the Paragraph Styles palette (see Figure
4-55). Alternatively, if you've defined a keyboard shortcut for the
paragraph style, you can press the shortcut.

FIGURE 4-55

Applying a
paragraph style

Select the paragraphs you
want to format (remember,
you don't need to select the
entire paragraph).

Click a style name in the
Paragraph Styles palette.
InDesign applies the paragraph style to the selected
paragraphs.

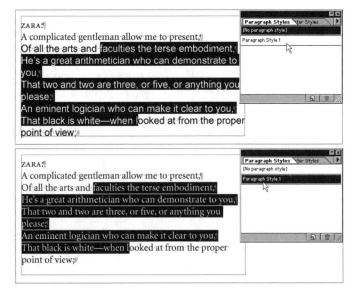

When you simply click a paragraph style to apply it, InDesign retains character styles applied to the text, but overrides any local formatting with the formatting defined in the paragraph style. To retain local formatting as you apply a paragraph style, hold down Option-Shift/Alt-Shift as you click the paragraph style name. To remove local formatting as you apply a paragraph style, hold down Option/Alt as you click the paragraph style name.

To remove a paragraph style from a text selection, click No Paragraph Style in the Paragraph Styles palette. Note that this does not change the formatting of the selected text—it simply applies the formatting applied by the paragraph style as local formatting.

To remove a paragraph style and reset the formatting to the publication's default formatting, hold down Option/Alt as you click No Paragraph Style in the Paragraph Styles palette.

Editing paragraph styles. To edit a paragraph style, hold down Command-Option-Shift/Ctrl-Alt-Shift and double-click the paragraph style name in the Paragraph Styles palette. InDesign will display the Edit Paragraph Style dialog box.

All of the other methods for editing a paragraph style (you can double-click the style name, or select the style name and choose Edit Style from the Paragraph Styles palette menu) apply the style. This means that the only time you can use these methods safely (i.e., without applying the style) is when the selected paragraph has been tagged with the style (because clicking the style name when no text is selected sets the publication's default text formatting).

Redefining paragraph styles. The easiest way to *create* a paragraph style is to base the style's definition on the formatting of an example paragraph. The easiest way to update the style definition? The same. Here's what you do (see Figure 4-56).

1. Apply local formatting to an example paragraph tagged with the paragraph style you want to change (a "+" will appear next to the style name in the Paragraph Styles palette).

2. Choose Redefine Style from the Character Style palette menu (or press Command-Option-Shift-R/Ctrl-Alt-Shift-R). InDesign redefines the style based on the selected paragraph.

Selecting unused paragraph styles. Choose Select All Unused from the Paragraph Styles palette menu to select all paragraph styles that are not applied to any text in the publication.

FIGURE 4-56

Redefining a
paragraph style

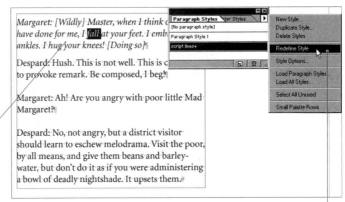

*Change the formatting of an
example paragraph tagged
with the paragraph style
you want to change. A
"+" appears next to
the style name in the
Paragraph Styles palette.*

Choose Redefine style from the Paragraph Styles palette menu.

*InDesign updates all
instances of the style
with the formatting of
the selected paragraph.*

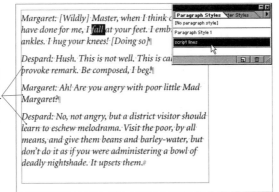

Deleting paragraph styles. To remove a paragraph style, first deselect everything (press Command-Shift-A/Ctrl-Shift-A) then select
the style name in the Paragraph Styles palette and choose Delete
Styles from the palette's menu (or click the Delete Style button at the
bottom of the palette). InDesign deletes the style.

When you remove a paragraph style, the formatting you applied
using the style does not change, but becomes local formatting.

Copying Styles from Other Publications

One of the great things about character and paragraph styles is that
you can use them to unify standard formatting across a range of
publications—the chapters of this book, for example. While you
can't define a "master" style sheet and have all publications get their
style definitions from it (as you can in QuarkXPress and Frame-
Maker), you can easily copy styles from one InDesign publication to
another.

To copy character styles from another publication, display the Character Styles palette and choose Load Character Styles from the palette menu. InDesign displays the Open a File dialog box. Locate and select the InDesign publication file containing the styles you want and click the Open button. InDesign copies the styles from the publication you selected into the current publication.

To copy paragraph styles from one publication to another, display the Paragraph Styles palette. Choose Load Paragraph Styles from the Paragraph Styles palette menu. InDesign displays the Open a File dialog box. Select the file containing the styles you want to import, then click the Open button. InDesign imports any paragraph styles found in the publication.

To import both character and paragraph styles from another publication, choose Load All Styles from the palette menu of either the Character Styles palette or the Paragraph Styles palette.

When you import styles that have the same name as styles that already exist in the publication , InDesign overrides the attributes of the existing styles with the attributes of the incoming styles.

You can also move styles from one publication to another: select and copy text tagged with the styles you want in one publication; then paste the text into another publication. If the styles do not exist in the publication you've pasted the text into, InDesign adds the style names to the Character Styles and Paragraph Styles palettes. If the styles already exist, InDesign overrides the style definitions in the incoming text with the style definitions of the existing styles.

Optical Margin Alignment

Ever since Gutenberg set out to print his Bible, typesetters have looked for ways to "balance" the edges of columns of text—particularly lines ending or beginning with punctuation. Because the eye doesn't "see" punctuation, it can sometimes appear that the left or right edges of some columns of type (especially justified type) are misaligned. Some other programs compensate for this problem by using a "hanging punctuation" feature, which pushes certain punctuation characters outside the text column. But there's more to making the edges of a column look even than just punctuation. Some characters can create a "ragged" look all by themselves—think of a "W," at the beginning of a line, for example.

When you select an InDesign story and turn on the Optical Margin Alignment option in the Story palette (choose Story from the Type menu to display the Story palette), the program balances the edges of the columns based on the appearance of *all* of the characters at the beginning or end of the lines in the column. This adjustment makes the columns appear more even—even though it sometimes means that characters are extending *beyond* the edges of the column (see Figure 4-57).

The amount that InDesign "hangs" a character outside the text column depends on the setting you enter in the Base Size field of the Story palette. In general, you should enter the point size of your body text in this field.

FIGURE 4-57
Optical margin alignment

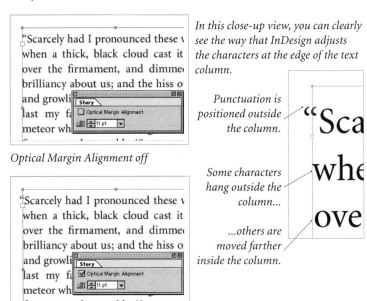

In this close-up view, you can clearly see the way that InDesign adjusts the characters at the edge of the text column.

Optical Margin Alignment off

Punctuation is positioned outside the column.

Some characters hang outside the column...

...others are moved farther inside the column.

Optical Margin Alignment on

An Old Typesetter Never...

Late night. The sound of the espresso machine in the kitchen about to reach critical mass and melt down, destroying the office and civilization as we know it. The office is different, the equipment and the coffee are better, but I still seem to be up late at night setting type.

And, to tell you the truth, I'm not sure I'd have it any other way.

5

Where Text Meets Graphics

Usually, we think of text and graphics as occupying two different, but parallel, universes. But there's an area, a Twilight Zone, a Bermuda Triangle of page layout, where the boundary between text and graphics blurs, frays, or becomes thin.

In this strange dimension, text characters can be bound to paths, or become paths, graphics can be embedded in text and behave as if they were text characters, and nothing, nothing is what it seems.

In spite of the repeated warnings of my scientific colleagues, I must, for the sake of humanity, tell what I have found in this alien landscape.

Paragraph Rules

I haven't looked at the PageMaker 3.0 documentation recently. I don't have to—I remember it too well.

A feature of the design is a rule drawn below a particular, and very common, heading. I know this, because I was one of the four people who put those rules there. For every one of those headings, one of us had to zoom in, measure from the baseline of the text in the heading, position a ruler guide, and then draw a rule. When the position of the heading changed, as it often did, we had to zoom in again, measure again, and move or redraw the rules.

I still dream about it.

Which is part of the reason I like the paragraph rules feature found in PageMaker, QuarkXPress, and InDesign. Rules can be part of your paragraph's formatting (or, better yet, part of a style definition), and the rules you specify follow your paragraph wherever it happens to go.

Applying Paragraph Rules

To apply a paragraph rule to a paragraph, follow these steps (see Figure 5-1):

1. Select the paragraph (remember, you don't need to highlight the entire paragraph—all you need to do is click the Text tool somewhere inside the paragraph).

2. Press Command-M/Ctrl-M to display the Paragraph palette, if it's not already visible, and then choose Paragraph Rules from the Paragraph palette menu. InDesign displays the Paragraph Rules dialog box.

3. Choose the type of paragraph rule (Rule Above or Rule Below) from the Rule Type pop-up menu, then turn on the Rule On option.

4. Set the rule options you want using the controls in the panel. If you turn on the Preview option, you can watch InDesign apply the paragraph rule to the paragraph as you adjust the settings.

5. Click OK to apply the paragraph rule settings to the selected paragraph, or click Cancel to close the dialog box without applying the rule.

Ground Rules for Paragraph Rules

Paragraphs can have up to two rules attached to them. One rule can be positioned on or above the baseline of the first line of text in a paragraph (InDesign calls this the "Rule Above"), the other line

FIGURE 5-1

Applying a paragraph rule

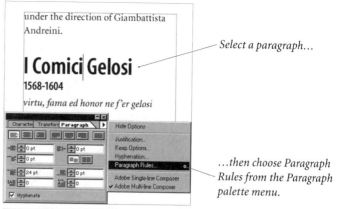

Select a paragraph…

…then choose Paragraph Rules from the Paragraph palette menu.

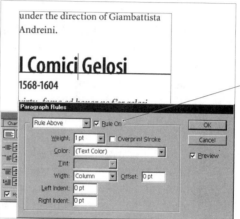

Turn on the rule you want (in this case, a paragraph rule above).

The width of this rule…

…is set to the width of the column.

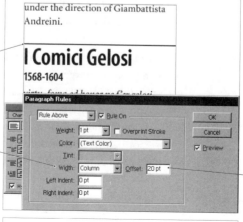

Adjust the rule options (in this example, I've used the Offset field to move the rule above the text).

The width of this paragraph rule above is set to the width of the text in the first line of the paragraph.

can be positioned at or below the baseline of the last line of the paragraph (the "Rule Below"). You can't have two rules above a single paragraph, or two rules below, without trickery (see below). Note that these rule positions specify only the starting point of the rule—by manipulating the rule width, it's easy to create a rule below that extends far above the baseline, or a rule above that extends far below the baseline of the last line.

Paragraph rules, like any other paths you can draw in InDesign, can be up to 1000 points wide, and the stroke width can be specified in .001-point increments. Unlike other paths, however, you can't use a dashed stroke.

You set the position at which InDesign starts drawing a paragraph rule using the controls in the Paragraph Rules dialog box (choose Paragraph Rules from the Paragraph palette menu).

Paragraph rules above grow *up* (that is, toward the top of the text frame) from the position you specify in the Offset field in the Paragraph Rules dialog box; rules below grow *down* (toward the bottom of the text frame) as you increase their stroke weight.

InDesign draws paragraph rules *behind* the text in the text frame.

You can base the width of a paragraph rule on the width of the text column or on the width of the text in the first (for paragraph rules above) or last (for rules below) line of the paragraph. Paragraph rules can also be indented from either the width of the column or the width of the text—the value you enter in the Left Indent and Right Indent fields in the Paragraph Rules dialog box determines the indent distance. You can even make paragraph rules extend beyond the width of the text or column by entering negative numbers in the Left Indent and Right Indent fields.

You can't select paragraph rules using the Selection tool or the Direct Selection tool. Everyone tries this at least once.

Paragraph rule positions have no effect on the vertical spacing of text. If you want to make room above a paragraph for a paragraph rule above, or below a paragraph for a rule below, you can use paragraph space before and after.

Tinting Paragraphs   When you want to put a tint behind a paragraph (which you might want to do for a sidebar, a line in a table, or for a note or warning paragraph in your text), paragraph rules are the way to go. Provided, or course, that your paragraph isn't taller than 1000 points or so (the maximum paragraph rule width), and provided the paragraph fits inside a single text frame or text column.

How do you do it (see Figure 5-2)?

FIGURE 5-2
Placing a tint behind a paragraph

Select a paragraph.

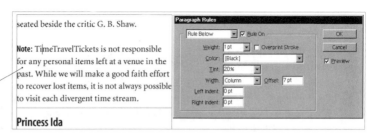

Display the Paragraph Rules dialog box and add a rule below.

Make the stroke weight of the rule at least equal to the sum of the leading of the lines in the paragraph.

Move the rule up or down by entering values in the Offset field (I usually start with the stroke weight, then add or subtract smaller values to "fine tune" the rule position).

1. Calculate the height of the paragraph by adding up the leading of the lines in the paragraph.

2. Select the paragraph, then use the Paragraph Rules dialog box to apply a paragraph rule below. Use the Weight field to set the stroke width of the rule to at least the height of the paragraph.

3. Use the Color pop-up menu to set the color of the paragraph rule.

4. Enter a value in the Offset field to move the paragraph rule up or down behind the paragraph (remember, a negative value in the Offset field moves a paragraph rule below toward the top of the paragraph).

5. When the paragraph rule looks the way you want it to, click the OK button to apply it to the selected paragraph.

Putting a Box Around a Paragraph Using Paragraph Rules

Are you thinking what I'm thinking? If the paragraph rule below overprints the paragraph rule above, and both rules fall behind the text in the paragraph, then you ought to be able to create a "box" around a paragraph by cleverly manipulating the width, height, and offset of the paragraph rules above and below. You can do just that, as shown in Figure 5-3.

FIGURE 5-3

Using paragraph rules to create a box around a paragraph

Set the rule above so that it covers the area behind the paragraph.

Set the rule below so it covers an area slightly smaller (in this example, two points smaller on all sides. Set the rule color to "Paper."

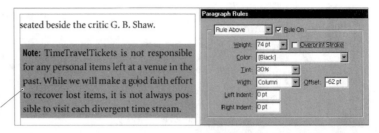

Look at the values in the Left Indent, Right Indent, Weight, and Offset fields) than the rule above.

Hanging Your Head in a Bar

Here's an effect you see often—a heading, set in a hanging indent, and knocked out of a paragraph rule. There's no trick to it—you use the same approach described in the previous section ("Tinting Paragraphs"), but you use a paragraph rule above and set the width of the rule so that it falls behind any text in the hanging indent (but not behind the text in the body of the paragraph).

To do this, set the right indent for the rule to at least the width of the body of the paragraph. Set the weight of the stroke to at least the height of the heading. Apply the paragraph rule, and you've got the effect you're looking for (see Figure 5-4).

Instant "Bullets"

Earlier, I mentioned that you can "hang" paragraph rules outside the text block containing the paragraphs containing the rules. Of what conceivable use is this?

Wouldn't it be great if you could make a bullet part of a paragraph style? There's a sleazy way to accomplish this using paragraph rules—provided all you want is a square bullet.

Here's what you do: apply a thick rule above to the paragraph, setting its right indent to a value equal to the width of the text column minus the width of the left indent. InDesign positions the paragraph rule to the left of the paragraph. Work with the offset, stroke width, and right indent until the square bullet looks the way you want it to (see Figure 5-5).

FIGURE 5-4
**Hanging headings
and paragraph rules**

*Set the text color of
the heading to "Paper."*

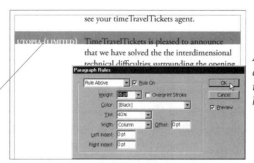

*Add a paragraph rule
above that's (roughly)
the height of the
heading.*

*Set the value in the Right
Indent field to the width of
the body text column (plus a
bit, if you want some space
between the heading and the
body copy).*

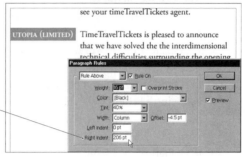

FIGURE 5-5
**One (very sleazy) way to
get square bullets**

*Select a paragraph
or series of paragraphs.*

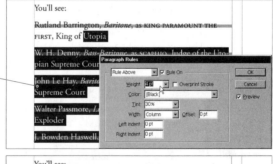

*Add a paragraph
rule above. Set
the stroke weight
of the paragraph
rule above to the
height of the
"bullet" you want
to add.*

*Enter a value in the Left
Indent field that's equal to
the distance from the left
edge of the bullet to the text.*

*Enter a value in the Right
Indent field that's equal to
the width of the column plus
the left indent, minus the
width of the paragraph rule.*

*What's so great
about this
technique? Why
not just type a
bullet character?
Simple: You can't
make a bullet
character part of
a paragraph style.*

When you work with a paragraph rule (or anything else) that
extends beyond the edges of a text frame, InDesign sometimes for-
gets to redraw the rules when you edit text in the text frame. Don't
worry—the rules are still there. To see them again, force InDesign
to redraw the screen by pressing Shift-F5.

Vertical
Paragraph Rules

What if your design calls for a vertical rule next to a specific type of paragraph? It's easy to automate this with paragraph rules—using a trick that borrows from other tricks I've already discussed above. Set a paragraph rule below that's equal to the height of the paragraph (or thereabouts)—just as you would if you were placing a tint behind the paragraph. Next, make the rule's right indent (or left, if you want the rule to fall to the right of the paragraph) equal to the width of the paragraph minus the width of the vertical rule you want. If, for example, you want a 1-point rule at the left of the text frame, and the text column is 18 picas wide, enter "17p11" in the Right indent field (see Figure 5-6).

This technique works especially well when you position the rules outside the text frame. To do this, enter a negative number in the Left field (this sets the position of the left edge of the rule). Enter a value in the Right field that's equal to the width of the text column plus the value you entered in the Left field minus the width of the "vertical" ruler you want to create. If you want a 1 point rule 3 points to the left of an 18-picas-wide text column, enter "-0p3" in the Left field and enter "18p2" in the Right field.

Want to position rules on both sides of the text column? Add a paragraph rule above that's the same weight as the rule above. You should be able to get the two rules to align by adjusting the values of the Offset fields for both rules (see Figure 5-7).

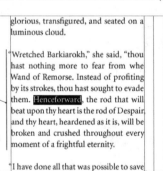

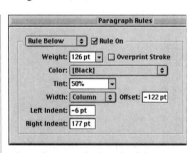

The indents set the length of the paragraph rule to a single point.

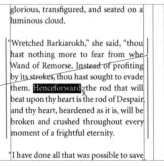

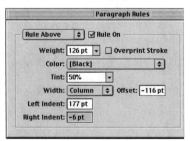

These indent settings create a rule to the right of the paragraph.

Two Rules Above

What can you do when one rule above isn't enough—when your design calls for two rules above your paragraph? A very common design specification calls for two rules above a heading: a thin rule that's the width of the column and a thick rule that's the width of the text in the heading. How can you accomplish this using InDesign's paragraph rules? It's easy, as shown in the following steps (see Figure 5-8).

1. Select a paragraph.

2. For the paragraph rule below, choose Column from the Width pop-up menu, then enter a value in the Offset field that positions the rule above the tops of the characters in the first line of the paragraph (this will be something like the sum of the leading values in the paragraph). Set the line weight to a hairline (.25 points) or so.

FIGURE 5-8
Thick/thin rule above

For the paragraph rule above...

For the paragraph rule below (which we're going to place above the paragraph—don't get confused)...

...enter a thin stroke weight (such as a hairline)...

When you change the text in the first line, InDesign changes the width of the thicker rule.

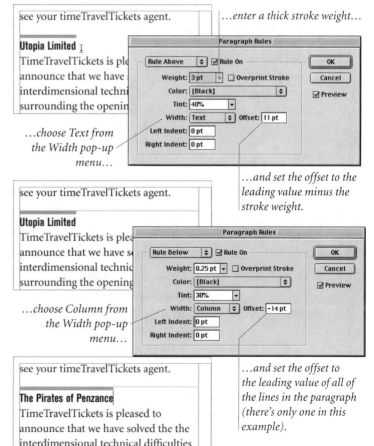

...enter a thick stroke weight...

...choose Text from the Width pop-up menu...

...and set the offset to the leading value minus the stroke weight.

...choose Column from the Width pop-up menu...

...and set the offset to the leading value of all of the lines in the paragraph (there's only one in this example).

3. For the paragraph rule above, choose Text from the Width pop-up menu, then set the stroke weight of the paragraph rule to something thicker than the stroke weight of the rule below—4 points, for example. Set the value in the Offset field so that the top edge of the rule above touches the bottom of the rule below.

More Than Two Rules

When you need to attach more than two rules above or below a paragraph, enter extra carriage returns before or after the paragraph, then apply paragraph rules to the resulting "blank" paragraphs. You can even set the leading of the empty paragraphs to zero, which keeps the empty paragraphs from disturbing the leading of the other text in the text column (see Figure 5-9). You can then use the Keep with Next settings of the empty paragraphs to make them "stick" to the original paragraph.

FIGURE 5-9
Combining paragraph
rules from more than
one paragraph

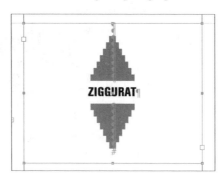

The range of possible design effects is limited only by your imagination. (And my imagination is running a little thin, right at the moment.)

Text Wrap

Any independent object in an InDesign publication can have a text wrap—a boundary that repels text—applied to it. Wrapping text around an object is something like the opposite of flowing text inside a path. When you flow text inside a path, you want text to stay inside a path; when you apply a text wrap, you want to keep it out. To set the text wrap for an object, follow these steps (see Figure 5-10).

1. Select an object—any frame or group—on an InDesign page.

2. Display the Text Wrap palette, if it's not already visible (press Command-Option-W/Ctrl-Alt-W).

FIGURE 5-10

Text wrap

To wrap text around an object, select the object and then click one of the text wrap options in the Text Wrap palette (I've listed the "official" name of the text wrap type below each example).

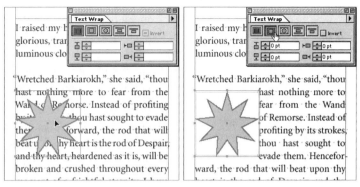

No Text Wrap

Wrap Around Bounding Box

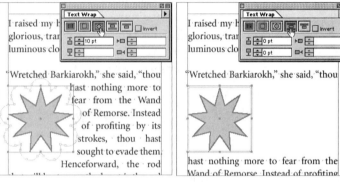

Wrap Around Object Shape

Jump Object

When you choose one of the rectangular text wrap options (Wrap Around Bounding Box, Jump Object, or Jump to Next Column), you can adjust the offset values for the top, right, left, and bottom independently. If you choose Wrap Around Object Shape, you can only enter a single offset value that applies to all sides of the text wrap.

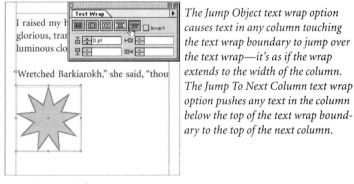

Jump To Next Column

The Jump Object text wrap option causes text in any column touching the text wrap boundary to jump over the text wrap—it's as if the wrap extends to the width of the column. The Jump To Next Column text wrap option pushes any text in the column below the top of the text wrap boundary to the top of the next column.

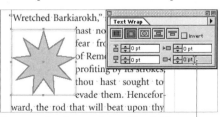

Enter a value in one of the offest fields...

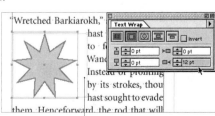

InDesign changes the offset for the corresponding side.

3. Click one of the Text Wrap buttons in the Text Wrap palette. InDesign displays the text wrap boundary around the selected object, and pushes any text falling inside the text wrap boundary to the outside of the boundary. If you applied the text wrap to a text frame, the text in that frame is unaffected by the text wrap boundary.

4. Set the text wrap offset distances using the Top, Left, Bottom, and Right fields in the Text Wrap palette. If you've selected anything other than a rectangular frame, you'll only be able to adjust a single field (the Left field) to set the offset distance.

You can make individual text frames immune to text wrap—select the frame and turn on the Ignore Text Wrap option in the Text Frame Options dialog box.

InDesign can apply an *inverted* text wrap to an object, which causes text to wrap to the inside of the text wrap (see Figure 5-11).

FIGURE 5-11
Inverted text wrap

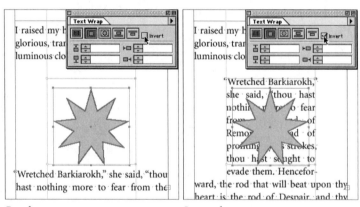

Regular text wrap   Inverted text wrap

The text wrap boundary is a path, and can be edited and adjusted just as you'd change the shape of any path in InDesign (see Figure 5-12). You can draw new line segments using the Pen tool, or change the location of path points using the Direct Selection tool.

Converting Text to Outlines

When you work in graphic design, you frequently need to alter character shapes for logos or packaging designs. For years, we dreamed about the ability to turn type into paths (or "outlines") we could edit. Finally, applications such as FreeHand and Illustrator added the feature. And, as you'd expect in a modern page layout program, InDesign has it.

FIGURE 5-12

Editing a text wrap

The text wrap boundary appears in a tint (I think it's 50 percent) of the selection color of the layer containing the object—this can make it difficult to see.

You can also use the Pen tool to add points, delete points, or change the control handles of points of a text wrap boundary.

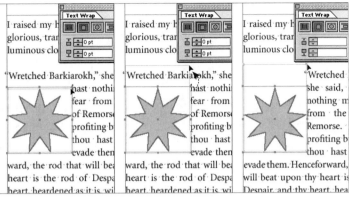

Select points on the text wrap boundary just as you would select points on any path.

Drag the points to a new location.

InDesign wraps the text around the edited text wrap boundary.

You can convert characters from just about any font (TrueType, PostScript Type 1 and OpenType fonts) for which you have the printer (outline) font.

Once you've converted the characters into outlines, you lose all text editing capabilities, but you gain the ability to paste things inside the character outline, to use the path as a frame, and to change the shapes of the characters themselves.

To convert characters of text into paths, follow these steps (see Figure 5-13).

1. Select the text you want to convert. You can select text using either the Text tool, or select the text frame using the Selection tool or the Direct Selection tool.

2. Choose Convert to Outlines from the Type menu (or press Command-Shift-O/Ctrl-Shift-O). InDesign converts the characters into paths. If you selected the characters using the Text tool, InDesign positions the paths on the current line as an inline graphic; if you selected the text frame using the Selection tool or the Direct Selection tool, InDesign joins the resulting outlines into a compound path.

When you convert individual characters containing interior space (such as "P," or "O") into paths, InDesign turns them into composite paths (see "Composite Paths" in Chapter 6, "Drawing"). This is handy. Not only are multiple-part characters (such as i, é, and ü) treated as single paths, but characters with interior paths (such as O, P, A, and D) are transparent where they should be, and fill properly.

FIGURE 5-13
Converting text
to outlines

*Select a text frame
with the Selection tool...*

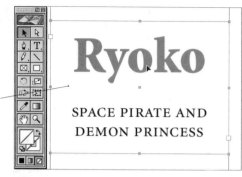

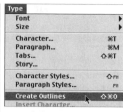

*...and choose Create
Outlines from the
Type menu.*

*InDesign converts the
characters in the
selected text frame to a
compound path.*

*To see the individual
paths and points, select
the compound path
using the Direct
Selection tool.*

*You can also select text using
the Text tool, then convert
the selected text to outlines.*

*When you do this, the
resulting compound path
will be inserted into the
text as an inline frame.*

You can always make the characters into normal (not composite) paths. To do this, select the character and choose Release from the Compound Paths submenu of the Object menu (see Figure 5-14).

FIGURE 5-14
Working with character outlines

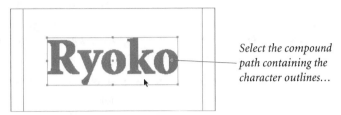

Select the compound path containing the character outlines...

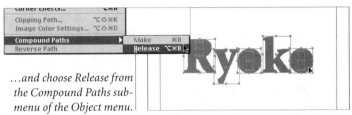

...and choose Release from the Compound Paths submenu of the Object menu.

InDesign converts the compound path into normal paths.

The same formatting (fill and stroke) is applied to all of the resulting paths—even the paths that create the hollow areas inside characters.

To put the characters back together again, select the path representing the hollow area or areas for a character...

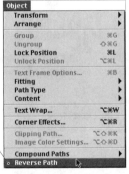

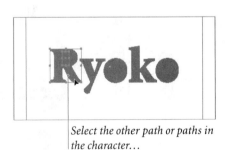

...and choose Reverse Path from the Object menu.

Select the other path or paths in the character...

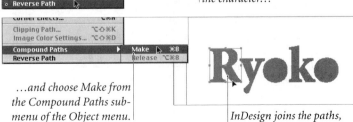

...and choose Make from the Compound Paths submenu of the Object menu.

InDesign joins the paths, restoring the interior space.

If Your Characters Won't Convert

If you weren't able to convert the text into paths, make sure that you have the outline (printer) fonts and that they're somewhere InDesign can find them. If you don't have the outline fonts, InDesign won't be able to convert your text into paths.

Making Type Glow

When you want to add a glowing outline to your type, follow these steps (see Figure 5-15).

1. Convert the text to outlines. In this case, select the text using the Selection tool.

2. Select the compound path containing the paths.

3. Increase the stroke weight to something fairly heavy—say, 6 points or more.

4. Display the Stroke palette and choose Width Changes Bounding Box from the Stroke palette menu.

5. Run the "Neon Glow" script (it's on your InDesign CD, inside the Scripting folder in the Adobe Technical Info folder).

InDesign creates a series of copies of the selected paths, changing the stroke weight and stroke color of each copy as it does so. When it's done adding paths, InDesign groups the "neon glow" effect.

FIGURE 5-15
Glowing type

Select a text frame with the Selection tool and convert the text to outlines.

Apply a thick stroke to the converted characters.

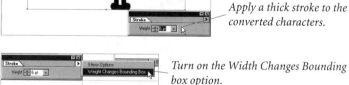

Turn on the Width Changes Bounding box option.

Run the "Neon" script.

If you're using Windows, you'll see a dialog box—you won't if you're using the AppleScript version of the script.

InDesign creates a group containing the objects

Inline Frames

It was the Dark Age of page layout. The flame of classical desktop publishing knowledge flickered but dimly, kept barely alive by devoted acolytes in isolated monasteries. Pestilence and famine stalked the narrow aisles between our unheated cubicles. And, almost worst of all, page layout programs could not paste graphics into text. Producing publications featuring graphics "anchored" to a specific piece of text was a nightmare. It went something like this. Scroll. Zoom in. Measure. Pull a guide down from a ruler. Select a graphic. Drag the graphic until it snaps to the guide. Sigh heavily. Repeat.

These days, I embed graphics in lines of text whenever the graphics have some defined relationship to the text. You know what I mean—illustrations that should appear immediately after a paragraph (think of the screen shots in a typical manual), or icons "hanging" to the left of a column of text, or graphic symbols in a line of text. If I embed the graphics in the text, they'll follow the text as it flows through the text blocks or text frames containing the story.

With InDesign, you can paste any kind of frame into a text frame. You're not limited to graphic frames—you can use text frames and groups as well, opening up new ways to solve old problems and adding capabilities that are entirely new. You can even create inline frames using frames that already contain other frames or other inline frames.

Using inline frames does more than just "stick" a frame to a particular location in a story—it also makes it easier for you to control the space between the graphic and the text. Complicated spacing arrangements that would be difficult (and involve lots of measuring, moving, and sighing) without inline frames become easy to implement using leading, tabs, indents, and paragraph space above and below.

Creating an Inline Frame

You can use any of the following methods to create an inline frame (see Figure 5-16).

◆ Paste a frame into a text frame.

◆ Use the Text tool to select a character or a range of characters and choose Convert to Outlines from the Type menu. InDesign creates a path for each character in the selection and embeds the paths, as a group, in the text.

Creating an inline frame

Select the object (graphic frame, text frame, or group) you want to embed in the text and cut or copy it to the Clipboard.

Select the Text tool and click it in a text frame.

Paste the object into the text. At this point, you can select the object using the Selection tool (or select object contents using the Direct Selection tool) and adjust the object's vertical position relative to the line of text.

You can also select the object as if it were a single character of text by using the Text tool.

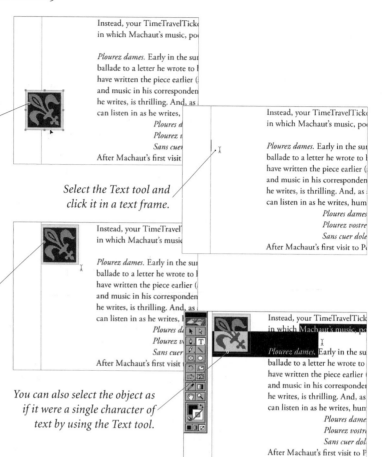

◆ Place a graphic when you have a text insertion point active in a text frame.

InDesign treats each inline frame as a single character of text. You can select an inline frame using the Text tool, and adjust its leading and baseline shift using the Character palette. You can adjust the horizontal distance between the inline frame and the other characters on the line using kerning or tracking—you can even kern text following the inline frame back into frame (you can't, however, kern the frame back into characters preceding it on a line).

You can select an inline frame using the Selection or Direct Selection tools, and you can edit the shape of the inline frame using the path drawing tools (the Pen, Add Point, Delete Point, and Convert Point tools). You can also drag an inline frame up or down in the text frame using either of the selection tools. This produces the same effect as applying a baseline shift amount using the Character palette (see Figure 5-17).

FIGURE 5-17

Adjusting the position of
an inline frame

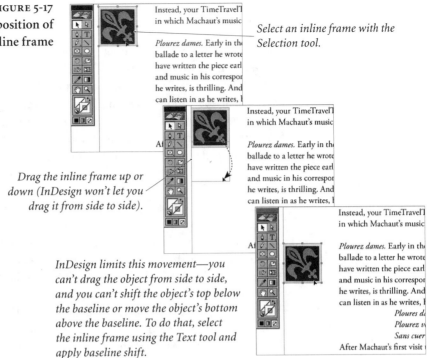

FIGURE 5-17

Adjusting the position of
an inline frame

*Select an inline frame with the
Selection tool.*

*Drag the inline frame up or
down (InDesign won't let you
drag it from side to side).*

*InDesign limits this movement—you
can't drag the object from side to side,
and you can't shift the object's top below
the baseline or move the object's bottom
above the baseline. To do that, select
the inline frame using the Text tool and
apply baseline shift.*

**Inline Frames
and Leading**

When you insert an inline frame into a text frame, InDesign gives
it the leading value of the surrounding text. If you're using "auto"
leading, and if the inline frame is taller than the height of the text,
InDesign pushes the line down to prevent the inline frame from
overlapping the text on the lines above it. If, on the other hand,
you're using a fixed leading value, you'll see the inline frame overlap the text. By default, InDesign positions the bottom of the inline
frame at the baseline of text.

This works perfectly for me—when the inline frame shares a line
with other text, I usually want the leading of the line to stay the
same as the other lines in the paragraph—and I can get this effect
using fixed leading values. When I place an inline frame in a paragraph by itself, however, I usually want the height of the paragraph
to equal the height of the inline frame—and I can get that effect by
using "auto" leading for the paragraph.

The rules are a little different when an inline frame falls on the
first line of text in a text frame. The position of the baseline of the
first line of text is controlled by the First Baseline option in the Text
Frame Options dialog box.

If the height of the inline frame is greater than the height of the
characters in the line (and it usually is), choosing "Ascent" positions
the top of the inline frame at the top of the text frame. This pushes

the first line down to accommodate the height of the inline frame. If you adjust the vertical position of the inline frame, the position of the first line of text moves up or down. The same thing happens when you choose "Cap Height" (note that these two settings produce different results for text, but not for inline frames).

When you choose "Baseline," however, InDesign positions the baseline of the first line of text according to the largest leading value in the line. If you're using a fixed leading value, and you've set the leading of the inline frame to the leading of the surrounding text, the position of the baseline of the first line of text won't change, regardless of what you do with the inline frame.

I always use the "Baseline" option for my first baseline position, and I always set the leading of a graphic that shares a line with text characters to the leading of those characters. This way, I always know where the first baseline of text will fall, and I don't have to worry that changes I make to the shape, size, or baseline position of the inline frame will mess up the leading.

The only time I use "auto" leading is when I'm working with a paragraph that contains only an inline frame. The only trouble is that I want the vertical distance taken up by the paragraph to be exactly equal to the height of the inline frame—no more, no less. By default, InDesign's "auto" leading value is equal to 120% of the point size of the type (or, in this case, the height of the inline frame). How can I get the base "auto" leading percentage down to 100%?

The percentage used to calculate "Auto" leading, as it turns out, is a paragraph-level attribute. To view or adjust this percentage, choose Justification from the Paragraph palette's menu. InDesign displays the Justification dialog box. Enter 100 in the Auto Leading field and click OK to close the dialog box (see Figure 5-18). Once you've done this, the leading of the paragraph will be equal to the height of the inline frame. If you want, you can add this to a paragraph style definition.

What Can't You Do with Inline Frames?

In spite of their tremendous flexibility, there are a few things you can't do with inline frames.

◆ You can't link (or "thread") a text frame you've pasted inline to another text frame.

◆ You can't apply a text wrap to an inline frame.

◆ When you select an inline frame using one of the selection tools, the InDesign selects the center point of the Proxy in the Transform palette—you can't choose any other point.

FIGURE 5-18
**Inline frames and
"Auto" leading**

*Height of inline graphic = 56
points (4 * 14).*

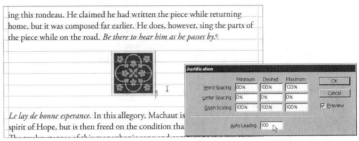

Leading = 14.

*In this example, the leading of the paragraph containing the inline frame is
set to "Auto," and the Auto Leading value is set to 120 percent, which means
that the lines following the graphic do not align to the 14-point baseline grid.*

*Set the Auto Leading value to 100 percent, and InDesign makes the vertical
space occupied by the inline frame equal to the height of the frame.*

◆ You can't adjust the horizontal position of a frame away from
the frame's position in text. Instead, you have to move the
graphic as if it were a text character.

**Creating Hanging
Side Heads**

If there's one thing that inline frames make easier, it's hanging side
heads. You know—the headings that appear to the left of a column
of text (like the one to the left of this paragraph). In InDesign, you
can create a hanging side head that follows a paragraph of text as
it flows through a publication—no more dragging the headings to
a new position when text reflows. You use a hanging indent and an
inline frame, as shown in the following steps (see Figure 5-19).

1. Create a hanging indent. To do this, set a left indent that's
   the width of the "companion column" you want to the left of
   the paragraph, then set a negative first line indent equal to the
   width of the left indent. Place a tab stop at the left indent.

2. Enter a tab character before the first character of the paragraph.
   This pushes the text to the left indent.

3. Paste a text frame before the tab character you just entered.
   Adjust the position of the inline text frame, if necessary.

FIGURE 5-19
Creating a hanging side head

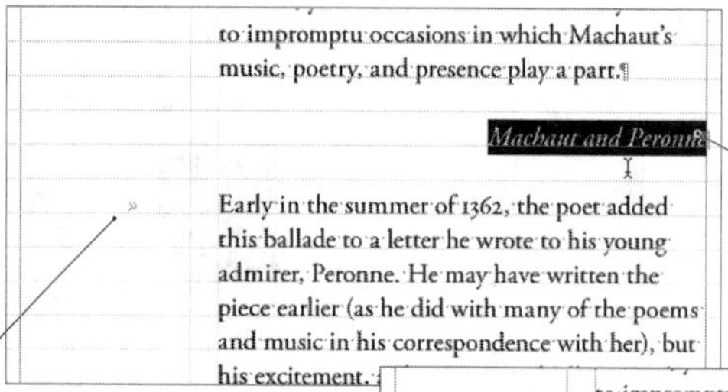

Use the Text tool to select the text you want to format as a hanging side head.

This paragraph has a negative first line indent to accommodate the heading, and I've already entered a tab character before the first line of the paragraph.

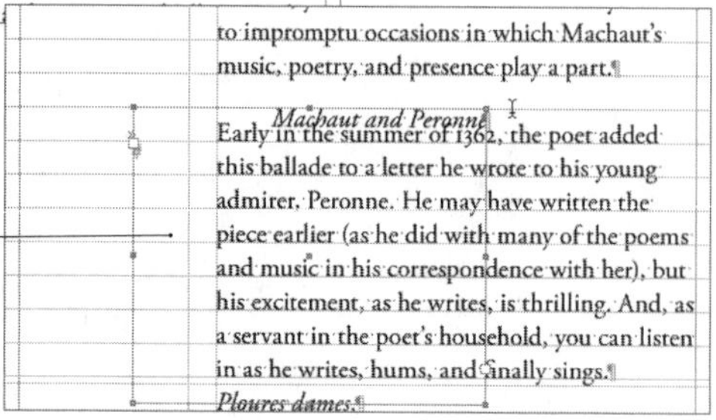

Cut or copy the heading to the Clipboard, then press Command-Shift-A/Ctrl-Shift-A (to deselect all), and then paste. InDesign places the text from the Clipboard in a new text frame.

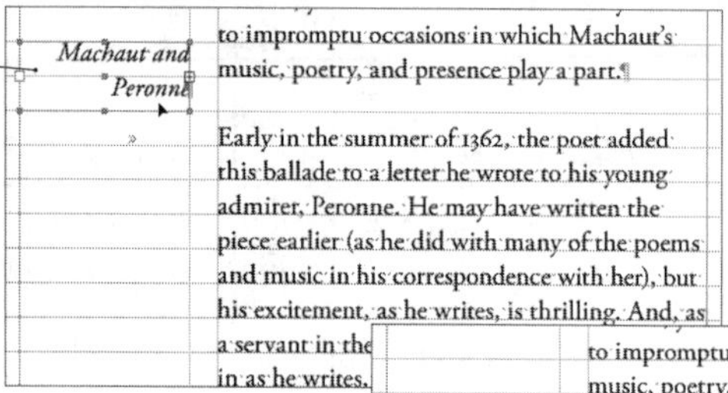

Adjut the size of the text frame, if necessary.

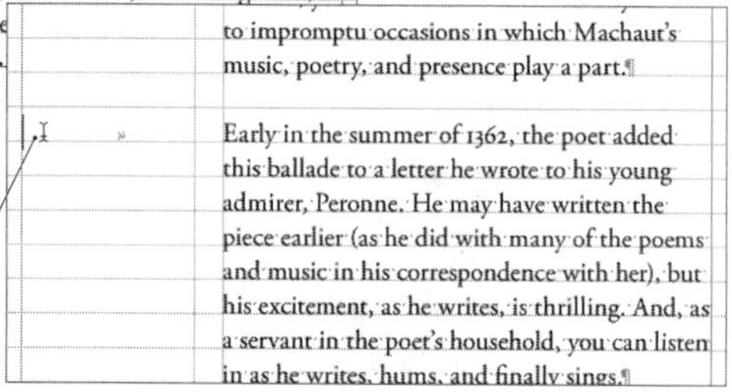

Cut or copy the text frame to the Clipboard, then click the Text tool in the text (before the tab character) and paste the text frame from the Clipboard.

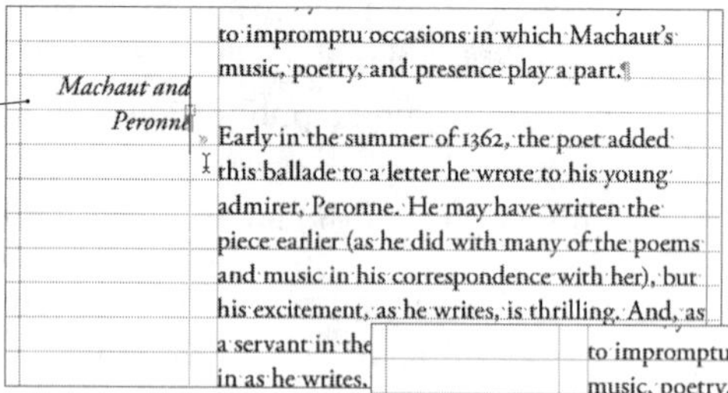

Adjust the size and/or position of the inline text frame until it looks the way you want it to.

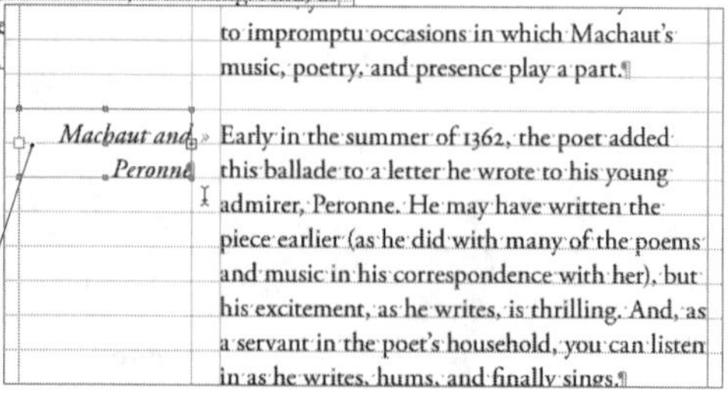

You've created a hanging side head that will move with the paragraph of body text as that paragraph moves in response to editing or layout changes.

4. Enter the heading's text in the inline text frame.

5. Format the heading.

That's all there is to it—you now have a hanging side head that will follow the paragraph anywhere it goes.

This same technique can also be used to position graphics frames, and comes in handy when you need to "hang" an icon or a vertical rule to the left of a particular paragraph.

Putting a Box Around Text

While you can use InDesign's paragraph rules to place a tinted box behind a paragraph (use a rule above set to the height of the paragraph), there's no immediately obvious way to put an outlined box around a paragraph that will follow the paragraph. You can use paragraph rules (as shown earlier in this chapter), or you can use an inline rectangle, as shown below (see Figure 5-20).

1. Create a paragraph above the paragraph you want to put the box around.

2. Draw a rectangle, then paste the rectangle into the empty paragraph you just created.

3. Set the leading of the paragraph and the inline frame to some fixed value (anything other than "auto").

4. Adjust the size and baseline position of the inline frame so that it falls around the following paragraph.

FIGURE 5-20
Another way to put a box around a paragraph

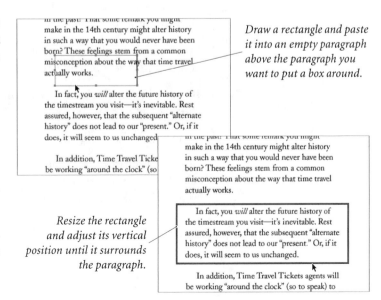

Draw a rectangle and paste it into an empty paragraph above the paragraph you want to put a box around.

Select the paragraph containing the rectangle, display the Keep Options dialog box, and then set the value in the Keep with Next field to something greater than zero—this will "stick" the paragraph to the following paragraph.

Resize the rectangle and adjust its vertical position until it surrounds the paragraph.

5. Use the Keep With Next option to "stick" the paragraph containing the inline frame to the following paragraph.

Tables and Inline Frames

Now, given that a table is just a bunch of frames joined together in a series of rows and columns, you'd think that inline frames might be a good way to create tables in your InDesign publications. I think you'd be right—provided your table is too complicated to create using tabs, but too simple to merit using a table-making plug-in. While table-making plug-ins for InDesign exist (there's even a demo version of one on your InDesign CD), you might want to use InDesign's inline frames to take care of most—if not all—of your table-creation needs. (Just to state what might not be immediately obvious: if your tables don't need to flow along with your text, you don't need to use inline frames—just create a table using independent text frames.)

By now, some of you may be spluttering, "But, I thought you said you couldn't link inline text frames! How can I create a table without linking frames?" It's true that you can't link an inline text frame to other text frames (inline or otherwise)—but we'll cheat (see Figure 5-21).

1. Create the table, one row at a time. If the columns in the table are of unequal width, make each row a series of linked text frames. If the table consists of a series of columns of equal width, our task becomes even easier—we can use a single inline text frame for each row, and adjust the number of columns in the text frame to give us the number we need for our table.

2. Fill the row with the table's content for that row (each cell can contain either text or a graphic).

3. If you've used multiple frames, group the frames that make up the row. Cut or copy the row.

4. Paste the row into a text frame.

6. Repeat this process for the other rows in the table. When the table has to break across pages, you can copy the heading row, if necessary, and paste it into position at the top of each page.

FIGURE 5-21
Tables as inline frames

Create a table using a series of linked frames.

Group the frames, then paste the table into text. To allow for breaks in a multi-page table, group each row and paste each row into the text as an inline frame.

Placing Text on a Path

InDesign 1.5 can place text *on* a path, as well as placing text *inside* a path (which is what a text frame is, after all). Once you've joined text to a path, you can select the text just as you would select any other text—select the Text tool and drag it through the characters you want to select, or click the Text tool in the text and use keyboard shortcuts. To select the path, click on the path using the Selection tool or the Direct Selection tool.

To attach text to a path, follow these steps (see Figure 5-22).

1. Select the Path Type tool.

2. Move the tool over a path. The cursor changes to indicate that InDesign is ready to place text on the path.

3. Click the tool on the path. InDesign places the cursor on the path. The position of the cursor depends on the document's default paragraph alignment (if the default alignment is left, for example, the cursor will appear at the start of the path).

    Instead of clicking, you can drag the tool along the path to define the area of the path you want to fill with text.

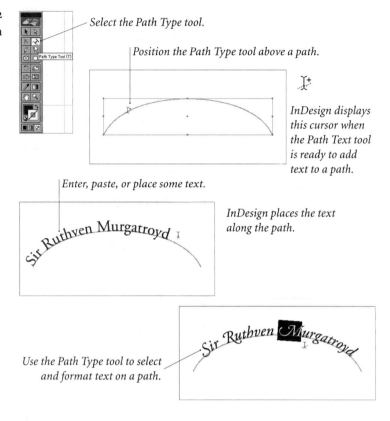

FIGURE 5-22

Adding text to a path

Select the Path Type tool.

Position the Path Type tool above a path.

InDesign displays this cursor when the Path Text tool is ready to add text to a path.

Enter, paste, or place some text.

InDesign places the text along the path.

Use the Path Type tool to select and format text on a path.

If InDesign cannot fit all of the text onto the path, the extra text is stored as overset text.

4. Add text to the path just as you would add text to a text frame—by typing, pasting text from the Clipboard, or importing text from a text file. This creates a new kind of object—not a text frame, not a path, but a blending of the two I'll refer to as a "path text object" from here on out.

Once you've attached text to a path, you can change its position on the path by dragging the Start Indicator or the End Indicator (see Figure 5-23), or change its orientation relative to the path using the Center/Flip Direction Indicator (see Figure 5-24).

Like text frames, path text objects feature an in port and an out port you can use to link the text to other text containers (text frames or other text path objects). You can even link text from a path text object to the interior of the path text object.

Note: InDesign does not apply paragraph rules to text in path text objects.

FIGURE 5-23
Changing the position of text on a path

Select the Selection tool and position the cursor above the Start indicator…

…or the End indicator…

…and drag the indicator along the path.

InDesign repositions the text on the path.

FIGURE 5-24
Flipping text on a path

Select the Selection tool and position the cursor above Flip indicator…

…and drag the indicator to the other side of the path.

InDesign flips the text on the path.

Path Text Options

You can control both the baseline position of text on a path and the relationship of the text to the shape of the path. To do this, select a path text object (or some of the text on a path) and then choose Options from the Path Type submenu of the Object menu. InDesign displays the Path Type Options dialog box (see Figure 5-25).

Effect. Do the character shapes distort in some way, or do they remain unchanged? That's the question you're answering when you make a choice from the Effect pop-up menu. What, exactly, do these oddly-named options do?

FIGURE 5-25

Path type options

To set options for a path text object, select the object using the Selection tool...

...then display the Context menu and choose Options from the Path Type submenu.

InDesign displays the Path Type Options dialog box.

Drag the dialog box out of the way (if necessary) and turn on the Preview option so that you can see the effect of the changes you make in the dialog box.

◆ Rainbow rotates the center point of each baseline to match the angle of the path at the location of the character.

◆ Skew skews the horizontal axis of the character to match the angle of the path at the location of the character, but leaves the vertical axis of the character unchanged.

◆ 3D Ribbon skews the vertical axis of each character to match the angle of the path at the location of the character, but leaves the character's horizontal axis unchanged.

◆ Stair Step aligns the center point of each character's baseline to match the angle of the path at the location of the character, but does not rotate the character.

◆ Gravity rotates the center of the baseline of each character to match the angle of the path at the character, skews the horizontal axis of the character to match that angle, and skews the vertical axis of each character around the geometric center point of the path.

These options are a bit difficult to describe with words, so take a look at Figure 5-26.

Flip. You've probably noticed that path text follows the direction of the path—the first character of the text typically appears at (or, if you've dragged text Path Text tool, nearest) the first point in the path. Given this, you'd think that you could select the path and

FIGURE 5-26
Effect option

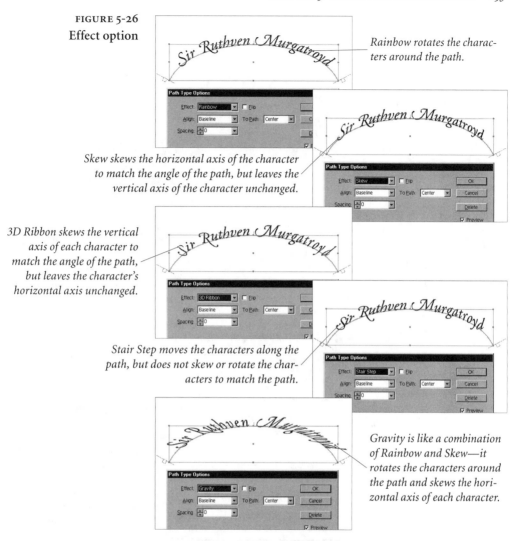

Rainbow rotates the characters around the path.

Skew skews the horizontal axis of the character to match the angle of the path, but leaves the vertical axis of the character unchanged.

3D Ribbon skews the vertical axis of each character to match the angle of the path, but leaves the character's horizontal axis unchanged.

Stair Step moves the characters along the path, but does not skew or rotate the characters to match the path.

Gravity is like a combination of Rainbow and Skew—it rotates the characters around the path and skews the horizontal axis of each character.

choose Reverse Path from the Options menu to make the text read from the opposite end of the path. But you can't (not without first removing the text from the path, anyway). To do what you're trying to do, turn on the Flip option (see Figure 5-27).

Align. These options control the way the text aligns to the path itself. Choose Ascender to align the top of the capital letters in the text (more or less) to the path, or choose Descender to position the bottoms of the characters on the path. Choose Center to align the text to the path at a point that's half of the height of the capital characters in the font, or choose Baseline to align the baseline of the characters to the path (see Figure 5-28).

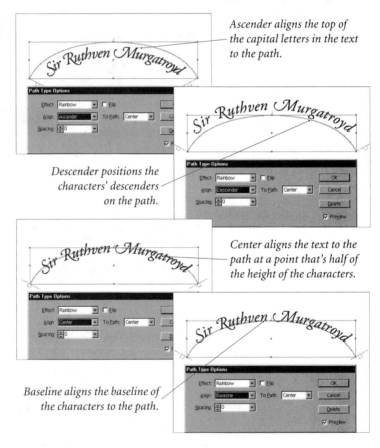

Select a path text object.

*Turn on the Flip option, and
InDesign flips the text across
the path.*

FIGURE 5-28
Align options

*Ascender aligns the top of
the capital letters in the text
to the path.*

*Descender positions the
characters' descenders
on the path.*

*Center aligns the text to the
path at a point that's half of
the height of the characters.*

*Baseline aligns the baseline of
the characters to the path.*

To Path. The options on the To Path pop-up menu control the way
that the text aligns to the *stroke* of the path. Choose Top to place the
alignment point (whatever it was you chose from the Align pop-up
menu) of the text at the top of the stroke; or Bottom to place the

alignment point at the bottom of the stroke; or Center to align the alignment point of the text with the center of the path (see Figure 5-29). For more precise control of the text position, use baseline shift.

FIGURE 5-29
To Path options

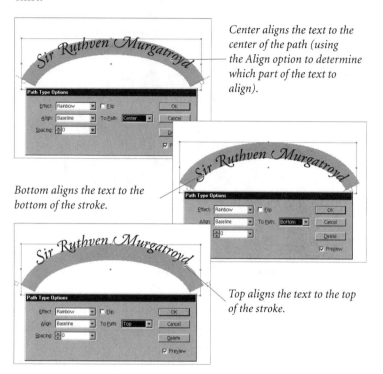

Center aligns the text to the center of the path (using the Align option to determine which part of the text to align).

Bottom aligns the text to the bottom of the stroke.

Top aligns the text to the top of the stroke.

Spacing. The Spacing field (and attached pop-up menu) control the spacing of text around curves in the path. Enter a value (in points) in this field to tighten or loosen character spacing around curves (see Figure 5-30). Note that this setting has no effect on the kerning or tracking of text on straight line segments.

FIGURE 5-30
Spacing

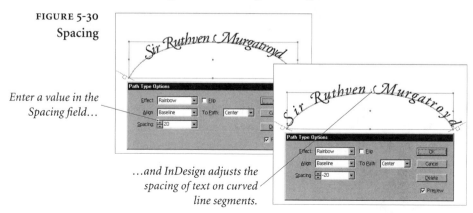

Enter a value in the Spacing field...

...and InDesign adjusts the spacing of text on curved line segments.

Removing Type from a Path

To remove the text from a path type object and convert the object back into a "normal" path, you need to do more than simply delete the text characters. If you do this, the object remains a path type object. Instead, select the path (or some of the text on the path) and choose Delete from the Path Type submenu (of the Object menu or the context menu). See Figure 5-31.

FIGURE 5-31
Removing text on a path

Select the path text object...

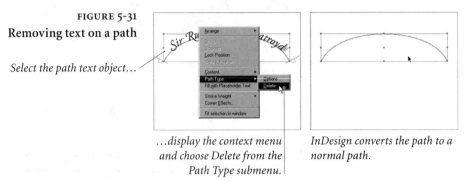

...display the context menu and choose Delete from the Path Type submenu.

InDesign converts the path to a normal path.

Alternate Reality

What wonders—or horrors—exist in this weird place, where the boundary between text and graphics breaks down? Where magic works, and previously immutable laws of physics no longer apply? I have been there, reader, and, as it turns out, I have discovered new and useful techniques that can be put to immediate use in the "normal" world.

6

Drawing

Fifteen of the twenty-seven tools in the InDesign toolbox are drawing tools. Using these tools, you can draw almost anything—from straight lines and boxes to incredibly complex freeform shapes.

The drawing tools can be divided into three types: the Rectangle, Polygon, Oval, and Line tools are for drawing basic shapes; the Pencil, Smooth, Eraser, Pen, Add Point, Delete Point, and Convert Point tools draw or edit more complex, or "freeform," paths (see Figure 6-1). The Scissors tool gives you a way of cutting paths.

Some of the path drawing tools (the Rectangle, Oval, and Polygon tools) have counterparts that draw frames (the Rectangular Frame, Oval Frame, and Polygonal Frame tools). The only thing different about these tools is that the "frame" versions draw paths whose content type has been set to "Graphic" (the "regular" versions of these tools draw paths whose content type is "Undefined"). That's it.

Throughout this book, I'll use the default variant of the tool to refer to both tools—when I say "the Rectangle tool," I'm referring to both the Rectangle tool and the Rectangular Frame tool.

FIGURE 6-1
Drawing tools

Freeform path drawing tools

Pen tool

Pencil tool

Path editing tools

Add Point tool

Delete Point tool

Scissors tool

Convert Point tool

Smooth tool

Eraser tool

Basic shapes tools

Rectangle tool

Oval tool

Polygon tool

Rectangle Frame tool

Oval Frame tool

Polygon Frame tool

Line tool

Which path drawing tools should you use? Don't worry too much about it—the basic shapes can be converted into freeform paths, and the freeform drawing tools can be used to draw basic shapes.

The paths you draw in InDesign are made up of points, and the points are joined to each other by line segments (see Figure 6-2). An InDesign path is just like a connect-the-dots puzzle. Connect all the dots together in the right order, and you've made a picture, or part of a picture. Because points along a path have an order, or winding, you can think of each point as a milepost along the path. Or as a sign saying, "Now go this way."

A brief note on path drawing terminology. Adobe likes to refer to points on a path as "anchor points," and to control handles as "direction lines." I don't.

FIGURE 6-2
Parts of a path

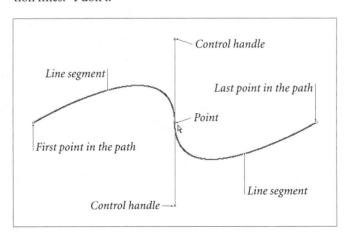

Control handle

Line segment

Last point in the path

Point

First point in the path

Line segment

Control handle →

Drawing Basic Shapes

The basic shapes tools (the Rectangle, Polygon, Oval, and Line tools, and their frame-drawing counterparts) don't draw anything you couldn't draw using the Pen tool (discussed later in this chapter) or (even) the Pencil tool; they just make drawing certain types of paths easier. They're shortcuts.

The operation of the basic shapes tools is straightforward: drag the tool and get a path of the corresponding shape. If you want to draw a frame, you can either use the frame-drawing variant of the tool, or draw the path and then convert it to a frame.

To draw a rectangle, oval, polygon, or line, follow the steps below (see Figure 6-3).

1. Select the appropriate tool from the Toolbox.

    To specify what type of polygon you'll be drawing, double-click the Polygon tool and choose the shape you want in the Polygon Settings dialog box before you start drawing.

2. Position the cursor where you want one corner of the shape, then drag. InDesign draws a path, starting where you first held down the mouse button.

    To draw squares, hold down Shift as you drag the Rectangle tool. To draw circles, hold down Shift as you drag the Oval tool. When you hold down Shift as you drag, the Polygon tool produces equilateral polygons. Holding down Shift as you drag the Line tool constrains the angle of the line to 45-degree tangents from the point at which you started dragging.

    Hold down Option to draw a basic shape from its center point.

3. When the basic shape is the size and shape you want it to be, stop dragging and release the mouse button.

FIGURE 6-3
Drawing a basic shape

 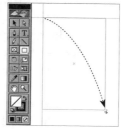 

Select a basic shape tool (in this example, the Rectangle tool).   *Drag the tool on the page.*   *InDesign creates a basic shape.*

You can also create rectangles and ellipses by specifying their width and height (see Figure 6-4).

1. Select the Rectangle tool or the Ellipse tool from the Toolbox.
2. Position the cursor where you want to place one corner of the basic shape, or hold down Option/Alt and position the cursor where you want to place the center point of the shape.
3. Click. InDesign displays the Rectangle dialog box (if you've selected the Rectangle tool) or the Ellipse dialog box (if you've selected the Ellipse tool).
4. Enter values in the Width and Height fields, then click the OK button.

FIGURE 6-4
**Adding a basic shape
"by the numbers"**

Select a basic shape tool.

*You can control the origin of
the basic shape by selecting
a point on the Transform palette's Proxy before you click.*

*Click the tool on the
page or pasteboard.*

*InDesign displays a
dialog box (Rectangle,
Polygon, or Ellipse).
Enter the dimensions of
the basic shape and click
the OK button.*

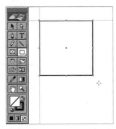

*InDesign creates a basic
shape with the dimen-
sions you entered.*

Points and Paths

Why is it that the most important things are often the most diffi-cult to learn? Drawing by manipulating Bezier paths—the geomet-ric construct used to represent path shapes in most of today's vector drawing programs—is one of those difficult things. When I first approached FreeHand and Illustrator, the process of drawing by placing points, and manipulating control handles struck me as alien, as nothing like drawing at all. Then I started to catch on.

In many ways, when I used pens and rulers to draw I was draw-ing lines from the point of view of everything *but* the line; in a Bezier-path-drawing program such as InDesign, I draw lines from the point of view of the line itself. This is neither better nor worse; it's just different and takes time to get used to. If you've just glanced at the Pen tool and are feeling confused, I urge you to stick with it. Start thinking like a line.

Thinking Like a Line   Imagine that, through the action of some mysterious potion or errant cosmic ray, you've been reduced in size so that you're a little smaller than one of the dots in a connect-the-dots puzzle. For added detail and color, imagine that the puzzle appears in a *Highlights for Children* magazine in a dentist's office.

The only way out is to complete the puzzle. As you walk, a line extends behind you. As you reach each dot in the puzzle, a sign tells you where you are in the puzzle and the route you must take to get to the next dot in the path.

Get the idea? The dots in the puzzle are points. The route you walk from one point to another, as instructed by the signs at each point, is a line segment. Each series of connected dots is a path. As you walk from one dot to another, you're thinking like a line.

Each point—from the first point in the path to the last—carries with it some information about the line segments that attach it to the previous and next points along the path.

Paths and their formatting (fill and stroke) attributes are different things. Even if the fill and stroke applied to the path is "None" or the stroke weight is 0 there's still a path there.

When you select a point, the point "fills in," becoming a solid square (see Figure 6-5). Note that this is the way that Illustrator displays a selected point, but the opposite of FreeHand's method.

FIGURE 6-5
Selected and unselected points

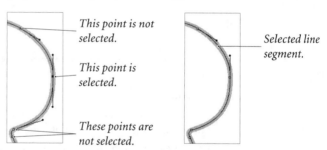

This point is not selected.

This point is selected.

These points are not selected.

Selected line segment.

Point Types

Points on an InDesign path are either *corner points* or *curve points*. Each type of point has its own special properties.

♦ A curve point adds a curved line segment between the current point and the preceding and following points along the path. Curve points have two control handles extended from them, and moving one control handle affects the position of the other control handle. The control handle following the point controls the curve of the line segment following the curve point on the path; the control handle preceding the point controls the curve of the line segment preceding the curve point on the path. Curve points are typically used to add smooth curves to a path (see Figure 6-6).

◆ A corner point adds a straight line segment between the current point and the preceding point on the path (see Figure 6-7). Corner points are typically used to create paths containing straight line segments.

FIGURE 6-6
Curve points

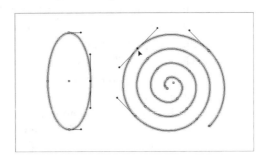

Curve points curve the line segments attached to the point. All of the points in this example are curve points.

FIGURE 6-7
Corner points

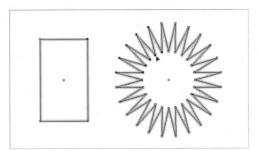

Corner points, by default, apply no curve to the line segments attached to the point. All of the points in this example are corner points.

What type of points should you use? Any type of point can be turned into any other type of point, and anything you can do with one kind of point can be done with the other kind of point. Given these two points (so to speak), you can use the kinds of points and drawing tools you're happiest with and achieve exactly the results you want. There is no "best way" to draw with InDesign's Pen tool, but it helps to understand how the particular method you choose works.

Winding   Paths have a direction, also known as "winding" (as in "winding a clock"—nothing to do with the weather) that generally corresponds to the order and direction in which you placed their points (see Figure 6-8). In our connect-the-dots puzzle, winding tells us the order in which we connect the dots.

FIGURE 6-8
Winding

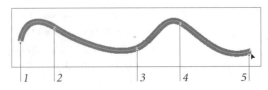

The order in which you create points determines the direction (or "winding") of the path.

To reverse the direction of a path, select the path and choose Reverse Path from the Object menu (in InDesign 1.0, you had to use the Direct Selection tool to select a point before InDesign would let you reverse the path). InDesign reverses the direction of the path.

Control Handles You control the curvature of the line segments before and after each point using the point's control handles. Points can have up to two control handles attached to them. By default, new corner points have none and curve points have two. Note that each line segment has up to two control handles defining its curve—the "outgoing" control handle attached to the point defining the start of the line segment and the "incoming" control handle attached to the next point.

If you retract the control handle (by dragging it inside the point), the control handle has no effect on the curvature of the path. This doesn't necessarily mean that the line segment is a straight line, however—a control handle on the point at the other end of the line segment might also have an effect.

The most significant difference between corner points and curve points is that the control handles attached to a corner point can be adjusted independently, while changing the angle of one control handle of a curve point changes the angle of the other control handle (see Figure 6-9). This difference, in my opinion, makes corner points much more useful than curve points—you can do anything with a corner point you could do with a curve point or a connector point.

To convert a point from one point type to another, click the point using the Convert Point tool. If you click a curve point, this retracts both control handles. To convert a curve point to a corner point while leaving one of its control handles in place, drag the other control handle using the Convert Point tool (see Figure 6-10).

FIGURE 6-9
Curve points vs.
corner points

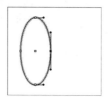 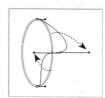 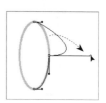

When you adjust one control handle on a curve point, InDesign adjusts the other control handle, as well.

To adjust the curvature of a line segment without changing the curve of the following line segment, use a corner point.

FIGURE 6-10
**Converting from one
point type to another**

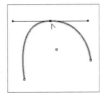  

*Position the Convert
Point tool over a
curve point...*

*...and click. InDesign
converts the curve point
to a corner point.*

*To convert a corner point
to a curve point, drag the
Convert Point tool over
the point.*

 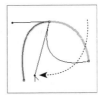 

*To convert a curve
point to a corner point,
drag one of the control
handles using Convert
Point tool.*

*InDesign converts the
curve point to a corner
point. As you drag the
control handle...*

*...InDesign adjusts the
curve of the correspond-
ing line segment, but
leaves the other line
segment unchanged.*

Drawing Paths with the Pencil Tool

The quickest way to create a freeform path on an InDesign page is
to use the Pencil tool. Click the Pencil tool in the Toolbox (or press
N), then drag the Pencil tool on the page. As you drag, InDesign creates a path that follows the cursor, automatically placing corner and
curve points as it does so (see Figure 6-11).

FIGURE 6-11
**Drawing with
the Pencil tool**

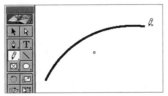 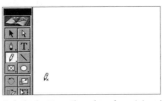

*Select the Pencil tool and position it
where you want the path to start.*

*Drag the Pencil tool on the page or
pasteboard.*

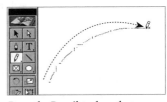 

*When the path looks the way you
want it to, stop dragging.*

*As you drag the Pencil tool, InDesign
positions curve and corner points.*

Drawing Paths with the Pen Tool

You use the Pen tool and its variants (the Remove Point, Add Point, and Convert Point tools)—to create and edit paths.

When you *click* the Pen tool in the publication window, InDesign places a corner point. *Drag* the Pen tool, and InDesign places a curve point where you started dragging—you determine the length of the control handles (and, therefore, the shape of the curve) by dragging as you place the curve point (see Figure 6-12).

FIGURE 6-12
Placing curve
and corner points

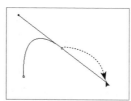

Drag the Pen tool...

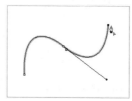

...and InDesign creates a curve point.

Click the Pen tool...

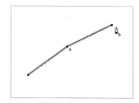

...and InDesign creates a corner point.

To curve the line segment following a *corner* point, place the corner point, position the Pen tool above the point (this switches to the Convert Point tool), and then drag. As you drag, InDesign extends a control handle from the point (see Figure 6-13).

The trickiest thing about using the Pen tool this way is that you don't see the effect of the curve manipulation until you've placed the next point. This makes sense in that you don't need a control handle for a line segment that doesn't yet exist, but it can be quite a brain-twister.

FIGURE 6-13
Dragging a control
handle out of
a corner point

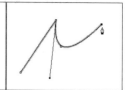

Position the Pen tool above a point (it'll change into the Convert Point tool).   *Drag a control handle out of the point.*   *Click the Pen tool to add a point. InDesign curves the line segment connecting the points.*

To convert a curve point you've just placed to a corner point, position the Pen tool above the point (to switch to the Convert Point tool) and then click the point. InDesign converts the point to a corner point and retracts the point's control handles.

You can change the position of points, as you'd expect, by selecting the point with the Direct Selection tool and then dragging the point to a new location.

Drawing Techniques

Now that you know all about the elements that make up paths, let's talk about how you actually use them.

Path Drawing Tips   When you're drawing paths, don't forget that you can change the path after you've drawn it. I've often seen people delete entire paths and start over because they misplaced the last point on the path. Go ahead and place points in the wrong places; you can always change the position of any point on the path. Also, keep these facts in mind:

◆ You can always split the path using the Scissors tool.

◆ You can always add points to or subtract points from the path.

◆ You can always change tools while drawing a path.

It's also best to create paths using as few points as you can—but it's not required. I've noticed that people who have just started working with Bezier drawing tools use more points than are needed to create their paths. Over time, they learn one of the basic rules of vector drawing: Any curve can be described by two points and their associated control handles. No more, no less.

Manipulating Control Handles   The aspect of drawing in InDesign that's toughest to understand and master is the care, feeding, and manipulation of control handles. These handles are fundamental to drawing curved lines, so you'd better learn how to work with them.

To adjust the curve of a line segment, use the Direct Selection tool to select a point attached to the line segment. The control handles attached to that point—and to the points that come before and after the selected point on the path—appear. If you don't see control handles attached to the point you selected, the curve of the line segment is controlled by the points at the other end of the line segments. Position the cursor over one of the control handles and drag.

The curve of the line segment associated with that handle changes as you drag. When the curve looks the way you want it to, stop dragging (see Figure 6-14).

To retract (delete) a control handle, drag the handle inside the point it's attached to.

You can also adjust the curve of a curved line segment by dragging the line segment itself. To do this, select the line segment (click the line segment with the Direct Selection tool, or use the tool to drag a selection rectangle over part of the line segment) and then drag. As you drag, InDesign adjusts the curve of the line segment (see Figure 6-15).

FIGURE 6-14
Adjusting curve points

  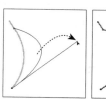

Select a point using the Direct Selection tool.   *Drag the control handle attached to the point to a new location.*   *InDesign curves the line segment.*

FIGURE 6-15
Another way to adjust the curve of a line segment

Select a line segment using the Direct Selection tool (drag a selection rectangle over the line segment).   *Drag the line segment. As you drag, InDesign adjusts the curve of the line segment.*

Adding Points to a Path

To add a point to an existing line segment, select the path, switch to the Pen tool, and then click the Pen tool on the line segment. InDesign adds a point to the path (see Figure 6-16).

You don't need to select the Add Point tool—InDesign will switch to it when you move the Pen tool above a line segment.

FIGURE 6-16
Adding a point to a path

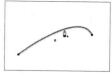 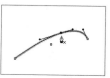

Position the Pen tool above a line segment. InDesign switches to the Add Point tool.   *Click on the path, and InDesign adds a point to the path.*

Removing Points from a Path

To remove a point from a path, select the path, switch to the Pen tool, and then click the Pen tool on the point. InDesign removes the point from the path (see Figure 6-17).

FIGURE 6-17
Removing a point
from a path

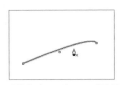

Position the Pen tool above an existing point on a path. InDesign switches to the Delete Point tool.

Click the point, and InDesign removes the point from the path.

Selecting and Moving Points

If you've gotten this far, you probably know how to select points, but here are a few rules to keep in mind.

♦ To select a point, click it with the Direct Selection tool, or drag a selection rectangle over it (using the same tool).

♦ You can select more than one point at a time. to do this, hold down Shift as you click the Direct Selection tool on each point, or use the Direct Selection tool to drag a selection rectangle over the points you want to select.

♦ You can select points on paths inside groups or compound paths by using the Direct Selection tool.

♦ When you move a point, the control handles associated with that point also move, maintaining their positions relative to the point. Note that this means that the curves of the line segments attached to the point change, unless you're also moving the points on the other end of the incoming and outgoing line segments.

♦ To move a straight line segment and its associated points, select the line segment with the Direct Selection tool and drag.

Opening and Closing Paths

Paths can be open (which means that there's no line segment between the beginning and ending points on the path) or closed (see Figure 6-18). You don't have to close a path to add contents (text or a graphic) or apply a fill to the path.

To close an open path, select the path, select the Pen tool, and then click the Pen tool on the first or last point on the path (it doesn't matter which). Click the Pen tool again on the other end point. InDesign closes the path (see Figure 6-19).

To open a closed path, select the Direct Selection tool and click the line segment between two points on the path (you can also drag a selection rectangle over the line segment. Press Delete, and InDesign removes the line segment, opening the path between the points on either side of the line segment (see Figure 6-20).

To open a path *without* removing a line segment, select the Scissors tool and click the path. Click on a point to split the path at that point, or click a line segment to split the path at that location (see Figure 6-21).

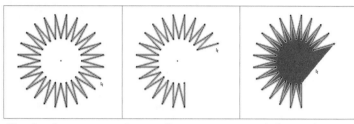

Closed path.   *Open path.*   *A path does not have to be closed to have a fill.*

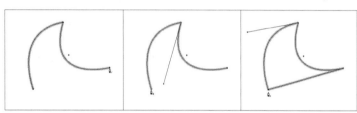

Move the Pen tool over an endpoint of an open path.   *Click the Pen tool, then move it over the other endpoint on the path.*   *Click on the endpoint. InDesign closes the path.*

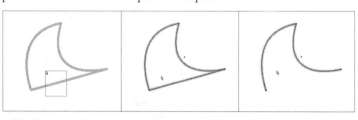

Select the Direct Selection tool, then drag a selection rectangle over a line segment.   *Press the Delete key to delete the line segment.*

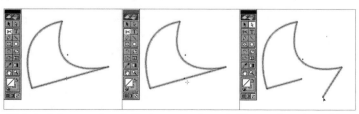

Click the Scissors tool on a line segment or point.   *InDesign opens the path. You can drag the path's endpoints apart, if necessary.*

The point closest to the start of the path (following the path's winding) becomes the point farther to the back, and the point farthest from the start of the path is on top of it.

Joining Open Paths

You can join two open paths to create a single path, or you can join two closed paths to create a compound path. In this section, I'll talk about joining open paths. For more on joining closed paths to create compound paths, see the section "Compound Paths," below.

To join two open paths, follow these steps (see Figure 6-22).

1. Select the Pen tool.

2. Position the Pen tool above the start or end point of one of the open paths (you don't need to select either path). InDesign changes the cursor to indicate that it's ready to add a point to the path.

3. Click the Pen tool, then position the cursor over the start or end point of the second path. InDesign changes the cursor to show that it's ready to connect the current path to the point.

4. Click the Pen tool. InDesign joins the two paths.

5. Repeat this process for the other two end points to close the path, if necessary.

FIGURE 6-22
Joining open paths

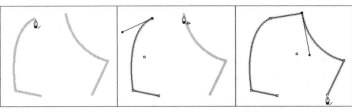

Position the Pen tool over an endpoint of an open path.

Click the Pen tool to continue the path, then move the cursor over the endpoint of another open path.

Click the Pen tool on one of the remaining endpoints.

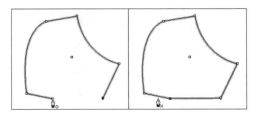

Click on the other endpoint to close the path.

Compound Paths

In the old days, not only did I have to walk miles to school in freezing cold weather, but I also had to work my way through an impossibly difficult series of steps just to create holes inside closed paths. While the process was kind of fascinating, it did nothing to help me hit my deadlines.

These days, creating holes in paths is easier—just make them into compound paths. Compound paths are made of two or more paths (which must be unlocked, ungrouped, and closed) that have been joined using the Make option on the Compound Paths submenu of the Object menu. Areas between the two paths, or areas where the paths overlap, are transparent. The following steps show you how to make a torus, or "doughnut" shape (see Figure 6-23).

1. Select the Oval tool from the toolbox.

2. Draw two ovals, one on top of the other.

3. Fill the ovals with a basic fill.

4. Select both ovals.

5. Press Command-8/Ctrl-8 to join the two ovals.

FIGURE 6-23
Creating compound paths

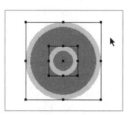

Select the paths you want to turn into a compound path.

Choose Make from the Composite Paths submenu of the Object menu.

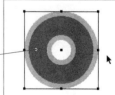

InDesign creates a compound path from the selected objects.

Compound paths don't have to have holes in them—this example shows a compound path that I've used as a container for an image.

If you decide you don't want the paths to be compound paths, you can change them back into individual paths by selecting the compound path and then choosing Release from the Compound Paths submenu of the Object menu.

When you join paths with different lines and fills, the compound path takes on the stroke and fill attributes of the path that's the farthest to the back.

Compound paths can be transformed just as you'd transform any other path.

When you convert characters to paths, InDesign automatically converts the characters into compound paths.

Editing Compound Paths

You can subselect the individual points that make up a compound path in the same way that you subselect objects inside a group—select the Direct Selection tool and click on the point. Once a point is selected, you can alter its position (see Figure 6-24).

FIGURE 6-24
Editing a
compound path

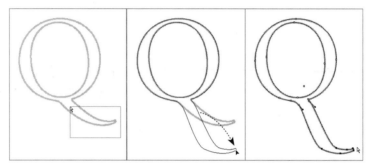

Use the Direct Selection tool to select some points.

Transform (move, scale, shear, or rotate) the points, In this example, I've dragged the points to a new location.

Splitting Compound Paths

To convert a compound path back into two or more normal paths, select the compound path and choose Release from the Compound Paths submenu of the Object menu (or press Command-Option-8/ Ctrl-Alt-8). InDesign converts the compound path into its component paths. Note that the paths do not return to their original formatting when you do this.

Smoothing Paths

You like using the Pencil tool. But your mouse hand isn't perfectly steady. Or the jerk you share office space with can't resist the urge to bump your arm while you're drawing. Either way, you need a way to smooth the path you've drawn in InDesign. Are you doomed to an after-hours workout with the Pen tool? Not with the new (in InDesign 1.5) Smooth tool. With the Smooth tool, you can smooth out the rough patches in your InDesign paths.

To use the Smooth tool, select the tool from the Tools palette (or press Shift-N until InDesign selects the tool for you). Alternatively, you can select the Pencil tool and hold down Option/Alt to change the Pencil tool to the Smooth tool. Drag the tool along the path you want to smooth (see Figure 6-25). As you drag, InDesign adjusts the control handles and point positions on the path (sometimes deleting points as you drag).

FIGURE 6-25
Smoothing a path

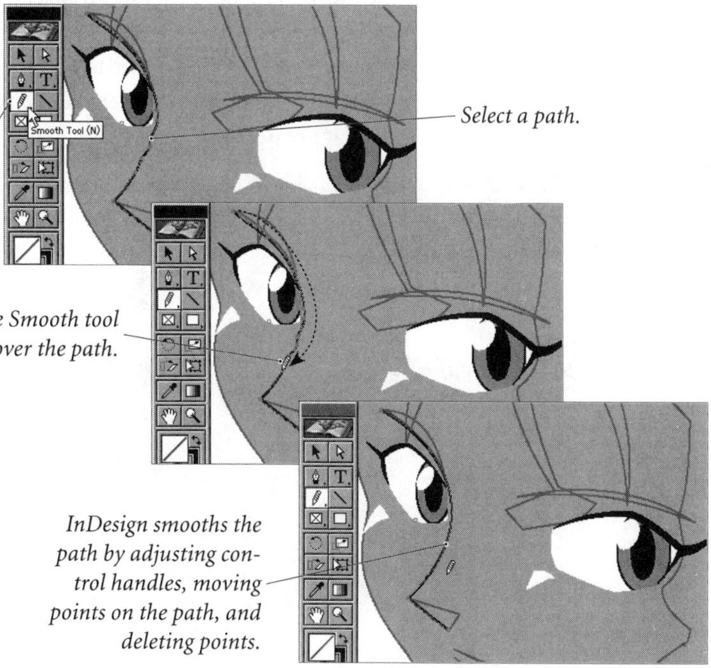

Select the Smooth tool from the Tools palette (or press Shift-N until InDesign selects the tool for you).

Select a path.

Drag the Smooth tool over the path.

InDesign smooths the path by adjusting control handles, moving points on the path, and deleting points.

To control the operation of the Smooth tool, double-click the Smooth tool in the Tools palette. InDesign displays the Smooth Tool Preferences dialog box (see Figure 6-26). The Fidelity slider controls the distance, in screen pixels, that the "smoothed" path can vary from the path of the Smooth tool (higher values equal more adjustment and greater variation from the existing path). The Smoothness slider controls the amount of change applied to the path (higher values equal greater smoothing).

FIGURE 6-26
Smooth Tool Preferences

Erasing Paths

Imagine that you want to remove an arbitrary section of a path, and that the beginning and end of the section do not correspond to existing points on the path. In InDesign 1.0, deleting this section of the path would have involved splitting the path using the Scissors tool (at either end of the section you wanted to delete) and then deleting the path segment between the two points.

In InDesign 1.5, it's much easier. Select the Erase tool from the Tools palette (or press Shift-N until InDesign selects the tool for you), then drag the tool over the area of the path you want to delete (see Figure 6-27).

FIGURE 6-27
Erasing part of a path

Select the Erase tool from the Tools palette (or press Shift-N until InDesign selects it for you).

Select a path.

Drag the Erase tool over the parts of the path you want to erase.

When you drag the Erase tool over a line segment on a closed path, InDesign opens the path. When you drag the Erase tool over an open path, InDesign splits the path into two paths.

Corner Effects

InDesign can apply a number of distortions to the corners of the paths in your publication. These distortions are known as "Corner Effects," and are controlled by the settings you enter in the Corner Effects dialog box. The most common use of this feature is to add rounded corners to rectangles and squares.

To apply a corner effect, select a path and then choose Corner Effects from the Object menu. InDesign displays the Corner Effects dialog box. Choose the effect you want from the Effect pop-up menu, then enter a value in the Size field and then press Return to apply your change. InDesign changes the corners of the path based on the corner effect you selected (see Figure 6-28).

FIGURE 6-28
Corner effects

Select a path, then display the context menu and choose Corner Effects (or press Command-Option-R/Ctrl-Alt-R).

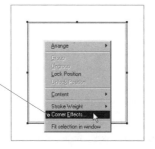

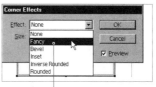

Choose a corner effect from the Effect pop-up menu.

InDesign's corner effects

Fancy *Inset* *Inverse Rounded* *Rounded* *Bevel*

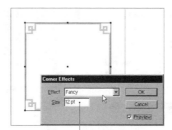 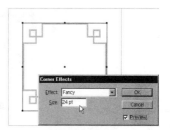

InDesign's corner effects can be applied to any corner point. Try them with polygons for interesting geometric shapes.

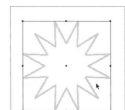 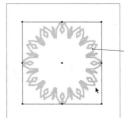

Enter a value in the Size field to set the size of the corner effect

Patterns created by overlapping corner effects

Strokes

Once you've created a path, you'll probably want to give the path some specific line weight, color, or other property. The process of applying formatting to a path is often called "stroking a path," and we refer to a path's appearance as its "stroke." Strokes specify what the outside of the path *looks like.*

To define a stroke for a path, select the path, then display the Stroke palette by pressing F10 (see Figure 6-29). Use the Type pop-up menu to choose the type of stroke you want to use—solid, dashed, or any of the "scotch" (i.e., multi-stroke) types.

FIGURE 6-29
Stroke palette

Stroke types

Thick-Thin-Thick

Thin-Thick-Thin

Thick-Thick

Thick-Thin

Thin-Thick

Thin-Thin

Solid

Dashed

Choose a stroke type from the Type pop-up menu.

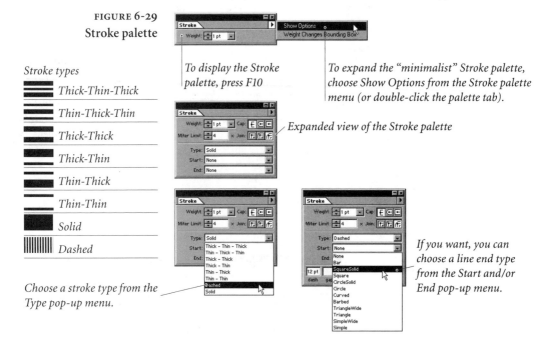

To display the Stroke palette, press F10

To expand the "minimalist" Stroke palette, choose Show Options from the Stroke palette menu (or double-click the palette tab).

Expanded view of the Stroke palette

If you want, you can choose a line end type from the Start and/or End pop-up menu.

Weight   You can enter a line weight for the stroke of the selected path using the Weight field, or you can choose a predefined line weight from the pop-up menu associated with the field. To remove a stroke from a path, enter zero in the Weight field.

Historical note: In the old days of desktop publishing, some programs created hairlines using the PostScript command "0 setlinewidth," which generates a one-pixel wide stroke on a PostScript printer. Provided you were printing to a 300-dpi laser printer, this worked pretty well—you'd get a stroke that was approximately the width of a hairline (between .2 and .25 points). When imagesetters appeared, however, this approach led to strokes that were $1/1200^{th}$ of an inch wide or even smaller—stroke weights too fine to be printed on most presses. So we grizzled graybeards advised all of our younger cohorts to avoid entering zero for the weight of a stroke. In InDesign, at least, it doesn't matter—entering zero won't result in a "0 setlinewidth" stroke.

Weight Changes Bounding Box

By default, changing the weight of a stroke changes the position of the points on the path. This means that increasing the stroke weight of, say, the border of an ad in your magazine layout keeps the stroke inside the area the advertiser is actually paying for (see Figure 6-30). That's the way that QuarkXPress works, so I guess people must like it.

FIGURE 6-30
Weight Changes Bounding Box

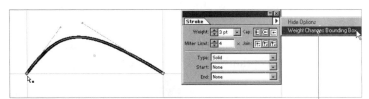

The starting and ending points of this path fall exactly on ruler guide intersections. What happens when you change the width of the stroke?

That depends on the state of the Width Changes Bounding Box option.

Width Changes Bounding Box off.

Width Changes Bounding Box on.

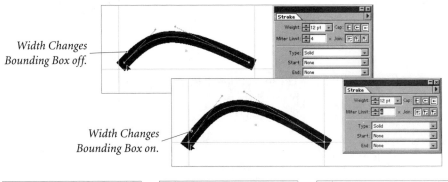

Here's a rectangle with a stroke width of zero points. If I increase the stroke width...

...InDesign makes the stroke width increase equally around the path when I have the Width Changes Bounding Box option turned on...

...or increases the stroke weight inside the path when I have Width Changes Bounding Box turned off.

It also enrages and upsets geometric purists (like the author), who believe that the positions of the points on a path are sacred and should not be altered just to keep a path inside its bounding box. Not by some smartypants page layout program, anyway—I'll change the shape of the path myself if I, the omnipotent user, feel I should. Luckily, someone at Adobe agrees with me, and added the Stroke Weight Changes Bounding Box option to the Stroke palette.

When you turn on the Stroke Weight Changes Bounding Box option, InDesign leaves the position of the path alone when you increase or decrease stroke weight. Choosing this option has no effect on existing paths.

Cap   Select one of the Cap options to determine the shape of the end of the stroke (see Figure 6-31). The Cap option you choose has no visible effect on a closed path.

FIGURE 6-31
Cap options

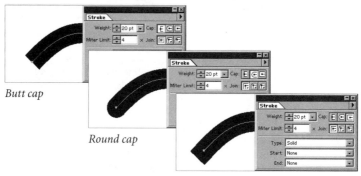

Butt cap

Round cap

Projecting cap

Join   The Join option determines the way InDesign renders corners—the place where two line segments in a path meet in a corner point (see Figure 6-32).

FIGURE 6-32
Join options

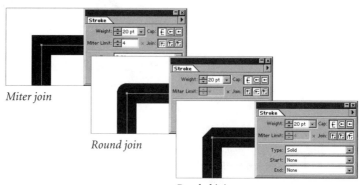

Miter join

Round join

Beveled join

Miter Limit   When paths go around corners, some weird things can happen. Asked to corner too sharply, the stroke skids out of control, creating spiky elbows that increase the effective stroke weight of a path's corners. The value you enter in the Miter Limit field sets the distance, as a multiple of the stroke weight, that you'll allow the corner to extend before InDesign applies a beveled join to the corner (see Figure 6-33). If, for example, you enter "2" in the Miter Limit field, InDesign will flatten corners when the stroke weight of the corner is equal to or greater than two times the weight of the stroke.

The Miter Limit field is only available when you're using the Miter Join option, and applies only to corner points.

FIGURE 6-33
Miter Limit

When angles get small, corners go out of control. In this example, a Miter Join creates a projecting "elbow."

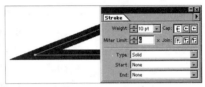

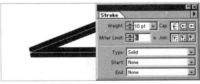

Increase the value in the Miter Limit field to cause corners with tight angles to be rendered using a Beveled miter join.

Dash   If you want a dashed line, choose Dashed from the Type pop-up menu, and use the Dash and Gap fields that appear at the bottom of the Stroke palette to specify the appearance of the dashed stroke (see Figure 6-34).

FIGURE 6-34
Applying a dashed stroke

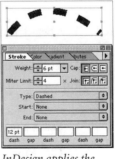

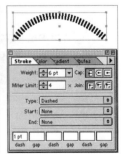

To apply a dashed stroke, choose Dashed from the Type pop-up menu.

InDesign applies the default dashed stroke pattern.

Edit the dashed stroke pattern, if necessary, by entering new values in the Dash and Gap fields (these fields use standard measurement units).

Creating a Dotted Stroke

You've probably noticed that there's no "dotted" stroke option available on the Type pop-up menu in the Stroke palette. Does that mean you can't create dotted lines? Not if you cheat. Here's what you do (see Figure 6-35).

1. Select a path.

2. Display the Stroke palette if it's not already visible (press F10).

3. Click the Round Cap option.

4. Choose Dashed from the Type pop-up menu. InDesign displays the Dash and Gap fields at the bottom of the Stroke palette.

5. Enter zero (yes, that's right, *zero*) in the first Dash field, and then enter a value equal to two or more times the stroke weight in the first Gap field. InDesign creates a dotted stroke where each dot is equal in diameter to the weight of the stroke.

FIGURE 6-35
Dashed strokes and cap options

Each dash in a dashed stroke has a line cap...

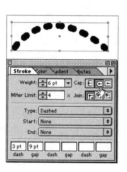
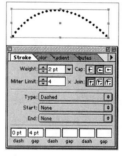

...which means you can create a dotted stroke by entering a dash pattern and choosing the Rounded line cap.

Creating Layered Strokes

I've heard a number of people complain that InDesign doesn't include their favorite "fancy" rules—if you can't find what you're looking for on the Type menu in the Stroke palette, you can make your own. To create a simple multi-stroke effect, follow these steps (see Figure 6-36).

1. Select a path.

2. Clone the path. To do this, press Command-C/Ctrl-C to copy the path, then press Command-Option-Shift-V/Ctrl-Alt-Shift-V. InDesign creates a copy of the selected path exactly on top of the original path.

3. Turn on the Stroke Weight Changes Bounding Box option on the Stroke palette menu (if it's not already on).

FIGURE 6-36
Creating a complex stroke by stacking paths

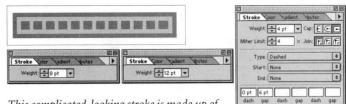

This complicated-looking stroke is made up of three separate strokes applied to three paths.

4. Change the stroke weight, stroke type, or color of the copy of the path.

5. Select the original path and the clone and group them (note that you can't make them a compound path, as that would apply one of the two strokes to both paths and would undo your multi-stroke effect).

Arrowheads   You can add arrowheads or (I guess) tailfeathers to any open path you want by choosing an arrowhead from the Start and End pop-up menus at the bottom of the Stroke palette. The Start pop-up menu applies to the first point in the path (according to the direction of the path); the End pop-up menu applies to the last point in the path. You don't have to make choices from both of the pop-up menus (see Figure 6-37).

FIGURE 6-37
Applying an arrowhead

Select a path.

Choose an arrowhead type from the Start or End pop-up menus in the Stroke palette.

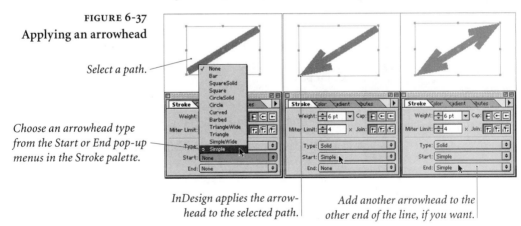

InDesign applies the arrowhead to the selected path.

Add another arrowhead to the other end of the line, if you want.

To swap the arrowheads on the beginning and end of a path, select the path and choose Reverse Path from the Object menu (see Figure 6-38).

Overprint   You won't find this basic stroke option in the Stroke palette, so stop looking. Instead, it's in the Attributes palette (choose Attributes

FIGURE 6-38
Reversing the
direction of a path

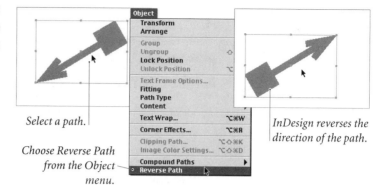

Select a path.

Choose Reverse Path
from the Object
menu.

InDesign reverses the
direction of the path.

from the Window menu). Checking the Overprint Stroke option makes the stroke overprint (rather than knock out of) whatever's behind it. This might not seem like much, but if you're creating color publications, you'll find it's one of the most important features in InDesign (see Chapter 8, "Color").

Editing Strokes   Once you've applied a stroke to a particular path, you can change the stroke using any of the following methods. Again, there's no "right" way to edit a stroke—which method is best and quickest depends on how you work and which palettes you have open at the time you want to change the stroke.

◆ Press F10 to display the Stroke palette, then make changes in the palette.

◆ Click a swatch in the Color palette to apply a color to the path (see Chapter 8, "Color," for more on applying colors using the Color palette).

◆ Use the Fill and Stroke buttons at the bottom of the Toolbox to apply or remove colors and gradients from the path.

◆ Use the Eyedropper tool to pick up the formatting of a path and apply that formatting to another path.

Removing Strokes   To quickly remove a stroke from a path, use one of the following techniques.

◆ Select the path, then click the Stroke selector (at the bottom of the Toolbox), then click None.

◆ Select the path, then display the Swatches palette and choose None from the Stroke Type pop-up menu.

◆ Enter 0 in the Weight field of the Stroke palette.

Fills

Just as strokes determine what the *outside* of a path looks like, fills specify the appearance of the *inside* of a path. Fills can make the inside of a path a solid color, or a linear or radial gradient. Any path you create can be filled.

To apply a fill to a path, select the path and do one of the following (see Figure 6-39).

◆ Click the Fill selector in the Tools palette, then click the Apply Color button (or press comma).

FIGURE 6-39
Applying a fill

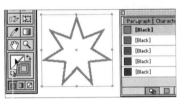

Click the Fill selector in the Tools palette.

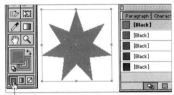

Click the Apply Color button...

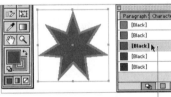

...or click a color or tint swatch in the Swatches palette...

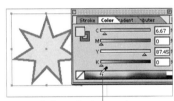

...or click a color in the Color palette.

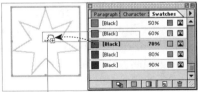

Drag a color swatch out of the Swatches palette...

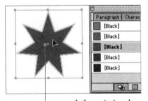

...and drop it in the interior of a path.

Use the Eyedropper tool to pick up the color you want from another path...

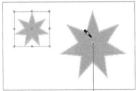

...and then click the Eyedropper tool on the path.

- Click a color or tint swatch in the Swatches palette (press F5 to display the Swatches palette). You can also drag the swatch out of the Swatches palette and drop it on a path (the path doesn't have to be selected).

- Display the Color palette and define a color.

- Select the Eyedropper tool and click an object formatted with a fill, then click the tool again on the selected path.

Removing Fills   To quickly remove a fill from a path, do one of the following:

- Click the Fill button at the bottom of the Toolbox, then click the None button.

- Click the Fill button in the Color palette and then click the None swatch (if you can't see the None swatch, it's because you've hidden the Color palette's option—choose Show Options from the Color palette menu to expand the palette and display the options).

- Click the Fill button at the bottom of the Toolbox, then click the None swatch in the Swatches palette.

Gradients

A "gradient" is a type of fill or stroke that creates a graduation from one color to another—an effect also known as a "fountain" or a "vignette." InDesign offers two types of gradients: "Linear" and "Radial." For either type of gradient fill, you can set the colors used in the gradient, the speed with which one color blends into another, and the colors used in the gradient (gradients can contain two or more colors). For Linear gradients, you can set the angle that the graduation is to follow.

Linear gradients create a smooth color transition (or series of transitions) from one end of a path to another; Radial gradients create a graduation from the center of a path to its edges. Gradients applied to paths are calculated relative to the geometric bounds of the path; gradients applied to text characters use the geometric bounding box of the text frame containing the text (not the individual characters themselves).

Applying Gradients   To apply a gradient to a path, follow these steps (see Figure 6-40).

1. Select the path using the Selection tool or the Direct Selection tool, or select text using the Text tool or Path Text tool.

2. Do one of the following.

♦ Click the Fill or Stroke selector in the Toolbox (to determine what part of the path you want to apply the gradient to). Click the Apply Gradient button at the bottom of the Toolbox.

♦ Display the Gradient palette (choose Gradient from the Window menu), and then click the gradient ramp.

♦ Click an existing gradient swatch in the Swatches palette (press F5 to display the Swatches palette). You can also drag the gradient swatch out of the Swatches palette and drop it on a path (the path doesn't have to be selected).

♦ Select the Eyedropper tool and click an object formatted with a gradient, then click the tool again on the selected path.

♦ Select the Gradient tool and drag the tool inside the path.

FIGURE 6-40

Applying a gradient

Click the Fill or Stroke selector...

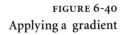

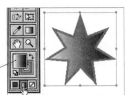

...then click the Apply Gradient button.

Select an object, then click a gradient swatch in the swatches palette.

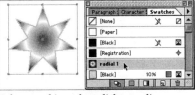

Display the Gradient palette, then click the gradient ramp.

Drag a gradient swatch out of the Swatches palette and drop it on a path (the path does not have to be selected).

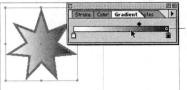

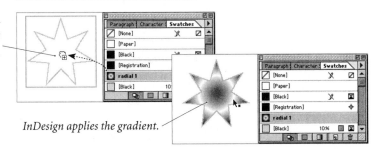

InDesign applies the gradient.

Gradient Controls

When you create or edit a gradient, you work with InDesign's gradient controls: the gradient ramp, gradient stop icons, and centerpoint icons. What the heck am I talking about? See Figure 6-41.

FIGURE 6-41
Gradient controls

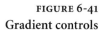

Unselected gradient stop

Selected gradient stop

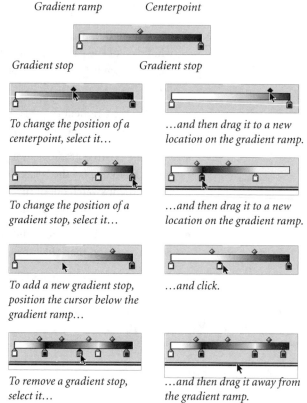

Gradient ramp   *Centerpoint*

Gradient stop   *Gradient stop*

To change the position of a centerpoint, select it...   *...and then drag it to a new location on the gradient ramp.*

To change the position of a gradient stop, select it...   *...and then drag it to a new location on the gradient ramp.*

To add a new gradient stop, position the cursor below the gradient ramp...   *...and click.*

To remove a gradient stop, select it...   *...and then drag it away from the gradient ramp.*

Creating a Gradient Swatch

In my opinion, the best way to apply gradients is to use the Swatches palette. Just as applying a color from the Swatches palette establishes a link between the color swatch and the object you've applied it to, so applying a gradient swatch links the swatch and the objects you've formatted with it. This means that you can edit the definition of the gradient swatch and update the formatting of all of the objects you've applied the swatch to.

To create a gradient swatch, follow these steps (see Figure 6-42).

1. Select an object formatted using a gradient that has the attributes you want (this step is optional).

2. Display the Swatches palette, if it's not already visible, then choose New Gradient Swatch from the Swatches palette menu. InDesign displays the New Gradient Swatch dialog box. If you selected an object in Step 1, InDesign picks up the attributes

FIGURE 6-42
Creating a
gradient swatch

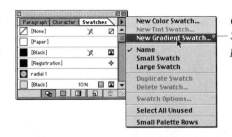

*Choose New Gradient
Swatch from the Swatches
palette menu.*

*InDesign displays the New
Gradient Swatch dialog box.*

*Enter a name for the gradient
(optional, but a good idea).*

*Set up the gradient. If
you selected an object
formatted using a
gradient, that gradient's
properties will appear here.*

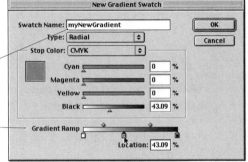

*Click the OK button,
and InDesign adds the
gradient to the list of
available swatches.*

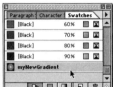

of the gradient applied to the object and displays them in this
dialog box. If you did not select an object, the controls in the
dialog box reflect the document's default gradient formatting.

3. If you're creating a gradient based on the gradient applied to a
selected object, enter a name for the gradient swatch (this step
is optional) and click the OK button to save the gradient swatch.
If you're creating a new gradient swatch "from scratch," specify
the colors and gradient stop positions for the gradient. Once the
gradient looks the way you want it to, click the OK button to
save the gradient swatch. InDesign adds the gradient swatch to
the list of swatches in the Swatches palette.

**Using the
Gradient Palette**

You can also apply and edit gradients using the Gradients palette
(see Figure 6-43). Like the New Gradient Swatch and Gradient
Options dialog boxes, the Gradient palette contains a gradient ramp,
with centerpoints above the ramp and gradient stops below.

To apply a gradient, select a path, then display the Gradient palette, then click the gradient ramp. InDesign applies the gradient to
the selected object.

To edit a gradient you've applied to a path, select the path, then
display the Gradient palette (if it's not already visible). InDesign
loads the gradient applied to the selected path into the Gradient palette. Adjust the gradient stop positions, or add gradient stops, or

FIGURE 6-43
Using the
Gradient palette

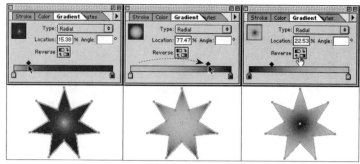

*You can use the Gradient
palette to edit the gradient
applied to an object. You
could, as shown in this
example, change the
position of a centerpoint
on the gradient ramp.*

*One thing that the Gradient palette has that you
won't find elsewhere—the Reverse button, which
reverses the direction of the gradient.*

change the position of centerpoints or colors, and InDesign applies
the changes to the selected path.

Editing Gradients

To edit the color, gradient type, or angle of a gradient you've applied
to an object, select the object and then display the Gradient palette
(see Figure 6-44). You can use any or all of the following techniques
to change the gradient.

◆ Drag a gradient stop to a new position on the gradient ramp.
Alternatively, you can select the gradient stop and enter a new
value in the Location field.

◆ Add a new gradient stop by clicking below the gradient ramp.

FIGURE 6-44
Getting a swatch color
into a gradient stop

*It's something every InDesign
user has done at least
once—you select a gradient
stop, then click a color swatch
in the Swatches palette,
expecting to apply the color
to the gradient stop. Instead,
InDesign fills (or strokes) the
path with the color. How the
heck do you get a swatch
color into a gradient swatch?*

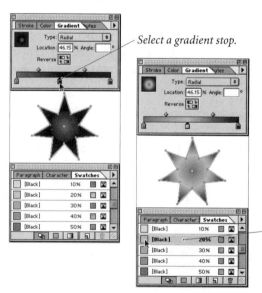

Select a gradient stop.

*Hold down
Option/Alt and click
the color swatch in
the Swatches palette.
InDesign assigns the
color to the gradient
stop.*

◆ Change the position of the centerpoint by dragging it above the gradient ramp. Or you can select the centerpoint and enter a new value in the Location field.

◆ Remove a gradient stop by dragging it away from the gradient ramp.

◆ Reverse the gradient ramp by clicking the Reverse button.

◆ Change the angle of a linear gradient by entering a new value in the Angle field.

◆ Change the color of a gradient stop using a color from the Swatches palette. To do this, select the stop, then hold down Option/Alt and click a color swatch in the Swatches palette.

◆ Change the color of a gradient stop to an unnamed color. To do this, select the gradient stop, then display the Color palette. Specify a color. As you change color values in the Color palette, InDesign changes the color applied to the gradient stop.

◆ Change the gradient type using the Type pop-up menu.

Applying a Gradient to Multiple Paths

To apply a gradient to more than one path, select the paths (which need not already have gradients applied to their fills or strokes), then drag the Gradient tool. The point at which you start dragging defines the starting point of the gradient (see Figure 6-45).

FIGURE 6-45
Applying a gradient to multiple objects

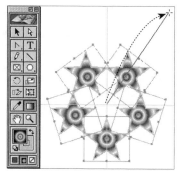

Select a series of paths. In this example, each path has been formatted using a radial gradient fill. Position the Gradient tool over the point at which you want to place the center point (for a radial gradient) or start (for a linear gradient), and then drag the tool.

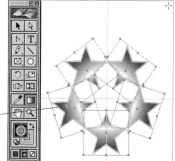

InDesign applies a single gradient to the selected paths.

Drawing Conclusions

Earlier in this chapter, I noted that I found the process of drawing paths using Bezier curves confusing when I first encountered it. As I worked with the tools, however, I found that the parts of my brain that were used to using rapidographs (an obsolete type of pen used by the ancient Greeks), triangles, curves, and rulers quickly adapted to the new drawing environment. Eventually, I realized that this was the easier way to draw.

Then, after reading a related article in a tabloid at the supermarket, it dawned on me that the archaic methods I'd learned were nothing less than an extraterrestrial plot, forced on us in classical antiquity by evil space gods, to some cosmic purpose which I cannot—as yet—reveal.

Just keep at it.

Importing
and Exporting

Someday, you'll need to do something that's beyond the drawing and typesetting capabilities of InDesign. You'll need to edit TIFF images, or do serious 3-D rendering, or create Web pages. Other applications do these things better than InDesign does. But you can add the files you create in other applications to your InDesign publication. And you can export InDesign pages for use in other page-layout and drawing programs.

You can scan an image, edit it with an image-editing program, and then import it into an InDesign publication. You can color-separate imported images as you print—or before you print, if you prefer. You can import graphics created in Macromedia FreeHand, Adobe Illustrator, or almost any other drawing program. If you're working with Illustrator or FreeHand, you can copy and paste paths (or drag and drop) out of those programs and paste them into InDesign to produce editable InDesign paths.

InDesign can also place pages from Adobe Acrobat Portable Document Format (PDF) files as graphics. As you'll see, this makes PDF a great format for getting graphics out of just about any kind of program and into InDesign.

Importing

InDesign offers three ways to bring files from other applications into your publications. Here are your options:

◆ Place the file. What, exactly, happens when you place a graphic depends on the file's format and size. If the file is 48Kb or smaller, InDesign copies the file into the publication. Note that though the graphic is embedded, InDesign maintains a link to the original file—this is not true for most embedded graphics.

When the graphic is larger than 48Kb, InDesign creates a link to the file you imported, and stores only a low-resolution, "proxy" (or "preview") image in the publication (though you can change the resolution of this preview image if necessary). When you print, InDesign gets the information it needs to print the graphic from the file on your disk. You can change this behavior, if you want—and make InDesign store the file inside your publication—see "Linking and Embedding," later in this chapter.

◆ Copy and paste. The most obvious, simplest, and least reliable method of getting information from another application is to copy it out of the application and paste it into InDesign. While this technique works well for small amounts of text, it can spell disaster for graphics and images created in other programs. I don't mean to imply that you should *never* use copy and paste, just that you should approach it with caution.

Another thing about copy and paste is that InDesign is very picky about what it'll let you paste into a publication. Overly picky, in my opinion. You can't, for example, copy an image out of Photoshop and paste it into InDesign. Even though this is the wrong thing to do, and is likely to result in printing problems, I still believe that InDesign should let you to do it (you might have a perfectly good reason for doing so).

A good reason to use copy and paste however, appears when you're working with Illustrator or FreeHand—when you copy paths out of these programs and paste them into InDesign, you get editable InDesign paths.

◆ Drag and drop. As I mentioned in Chapter 2, "Page Layout," you can drag objects out of one InDesign publication and drop them into another. You can drag files from your desktop (the Macintosh Finder or the Windows Explorer) and drop them into your InDesign publication window. This is essentially same as importing the files using the import command (except that you won't be able to set import options for the files, as you can if you place them). You can also drag objects from other programs and drop them into InDesign. This, in general, is the same as copying and pasting, and comes with the same cautions.

Note that you can also open QuarkXPress and PageMaker files—that's covered in Chapter 2, "Page Layout."

Placing Anything

To get a graphic file into an InDesign publication, follow these steps (see Figure 7-1).

1. Before you leap to the Place command on the File menu, take a second to think about where you want the graphic to appear.

   ◆ Do you want the graphic to fill an existing frame? If so, select the frame.

   ◆ Do you want the graphic to appear as an inline frame in a text frame? If so, select the Text tool and click it inside the text frame.

   ◆ Do you want to place the graphic in a new frame? If so, press Command-Shift-A/Ctrl-Shift-A to deselect everything before placing the graphic.

2. Press Command-D/Ctrl-D (or choose Place from the File menu). The Place dialog box appears.

3. Locate and select a file. To view the available import options for the file type you've selected *before* you place the file, turn on the Show Filter Options option.

4. If you have a frame selected, and want to place the file inside the frame, make sure you turn on the Replace Selected Item option. If you don't want to replace the selection, turn this option off.

5. Click the Open button (or press Enter). If you turned on the Show Filter Options option, InDesign displays the Import Filter Options dialog box for the relevant import filter. Make any changes you want in this dialog box and then click the OK button (the import filter options for each file type will be discussed later in this chapter). What happens next depends on the choice you made in Step 1.

FIGURE 7-1
Placing a graphic

*Placing a graphic in a frame
(similar to the QuarkXPress
"Get Picture" method).*

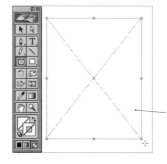

*Create a frame using one of
the frame drawing tools.*

*Choose Place from the File
menu (or press Command-
D/Ctrl-D).*

*InDesign displays the
Place dialog box.*

Locate and select a file.

Click the Open button.

*InDesign places the graphic
in the frame, cropping the
graphic into the frame (if
the graphic is bigger than
the frame).*

*Creating a frame
dynamically.*

*Choose Place from the File
menu (or press Command-
D/Ctrl-D). InDesign displays
the Place dialog box (see
above). Locate and select a
file, then click the Open
button.*

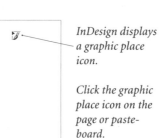

*InDesign displays
a graphic place
icon.*

*Click the graphic
place icon on the
page or paste-
board.*

*InDesign places the graphic on
the page, creating a frame that is
exactly the size of the graphic.*

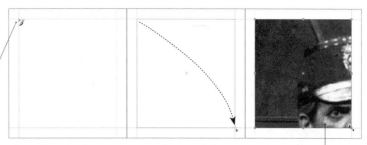

When you position the place icon near a ruler guide or grid line, InDesign changes the appearance of the place icon to show that clicking or dragging the icon will "snap" the incoming graphic to the guide or grid.

If you drag the place icon as you place a graphic...

...InDesign places the graphic inside a frame that's the width and height you define by dragging. This does not scale the graphic itself.

When you position the place icon over an existing frame, InDesign changes the appearance of the icon to indicate that clicking the icon will place the file inside the frame.

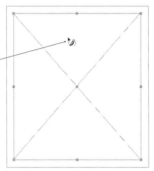
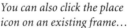

You can also click the place icon on an existing frame...

...to place the graphic inside the frame.

- If you had a frame selected, and turned on the Replace Selected Item option, the graphic appears inside the frame.

- If you had an active text insertion point in a text frame, and if you turned on the Replace Selected Item option, InDesign places the graphic into the text frame (at the location of the cursor) as an inline graphic.

- If you deselected everything before placing, or if you turned off the Replace Selected Item option, InDesign displays the place icon. Click the place icon on a page or on the pasteboard, and InDesign imports the file you selected and positions the upper-right corner of the file at the point at which you clicked the place icon. InDesign places the graphic on the page or pasteboard at its original size.

    Instead of clicking, you can *drag* the place icon. This produces a frame that's the width and height you define by dragging. Note that this does not scale the graphic itself.

    To place the graphic inside an existing frame, click the place icon in the frame. This frame doesn't have to be a graphic frame, and it doesn't have to be selected. When you click inside the frame, InDesign replaces any frame content with the incoming graphic.

If you accidentally placed the graphic inside a frame, don't panic. Instead, press Command-Z/Ctrl-Z to "undo" the action. InDesign displays the place icon, and is ready to place the graphic. At this point, you can cancel the Place operation by pressing Command-Z/Ctrl-Z again, or by clicking the place icon on any tool in the Tools palette.

About Graphic File Formats

InDesign can import a range of graphic file formats, including Adobe Illustrator formats, TIFF images, JPEG images, GIF images, EPS files, and PICT or WMF-type graphics. From InDesign's point of view, there are certain limitations and advantages to each of these file formats.

Just to refresh everyone's memory, here are a few quick definitions, rules, and exceptions regarding graphic file formats.

There are three fundamental graphics file format types:

◆ Bitmap files store pictures as matrices (rows and columns) of squares known as pixels, with each pixel having a particular gray or color value (also known as a gray depth, color depth, or bit depth). Bitmap files are typically created by image editing programs such as Adobe Photoshop, or by the software you use to run your scanner. TIFF, BMP, MacPaint, and GIF are all bitmap graphic file formats.

◆ Vector files contain sets of instructions for drawing graphic objects—typically geometric shapes, such as lines, ellipses, polygons, rectangles, and arcs. The drawing instructions say, "Start this line at this point and draw to that point over there"; or, "This is a polygon made up of these line segments." PostScript paths, such those as you'd find in an EPS, are another example of a vector format, but they're usually contained in a metafile (see below).

◆ Metafiles can contain both vector and bitmap graphics. Macintosh PICT, Adobe Illustrator, EPS, and WMF (Windows metafile) formats are all examples of metafiles. Metafiles don't have to contain *both* vector and bitmap objects. Sometimes you'll find metafiles that contain only an image, or metafiles that contain only vector artwork.

There are a lot of different ways to talk about the files saved in these three format types. I usually refer to bitmap files as "images," and vector files as "drawings."

Note that these formats are all "interchange" formats—they're for moving information from one application to another. All programs support their own, "native," file format, but many can read or write files in other formats. Some programs can open or import files saved in the native formats of other programs. InDesign can also place native Illustrator and Photoshop files—which might mean that you don't have to use an interchange format at all.

Some programs are real "Swiss Army knives," and can open and save files in lots of different formats. Photoshop, for example, can open and save files in a dozen different bitmap formats. Photoshop is a great program to have around even if you use it for nothing more than file conversions.

A Philosophical Note

There's always a temptation, as an explaining parent or as a computer book author, to simply say, "Because I say so." I feel that you deserve better. At the same time, a basic explanation of the problems inherent in, say, the Macintosh PICT vector format would consume all of the pages of this chapter. And then there's WMF, PICT's Windows counterpart, to think about.

There's just not room, so I'll try to be brief.

The biggest problem is that many graphics file formats, in spite of their being designed as "interchange" formats, make too many assumptions about the system they'll be viewed on or printed from. We say such formats are *device specific*, because they're tied to some feature of a particular video display system or printer (the "device"). Most of these formats assume that files stay on the computer system they're created on—not a reasonable assumption to make for anyone doing any kind of publishing. PostScript files (including EPS files) are practically the definition of a *device independent* file format.

In many cases, it's not the specification of the file format itself that's the problem—it's the way the import and export filters that read and write the files have been written. There's no reason (any more) to convert curves into a series of straight line segments when you export a vector drawing as a Windows Metafile—yet many export filters do just that.

Many bitmap formats incorrectly assume that the color palette of the system they're on will remain the same—this is particularly true of bitmap-only PICT files. This means that colors can shift as you move the file from computer to computer—which means that the colors change when you print. This can mean that you lose colors or levels of gray when you print.

Most metafile and vector formats—except EPS—assume that the font list of the system they're created on will remain the same, and refer to fonts by their *number* (as they appear in the list of fonts at the time the file was created) rather than by their *name*. This can cause problems when you move to another system, or even when you install a new font.

It all comes down to using the formats for what they were intended for. BMP files were intended to be viewed onscreen, in Windows—not printed. PICT and WMF files were intended for printing on (different types of) non-PostScript printers. EPS and TIFF were designed to work well on high resolution PostScript printers; GIF and JPEG were designed to carry a great deal of image information in the smallest possible package—which makes them ideal for on-line publishing. In addition, EPS, TIFF, JPEG, and GIF were designed for interchange between different computing environments and platforms—something you can't say of PICT (Macintosh-only) and WMF (Windows-only).

WMF is a file format for saving commands written in the Windows Graphic Device Interface (or GDI)—the language Windows uses to draw objects onscreen (or print to non-PostScript printers). PICT is based on QuickDraw, the native drawing language of the Macintosh. When you send files in these formats to a PostScript printer, they have to be translated into PostScript commands. This process isn't perfect, which means that what you see on your screen may not be what you get from your printer.

Graphic Display Properties

While the state of the Display pop-up menu in the General Preferences dialog box sets the default resolution InDesign uses to display graphics in a publication, you can vary the display resolution for individual images. This can come in handy when you need to see more detail in one image than in others, or when you want to speed up the redraw of a specific slow-drawing graphic.

To control the display properties of a graphic, select the graphic, and then display the context menu (hold down Control before you press the mouse button on the Macintosh; press the right mouse button in Windows). Choose one of the display options from the Display submenu (see Figure 7-2). These options affect all graphic file types—they're not just for images only.

◆ Full Resolution. For an image file, turning on this option means that InDesign gets image data from the original file on your hard drive to render the best possible preview for the current screen magnification. For an EPS or PDF, it means that InDesign will reinterpret the file to create a new preview (this is where those beautiful EPS previews come from). As you'd expect, either process takes more time than simply slamming a fixed resolution preview onto the screen (which is what the Proxy option does).

◆ Optimized Resolution. This option attempts to strike a balance between Full Resolution (see above) and Proxy (see below), by creating a new preview image (with a minimum resolution of 72 pixels per inch and a maximum resolution determined by the amount of available memory). InDesign then stores this preview image and uses it as it does a proxy image (i.e., InDesign does not generate a new image as you change screen magnifications).

FIGURE 7-2

Setting the display resolution for a graphic

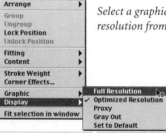

Select a graphic, then choose a display resolution from the Context menu.

Choose Set to Default to display the graphic using the display resolution you chose from the Display pop-up menu of the General panel of the Preferences dialog box.

Gray Out   *Proxy*   *Optimized Resolution*   *Full Resolution*

◆ Choose Proxy to have InDesign use the Proxy image InDesign
generated when you placed the file (or to construct a preview
image, if no preview was created). InDesign uses this preview
image to display the graphic at all magnification levels—which
means that images are going to get pretty ugly as you zoom in
on them. The advantage? The screen display of proxy images is
much faster than generating new previews for every magnification change.

◆ Gray Out. Choose this option to draw the selected graphic as
a gray box. The display of these gray boxes is very fast, but
somewhat lacking in detail.

◆ Set to Default. Choose this option to set the display of the
graphic to the display method selected in the Display pop-up
menu of the General Preferences dialog box.

To switch from one display setting to another without displaying
the context menu, select the graphic and press Commmand-Shift-
F5/Ctrl-Shift-F5. With each press of this shortcut, InDesign cycles
to the next display setting.

Working with Images

We don't think too much about the process of taking a photograph,
scanning it, incorporating it into a page layout, printing color separations of the publication, and then printing it on a commercial
offset printing press. But it's an amazing process.

First you record the visible light that's bouncing off of physical
objects. To do this, you use a lens to project the light onto a piece
of film that's coated with a chemical compound that changes on
contact with light. After you expose the film to some other chemicals, an image appears. Next, you turn the photographic image into
pixels using a scanner. Or you skip the film altogether and take the
picture with a digital camera.

When you print from your page layout program, you turn the
pixels into color halftone screens—overlapping patterns of dots,
which, when printed using certain inks, produce something that
resembles what you saw in the first place.

Given all of the above, is it any surprise that there are lots of
things for us to talk about when it comes to images?

Image Import Options   When you place an image, you can use the Image Import Options dialog box to specify a number of important things about the image (see Figure 7-3).

FIGURE 7-3
Image Settings

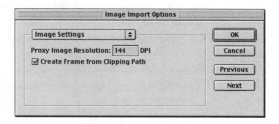

Proxy Image Resolution. What you see when you look at an imported graphic in an InDesign publication window depends on the option you've chosen from the Display pop-up menu of the Display section of the General Preferences dialog box (see Chapter 1, "Basics," for more on image display preferences). Or you can set the display resolution of individual images using the Display submenu of the context menu (see "Graphic Display Properties" earlier in this chapter). In either case, choosing Proxy tells InDesign to display a fixed (usually, but not necessarily, low) resolution version of the image for display at all screen magnifications. These preview images won't change as you zoom in or zoom out.

The resolution of the proxy images is controlled by the value you enter in the Proxy Image Resolution field in the Image Import dialog box as you place the image (you won't see the dialog box if you haven't turned on the Show Import Options option in the Place dialog box). In addition, InDesign uses the proxy image to print when you have the Low Resolution print option turned on.

Create Frame from Clipping Path. If the image you're placing contains a clipping path, InDesign makes available the Create Frame from Clipping Path option. When you turn this option on as you place the image, InDesign turns the clipping path into a frame and then positions the image inside the frame.

If the image does not contain a clipping path, this option won't be available. You can always create a clipping path for the image in InDesign, or choose another path saved with the image as the clipping path (as shown in "Creating a Clipping Path," later in this chapter).

Color Settings   You can apply InDesign's color management to a graphic as you place it, or you can choose to use a color management profile embedded in the graphic. Or you can choose to turn color management off for a graphic. Either way, the Color Settings panel of the Image Import Options dialog box is where you'll find the controls you're looking for (see Figure 7-4).

Color management is a very complicated topic, and the following control descriptions do not attempt to discuss the finer points of each topic. For more on color management, see Chapter 9, "Color."

FIGURE 7-4
Color Settings panel

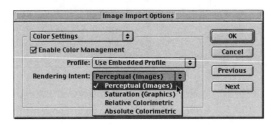

Enable Color Management. When you're importing a color image, InDesign activates the Enable Color Management option in the Color Settings panel of the Image Import Options dialog box. Turn this option on to apply color management to the incoming image; turn it off if color consistency is not important (to you or to the graphic).

Profile. If the image file you've selected contains a color management profile, InDesign selects Use Embedded Profile from the Profile pop-up menu. If you know that the embedded profile is not the one you want, choose another profile from the pop-up menu.

Rendering Intent. Choose the gamut scaling method you want to use to render the colors in the image. For most photographic images, you'll probably want to choose Perceptual (Images).

Images and Halftoning   Commercial printing equipment can only print one color per printing plate at one time. We can get additional "tints" of that color by filling areas with small dots; at a distance (anything over a foot or so), these dots look like another color. The pattern of dots is called a halftone (for more on digital halftoning and commercial printing, see Chapter 9, "Color").

We use halftoning to print the different shades inside images, or the different colors in vector artwork. The eye, silly and arbitrary thing that it is, tells our brain that the printed photograph is made up of shades of gray (or color)—not different patterns of large and small dots.

About Gray Levels

In the following sections, I'm going to refer frequently to "gray levels." When I do this, I'm not necessarily talking about the *color* gray—I'm talking about halftone screen values less than 100 percent and greater than 0 percent that appear on a printing plate. You still need gray levels when you're printing color separations, because almost all of the colors you'll find in a typical printed color image are made up of overlapping tints of two or more inks.

Images, Halftone Screen Frequency, and Resolution

Let me introduce you to the image balancing act (in case you haven't already met). It goes like this: for any printer resolution (in dots per inch, or dpi) there's an ideal halftone screen frequency (in lines per inch, or lpi)—a frequency that gives you the largest number of grays available at that printer resolution. If you go above this screen frequency, you start losing gray levels. To find the line screen that'll give you the largest number of grays for your printer's resolution, use this equation.

number of grays = (printer resolution in dpi/screen ruling in lpi)^2+1

If the number of grays is greater than 256, the number of grays equals 256. Most PostScript printers (any printer not equipped with PostScript 3) have a limit of 256 gray shades at any resolution.

So if you want 256 grays, and your printer resolution is 1200 dpi, the optimum screen ruling would be around 80 lpi.

What if you want to use a higher screen frequency? Something's got to give—and, usually, what gives is resolution. When you print at higher resolutions, you can use much higher line screens before you start losing grays.

The next factor in the balancing act is the resolution of your images. It's natural to assume that scanning at the highest resolution available from your scanner will give you the sharpest images. This bit of common knowledge, however, doesn't hold true for grayscale or color images; for these, scan at no more than twice the screen frequency you intend to use. Higher scanning resolutions do not add any greater sharpness (believe me, I've spent a lot of money printing test files to make *sure* that this is true), but the size of your image files increases dramatically. To determine the size of an image file, use this equation.

file size = (dpi^2 × bit depth × width × height)/8192 (bits in a kilobyte)

Bit depth is eight for an eight-bit image, 24 for an RGB color image, and 32 for a CMYK image. The result is in kilobytes.

There's one guy I know who always complains about the size of his TIFF files. He told me the other day about a color magazine cover that took up 60 MB on his hard drive. I think he's using too high a scanning resolution. Here's why—if the size of his image is 8.5 × 11 inches, he's using a 150 lpi halftone screen, and he's working with an RGB image, his file should be 21.4 MB, because $300^2 \times 24 \times 8.5 \times 11 \div 8192 = 24653.3$ (divide the result by 1024 to get megabytes). If he's working with a CMYK TIFF, his file size should be $300^2 \times 32 \times 8.5 \times 11 \times 8192 = 32871.1/1024$, or 32.1 megabytes—still nowhere near the file size he's griping about.

Ideally, you should scan at the same size as you intend to print the image. Resolution changes when you change the size of the image, so if your scanner won't create an image at the size you want, you can compensate for the effect of scaling the image in InDesign using this equation.

(original size/printed size)$^\prime$ original (scanning) resolution = resolution

If you'd scanned a three-by-three-inch image at 300 dpi and reduced it to 2.25 inches square (a reduction of 75 percent), the resolution of the image is 400 dpi.

Scanning Line Art

When you're scanning line art, save the files as bi-level TIFFs rather than as grayscale. You'll save lots of disk space, and your line art TIFFs will be just as sharp as if you saved them as grayscale TIFFs. Also, scan your line art at the highest resolution you can get out of your scanner. Line art, unlike grayscale and color images, benefits from increased resolution, because you're not creating halftones.

Increasing Line Art Resolution. Sometimes, your scanner can't scan at a high enough resolution to give you a good scan of line art. This is especially true when you're scanning those great, copyright-free engravings from Dover's clip art books. In this case, try this trick, which I stole (with permission) from *Real World Scanning and Halftones* by Steve Roth, Glenn Fleishman and David Blatner (Peachpit Press). This process produces a bi-level image at twice the resolution of your scanner.

1. Scan the image as grayscale at the highest optical resolution your scanner offers.

2. Resample the image to twice its original resolution using Photoshop (or other image editing program).

3. Sharpen the image.

4. Select Threshold from the Adjust submenu of the Image menu. Drag the arrow back and forth to adjust the break point for black and white. Click OK.

5. Convert the image to a bilevel TIFF and save it.

Preseparating Color Images

If you prefer, you can use another program—Adobe Photoshop comes to mind—to create color separations of images. Save the separated image as either an EPS, DCS, or as a CMYK TIFF, and you'll be able to import it into InDesign. When you print your publication, InDesign sends the color separations of the image to the printer. In a way, InDesign isn't really creating color separations of the image—it's just passing along the separations stored in the file. This is what's meant by a "preseparated host based workflow."

EPS files created by Photoshop (or other applications) contain all of the information needed to print color separations of an image. DCS is a variation of the EPS format, and exists in (at least) two versions. DCS1 files store the color-separated image as five separate files (one for each color, plus a "header" file that's the part you work with). DCS2 files generally contain all of the separations in a single file (although they, too, can be split into multiple files). If you're working with spot colors in Photoshop, you'll have to save the image using the DCS format to print color separations from InDesign.

CMYK TIFFs contain the separated image data, but don't contain any halftoning information from the application that created the separations. In most cases, in my opinion, that's fine.

Importing EPS and PDF Graphics

How did PDF and EPS get to be the industry-standard graphic file formats for vector graphics and type? It's because they're both based on the PostScript language—which, as you'll recall, is the language of high resolution imagesetters. When you have to convert drawing instructions from another vector format—WMF, for example—into PostScript, you're asking for trouble. And trouble is expensive when you're printing on film at 3600 dots per inch.

Graphics saved in the PDF or EPS formats are *resolution independent*, and so paths print as smoothly as possible on whatever printer you happen to be printing to. Both formats can include color definitions (including spot colors), and store the positions of graphics and type with a very high degree of precision. All of the above make these formats ideal for prepress use.

The difference between the two formats is that EPS graphics can contain "active" PostScript code—routines that generate paths when the graphic reaches a PostScript interpreter.

A graduated fill from FreeHand (or a gradient from Illustrator), for example, is really a piece of PostScript code that tells a PostScript interpreter to fill a path with a series of paths filled with varying colors. This means that the PostScript interpreter has to work a bit—calculating the positions of the points on the generated paths, setting their color, and so on. By contrast, a gradient in a PDF is literally a series of paths—all the PostScript interpreter has to do is draw them into the image of the page it's creating in the printer's memory.

EPS Import Options

When you import an EPS graphic, and have turned on the Show Import Options option in the Place dialog box, InDesign displays the EPS Import Options dialog box (see Figure 7-5).

FIGURE 7-5
EPS Import Options
dialog box

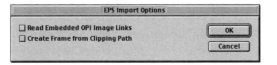

Read Embedded OPI Image Links. Open Prepress Interface (OPI) is a standard for maintaining image links between desktop page layout and illustration software and dedicated color prepress systems, such as those manufacturered by Kodak and Scitex. When you work with an OPI system, you typically work with low resolution proxy images as you lay out a page, and then link to higher resolution images saved on the prepress system when you print (or otherwise hand the job off to the prepress system). OPI concerns imported images only, and has nothing to do with vector graphics or type.

Turn this option off if the prepress system will take care of replacing any OPI images in the EPS; turn it on if you want InDesign to replace the images as you print. InDesign will store the OPI image information regardless of the setting of this option.

Create Frame from Clipping Path. Turn on this option when you want to place the contents of the graphic inside the clipping path defined in the EPS graphic.

PDF Import Options

When you import a PDF graphic, and have turned on the Show Import Options option in the Place dialog box, InDesign displays the Place PDF dialog box (see Figure 7-6).

FIGURE 7-6

Place PDF dialog box

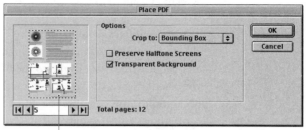

The Place PDF dialog box displays a preview of the pages of the PDF you've selected.

Page. PDF files can contain multiple pages (unlike EPS, which is, by definition, a single-page-per-file format), so you need some way to select the page you want to place. Scroll through the pages until you find the one you want. When you place a PDF without displaying the Place PDF dialog box, InDesign places the first page in the PDF.

Crop To. Do you have to import the whole page? No—you can use this pop-up menu to define the area of the page you want to place. Choose one of the following options (depending on the PDF, some options may be unavailable).

◆ Choose Bounding Box to crop the incoming PDF graphic to an area defined by the objects on the PDF page.

◆ Choose Art to place the area defined as an art box in the PDF graphic (if no art box has been defined, this option will not be available). For a PDF exported from InDesign, the art box is the same as the Trim area (see below).

◆ Choose Crop to crop the area of the incoming PDF graphic to the crop area defined in Acrobat (using the Crop Pages dialog box). If the PDF has not had a crop area defined, this area will be the same as the Media setting (see below).

◆ Choose Trim to import the area defined by any trim marks in the PDF.

◆ Choose Bleed to import the area defined by any bleed marks in the PDF

◆ Choose Media to import the area defined by the original paper size of the PDF.

Preserve Halftone Screens. When you turn this option on, InDesign uses the halftone screens defined in the PDF. Turn this option on to override the halftone screens defined in the PDF with the halftone screens you specify in the Colors panel of the Print dialog box.

Transparent Background. Turn this option on when you want to be able to see objects behind the imported PDF, or turn it off to apply an opaque white background to the PDF graphic. In general, I think you should leave this option turned on—if you want an opaque background, you can always apply a fill (of any color) to the frame containing the PDF graphic. If you turn this option off, on the other hand, the white background applied by InDesign cannot be changed by setting the fill of the frame.

Placed PDFs and Color Management. InDesign can't apply color management profiles to PDF graphics, but profiles embedded in the PDF will be used when you color separate the publication. If your PDFs require precise color matching, apply and embed the appropriate color profiles before saving the PDF for import into InDesign.

Creating Your Own EPS Graphics

If you think PostScript programming is fun, that makes two of us. You can create EPS graphics using a word processor or text editor, but you've got to remember two things.

◆ Try printing the file before you import it. If it doesn't print when you download it to your printer, it won't print after you've imported it into InDesign. Always test every change you make in your word processor by downloading the text file to the printer and seeing what you get before you bring the file into an InDesign publication, or at least before you take the file to a service bureau.

◆ InDesign can create a preview for any EPS graphic.z

Why would you want to create your own EPS graphics? There are lots of things you can do with PostScript that InDesign doesn't do (yet). And it's fun.

Because an EPS file is a text-only file, InDesign (and other programs) need some way to distinguish it from other text-only files. They get their clues from the first few lines of the EPS (also known as the file "header"). These lines should looks something like this:

```
%!PS-Adobe-2.0 EPSF-1.2
%%BoundingBox x1 y1 x2 y2
```

Where the values following the "BoundingBox" comment are the measurements of the EPS graphic in the following order: left, bottom, right, top. Points are the measurement system used in an EPS graphic (unless you make other arrangements), so the bounding box of an example US letter-sized EPS graphic would be:

```
%%BoundingBox 0 0 617 792
```

Figure 7-7 (on the next page) shows an example hand-coded EPS graphic, and what it looks like when you place it in InDesign.

Operators to Avoid. The PostScript code you use inside an EPS should not include any of the following PostScript operators.

banddevice	copypage	erasepage	exitserver
framedevice	grestoreall	initclip	initgraphics
initmatrix	legal	letter	note
nulldevice	quit	renderbands	setpageparams
setsccbbatch	stop		

Linking and Embedding

In InDesign, you can choose to embed (that is, store) imported graphics in your publication, or you can choose to store them externally and link to them. When you link to a graphic InDesign doesn't include the graphic file in your publication, but establishes a link between the publication and the imported file. InDesign creates a low resolution screen preview of the graphic, and uses that preview to draw the image on your page.

Linking means you don't have to store two copies of the original file—one on disk, and one in your InDesign publication—thereby saving disk space.

When you print, InDesign includes data from linked graphics in the stream of PostScript it's sending to your printer or to disk. This means that you need to take any externally stored graphics with you when you want to print your publication at an imagesetting service bureau.

Which method should you use? It's up to you. When you embed graphics, your publication size increases, but you don't have to keep track of the original files. When you link to externally-stored graphics, your publications will take up less space on disk, but you'll have to keep track of more than one file.

In some cases, InDesign embeds a copy of the graphic in your publication. This "automatic" embedding differs from "manual"

FIGURE 7-7
Writing your
own EPS graphics

```
%!PS-Adobe-2.0 EPSF-1.2
%%BoundingBox: 0 0 612 792
%%Creator:(G. Stumph & O. M. Kvern)
%%Title:(Fractal Tree)
%%CreationDate:(9-25-90)
%%EndComments
%% set up variables
/bdf
    {bind def} bind def
/depth 0 def
%% maxdepth controls how many branchings occur
%% exceeding 15 will be VERY time consuming
/maxdepth 10 def
%% after branching Òcutoff Ó times, the branch angles increase
%% set cutoff higher than maxdepth to supress this
/cutoff 4 def
/length
    {rand 72 mod 108 add} bdf
/ang
    {rand 10 mod 10 add} bdf
/sway
    {rand 60 mod 30 sub} bdf
/NewLine
    {sway length 3 div sway length 3 div
    0 length rcurveto currentpoint
    depth 1 sub maxdepth div setgray
    stroke translate 0 0 moveto} bdf
/down
    {/depth depth 1 add def
    depth cutoff gt
        {/ang
            {rand 30 mod 20 add} bdf
        } if
    } bdf
/up
    {/depth depth 1 sub def
    depth cutoff le
        {/ang
            {rand 10 mod 10 add} bdf
        } if
    } bdf
%% FractBranch is the loop that does all the work,
%% by calling itself recursively
/FractBranch
    {.8 .8 scale
    down NewLine
    depth maxdepth lt
        {ang rotate gsave FractBranch grestore
        ang 2 mul neg rotate gsave FractBranch grestore} if
    up
    } def
gsave
306 72 translate 0 0 moveto
10 setlinewidth
1 setlinecap
```

```
currentscreen 3 -1 roll
pop 65 3 1 roll setscreen
FractBranch
grestore
%%End of file
```

*Here's what the above
PostScript code looks
like when you place it
in InDesign or print it.*

embedding—you can maintain links to automatically embedded files, but not to manually embedded graphics.

When you move a linked file, or change its name (including any changes you might make to the name of the folder you've stored it in—or the volume you've stored it on), you break the link between the file and any InDesign publication you've placed it in. You can also break the link when you move the publication file to another volume.

If InDesign can't find a linked file when you're opening a publication, it looks in the folder containing the illustration for the linked file. If InDesign can't find the linked file there, it displays an alert stating that the publication contains missing or modified linked graphics. Click the Fix Links button to locate and link to the file or files (see Figure 7-8).

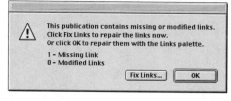

*When InDesign can't find
a linked file in a publication as it opens the publication, you'll see the Fix Links
dialog box.*

*Click the Fix Links button to
display the Relink dialog box.*

*Click the Browse button to display a standard file
dialog box, then locate and select the appropriate file.*

The key to InDesign's linking and embedding features is the Links palette (see Figure 7-9). To display the Links palette, press Command-Shift-D/Ctrl-Shift-D, or choose Links from the File menu. The Links palette displays the names of the linked files in the publication, and sometimes displays the following icons.

◆ If a graphic has been modified since its last update, you'll see a Caution icon (a yellow triangle with an exclamation mark inside it).

◆ If a graphic is missing, you'll see the Missing link icon—it's a red circle with a question mark in it. This means that InDesign can't find the file—it's been moved or deleted (or maybe you've lost your connection to the server that holds the file).

The file names of files you've embedded using the Embed option on the Layers palette menu do not appear in the Links palette.

You can change the order of the links in the Links palette—to do this, choose Sort by Status, Sort by Name, or Sort by Page from the Links palette menu.

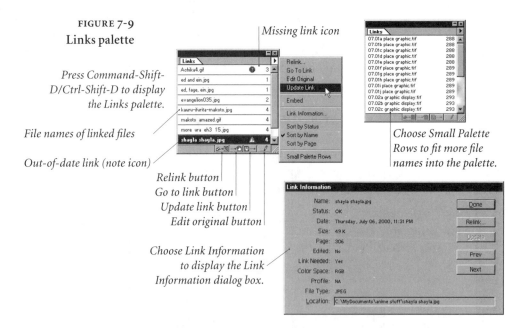

FIGURE 7-9
Links palette

Press Command-Shift-D/Ctrl-Shift-D to display the Links palette.

File names of linked files

Out-of-date link (note icon)

Relink button
Go to link button
Update link button
Edit original button

Choose Link Information to display the Link Information dialog box.

Missing link icon

Choose Small Palette Rows to fit more file names into the palette.

Getting Link Information Where the heck is that graphic file stored, anyway? Do I need it to print the publication? What color profile is attached to it, if any? The answers to these and other questions can be found in the Link Information dialog box. To display the Link Information dialog box, do one of the following.

◆ Select the graphic and choose Link Information from the Graphics submenu of the Context menu (to display the Context menu on the Macintosh, hold down Control and click; in Windows, press the right mouse button).

◆ Select the graphic's file name in the Links palette, then choose Link Information from the Links palette menu.

The meaning of most of the items in the Link Information dialog box is fairly straightforward—the Size field shows the amount of disk space taken up by the graphic, for example—but a couple of the fields deserve further explanation.

Date. The Date field shows when the original file was last saved.

Edited. This field shows when the original file was last edited.

Link Needed. Is the linked file needed to print the publication? If the graphic has been embedded by InDesign, you might not need the original file to print the publication (if you've embedded the graphic manually, you won't be able to display the Link Information dialog box).

Location. Note that the location field is the only editable field in the Link Information dialog box. While I say it's an "editable" field, I don't mean that you can change the path name in the field—you can't. But you can select the text and copy it out of the Links Information dialog box.

Of what possible use is this? Well—here are a few ideas.

◆ You can paste the text into your publication before embedding the graphic. When you embed the graphic, you'll lose all link information, including the name of the file (see "Embedding a Graphic," below). If you think you might, at some point, have to locate and edit the original file of an embedded graphic (and you will, believe me), having the name of the file around can be a big help. Put the text frame containing the file location on a non-printing layer, and you'll always have it to refer to (this is better than doing the "now where did I put that file/what did I name that file" mental exercise).

◆ You can paste the path name into the file name field of any Open, Save As, or Place dialog box. In Windows, you can also paste the path name into the Find dialog box—once you've found the file, you can use the context menu to copy it to another volume, or add it to an email message as an attachment, among other things.

◆ You can paste the path name into a database, spreadsheet, or word processing document.

The Next and Previous buttons display link information on the next or previous file shown in the Links palette. Note that the order of the links shown in this list does not necessarily have anything to do with the location of the graphics—the "next" link could be separated from the current link by many pages (unless you've chosen Sort By Pages from the Links palette menu).

Updating a Link   To update the link of an imported graphic, follow these steps (see Figure 7-10).

1. Display the Links palette, if it's not already visible.

2. Select the graphic you want to update, or select the corresponding link in the Links palette.

3. Choose Update Link from the Links palette menu (or cilck the Update Link button at the bottom of the Links palette). InDesign updates the link to the graphic file.

Updating a link

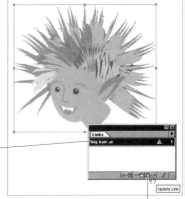
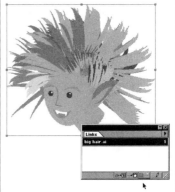

When the link to a graphic is out of date, InDesign displays an icon next to the filename in the Links palette.

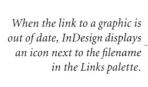

To update the link, select the filename and click the Update Link button.

InDesign updates the link to the graphic.

Linking to Another File   To link an imported graphic to another file, or to the original file in a new location, follow these steps (see Figure 7-11).

1. Display the Links palette, if it's not already visible.

2. Select the graphic you want to update, or select the corresponding link in the Links palette.

FIGURE 7-11

Linking to another file

Select an imported graphic and then choose Relink from the Links palette menu (or click the Relink button at the bottom of the palette).

InDesign displays the Relink dialog box. Enter a filename in the Location field, or click the Browse button...

...and select a file in the Locate file dialog box.

InDesign replaces the original graphic with the graphic you selected.

If the original graphic and the replacement graphic have different dimensions, use the Fitting options (on the Object menu, or the context menu, or on the Links palette menu) to fit the graphic to the frame...

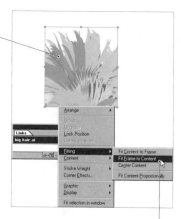

...or, as in this example, to fit the frame to the graphic.

The filename of the new graphic replaces the filename of the original graphic in the Links palette.

3. Click the Relink button (or choose Relink from the Links palette menu). InDesign displays the Relink dialog box.

4. Locate and select a file.

5. Click the OK button.

When InDesign cannot find the original file, you won't be able to choose Update Link from the Links palette menu. In this case, choose Relink and link to the graphic file in its new location.

Updating All Links To update all of the links in a publication, select all of the file names in the Links dialog box, then choose Update Link from the Links palette menu. InDesign updates all of the links.

Embedding a Graphic

To store a graphic inside the publication, select the name of the graphic in the Links palette and choose Embed from the Links palette menu. When you embed a graphic, the graphic's filename disappears from the list of links in the Links palette. Embedding a graphic has the following effects.

◆ It breaks the link to the external file, which means you won't be able to update the embedded graphic when you make changes to the original file (except by replacing the embedded graphic using the Relink command).

◆ The size of your publication file increases by the size of the graphic file. When you copy and paste the embedded graphic, the publication grows again by the same amount. I've seen other authors state that an embedded graphic on a master page increases a publication's file size by the size of the embedded file for each application of that master page—this isn't true. File size does increase by the size of the graphic if you apply a manual override to the master page item (this is as you'd expect, as an override *copies* the master page item to the document page).

◆ You can't use the Edit Original command to open and edit the graphic file.

◆ You can't get link information for the embedded graphic. This means that you won't be able to find the name of the embedded graphic—which can be a real problem when you need to edit the original file.

If you're embedding a graphic because you want to take your publication to another system or to an imagesetting service bureau, you should try using InDesign's Package and Preflight plug-ins, instead. These plug-ins can create packages containing all of the files necessary to print your publication. In addition, embedding confuses service bureaus, who are used to working with QuarkXPress (which cannot embed graphics). See Chapter 9, "Printing," for more on using the Package and Preflight plug-ins.

Navigating with the Links Palette

One very nice feature of the Links palette is the Go to Link button. To display any file that appears in the Links palette, select the file and click the Go to Link button. InDesign displays the graphic you selected, centered in the publication window (jumping to another spread, if necessary, to do so).

Working with Graphic Frames

Getting used to the way that InDesign works with graphics and graphics frames can take some time—especially for users of Free-Hand and PageMaker (where graphics are not necessarily stored inside frames). I hope that the following sections help.

Selecting Frames and Graphics

You can modify the size, shape, and formatting of a graphic frame, or you can modify the frame's contents, or you can change both at once. The key to making these adjustments lies in the selection method you use (see Figure 7-12).

◆ When you click the frame or frame contents using the Selection tool, or when a selection rectangle created by dragging the Selection tool touches the frame, you're selecting both the frame and its contents.

At this point, any changes you make (using the Transform palette or transformation tools) affect both the frame and its contents. For more on transforming objects, see Chapter 8, "Transforming."

FIGURE 7-12

Selecting a graphic

Click the Selection tool on the frame or graphic to select the frame and the graphic (note solid selection handles).

Click the Direct Selection tool on the frame to select the frame (note hollow selection handles).

Click the Direct Selection tool inside the frame to select the graphic. When the frame and the graphic are exactly the same size, it can be difficult to tell which is selected (in this example, it's easy, because the graphic is larger than the frame).

◆ When you click the outline of the frame with the Direct Selection tool, you're selecting the frame only—not its contents. Select the frame when you want to edit the shape of the frame using the drawing tools, or transform the frame using the transformation tools or the Transform palette, or when you want to move the frame without moving its contents.

◆ When you click *inside* the frame with the Direct Selection tool, you're selecting only the frame contents—not the frame itself. Select the graphic when you want to transform (rotate, scale, move, or skew) the graphic inside the frame, or when you want to apply color to the graphic.

Resizing Imported Graphics

When you select a graphic frame with the Selection tool and drag the corner handle, InDesign resizes the frame *but does not scale the graphic*. To scale the graphic inside the frame as you scale the frame, hold down Control/Ctrl as you drag the corner handle (see Figure 7-13). Hold down Shift as you drag to proportionally resize the frame and graphic.

You can also resize both the frame and the graphic using the Scaling tool or the Scale Horizontal and Scale Vertical fields in the Transform palette, provided you've selected the frame using the Selection tool. Or use the Free Transform tool or the Scale dialog box (see Chapter 8, "Transforming").

FIGURE 7-13
Scaling a graphic with the Selection tool

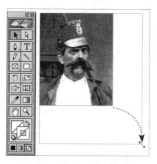

When you simply drag one of the selection handles of a frame containing a graphic, InDesign scales the frame, but does not scale the graphic.

Hold down Command/Ctrl as you drag a selection handle, and InDesign will scale the graphic as it scales the frame.

Panning a Graphic   When you "pan" a graphic, you move the graphic without moving the graphic's frame. To do this, select the graphic with the Direct Selection tool, then drag. As you drag, InDesign repositions the graphic inside the frame (see Figure 7-14).

Note that it's possible to move the graphic entirely outside the frame, off the page, and beyond the edge of the pasteboard. Don't.

FIGURE 7-14
Panning a graphic

Use the Direct Selection tool to select an image inside a frame…
…then drag the image. If you wait a second before you start dragging, you'll be able to see the image as you drag.

Working with Clipping Paths

Earlier in this chapter, I talked about InDesign's ability to create a frame from a clipping path stored in a graphic as you place the graphic—but what about creating a clipping path for a graphic that doesn't have one? First, there's nothing magical about clipping paths—they're just graphic frames. In fact, you could say that every graphic you place in InDesign is inside a clipping path—its graphic frame.

In InDesign, there are really two types of clipping paths—frames you draw or adjust using InDesign's drawing tools, or frames created using the Clipping Path command on the Object menu. The latter is a frame within a frame—and behaves just as if you'd created a frame and then pasted it into a rectangular frame.

Selecting an Existing Clipping Path   If the selected graphic contains a clipping path or multiple clipping paths, you can select the clipping path you want to apply. To do this, select the graphic, then display the Clipping Path dialog box (choose Clipping Path from the Object menu). Select the clipping path you want from the Type pop-up menu (see Figure 7-15).

Creating a Clipping Path   To create an "automatic" clipping path, follow these steps (see Figure 7-16).

1. Select a graphic. You'll have the best luck with a graphic whose background is white. In addition, it's a good idea to select the

FIGURE 7-15

Using an existing clipping path

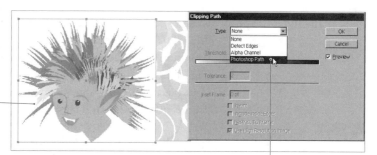

Place a graphic containing a clipping path (in this example, I've used a Photoshop file).

Select the graphic, then press Command-Option-Shift-K/Ctrl-Alt-Shift-K (or choose Clipping Path from the Object menu) to display the Clipping Path dialog box.

Choose Photoshop Path from the Type pop-up menu.

InDesign displays the Path pop-up menu.

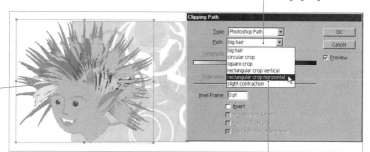

InDesign applies the first clipping path defined in the graphic (in this example, the path named "big hair").

If that's not the clipping path you want, select one of the other clipping paths.

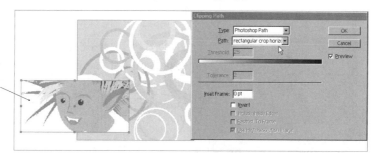

InDesign applies the clipping path (in this example, the path named "rectangular crop horizontal").

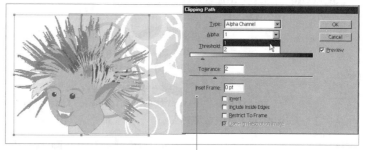

You can also use alpha channels defined in the graphic as clipping paths. When you choose Alpha Channel from the Type menu, InDesign displays the Alpha pop-up menu.

InDesign activates several options that are not available when you use a Photoshop path.

FIGURE 7-16

Creating a clipping path

Select a graphic, then press Command-Option-Shift-K/ Ctrl-Alt-Shift-K (or choose Clipping Path from the Object menu) to display the Clipping Path dialog box.

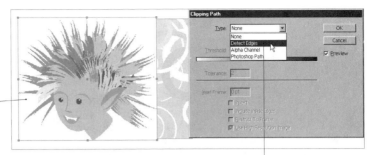

Choose Detect Edges from the Type pop-up menu.

InDesign attempts to find the edges in the graphic. It should be obvious that InDesign will do a better job of this when the graphic has a simple out- line and a simple background (as in this example).

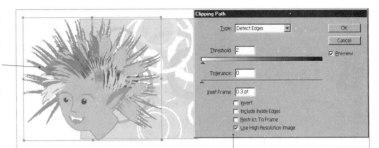

You can fine tune the clipping path using the controls in the Clipping Path dialog box.

graphic using the Selection tool and then switch to the Direct Selection tool (or click on the frame with the Direct Selection tool). I know this seems odd, but bear with me. I'll tell you why later.

2. Choose Clipping Path from the Object menu (or press Com- mand-Option-Shift-K/Ctrl-Alt-Shift-K). InDesign displays the Clipping Path dialog box.

3. Choose Detect Edges from the Type pop-up menu. Turn on the Preview option, if it's not already on, and drag the Clipping Path dialog box out of the way (if necessary) so that you can see the selected image. Look at the clipping path that InDesign has built around the image. What? You can't see the clipping path? That's because you didn't select the image using the Direct Selection tool, like I told you to in Step 1. If you had, you'd be able to see the clipping path as you adjust the settings in the Clipping Path dialog box.

4. Work with the controls in the dialog box.

   ◆ Adjust the values in the Threshold and Tolerance fields (either enter values in the fields or drag the associated slid- ers) until the clipping path looks the way you want it to.

◆ Turn on the Include Inside Edges option to create "holes" inside the clipping path for any blank (as defined by the value you entered in the Threshold field) areas inside the graphic.

◆ Turn on Invert to turn the clipping path "inside out."

◆ Most of the time, you'll probably want to turn on the Use High Resolution Image option—it uses data from the image file on disk (rather than simply using the screen preview image) to create a more accurate clipping path.

◆ If necessary (and it usually will be), enter a value in the Inset Frame field to shrink (enter positive values) or expand (enter negative values) the clipping path.

5. Once the clipping path looks the way you want it to, click the OK button.

Removing a Clipping Path   To remove a clipping path, select the image, display the Clipping Path dialog box, and choose None from the Type pop-up menu. InDesign removes the clipping path.

Applying Color to an Imported Graphic

You can't apply a color to just any imported graphic—but you can apply colors to bi-level (i.e., black-and-white) and grayscale TIFF images. To apply a color to an image, select the image using the Direct Selection tool, then apply a color as you normally would—probably by clicking a swatch in the Swatches palette (see Chapter 9, "Color," for more on applying colors).

In InDesign 1.0, you could apply tints to images, but InDesign would always apply the color the tint was based on (i.e., the 100% tint) to the image. In InDesign 1.5, this limitation departs (good riddance!), and you can apply tints to grayscale and bi-level images.

If you want the image to overprint any objects behind it, select the image using the Direct Selection tool, display the Attributes palette (if it's not already visible), and then turn on the Overprint Fill option. You can use this technique to create duotones from grayscale images you've placed in a publication, as shown in Color Figure 7.

Exporting

Sometimes, you've got to get your pages out of your InDesign publications and into some other application or format. You can export InDesign pages as EPS, PDF, or HTML (in addition to the text export options described in Chapter 3, "Text").

Exporting EPS   To export an InDesign page (or series of pages) as an EPS graphic (or series of graphics—EPS is, by definition, a single-page-at-a-time format), choose EPS from the Formats pop-up menu (on the Macintosh) or the Save as Type field (in Windows) and click the Save button. InDesign displays the Export EPS dialog box. This dialog box has two panels: EPS Options and Pages. Here's a quick description of the options in each panel.

EPS Options. The controls in this panel define the way that InDesign exports objects to the EPS file (see Figure 7-17).

FIGURE 7-17
EPS Options panel

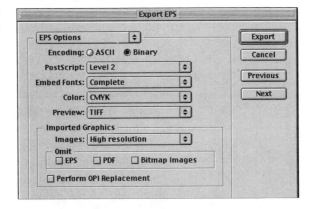

◆ Encoding. Choose ASCII if you expect to print the EPS on a system connected to a printer via a serial cable, or if you plan to edit the EPS using a text editor or word processor—otherwise, choose Binary to create a compressed version of the file.

◆ PostScript. Choose the PostScript version of the printer you expect to use to print the EPS. Choose Level 2 if you'll be printing on a PostScript Level 2 or PostScript 3 printer, choose Level 1 *only* if you'll be printing on a PostScript Level 1 printer, and choose Level 1, 2, and 3 Compatible if you don't know the printer type that will be used to print the EPS. The main difference here lies in the way that the different versions of the PostScript language print gradients. PostScript Level 2 and

PostScript 3 printers can generally print smooth gradients; PostScript Level 1 printers will probably show noticeable banding in gradients. In addition, PostScript Level 1 printers often have trouble printing multiple master fonts.

◆ Embed Fonts. To make sure that the EPS contains all of the fonts you've used, choose Complete from the Embed Fonts pop-up menu. Why not do this every time? Because your EPS files can become huge, bloated, swollen with included fonts. To reduce the size of the EPS, choose Subset to include only the characters needed to print the text in the EPS. Choose None when you don't want or need to include any fonts in the EPS.

Some fonts cannot be embedded—the font manufacturer has included information in the font that prevents embedding. When InDesign reads this information, it will not include the fonts in the EPS, regardless of the choice you make from the Embed Fonts pop-up menu. If you find you're missing a font in an EPS, return to the InDesign publication and convert all of the characters that use the missing font to outlines and then export the EPS again.

◆ Color. Do you want to convert RGB images in your publication to CMYK as you create the EPS? If so, choose CMYK from the Color pop-up menu. The method InDesign uses for this conversion depends on the setting of the Enable Color Management option in the Document Color settings dialog box (choose Document from the Color Preferences submenu of the File menu). If the option is on, and you've assigned a color profile to an image, InDesign uses that profile to create separations of the image. If the option is turned off, or if you have not turned on color management for the image, InDesign uses its internal RGB to CMYK conversion method.

Choose Gray to convert all colors to their grayscale equivalents. Choose to convert all colors to their RGB equivalents.

Choose Device Independent (which won't be available unless you've turned on color management) to allow output devices to apply their own color management profiles to the exported EPS. When you do this, InDesign does not convert RGB images as during the export process.

◆ Imported Graphics. To keep InDesign from including a certain type of imported graphic file in the EPS, turn on the corresponding option in the Omit section (to omit placed PDF graphics, for example, turn on the PDF option).

Most of the time, you'll probably want to choose High Resolution from the Images pop-up menu—this includes all of the data in the image. If you're planning to print the EPS through an OPI system, and plan to replace the images, or if you're creating the EPS for on-screen viewing only, choose Low Resolution. Choose Omit to export OPI image links only.

◆ Perform OPI Replacement. Turn this option on to have InDesign perform OPI image replacement as you export the EPS. If you're exporting a page containing EPS graphics containing OPI image links, you'll probably need to turn this option on.

Pages. Which pages do you want to export? Bear in mind, as you work with the controls in this panel, that each page in the page range you specify will be exported as a separate EPS file (see Figure 7-18).

FIGURE 7-18
Pages panel

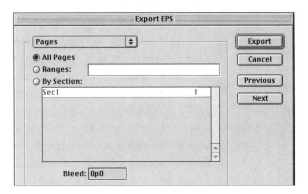

◆ All Pages/Ranges/By Section. Which pages do you want to export as EPS? (Again, remember that each page will become a separate EPS file on disk when you export.) Use these options to let InDesign know.

◆ Bleed. If you do not enter a value in the Bleed field, InDesign sets the edge of the EPS bounding box to the edge of the page you're exporting. Enter a value in the Bleed field to expand the area of the page.

An EPS-related Rant   It's inevitable—some of you are going to be asked by your imagesetting service provider to give them EPS files of your InDesign pages. This is because they want to import the EPSs into QuarkXPress 3.32. Why would they want to do this? Because it's the only way they know how to print *anything*. For what it's worth, they probably do the same thing with QuarkXPress 4.1 publications. In spite of the output disasters that this approach can cause, it's what they're familiar with, and is the only way they'll print your job. You're laughing now, but, believe me, these guys are out there.

So, while you're searching for a new imagesetting service bureau, you might as well give them what they want.

Exporting PDF

InDesign can export Adobe Acrobat Portable Document Format files (or PDF), which means you can use the PDF for remote printing, electronic distribution, or as a graphic you can place in InDesign or other programs. InDesign doesn't need to use the Acrobat Distiller (or the Distiller Assistant) to create PDF files.

Many of you have gotten the idea that PDF is great for putting publications on the World Wide Web, or for creating other sorts of on-line publications. Many of you, on thinking this, have to stifle a yawn whenever the topic comes up. Sure, it's a great format for that pie-in-the-sky "paperless office" stuff, but what's it got to do with the world of ink-on-paper where most of us spend our time?

I'll tell you. PDF isn't just for on-line publications. It makes a great format for moving laid-out pages from one publishing application to another—what's usually called an "interchange format" (RTF is another example of an interchange format). Having InDesign write PDF files makes it easy to take a page you've laid out in InDesign and place it in QuarkXPress, Illustrator, or PageMaker. To open or import the PDF using FreeHand, you'll have to either convert the PDF to an earlier format, or (at the time of this writing) wait for an update to FreeHand's PDF import filter.

InDesign exports PDF files in the Acrobat 1.3 format, which means you'll need the Acrobat 4 Reader to view the files (or Acrobat 4 to edit the files).

PDF files exported by InDesign do not include PDF navigational features such as article threads or bookmarks.

PDF Export Options

When you export a PDF, InDesign displays the Export PDF dialog box. This dialog box contains four panels for setting PDF export options, as shown in the sections following (see Figure 7-19).

◆ Style. Select a PDF export style from the Style pop-up menu to export the PDF using the settings defined in the style. See "Defining a PDF Export Style," later in this chapter.

◆ Subset Fonts Below. The value you enter in this field sets the threshold at which InDesign includes complete fonts in the PDF you're exporting. When you "subset" a font, you include only

FIGURE 7-19
PDF export options

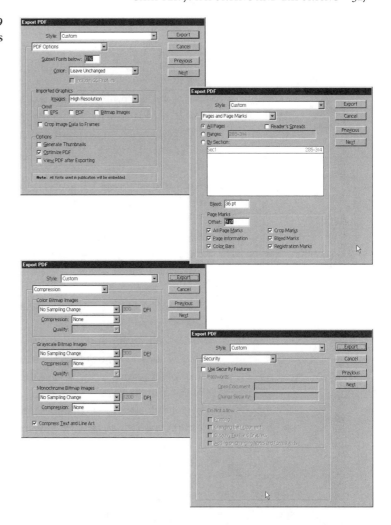

those characters that are used on the pages you're exporting. Enter 100 to force InDesign to always download a subset of the characters in a font (this well keep file sizes down), or enter 0 to force InDesign to include the entire font in the PDF, or enter some other percentage value to strike a balance between the two extremes.

◆ Color. Choose CMYK from the Color pop-up menu to convert any RGB images to CMYK in the exported PDF. If you've assigned a color profile to an image, InDesign uses that profile to create separations of the image. If you have not turned on color management for the image, InDesign uses its internal RGB to CMYK conversion method. Or choose RGB to convert the images in the publication to the RGB color model. Choose

Leave Unchanged to export the images using their current color model. The options on the Color menu have no effect on spot colors you've defined in your publication.

◆ Include ICC Profiles. Turn this option on if images and colors in the PDF file require color management for viewing or printing. If InDesign's color management system is not active, this option will not be available.

◆ Imported Graphics. Choose High Resolution to include all of the image data in the PDF—do this if you plan to print the PDF. If the PDF is intended for online use only, choose Low Resolution. Turn on the options in the Omit section to omit a particular graphic type (EPS, PDF, or Bitmap Images) from the exported PDF.

◆ Crop Image Data to Frames. When you turn this option on, InDesign sends only the visible parts of the images in the publication. This can result in a much smaller file for publications that contain cropped images. But it also means you won't have access to the image data if you edit the image in the PDF. Most of the time, this isn't a problem, but you might want to turn this option off if your PDF includes images that bleed (so that you can increase the bleed area, if necessary).

◆ Generate Thumbnails. Creates a preview image, or "thumbnail" of each page or spread (if you're exporting reader's spreads) you export. You can display thumbnails when you view the PDF using Acrobat or Acrobat Reader. They don't do much for me, and they increase the size of the file.

◆ Optimize PDF. When this option is off, InDesign includes repeated objects (such as objects from master pages) as individual objects on each page of the PDF. When you choose Optimize PDF, InDesign exports a single instance of each repeated item for the entire PDF. When the item appears on a page in the PDF, InDesign includes a reference to the "master" item. This reduces the file size of the PDF without changing the appearance of the exported pages.

◆ View PDF after Exporting. When you turn this option on, InDesign will open the PDF using Acrobat Reader or Acrobat after exporting the PDF.

Compression. The options in this panel define the compression and/or sampling changes applied to the images in your publication as it's exported as a PDF.

You can compress color and grayscale images using ZIP or JPEG compression. Which method should you use? I admit that I'm a bit conservative—I use 8-bit ZIP for everything. I do this because ZIP compression does not discard image data (it's "lossless"). JPEG compression, even at its highest quality setting, removes data from an image file (it's "lossy"). For scanned photographs, I guess you can get away with JPEG compression, but I still don't recommend it. You never know when you might need that image data! If you're working with image files where every pixel counts—screen shots, for example—you should never use JPEG compression.

You can also choose to downsample or subsample images (by selecting a resampling option from the Resample pop-up menus in each image section in the dialog box), but, again, I'm conservative. Unless you're creating a PDF for online use or proofing, I think you should avoid these options. Earlier in this chapter, I discussed the interaction between printer resolution, halftone screen frequency, and image resolution, and stated that you could safely reduce image resolutions to match a given halftone screen. Wouldn't it be easier to have InDesign do it for you by choosing to downsample or subsample images as it exports them to a PDF file?

Don't confuse the two resampling methods—they're very different from each other. When you *resample* an image, you turn an area of pixels into a single, larger pixel. When you *downsample* an image, InDesign takes the average color or gray value of all of the pixels in the area to set the color or gray value of the larger pixel. When you *subsample* an image, on the other hand, InDesign uses the color or gray value of a single pixel in the middle of the area. This means that subsampling is a much less accurate resampling method than downsampling, and shouldn't be used for anything other than proofing (see Figure 7-20).

I don't know that there's any actual problem with InDesign's downsampling—but I still don't like it. If I change the resolution of an image in Photoshop, I can see the result of resampling on the screen, and undo the change if necessary. When I use InDesign's downsampling while exporting a PDF, I won't see the result until I view the PDF. While I can always return to InDesign and export the PDF again, I'd rather just get the image resolution right in Photoshop before I place the image in my InDesign publication.

Remember that monochrome (or bi-level) images, do not have halftone screens applied to them by the printer, and, therefore, are

FIGURE 7-20
**Sampling methods
compared**

Normal   *Downsampled to 300   Subsampled to 300
                      pixels per inch   pixels per inch*

not subject to the same rules that govern grayscale and color image. In a monochrome image, the ideal resolution is the resolution of the printer—so don't resample the image unless you're creating the PDF for proofing or on-screen viewing.

If you've read the above arguments and *still* want to resample the images in your publication as you create a PDF, choose the resampling method from the appropriate Resample pop-up menu, then enter the resolution you want in the associated field.

The Compress Text and Line Art option applies to text and paths you've drawn in InDesign—I cannot think of any reason you should turn this option off.

Pages and Page Marks. Use the options in this panel to specify the pages you want exported to the PDF, and to set up any printers' marks you want applied to those pages.

- Page Ranges. Which pages do you want to export? Just as in the Advanced Page Control panel of the Print dialog box, you can specify all pages (turn on the All option) individual page ranges (135-182), non-contiguous pages (3, 7, 22), or export pages by section.

- Reader's Spreads. When you turn on the Reader's Spreads option, InDesign exports each spread in the page range you've specified (see above) as a single page of the exported PDF.

- Bleed. The value you enter in the Bleed field expands the boundary of the pages in the exported PDF by adding that value on all sides of the page bounding box.

- Page Marks. The options in this section option add printers' marks or page information outside the page area. For a complete description of InDesign's page marks, see Chapter 10, "Printing." You won't see these page marks when you open the PDF in Acrobat unless you expand the page boundaries, as shown in Figure 7-21.

FIGURE 7-21

Seeing your page marks in Acrobat

Here you are, in Acrobat, looking at a PDF you just exported from InDesign.

You could have sworn you turned on various printers' marks as you exported the file, but they aren't here. Did you forget to turn them on? Are you losing your mind?

To view your InDesign printers' marks in Acrobat, choose Crop Pages from Acrobat's Document menu. Acrobat displays the Crop Pages dialog box.

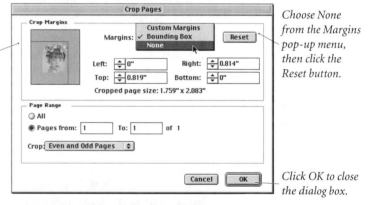

Choose None from the Margins pop-up menu, then click the Reset button.

Click OK to close the dialog box.

Acrobat displays the bleed area you defined when you exported the PDF, plus any printers' marks you specified.

Security. When you export a PDF, you can choose to limit access to the PDF. You can password protect the entire PDF—which means that anyone trying to open the PDF will have to enter a password. Or you can use a password to protect the PDF against editing. Or you can specify that the PDF cannot be printed, or even that text cannot be copied out of the PDF and pasted into another application.

In my view, PDF security features are for PDFs you're exporting for online distribution (that is, the PDF is the final product of your production process), and not for prepress use. Think about it—do you want your imagesetting service bureau calling you at four in the morning to ask for the password you used to lock up a PDF? I might have my paranoid moments, but my practicality gets the better of them most of the time—and it's just not practical to lock up a PDF that's headed for printing and prepress work.

Just my opinion, of course.

To activate security features for the PDF you're exporting, turn on the Use Security Features option. Enter a password for the PDF in the Open Document field, then enter a password for changing security settings in the Change Security field. Turn on the security options you want in the Do Not Allow section (these do exactly what they say—turn on the Printing field, for example, and you won't be able to print the PDF).

Defining a PDF Export Style

PDF export styles are like paragraph styles—they're bundles of attributes that can be applied in a single action. All of the attributes in the PDF Export dialog box are included in a PDF export style. To create a PDF export style, follow these steps (see Figure 7-22).

1. Choose Define PDF Style from the File menu. InDesign displays the Define PDF Styles dialog box.

2. Click the New button. InDesign displays the Edit PDF Export Style dialog box.

3. Enter a name for the PDF export style, then set up the PDF export options using the three panels of the dialog box. The panels contain the current PDF export settings—if you've recently exported a PDF using settings you want to use in the PDF export style, all you need to do is click the OK button. Otherwise, fill in the options as described in the section "Exporting a PDF," earlier in this chapter (note that you can't set the page range options in a PDF export style). Click the OK button when you're done. InDesign returns you to the Define PDF Styles dialog box and adds the new style to the list available styles.

FIGURE 7-22
Defining a PDF
export style

*Choose Define PDF Style
from the File menu. InDesign
displays the Define PDF
Styles dialog box.*

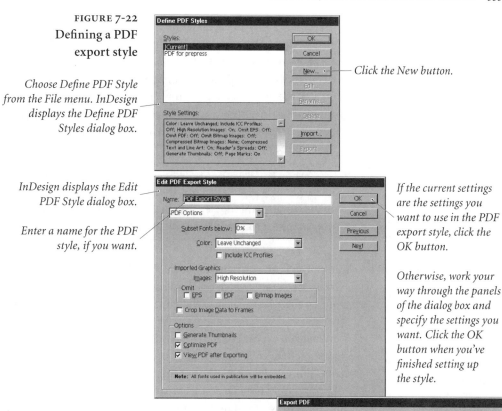

— *Click the New button.*

*InDesign displays the Edit
PDF Style dialog box.*

*Enter a name for the PDF
style, if you want.*

*If the current settings
are the settings you
want to use in the PDF
export style, click the
OK button.*

*Otherwise, work your
way through the panels
of the dialog box and
specify the settings you
want. Click the OK
button when you've
finished setting up
the style.*

*Choose a PDF export style from the
Style pop-up menu to export the PDF
using the settings defined in the style.*

To export a PDF using the settings in a PDF export style, choose
the style name from the Style pop-up menu in the Export PDF
dialog box. InDesign applies the settings of the PDF export style to
the controls in the Export PDF dialog box. You'll still need to enter
a page range in the Pages and Page Marks panel—the export style
does not include that information.

**Managing
PDF Export Styles**

You can use the Define PDF Style dialog box to add, delete, rename,
edit, and import or export PDF export styles.

◆ To delete a PDF export style, select the style name and click the
Delete button.

◆ To export PDF export styles, select the style names and click the
Export button. InDesign displays the Export PDF Styles dialog
box. Specify a file name and location for the document and click
the OK button.

◆ To import a PDF export style or set of styles, open the Define PDF Styles dialog box and click the Import button. InDesign displays the Import PDF Styles dialog box. Locate and select a document (or an InDesign publication containing PDF export styles), then click the OK button. If the PDF export styles you're importing already exist in the publication, InDesign will create copies of the styles (InDesign will append a number—usually "1"—to the duplicate styles).

◆ To rename a PDF export style, select the style name in the Define PDF Styles dialog box, then click the Rename button. InDesign displays the Rename PDF Style dialog box. Enter a new name for the style and click the OK button.

Exporting HTML

You can export your InDesign publication as HTML (hypertext markup language), which creates a page or pages that can be viewed using a web browser, such as Netscape Navigator or Microsoft Internet Explorer.

When you export as HTML, keep in mind that the resulting document might bear little resemblance to your laid out publication—if maintaining control over the appearance of your material is important, you should use PDF, rather than HTML. In addition, InDesign lacks the ability to add more than rudimentary (next page/previous page) navigational features, and cannot create hyperlinks in the exported HTML document(s).

To export pages from an InDesign publication as HTML, follow these steps (see Figure 7-23).

1. Choose Export from the File menu. InDesign displays the Export dialog box.

2. Enter a filename and navigate to the folder in which you want to save the file, then choose HTML from the Format (Macintosh) or Save As Type (Windows) pop-up menu.

3. Click the Save button. InDesign displays the Export HTML dialog box.

4. Set options in the four panels of the dialog box. As in other InDesign multi-panel dialog boxes, you can move to the next panel by pressing Command-Down Arrow/Ctrl-Down Arrow or to the previous panel by pressing Command-Up Arrow/Ctrl-Up Arrow.

FIGURE 7-23

Exporting as HTML

The Documents panel of the Export HTML dialog box changes depending on the Export As option you choose.

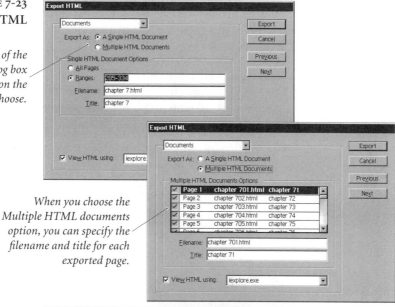

When you choose the Multiple HTML documents option, you can specify the filename and title for each exported page.

The options in the Formatting panel control the appearance of text and of the background of the page (or pages).

When you choose Appearance, InDesign will convert some text to graphics files during the export process.

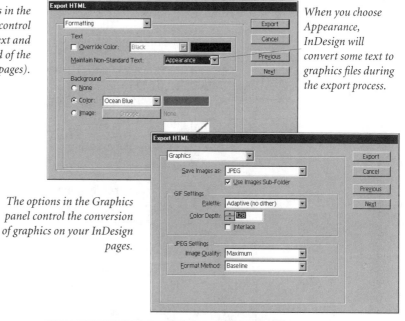

The options in the Graphics panel control the conversion of graphics on your InDesign pages.

The options in the Layou[t] panel control the conversion of your InDesign page layout to HTML.

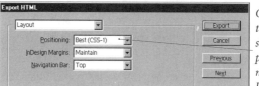

Choose Best (CSS-1) to use cascading style sheets, which will produce a closer match to your InDesign pages.

Documents. The options in this panel control the structure of the exported HTML document.

◆ To export all of the pages in the publication into a single (long, scrolling) HTML file, choose A Single HTML Document from the Export As pop-up menu. If you choose this option, InDesign makes more controls available.

  ◆ Choose the All Pages option when you want to include the entire document in the HTML file.

  ◆ Choose Ranges and enter a page range. When you enter a page range, you can use commas to indicate noncontiguous pages and dashes to indicate ranges, for example: "1, 3, 5-12, 14."

  ◆ InDesign enters the file name you entered in the Export dialog box in the FileName field, but you can change the name and file path using this field, if you want.

  ◆ Enter a title for the HTML page (or pages) in the Title field—this sets the text your browser displays in the title bar of the window containing the file.

◆ To export each page as a separate HTML file, choose Multiple HTML Documents. When you do this, InDesign displays the Multiple HTML Options section—a list of the pages in the publication.

  ◆ To export a page, turn on the option to the left of the page name.

  ◆ To set an export file name and file path for the HTML file, select the page and enter the file name in the Filename field.

  ◆ To set a title for the HTML file, enter the title in the Title field. When you open the page, your web browser will display the title in its title bar.

◆ Select a browser from the View HTML Using pop-up menu.

Formatting. The controls in the Formatting panel give you some (a little—I'm not promising much) control over the appearance of text and graphics in the exported HTML file.

◆ Text Override Color. The color you choose here changes the color of the text in the HTML file to the color you specify. The pop-up menu displays a list of colors matching some of the colors in the standard color lookup table in today's browsers (see the discussion of "web-safe colors" in Chapter 9, "Color"), or you can define a color by double-clicking the color swatch to the left of the pop-up menu.

◆ Maintain Non-Standard Text. When you choose Maintain Appearance from the Maintain Non-Standard Text pop-up menu, InDesign will convert any text characters using InDesign formatting not supported by HTML (ligatures, small caps, oldstyle figures, kerning, tracking, justification, tab stop locations, and so on—really, just about any InDesign formatting other than bold and italic is "non-standard," if you ask HTML) to GIF images. (Yes, you heard that right, GIF images.) To remove the "non-standard" formatting (in the HTML file, not in the InDesign file), choose Maintain Editability.

◆ Background. Use the controls in the Background section of the Formatting panel to define the background of the HTML file or files you're creating. You can choose to set the background to a color, or to an image. To apply a background color, choose the color from the Color pop-up menu (the pop-up menu displays a limited list of web safe colors) or double-click the color swatch to the right of the pop-up menu to display a system color picker. Turn on the Image option and click the Choose button to locate and select an image file. The image you select will be tiled across the background of the HTML pages you export.

Layout. The Layout panel contains controls for defining the page setup of the HTML file.

◆ Positioning. Choose Best (CSS-1) to include cascading style sheets definitions in the exported HTML file. If you do this, there's a better chance of your HTML pages resembling the InDesign pages they're based on.

◆ InDesign Margins. Choose Maintain if you want to write the margins of your InDesign publication into the HTML file(s) you're exporting, or choose None to use the browser's default margins.

◆ Navigation Bar. Choose the Top, Bottom, or Both option to place a simple navigational link at the specified position on the page. To omit the navigational links, choose None.

Graphics. The options in the Graphics panel control the way that InDesign exports images in your publication.

◆ Save Images As. Choose the image file format you want to use to export the images.

◆ Choose Automatic to have InDesign export RGB, CMYK, and grayscale bitmap images (such as TIFF) as JPEG and export indexed color images-and any images using clipping paths—as GIF.

◆ Choose JPEG or GIF to export the graphics in the publication using the corresponding format.

◆ Images already in a format supported by web browsers (JPEG, GIF, PNG) and having a resolution of 72 pixels per inch are not converted during export (unless they're embedded—see below).

◆ JPEG, GIF, and PNG whose resolutions are anything other than 72 pixels per inch will be exported in the corresponding format at that resolution—which can mean that JPEG images get compressed again. This is a bad thing, so either make sure the resolution of your JPEG graphics is 72 pixels per inch or choose GIF from the Save Images As pop-up menu (if your publication contains JPEG images at higher or lower resolutions).

◆ Embedded images (i.e., images stored inside the publication) are always converted, regardless of their resolution or format.

◆ Use Images Sub-Folder. Turn this option on when you want to create a folder named Images inside the folder to which you're exporting. InDesign will export any images on the page range you've selected to this folder. When this option is off, InDesign stores the images in the same folder as the HTML file.

GIF Settings. The options in this section control the way InDesign exports GIF images.

◆ Palette. Choose a color palette from the Palette pop-up menu.

  ◆ Adaptive (No Dither). Choose the Adaptive palette to create a color palette based on a sampling of the colors in the image. Because of the limited number of colors that can be used in a GIF palette (up to 256, depending on the value you enter in the Color Depth field—see below), programs that export GIF typically use dithering to simulate a larger number of colors. When you choose the Adaptive palette, InDesign does not use dithering, which means the appearance of the exported images can differ significantly from the original images. Use the Adaptive palette when you're exporting line art (monochrome bitmap images) or images containing fewer than 256 colors.

◆ Web. Choose the Web palette to export images using the "web safe" color palette (see "Web Safe Color," in Chapter 6, "Color"). As you might expect, this can create considerable changes in the appearance of the images in your publication (though the extent of the change depends on the content of the images).

◆ Exact. When you export an image in the GIF format using the Exact color palette, InDesign attempts to create a palette containing all of the color values used in the image. If the image contains more than 256 colors (or the value you entered in the Color Depth field—see below), InDesign displays a warning message.

◆ System. Choose System to use the system's default color palette to export the GIF image. Use this option only if you created the graphics using the system color palette, and if you do not plan to distribute the HTML file widely (i.e., to other platforms or other video systems).

◆ Color Depth. Sets the maximum number of colors used in the color palettes (see above) of the exported GIF images.

◆ Interlace. When you turn on the Interlace option, a browser opening the HTML file will first display a low resolution version of the GIF and will add more detail to the image as additional image information is downloaded. When you turn this option off, the browser will wait to display the GIF image until all of the image data has been downloaded.

JPEG Settings. The options in this section control the way

InDesign exports JPEG images.

◆ Image Quality. The options on the Image Quality pop-up menu control the amount of compression applied to exported JPEG images. Low applies the most compression and produces the smallest image file (and the lowest quality); Maximum retains image quality but produces larger files.

◆ Format Method. Choose Progressive to make the JPEG images display in increasing detail as image data are downloaded by the browser; choose Baseline to make the browser wait until all of the image data has been downloaded before displaying the JPEG.

4. Click the Export button to export the publication as HTML.

The Best of All Possible Worlds

Can you get there from here? When you're working with InDesign, you can almost always export or save files in a form you can use in another program, and you can usually produce files in other programs you can import or open using InDesign.

There are definitely bumps in the road—sometimes, you've got to go through an intermediate program to convert files from one format to another (particularly if the files came from another type of computer).

Someday, we'll have a more complete, universal, and sophisticated file format for exchanging publications. PDF is getting very close to being that format, and it's certainly making steps in the right direction. When the great day arrives, we'll be able to take page layouts from InDesign to FreeHand to QuarkXPress to Photoshop, using each program for what it's best at without losing any formatting along the way.

And the streets will be paved with gold, mounted beggars will spend the day ducking winged pigs, and the Seattle Mariners will win the World Series.

8

Transforming

In the previous chapters, I've covered the process of getting text and graphics into your InDesign publication. This chapter is all about what you can do with those elements once you've wrestled them onto your pages. The process of moving, rotating, scaling, reflecting, or shearing an object is called *transformation*.

Many of the topics in this chapter have been touched on in the preceding chapters—mainly because everything you can do in InDesign is interconnected. In the old days, software was entirely linear or modal: one had to proceed from this screen to that screen following a particular sequence of steps. These days, software is extremely nonlinear and nonmodal (that is, you can do things many different ways in many different orders), and, therefore much harder to write about. It's enough to drive a poor author mad! Your purchase of this book will make my time at Looney Farm that much more pleasant. Thank you.

Transformation Basics

There are many ways to transform an object on an InDesign page or pasteboard. Select the object using the Selection tool, then:

◆ Drag one of the object's selection handles to scale the object.

◆ Select a transformation tool from the Tools palette, set the center of transformation (if necessary), and drag the tool.

◆ Display the Transform palette and enter values in the palette field corresponding to the transformation you want to apply—or choose a preset value from the pop-up menu associated with that field.

◆ Choose one of the "preset" rotation or reflection options from the Transform palette menu.

◆ Double-click one of the transformation tools in the Toolbox to display the corresponding transform dialog box (double-click the Rotate tool, for example, to display the Rotation dialog box).

◆ Select the Free Transform tool, then apply a transformation by dragging the object's selection handles. See "Using the Free Transform Tool," later in this chapter.

◆ Scale an object by pressing keyboard shortcuts. See "Scaling an Object with the Keyboard," later in this chapter.

There's no "right" or "best" way to do transformations—you can experiment with the different methods and see which you like best. I change methods depending on the situation (and my mood).

Setting the Center of Transformation

When you select an object and then choose one of the transformation tools from the Tools palette, InDesign displays the center of transformation icon (it looks something like a small registration mark) on or around the object (see Figure 8-1). The initial position of the icon is determined by the point selected in the Transform palette's Proxy.

When you scale, rotate, or shear an object, InDesign transforms the object around the Center of Transformation. To reposition the center of transformation icon, either drag it to a new position or click a point on the Proxy in the Transform palette.

Adobe refers to the center of transformation icon as the "Point of Origin" icon. I think this is confusing, so I'll add to the confusion by calling it something different.

FIGURE 8-1
Center of transformation

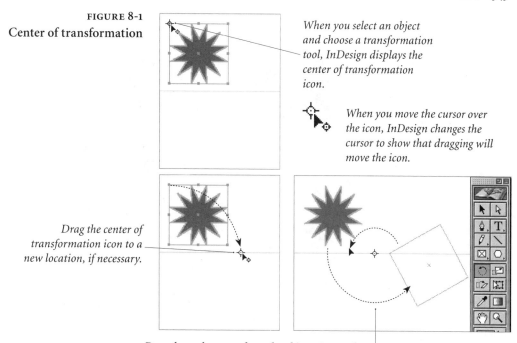

When you select an object and choose a transformation tool, InDesign displays the center of transformation icon.

When you move the cursor over the icon, InDesign changes the cursor to show that dragging will move the icon.

Drag the center of transformation icon to a new location, if necessary.

Drag the tool to transform the object. As you drag, InDesign transforms (in this example, rotates) the object around the center of transformation.

Transforming Line Segments and Points

To transform a point or line segment on a path, select the path or point using the Direct Selection tool, then transform it as you would any other object (drag it, or enter values in the X and Y fields of the Transform palette, or press the Arrow keys, or display the Move dialog box). This can produce some very interesting effects (see Figure 8-2).

When you select the points and/or line segments of a path and then copy as you transform the object, InDesign splits the path at the unselected points on the path. This takes a little getting used to, but might come in handy. If you want to transform line segments or points of a copy of a path, copy the path first, then apply the transformation.

Transforming Path Contents

When you transform a path that contains other objects (an image frame, for example, or a path you've pasted other paths or text blocks into), you can choose to apply the transformation to the path's contents (see Figure 8-3). To do this when you're scaling an object using the Transform palette, turn on the Scale Content option on the Transfrom palette menu. If you're using the Move, Scale, Rotate, or Shear dialog boxes to transform the object, turn on the transform content option in the dialog box.

FIGURE 8-2
Transforming
points, not paths

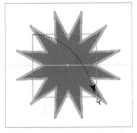

Select some points using the Direct Selection tool.

In this example, the points on the inside of the star polygon are selected; the outside ones aren't.

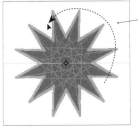

Apply a transformation. In this example, I've rotated the selected points.

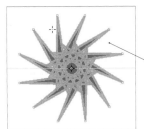

InDesign applies the transformation to the selected points; not to the entire path.

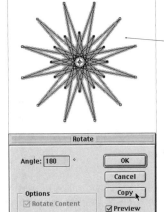

Note: If you're transforming selected points using one of the transformation dialog boxes and click the Copy button…

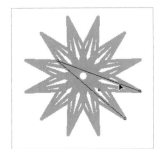

InDesign splits the path at the location of the unselected points.

The Transform Palette Is Your Friend

If numbers scare you, you're going to be scared by the Transform palette. Don't give in to math anxiety—the palette is too useful to avoid. The first step in taming the Transform palette is to understand what it is, exactly, that these controls are called, and what they can do for you. Take a look at Figure 8-4.

To display the Transform palette, press F9.

FIGURE 8-3
Transforming
path contents

Untransformed object

*Object scaled with the
Scale Content option
turned off.*

*Object scaled with the
Scale Content option
turned on.*

FIGURE 8-4
InDesign's
Transform palette

**Coordinates at those of the
point corresponding to the
point selected on the Proxy,
and are measured relative to
the current zero point.*

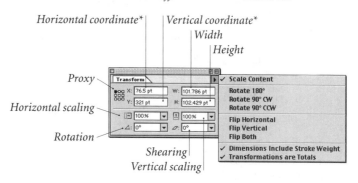

The Proxy

A "proxy" is something that stands in for something (or someone) else. The Proxy in the Transform palette stands in for the object or objects you've selected (see Figure 8-5). The points on the Proxy correspond to the selection handles InDesign displays around an object when you select it with the Selection tool (not the Direct Selection tool).

When you select a point on the Proxy, you're telling InDesign that whatever changes you make in the Transform palette affect that point (the X and Y fields), or are centered around that point (the Width, Height, Horizontal Scaling, Vertical Scaling, Rotation Angle, and Shear Angle fields).

FIGURE 8-5
The Transform
palette Proxy

*The point you select on the
Proxy also sets the center of
transformation.*

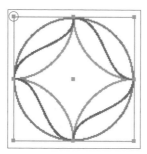

The points you see on the Proxy correspond to the selection handles you see when you select an object.

The point you select in the Proxy determines the content of the X and Y fields in the Transform palette—select the upper left corner (as in this example), and you'll see the coordinates of that corner of the selection.

Understanding Page Coordinates

An InDesign page—or any other flat object—is a two-dimensional surface; a plane. You can defined the position of any point on a plane using a pair of coordinates: the horizontal location (traditionally referred to as "X") and the vertical location ("Y"). The numbers you see in the X and Y fields of InDesign's Transform palette represent the horizontal and vertical distance of the selected point on the Proxy from the zero point.

As you move farther to the right of the horizontal zero point, the value in the X field increases; move the object to the right, and the value in the X field decreases. Horizontal locations to the left of the zero point are represented by negative numbers. As you move farther down on the page, the value in the Y field increases. Vertical locations above the zero point are represented by negative numbers. Note that this means that InDesign's vertical coordinate system is *upside down* relative to the two dimensional coordinate system you learned in junior high school geometry class (see Figure 8-6).

FIGURE 8-6
Page coordinates

InDesign's two dimensional coordinate system. All coordinates are measured from the zero point. X represents the horizontal location of a point; Y represents the vertical location.

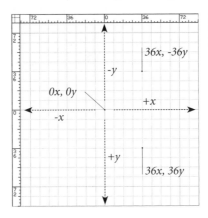

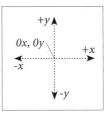

Traditional two dimensional coordinate system (note that values on the y axis increase as you go up—the opposite of InDesign's approach).

Scale Content

Choose Scale Content to scale the content of frames as you apply changes to the width, height, or scaling of a frame. This setting only affects transformations you apply using the Transform palette—if you're scaling an object by dragging a corner handle with the Selection tool, you'll still have to hold down Command/Ctrl.

Duplicating as You Transform

Hold down Option/Alt as you press Return/Enter to apply a change you've made to any of the Transform palette fields, and InDesign will apply the transformation to a duplicate of the selected object (see Figure 8-7).

Transformations Are Totals

When you select an object that's contained by a frame, should the Transform palette fields reflect the state of the selected relative to the pasteboard, or relative to the frame containing the object? That's

FIGURE 8-7
**Duplicating as
you transform**

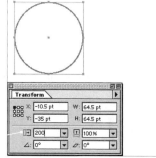 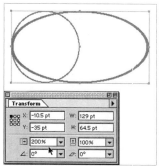

*Enter a value in the Horizon-
tal Scaling, Vertical Scaling,
Width, or Height fields…*

*…and press Option-Return (Macintosh) or Alt-Enter (Windows).
InDesign applies the transformation to a copy of the selected object.*

the question you answer with by turning the Transformations are
Totals option on the Transform palette menu on or off (it's on by
default). When you turn this option on, InDesign displays the rotation, scaling percentages, and shear angle of the selection relative to
the pasteboard. Turn this option off to display the information relative to the enclosing frame (see Figure 8-8).

FIGURE 8-8
**Transformations
are totals**

*The frame containing this
image has been rotated 20
degrees, as you can see by
looking at the Rotation field
in the Transform palette. If
you use the Direct Selection
tool to select the image…*

…InDesign displays its rotation relative to the parent frame…

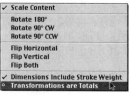

*…unless you turn on the
Transformations Are Totals
option on the Transform
palette menu.*

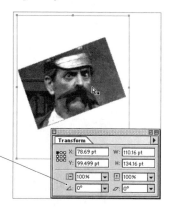

*When you do that, InDesign displays
the rotation angle (or skewing angle)
relative to the pasteboard. When
the Transformations Are Totals option
is on, InDesign displays the scaling
percentages relative to the original size
of the image.*

Dimensions Include Stroke Weight   What defines the dimensions of a path? Is it the geometric representation of the path itself? Or is it the area taken up by the path, including the stroke weight applied to the path? I prefer to work with the geometric bounds of a path, so I turn off the Dimensions Include Stroke Weight option. You might prefer to work with the visible bounds of objects—if you do, turn this option on (it's on by default).

Moving Objects

There are (at least) four ways to move objects in InDesign—select the object and then try any of the following.

◆ Drag the objects using the Selection tool or the Direct Selection tool.

◆ Enter values in the X and Y fields in the Transform palette.

◆ Drag the object using the Free Transform tool.

◆ Press the arrow, or "nudge" keys.

Moving Frame Content   To move the content of a frame without moving the frame itself, select the Direct Selection tool and click inside the frame. Then use any of the movement methods (dragging, entering values in the Transform palette, or pressing arrow keys) to move the object.

Moving Objects by Dragging   InDesign is just like any other program—if you want to move an object, select the object with the Selection tool or the Direct Selection tool and drag. Hold down Option/Alt as you drag to duplicate the object.

Dragging Things Quickly Versus Dragging Things Slowly. If you select an object and then immediately start dragging, you'll see only a box representing the object. If, on the other hand, you hold down the mouse button for a second before dragging, you'll see the object as you drag it. Dragging quickly is great for snapping objects into position by their outlines; waiting a second before dragging is best when you want to see the objects in a selection as you position them on the page.

Moving Objects with the Transform Palette   When I need precision, I always move objects by entering numbers in the X and Y fields of the Transform palette (see Figure 8-9). And

FIGURE 8-9
Moving objects with
the Transform palette

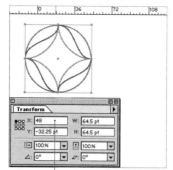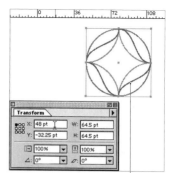

To move an object to a
specific location on the page
or pasteboard...

...enter the position
in the X or Y field.

Press Return/Enter, and InDesign moves
the object to the location you entered.

To move an object by
a certain amount add (to
move to the right or down)
or subtract (to move to the
left or up) the amount to the
value in the the X or Y field.

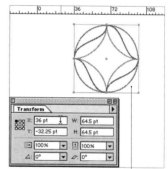

Press Return/Enter, and InDesign moves
the object relative to is current position.

it's not just because I'm a closet rocket scientist; it's because I don't trust the screen display, even at 4000 percent magnification. You shouldn't either, when it comes to making fine adjustments in your InDesign publication.

1. Select the object you want to move.

2. Display the Transform palette, if it's not already visible (press F9 to display the palette).

3. Enter values in the X field (to move the object horizontally), the Y field (to move the object vertically), or in both the X and Y fields. If you want to move the object to an *absolute* position (relative to the current position of the zero point), a new value in the field; to move the object some distance *relative* to its current location, add or subtract that distance from the value in the palette field.

4. Press Return/Enter. InDesign moves the selected object.

**Moving Objects with
the Move Dialog Box**

To move objects using the controls in the Move dialog box, follow these steps (see Figure 8-10).

FIGURE 8-10

Moving objects with the Move dialog box

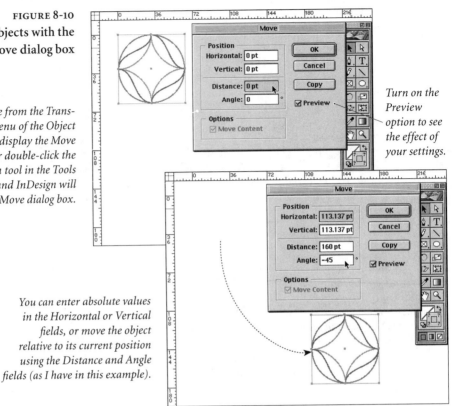

Choose Move from the Transform submenu of the Object menu to display the Move palette (or double-click the Selection tool in the Tools palette), and InDesign will display the Move dialog box.

Turn on the Preview option to see the effect of your settings.

You can enter absolute values in the Horizontal or Vertical fields, or move the object relative to its current position using the Distance and Angle fields (as I have in this example).

1. Select an object.

2. Double-click the Selection tool (or choose Move from the Transform submenu of the Object menu). InDesign displays the Move dialog box.

3. Set movement options using the controls in the dialog box.

   ◆ If you want to move the object to an *absolute* position (relative to the current position of the zero point), enter values in the Horizontal field, or in the Vertical field (to move the object vertically), or in both fields.

   ◆ To move the object *relative* to its current location, enter values in the Distance and Angle fields.

   ◆ To move the contents of a path, turn on the Move Content option.

   ◆ To see the effect of the current settings, turn on the Preview option.

4. Press Return/Enter to move the object, or click the Copy button to move a copy of the object.

Moving Objects with the Free Transform Tool

You can use the Free Transform tool to move objects—position the tool over any part of the object other than the selection handles, and the Free Transform tool will work just like the Selection tool. Drag an object by its center point, and InDesign will snap the center point to any active grids or guides. Hold down Option/Alt as you drag to duplicate the object as you move it.

Moving Objects by Pressing Arrow Keys

As if dragging by eye and specifying coordinates weren't enough (in terms of movement options), InDesign also sports "nudge" keys. Select an element and press one of the arrow keys, and the element moves in that direction in the increments you set in the Cursor Key field in the Units and Increments Preferences dialog box.

To move the selected object by ten times the distance you entered in the Cursor Key field, hold down Shift as you press the arrow key. To duplicate the selection as you move it, hold down Option/Alt as you press the arrow key.

Scaling

To change the size of an object, select the object and then use any of the following techniques.

◆ Drag the Scale tool.

◆ Drag a selection handle with the Selection tool.

◆ Drag one of the object's selection handles using the Free Transform tool.

◆ Enter values in the Width, Height, Horizontal Scale, or Vertical Scale fields in the Transform palette.

◆ Enter values in the Scale dialog box.

◆ Press a keyboard shortcut.

In addition to the above, you can change the width of text frames by changing the width of the columns in the text frame when you've turned on the Fixed Column Width option in the Text Frame Options dialog box (see Chapter 3, "Text").

Scaling with the Scale tool

When you want to scale an object until it "looks right," use the Scale tool (see Figure 8-11).

1. Select the object you want to scale.

2. Select the Scale tool from the Tools palette.

3. Change the location of the center of transformation icon, if necessary. To do this, either drag the icon to a new location or click one of the points in the Proxy in the Transform palette.

4. Drag the Scale tool horizontally to scale the object's width, or drag vertically to scale the object's height. Dragging diagonally sizes the object's width and height. Hold down Shift as you drag to scale the object proportionally. Hold down Option/Alt as you drag to duplicate the object and scale the duplicate.

5. When the object reaches the size you want it to be, stop dragging.

FIGURE 8-11
Scaling an object with the Scale tool

Select an object, move the center of tranformation icon (if necessary), and then drag the Scale tool on the page or pasteboard.

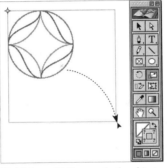

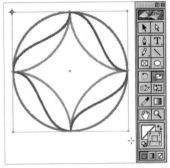

Hold down Shift to scale the object proportionally, or Command/Ctrl to scale object contents.

Once the object reaches the size you want, stop dragging.

Scaling with the Selection Tool

As in almost any other drawing or page-layout application, you can change the size of objects by dragging their corner handles with the Pointer tool (see Figure 8-12). As you drag, the object you're dragging gets larger or smaller. Hold down Shift as you drag to resize the object proportionally.

When you scale a frame, InDesign, by default, does not scale the frame's contents. To do this, hold down Command/Ctrl as you drag one of the selection handles.

Scaling with the Free Transform Tool

To scale an object using the Free Transform tool, follow these steps (see Figure 8-13).

1. Select an object.

FIGURE 8-12
Scaling an object using
the Direct Selection tool

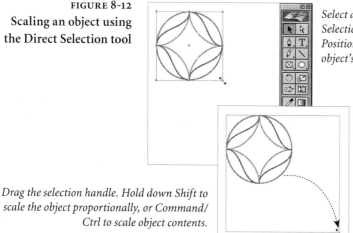

*Select an object, select the Direct
Selection tool from the Tools palette.
Position the cursor over one of the
object's selection handles.*

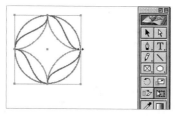

*Drag the selection handle. Hold down Shift to
scale the object proportionally, or Command/
Ctrl to scale object contents.*

*Once the object reaches the
size you want, stop dragging.*

FIGURE 8-13
Scaling an object using
the Free Transfrom tool

*Select an object, then select the
Direct Selection tool from the
Tools palette. Position the cursor
over one of the object's selection
handles…*

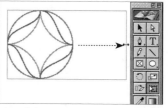

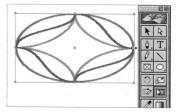

*…and drag. Hold down Option/Alt
as you drag to scale the object around
its center point. Hold down Shift
to scale the object proportionally,
and/or hold down Command/Ctrl
to scale the object's contents.*

*When the object reaches the size you
want, stop dragging.*

2. Select the Free Transform tool from the Tools palette.

3. Position the tool above one of the object's selection handles,
then drag. Hold down Option/Alt to scale the object proportionally around its center point, or hold down Shift as you drag a
corner handle to scale the object proportionally.

Scaling with the Transform Palette

When you know you want to make an object larger or smaller by an exact percentage, or to scale the object to a specific width or height, use the Transform palette (see Figure 8-14).

1. Select the object you want to scale.

2. Display the Transform palette if it's not already visible (to do this, double-click the Scale tool in the Tools palette or press F9).

3. Enter a new value in the Width or Height fields (or in both fields), or enter a scaling percentage in the Horizontal Scaling field or the Vertical Scaling field.

4. Press Return/Enter to scale the object. To apply proportional scaling, hold down Command/Ctrl as you press Return/Enter.

FIGURE 8-14
Scaling an object using the Transform palette

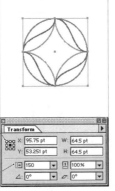 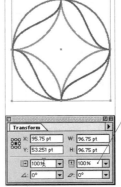

Set the center of transformation by selecting a point on the Proxy, if necessary.

Enter a scaling percentage in the Horizontal Scale or Vertical Scale field, or enter a new value in the Width or Height field.

Why do the scaling fields display 100% after I've applied the scaling? Because I have multiple objects selected. Select a single object, and you'll see the correct scaling percentage.

Press Return/Enter to apply the scaling change. Hold down Command/Ctrl as you apply the change (as I have here), and InDesign scales the object proportionally.

Scaling with the Scale Dialog Box

To scale objects using the Scale dialog box, follow these steps (see Figure 8-15).

1. Select an object.

2. Double-click the Scale tool (or choose Scale from the Transform submenu of the Object menu). InDesign displays the Scale dialog box.

3. Set scaling options using the controls in the dialog box.

   ◆ To scale the object proportionally, turn on the Uniform option and enter a scaling percentage in the Scale field.

   ◆ To scale an object non-proportionally, turn on the Non-Uniform option, then enter scaling percentages in the Horizontal and Vertical fields.

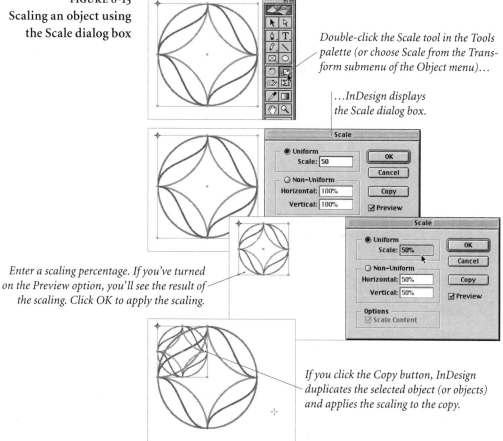

FIGURE 8-15
Scaling an object using
the Scale dialog box

Double-click the Scale tool in the Tools palette (or choose Scale from the Transform submenu of the Object menu)…

…InDesign displays the Scale dialog box.

Enter a scaling percentage. If you've turned on the Preview option, you'll see the result of the scaling. Click OK to apply the scaling.

If you click the Copy button, InDesign duplicates the selected object (or objects) and applies the scaling to the copy.

◆ To scale the contents of a path, turn on the Scale Content option.

◆ To see the effect of the current settings, turn on the Preview option.

4. Press Return/Enter to scale the object, or click the Copy button to scale a copy of the object.

Scaling with Keyboard Shortcuts

In InDesign 1.5, you can scale the selected object by pressing keyboard shortcuts.

◆ Press Command-. (period)/Ctrl-. to increase the size of the object by one percent.

◆ Press Command-, (comma)/Ctrl-, to decrease the size by one percent.

◆ Press Command-Shift-. (period)/Ctrl-Shift-. to increase the size by five percent.

◆ Press Command-Shift-, (comma)/Ctrl-Shift-, to decrease the size by five percent.

Rotating Objects

InDesign can rotate any object on a page, in .001-degree increments. The rotation angle is always shown relative to the pasteboard (where 0 degrees is horizontal) or to the frame containing the rotated object (unless you've turned on the Transformations are Totals option). If you rotate an object by thirty degrees, entering that rotation value again in the Rotation Angle field will not change the rotation of the object. To do that, you'd need to enter "+30" following the value shown in the Rotation Angle field—or use the Rotate dialog box.

Rotating with the Rotate tool

To rotate an object "by eye," follow these steps (see Figure 8-16).

1. Select the object you want to rotate.

2. Select the Rotate tool from the Tools palette.

3. Drag the Center of Transformation to the point you want to rotate around, or click a point in the Transform palette's Proxy. To rotate around the geometric center of an object, click the center point in the Proxy.

4. Drag the Rotate tool.

5. When the object looks the way you want it to, stop dragging.

Rotating with the Free Transform Tool

To rotate an object using the Free Transform tool, follow these steps (see Figure 8-17).

1. Select an object.

2. Select the Free Transform tool from the Tools palette.

3. Position the tool just outside one of the object's selection handles, then drag. InDesign rotates the object around its center point, or hold down Shift as you drag to constrain rotation to 45-degree increments.

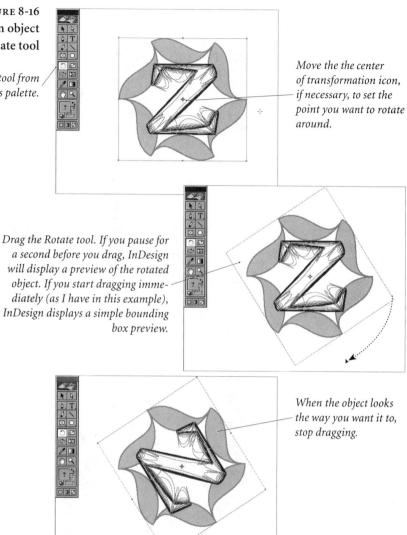

FIGURE 8-16
Rotating an object
using the Rotate tool

*Select the Rotate tool from
the Tools palette.*

*Move the the center
of transformation icon,
if necessary, to set the
point you want to rotate
around.*

*Drag the Rotate tool. If you pause for
a second before you drag, InDesign
will display a preview of the rotated
object. If you start dragging immediately (as I have in this example),
InDesign displays a simple bounding
box preview.*

*When the object looks
the way you want it to,
stop dragging.*

Rotating with the
Transform Palette

To rotate an object using the Transform palette, follow these steps
(see Figure 8-18).

1. Select the object you want to rotate.

2. Click a point on the Proxy to set the point you want to rotate
   around, if necessary.

3. Enter a new value in the Rotation Angle field of the Transform
   palette (if the palette is not already visible, press F9 or double-
   click the Rotate tool in the Tools palette). To rotate the object to

FIGURE 8-17
Rotating an object with the Free Transform tool

Select the Free Transform tool from the Tools palette.

Position the cursor outside one of the object's selection handles.

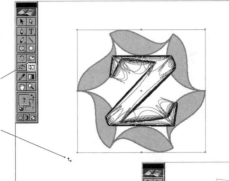

Drag the Free Transform tool. If you pause for a second before you drag, InDesign will display a preview of the rotated object. If you start dragging immediately (as I have in this example), InDesign displays a simple bounding box preview.

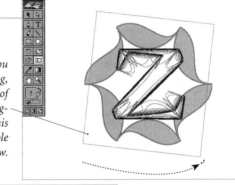

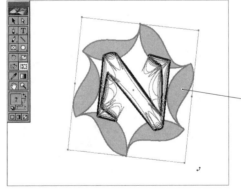

When the object looks the way you want it to, stop dragging.

a specific angle, enter that angle in the field. To rotate the object relative to its current rotation angle, add to or subtract from the value in the Rotation angle field.

You can enter positive numbers (such as "45") or negative numbers (such as "-270") between -360 and 360 degrees. Positive rotation angles rotate the selected object counterclockwise; negative values rotate the object clockwise. You enter rotation angles in .001 degree increments.

4. Press Return/Enter to rotate the object, or Option-Return/Alt-Enter to rotate a copy of the object.

FIGURE 8-18
Rotating an object using
the Transform palette

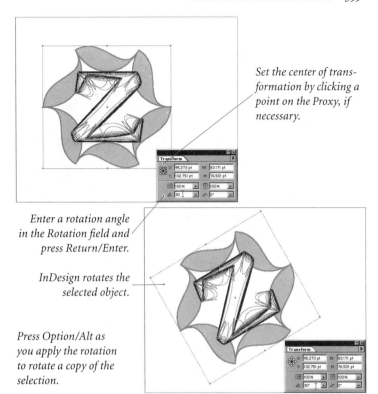

*Set the center of trans-
formation by clicking a
point on the Proxy, if
necessary.*

*Enter a rotation angle
in the Rotation field and
press Return/Enter.*

*InDesign rotates the
selected object.*

*Press Option/Alt as
you apply the rotation
to rotate a copy of the
selection.*

**Rotating with the
Rotate Dialog Box**

To rotate an object using the Rotate dialog box, follow these steps
(see Figure 8-19).

1. Select an object.

2. Double-click the Rotate tool (or choose Rotate from the Transform submenu of the Object menu). InDesign displays the
   Rotate dialog box.

3. Set rotation options using the controls in the dialog box.

   ◆ Enter a rotation angle in the Angle field.

   ◆ To rotate the contents of a path, turn on the Rotate
     Content option.

   ◆ To see the effect of the current settings, turn on the
     Preview option.

4. Press Return/Enter to rotate the object, or click the Copy button
   to rotate a copy of the object.

   If the Angle field in the Rotate dialog box has been set to something other than zero, and if you've turned on the Preview option

FIGURE 8-19

Rotating an object using the Rotate dialog box

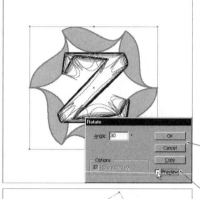

Select an object, then double-click the Rotate tool in the Tools palette (or choose Rotate from the Transform submenu of the Object menu, or hold down Option/Alt as you click the Rotate tool on the page or pasteboard).

InDesign displays the Rotate dialog box.

Turn on the Preview option so you can see the effect of the rotation you've specified.

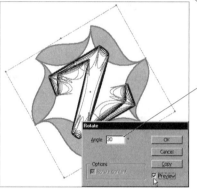

Enter a rotation angle in the Angle field.

When you're ready to apply the rotation, click the OK button, or click the Copy button to rotate a copy of the selection.

(in the Rotate dialog box), you'll see the object rotate to the specified angle. If that's what you want, click the OK button; otherwise, enter a new value in the Angle field (remember, you're seeing a preview—InDesign won't rotate the object until you click OK or Copy).

Rotating Multiple Selected Objects

When you rotate more than one object (in this sense, I'm counting groups as single objects), the objects rotate around a single point. This point can be their joint geometric center, or around any other point you've specified. They don't all rotate around their individual center points.

Reflecting Objects

Reflecting objects in InDesign is very simple—you can reflect, or "flip" an object over its vertical axis, its horizontal axis, or both its vertical and horizontal axes at once. That's it. There's no reflection tool, no need to enter a reflection angle anywhere (reflecting an object across an angle is the same as reflecting the object across its horizontal or vertical axis and then rotating).

To reflect an object, follow these steps (see Figure 8-20).

1. Select the object you want to reflect.

2. Choose Flip Vertical, Flip Horizontal, or Flip Both from the Transform palette menu. InDesign reflects the selected object.

FIGURE 8-20
Reflecting an object

Select an object...

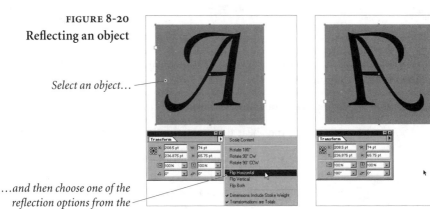

...and then choose one of the reflection options from the Transform palette menu.

Flip Horizontal

Flip Vertical

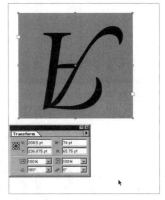

Flip Both

Shearing Objects

Shearing (or skewing) an object makes it appear that the plane the object's resting on has been rotated away from the plane of the page. It's good for creating perspective effects—but it's not a replacement for a serious 3D rotation program.

Shearing is hard to get used to at first, because vertical shearing seems to affect the horizontal lines in an object, while horizontal shearing affects the vertical lines in an object. It's just something you'll have to get used to (see Figure 8-21).

FIGURE 8-21
FigureTitle

No shearing   *Vertical shearing*   *Horizontal shearing*

Shearing with the Shear Tool

To shear an object using the Shear tool, follow the steps below (see Figure 8-22).

1. Select an object.

2. Choose the Shear tool from the Tools palette.

3. Change the location of the center of transformation icon, if necessary (you can either drag the icon to a new location, or click one of the points in the Transform palette Proxy).

4. Drag the Shear tool. As you drag the cursor, the skewing angles display in the Shearing Angle field of the Transform palette.

5. When the object looks the way you want it to, stop dragging.

FIGURE 8-22
Shearing an object with the Shear tool

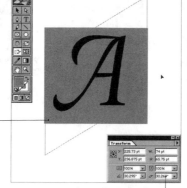

Select an object, then drag the Shear tool. As you drag, InDesign shears the selection.

As you drag, the Transform palette displays the shear angle.

When the object looks the way you want it to, stop dragging.

Shearing with the Transform Palette

To shear an object using the Transform palette, follow these steps (see Figure 8-23).

1. Select the object you want to shear.

2. Display the Transform palette, if it's not already visible.

3. Click one of the points on the Transform palette Proxy. This sets the center of transformation.

FIGURE 8-23
Shearing an object using
the Transform palette

FIGURE 8-23
Shearing an object using
the Transform palette

Select an object...

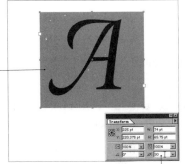 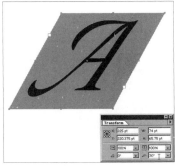

...enter a shear angle in the Shear field of the Transform palette.

Press Return/Enter to shear the selection. Press Option-Return/Alt-Enter to apply the transformation to a copy of the selection.

4. Enter an angle in the Shear Angle field, or add or subtract a value from the current content of the field.

5. Press Return/Enter to shear the selected object.

Shearing with the Shear Dialog Box

To shear an object using the Shear dialog box, follow these steps (see Figure 8-24).

1. Select an object.

2. Double-click the Shear tool (or choose Shear from the Transform submenu of the Object menu). InDesign displays the Shear dialog box.

FIGURE 8-24
Shearing an object using
the Shear dialog box

Select an object, then double-click the Shear tool in the Tools palette (or choose Shear from the Transform submenu of the Object menu, or hold down Option/Alt as you click the Shear tool on the page or pasteboard).

InDesign displays the Shear dialog box.

 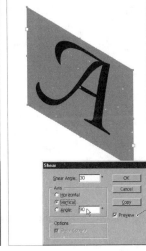

Turn on the Preview option so you can see the effect of the shearing you've specified.

Enter a shear angle in the Shear Angle field. Specify the shear axis you want to use.

Click the OK button, or click the Copy button to shear a copy of the selection.

3. Set shearing options using the controls in the dialog box.

◆ Enter an angle in the Shear Angle field.

◆ Choose a shear axis (the options are horizontal, vertical, or a specified angle).

◆ To rotate the contents of a path, turn on the Shear Content option.

◆ To see the effect of the current settings, turn on the Preview option.

4. Press Return/Enter to shear the object, or click the Copy button to shear a copy of the object.

Locking Object Positions

In InDesign, you can lock an object's position—which means that you can't transform it. You can, however, select the object, copy the object, or change its appearance.

To lock an object, select the object and press Command-L/Ctrl-L (or choose Lock Position from the Object menu). To unlock an object, press Command-Option-L/Ctrl-Alt-L (or choose Unlock Position from the Object menu).

Aligning and Distributing Objects

For many of us, MacDraw ushered in the era of object alignment. You could align the left, right, top, bottom, or center of selected objects. It was the greatest. I spent whole afternoons just aligning things. You couldn't do that in MacPaint.

I consider alignment and distribution to be transformations (in case you're wondering what the topics are doing in this chapter), by the way, because they amount to automated methods of moving objects.

InDesign features both object alignment and object distribution. InDesign aligns objects based on the object's bounding box—more or less what you see when you select the object with the Free Transform tool.

When you distribute objects you're telling InDesign to evenly arrange the selected objects. Objects can be distributed inside the area occupied by the objects, or by a specific distance.

Aligning Objects   When you've selected the objects you want to align, press F8 to display the Align palette. Click the alignment button to align the selected objects (see Figure 8-25).

If you've locked the position of an object in the selection, InDesign does not move that object when you apply an alignment. If an object doesn't seem to be following the herd, chances are good that it's locked—choose Unlock Position from the Object menu to apply alignment to it.

FIGURE 8-25
Aligning objects

Select the objects you want to align.

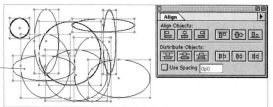

Display the Align palette, if it's not already visible, by pressing F8.

Click one of the alignment buttons. InDesign aligns the selected objects.

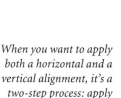

When you want to apply both a horizontal and a vertical alignment, it's a two-step process: apply one of the alignments, then apply the other.

In this example, I've aligned the objects to their horizontal centers, then to their vertical centers.

Distributing Objects   Have you ever wanted to space a bunch of objects at even distances from each other (from each other's centers, at any rate) across a particular horizontal measurement? If you have, InDesign's Distribute feature should make your day. To distribute the selected objects inside the rectangle defined by the objects, click one of the distribute buttons in the Align palette. InDesign distributes the objects as you've specified (see Figure 8-26).

To distribute (or space) the objects by a specified distance, use the Use Spacing option in either the Distribute Objects section of the Align palette or the Distribute Spacing section.

When you click one of the buttons in the Distribute objects section, the value you enter in the Use Spacing field sets the distance between the object sides (top, bottom, right, and left) or object centers (vertical or horizontal). If you enter 12 points, for example, and then click the Horizontal Distribute Lefts button, InDesign spaces the left edges of the objects in the selection 12 points apart.

When you use the Use Spacing option in the Distribute Spacing section, InDesign spaces the objects apart by the distance you enter in the Use Spacing field. Click the Vertical Distribute Space button to distribut the objects vertically, or click the Horizontal Distribute Space button to distribute the objects horizontally.

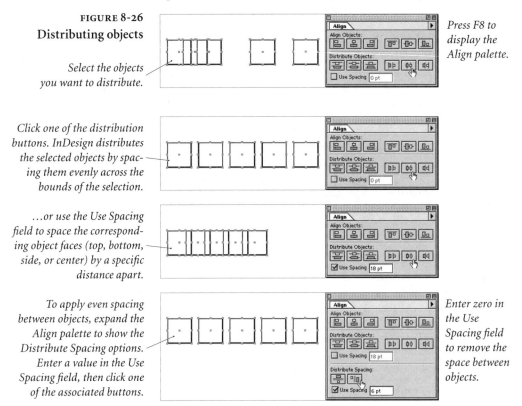

FIGURE 8-26
Distributing objects

Select the objects you want to distribute.

Press F8 to display the Align palette.

Click one of the distribution buttons. InDesign distributes the selected objects by spacing them evenly across the bounds of the selection.

...or use the Use Spacing field to space the corresponding object faces (top, bottom, side, or center) by a specific distance apart.

To apply even spacing between objects, expand the Align palette to show the Distribute Spacing options. Enter a value in the Use Spacing field, then click one of the associated buttons.

Enter zero in the Use Spacing field to remove the space between objects.

My Life Was Transformed

Fuzzy caterpillars turn into moths. Clark Kent jumps into a phone booth and emerges as Superman. Werewolves stalk the moors under the full moon. These transformations are all everyday, natural phenomena.

Make InDesign's transformation tools an integral part of how you work with the program, and you'll have their powerful, almost magical forces on your side. And that means you'll have more time for other things. Like howling at the moon.

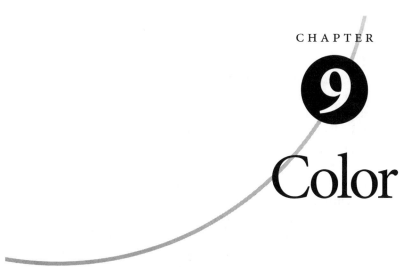

Color

Color communicates, telling us things about the object bearing the color. Without color cues, we'd have a hard time guessing the ripeness of a fruit or distinguishing a poisonous mushroom from an edible one. And many animals would have a hard time figuring out when to mate, or with whom.

We associate colors with human emotions: we are green with envy; we've got the blues; we see red. Colors affect our emotions, as well. Various studies suggest that we think best in a room of one color, or relax best in a room of another color.

What does all this mean? Color's important. A rule of thumb in advertising is that a color advertisement gets several times the response of a black-and-white ad. Designers of mail-order catalogs tell me that color is often cited as the reason for buying a product—and it's usually the reason a product is returned.

InDesign features a formidable array of features dedicated to creating, editing, applying, and printing colors. In addition, InDesign's color management can make what you see on your screen much closer to what you'll get when you print. Before I go any further, however, I have to talk about color printing.

Seeing Color, Printing Color

It's impossible to discuss the process of creating and using colors in InDesign without first talking a little about printing and visual perception. If you already know about those topics, feel free to skip ahead, though you'll miss all the jokes if you do. Everyone else should note that this is a very simple explanation of a pair of very bizarre and complex processes.

The Color Spectrum and Color Gamuts

The colors we see when we look at the world around us are the light reflected from objects in our field of view. In our eyes, the cornea, iris, and pupil conspire to cast this light on a rejoicing multitude of photoreceptive cells—the rods and cones at the back of the retina.

These cells, in turn, use chemical and electrical signals to pass information about the light striking them on to our visual cortex. And, after a series of profoundly *weird* things happen in the visual cortex (a friend of mine is an academic studying human visual perception—I haven't understood a word she's said for years), we see a picture.

The *visible spectrum* is the range of light wavelengths visible to the human eye (not your eye, or my eye, but an idealized, "normal" human eye) range from the top of the ultraviolet (wavelengths around $7 * 10^{-5}$ centimeters—or 700 nanometers) to the bottom of the infrared (wavelengths around $4 * 10^{-5}$ centimeters—or 400 nanometers). It's the job of our scanners, monitors, printers, inks, and printing presses to reproduce the colors we see in the visible spectrum.

Alas, they all fail miserably.

The range of color a device, color model, or printing method is capable of reproducing is referred to as its *color gamut.* There's no device, apart from your eye, that's capable of reproducing the range of light that your eye is capable of seeing. And even your eye isn't consistent from day to day.

We've settled, therefore, on a fairly well-known and well-understood set of compromises.

The Printing Process

After you've printed your InDesign publication on film and delivered it to your commercial printer (I like to walk in through the loading dock), the printer takes the film and uses it to expose (or "burn") a photosensitive printing plate. (These days, you might skip all of these steps and print directly to a printing plate.) The surface of the plate has been chemically treated to repel ink. When you expose the printing plate to light, the image areas from your film become able to accept ink. Once the plate's been exposed, the printer attaches the printing plate to the cylinder of a printing press.

As the cylinder holding the plate turns, the parts of it bearing the image become coated with ink, which is transferred (via another, rubber-covered cylinder—the offset cylinder) to the paper. This transfer is where we get the term "offset," as in "offset printing," because the printing plate itself does not touch your paper.

Printing presses put ink on paper one ink at a time. Some presses have more than one printing cylinder (also called a printing "head" or "tower") and can print several colors of ink on a sheet of paper in one pass through the press, but each printing cylinder carries only one color of ink. We can make it look like we've gotten more than one color of ink on a printing plate by using screens—patterns of dots that, from a distance, fool the eye into thinking it sees a separate color.

Spot and Process Inks

Spot-color printing is simple: your commercial printer uses inks that exactly match the color you want (or mixes inks to get the same result), then loads the press with that ink. In spot color printing, we sometimes use "tint builds"—screens of inks printed on top of each other—to create a new color without using another ink. In process-color printing, tint builds are where it's at; we use overlapping screens of four inks (cyan, magenta, yellow, and black) to simulate part of the spectrum of visible color. If everything's gone well, the dots of the different colored inks are placed near each other in a pattern called a rosette (see Color Figure 6 on the color pages for an example of a rosette).

Process-color printing can't simulate all the colors our eyes can see (notably very saturated colors, or metallic and fluorescent colors), but it can print color photographic images. Spot colors can print any color you can make with pigments, but aren't generally used to reproduce color photographic images (that's what process color printing was designed to be good at).

Color Management

When you aim at a target—and it doesn't matter whether you're aiming a rifle, a bow, a laser, or a camera—you have to make adjustments. You've got to consider the atmospheric conditions, the distance to the target, the characteristics of the target itself. Once you know what the variables are, and how they affect what you're trying to do, you've got a better chance of hitting the bullseye.

The same thing is true in color management. You need to under-stand the tools you have to work with, how they work together (or don't), and how they combine to produce the colors you see in the printed version of your publication.

It would be nice if we could make what we see on our screen exactly match what we'll get when we print. But we can't, for a vari-ety of practical and physiological reasons (not to mention simple lack of time and money). That said, I must also add that we can get very close—and we can also make the relationship between the dis-play and the printed piece more consistent and predictable.

The "device" (a printer, scanner, monitor, or printing press) is the key. Every device renders colors in a slightly different way. To adjust color in one environment so that it matches the color as seen in another environment, color management systems refer to a file containing information on the color characteristics of a device (how it displays or prints color). This file is called a "device profile." Device profiles are usually created by the manufacturers who make the hardware, though quite a few come with InDesign. The process of creating a device profile is called "characterizing" a device.

Once a device profile has been created for a device, you've got to maintain (or "calibrate") the device so that it doesn't vary from the profile. Imagesetter operators and commercial printers calibrate their equipment regularly (or should) to match industry standards.

InDesign's color management system uses device profiles approved by the International Color Consortium (ICC). If you're on the Macintosh, you can also use device profiles provided by Apple with the system-level ColorSync color management system (these profiles are also approved by the ICC).

For more on choosing device profiles, see "InDesign's Color Management Controls," later in this chapter.

Controlling Your Color-Viewing Environment

If it's important to you that what you see on your screen looks as much like the printed version of your publication as possible, there are a few rules you need to follow.

◆ Use a monitor and video system capable of displaying at least 24-bit color.

◆ Calibrate your monitor. Radius and Tektronix, for example, make color monitor calibration systems (hardware and soft-ware). If color is of critical importance to you and your publica-tions, find a system that works with your monitor, or buy a monitor that works with the calibration system you prefer.

◆ Control the lighting around your monitor and keep it consistent when you're working. Just about everyone agrees that the fluorescent lighting used in most of our office buildings is the worst possible lighting for viewing colors. Turn it off, if you can, and rely on incandescent lighting (desk lamps with one sort of bulb or another) to light your work area. If you can't turn it off, try getting some "full spectrum" (or "amber") fluorescent tubes to install above your monitor. These also reduce eye strain.

◆ Control the lighting of the area where you'll be viewing your color proofs. Ideally, you'd have a room or small booth equipped with "daylight" (or 5,000-degree Kelvin) lamps—but few of us can afford the money or space required.

Why is lighting important? Basically, the temperature of the light affects what a color "objectively" looks like. You can't assume ideal viewing conditions, but you have to work in them to be able to do consistent work.

These rules have been passed on to me by people who are serious about color, and whose opinions I respect. But, this being a "Real World" book, I have to point out that these conditions are difficult to achieve. My monitors are mostly left uncalibrated—let alone characterized. The lights above my desk are not "full spectrum" lighting (but at least I've lost the fluorescent tubes). And as for having a special booth or room for viewing color proofs—hah!

At the same time, I have to admit that I'm not doing work where color matching is crucially important—as it would be if I were producing clothing catalogs or coffee-table art books.

Is What You See Anything Like What You'll Get? Any time you're working with ink, refer to printed samples, rather than looking at the colors on your screen. Remember that, unlike the paper you'll be printing on, your screen is backlit, so it displays colors very differently from what they'll look like when printed. In addition, screens flicker—something I've never been able to get paper to do.

If you're using uncoated paper, look at samples of the ink (spot color) or ink mix (process color) printed on uncoated stock. If you're using coated paper, look at examples printed on coated paper. If you're using a colored paper, try to find an example of the ink printed on a colored paper—though these examples are much harder to find.

Pantone makes a line of swatch books showing their libraries of spot and process colors (including process color equivalents of the spot colors); they're printed on both coated and uncoated stocks, and, although they're kind of expensive, they're not as expensive as pulling a job off of a press because you didn't like the press check. They're downright cheap if you consider what it must cost to print them.

Don't use Pantone spot colors (the ones you find in the Pantone library) to specify a process color. The Pantone Matching System is a spot-color specifying system, and the colors don't convert to process colors particularly well because you can't make any given hue just using process colors (see the discussion earlier in this chapter). Still, Pantone has included the process color conversions for these colors (as seen in their *Process Color Imaging Guide*) in the definitions of these spot colors. The colors in the Pantone "ProSim" library are process-color simulations of Pantone spot inks.

Don't assume that color printers will automatically produce an accurate simulation of what the colors in your publication are going to look like when they're printed by your commercial printer. To do that, you'll have to do some work—you'll have to run test pages and adjust device profiles. And, at the same time, bear in mind that most color printers print using something akin to the process-color method, your spot colors will be converted to process colors during printing. Some of the six- and seven-color ink jet printers can produce good matches for most spot inks.

Note, however, that the color proofs you print on a color ink jet printer cannot show you the way that your pages will print on a printing press. In particular, they can't show you trapping problems. For that, you need to use one of the color proofing processes (such as Chromalin or Press Match) to create your proofs from the film you've gotten out of your imagesetter. Imagesetting service bureaus frequently offer color proofing as part of their business. Some of these proofing processes can give you a proof on the paper you're intending to use, or can give you transparent overlays that you can place on top of your selected paper to get an idea of what your publication will look like when printed.

InDesign's Color Management Controls

In InDesign, you use the Application Color Settings dialog box (choose Application Color Settings from the Color Settings submenu of the File menu) to choose the color management engine you want to use, and to set up the device profiles for your monitor, your separations printer, and your composite printer. You use the Document Color Settings dialog box (choose Document Color Settings from the Color Settings submenu of the File menu) to choose the source profiles you want to use.

Application Color Settings

The choices you make in the Application Color Settings dialog box form the basis of the way that InDesign displays and prints color (see Figure 9-1).

Engine. Color management engines are made by a variety of manufacturers—InDesign comes with two: the Adobe CMS and the Kodak Digital Science ICC CMS. If you're working with other Adobe applications, you should choose the Adobe CMS. If you're working with another application that uses the Kodak Digital Science ICC CMS, such as FreeHand, choose that CMS from the Engine pop-up menu.

Monitor. Choose a monitor profile that matches your monitor from the Monitor pop-up menu. If you can't find a matching profile, choose the Generic RGB Profile.

Composite. On the Composite pop-up menu, you'll see a list of color printers—choose the model of printer you use for printing color proofs. If you don't see a profile for your printer model, or if you're not planning to use a color composite printer, choose Adobe InDesign Default RGB.

Separations. The Separations pop-up menu contains a list of profiles for common commercial offset printing devices and methods. Choose the profile that most closely matches the way you'll be printing your publication (if you live and work in the United States, you'll probably want to scroll down to U.S. Sheetfed Coated, U.S. Sheetfed Uncoated, U.S. Web Coated, or U.S. Web Uncoated). If you don't know which separation profile to choose, try Adobe InDesign Default CMYK.

FIGURE 9-1
Application Color
Settings dialog box

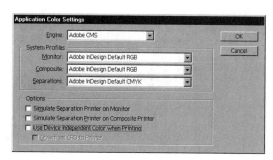

Simulate Separations Printer on Monitor. Your screen can display a far wider range of color than a typical commercial offset printing press can print. To make your screen better resemble your printed publication, turn on Simulate Separations Printer on Monitor.

Simulate Separations. A typical composite color printer can print a wider range of color than a commercial offset printing press. To force your composite printer to print using the color gamut of your separations printer profile, turn this option on.

Use Device Independent Color When Printing. Okay. This is where things get a bit theoretical for me, because I admit I have never worked with the hardware required to take advantage of this option. If you're using "in-RIP separations" (a feature of some PostScript Level 2 and PostScript 3 RIPs), you can have the printer create the separations for you using color rendering dictionaries (CRDs)—these are essentially the same thing as separations profiles.

Turn on the Download CRDs to Printer option to have InDesign create a CRD from your separations profile and send it to the printer; leave the option off to use the printer's default CRD.

When you want to use in-RIP separations, you do not turn on the Separations option in the Color panel of InDesign's Print dialog box—instead you print your publication as a composite. The RIP uses the default CRD (or the CRD you've downloaded) to determine how to separate the publication.

Document Color Settings

Once you've set up the color management system using the Application Color Settings dialog box, you can define the color settings of individual publications using controls in the Document Color Settings dialog box (see Figure 9-2).

Enable Color Management. Use the Enable Color Management option to turn color management on or off for a publication. If you're not planning to print color separations or color composite

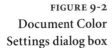

FIGURE 9-2
Document Color Settings dialog box

pages, you can turn InDesign's color management features off—you don't need them, and they do slow the program down.

Source Profiles. The profiles you choose from the CMYK, LAB, and RGB pop-up menus are the profiles InDesign will use for any objects you create in InDesign, and for any imported graphics that did not include a color management profile (and that you have not applied a profile to using the Image Color Settings dialog box).

Choose Use Separations Profile from the CMYK pop-up menu to have InDesign use the profile you selected from the Separations pop-up menu in the Application Color Settings dialog box.

If you're using a specific LAB profile in Photoshop, choose the corresponding profile from the LAB pop-up menu; otherwise, choose the Adobe InDesign Default LAB profile.

Choose a profile from the RGB pop-up menu that matches your monitor, or choose Adobe InDesign Default RGB.

Rendering Intent. What happens when the color management system encounters a color that is outside of the gamut of the selected printing device? The color management system changes the color to a color that's inside the printer's gamut. *How* it does that is the topic of the Rendering Intent section of the Document Color Settings dialog box.

When you choose Perceptual (Images) from either of the pop-up menus in this section, you're telling the color management system to bring out-of-gamut colors into the color gamut in a way that maintains a distinction between the colors. When you choose either Relative Colorimetric or Absolute Colorimetric, the out-of-gamut colors are moved to the nearest edge of the color gamut—which means that differences between out-of-gamut colors can disappear. When this happens, you'll see an effect similar to posterization in the more saturated areas of images. Saturation (Graphics), on the other hand, moves *in-gamut* colors toward the edge of the color gamut, resulting in more saturated color.

In general, you should choose Relative Colorimetric from the Solid Color pop-up, and Perceptual (Images) from the Images pop-up menu. If you want more intense color in business graphics (such as charts and graphs), you might try choosing Saturation (Graphics) from the Solid Color pop-up menu.

Applying Device Profiles to Images. When you select an RGB image in a InDesign publication, you can use the Image Color Settings option on the Graphic submenu of the context menu (or choose the corresponding option from the Object menu) to assign a device profile (a monitor or scanner profile) to the image. Why do this? When you use InDesign's color management system on an RGB image, you'll get better color separations (see Color Figure 10).

Color in InDesign

Now that you know all about color perception, color printing, and color management, it's time to get down to the process of specifying and applying colors in your InDesign publication.

Named and Unnamed Colors

InDesign has two basic methods for working with color: unnamed colors and color swatches. What's the difference? Both unnamed colors and color swatches can change the appearance of an object's fill or stroke, but swatches establish a relationship between the object and the named color swatch. Change the definition of the color swatch, and the color of all of the objects you've applied that swatch to will change, as well.

Here's another way to look at it: unnamed colors are to color swatches as local character formatting is to a character style. You get the *appearance* you're looking for, but you don't get the link between the style (in this case, the color swatch) and the object.

Why do you need that link? Because people change their minds. Your publication might have started its life intended for a two-color press, but, because of a recent change in management, it's now a six-color job (lucky you!). The client's corporate color may have been Pantone 327 when you started the job, but it's now Pantone 199. You get the idea—something like this has probably happened to you.

If you've used unnamed colors, there's nothing to do but claw your way through the objects in your publication, selecting and changing each affected object. If you've used named color swatches, on the other hand, making a change of this sort is a simple task: change the definition of the swatch, and you've changed the color applied to all of the fills and strokes formatted using the swatch.

Colors and Inks

Spot colors in your publication correspond directly to the inks you'll use to print the publication; process colors are made up of some or all of the four process inks (cyan, magenta, yellow, and black). When you create, edit, or import a color in InDesign, you're working with a single ink, or a tint of that ink, or (for a process color) a set of inks which, when printed, optically blend together to produce the color you want to see.

When it comes time to print, the ink list (in the Color panel of the Print dialog box) displays the inks needed to print the colors you have defined in your publication. You'll always see the process inks (cyan, magenta, yellow, and black) in the ink list, whether you've defined process colors or not. If you've defined spot colors, you'll see the spot inks associated with those colors in the ink list. If you want, you can print simulations of spot colors using process inks by clicking the All to Process button. This converts the colors as you print—the color definitions are not changed in your publication.

Spot Color or Process Color or Both?

Whether you use spot colors, process colors, or both depends on the needs of your specific publication—which has to do with your printing budget, your communications goals, and, most importantly, your mood. If you plan to use color photographs in your publication, you're going to have to use at least the four process inks. If you're printing on a tight budget, you'll probably want to use one or two inks.

When you're creating a color, you're offered a variety of choices: is the color a spot color, a process color, or a tint? Which color model should you use? Should you choose a color from a swatch library, or make up your own color definition? The following sections attempt to answer these questions.

Color Models

InDesign lets you define colors using any of three color models—CMYK, RGB, and LAB. Which color model should you use? That depends on how you plan to produce your publication.

Spot colors. If you're working with spot colors, it doesn't matter what color model you choose, and it really doesn't matter what the color looks like on the screen, as long as you let your commercial printer know what color of ink they need to use to print your publication. How do you know what ink to use? If you use Pantone colors (the most likely scenario), you can tell them the PMS color number. If you don't, it's trickier, but your printer can help you match the color you want to an ink they can mix.

If you plan to use Pantone spot colors, save yourself some trouble: choose swatches from the Pantone swatch libraries, rather than trying to mix the color yourself. Note that, in any case, you can't use the Color palette to create a spot color from scratch—to do that, you'll have to use the controls in the New Color Swatch dialog box.

Process colors. If you're working with process colors, *specify your color using the CMYK color model or a CMYK color-matching* *system*, or be ready for some surprises when your publication gets printed. Once again, look at a printed sample of the process color, and enter the values given in the sample book for the color. It might seem too obvious to state, but don't enter other CMYK values unless you want a different color!

If you plan to use Trumatch process colors, choose the colors from the Trumatch swatch library, rather than trying to mix them yourself.

On-screen colors. If you're creating a publication for online distribution (on a CD-ROM or on the web), use the RGB color model. If you're creating a publication for distribution on the web, you'll also want to stick with "browser safe" colors for any paths you draw in InDesign—colors that appear (more or less) the same on platforms supported by Microsoft Internet Explorer or Netscape Navigator. For more on picking browser-safe colors, see "Color and the Web," later in this chapter.

Tints. If you're trying to create a tint of an existing color (process or spot), use the Swatches palette—don't try to approximate the right shade by mixing colors. You can base your tint on a spot color, a process color, but you can't base tints on another tint.

Color Conversion Errors. When you convert a color from one color model to another—from RGB to CMYK, for example—a certain amount of error is introduced by the process of conversion. This is because the color models don't cover the same color gamut, and because the color models have differing approaches to defining colors. Each time you convert the color, the rounding error is compounded: if you convert 100C 10M 50Y 0K to RGB, you'll get 0R 230G 128B—converting that RGB color back to CMYK will yield a color defined as 90C 0M 40Y 10K. There's no "round trip" in color model conversion.

Swatch Libraries

InDesign's swatch libraries support the most frequently used color-matching systems in the graphic arts industry. There's nothing magical about these color libraries—they're just sets of agreed-upon industry standards. Colors from swatch libraries are always named colors, and appear in your publication as swatches.

DICColor. A spot-color specifying system corresponding to inks manufactured by Dainippon Ink and Chemicals, Inc. It's something like a Japanese version of Pantone—and not seen frequently in North America or Europe—except in printing subsidiaries of Japanese printers. Still, it's a nice set of colors, which you might want to use if you can get a printer to match them.

Focoltone. A process-color specification system (mostly used in Europe). Colors in the Focoltone library are organized in sets of colors with common percentages of at least one process color. The idea is to create a library of colors that, when applied to objects, are easy to trap, or don't need trapping at all.

HKS_E, HKS_N, HKS_D, HKS_K. Where do these colors come from, and what do they want? No one knows (except perhaps some secret U.S. government agency, and they're not telling). There's no mention of them in the documentation, and I haven't been able to find a reference to them anywhere. Snooping around in the library itself, I see that they're German, and that they're spot colors defined using the CMYK model.

Pantone Coated, Pantone Uncoated. Sets of spot-color inks manufactured by Pantone, Inc. These inks are the industry standard for spot color in the North American printing business (as always, ask your commercial printer).

Pantone Process. A set of Pantone process-color tint builds. These colors have no relation to the Pantone spot colors.

System (Macintosh), System (Windows). These two swatch libraries contain the 8-bit RGB color palettes for their respective systems.

TOYO Color Finder. A spot-color library for matching inks from the Toyo Ink Manufacturing Company, Ltd., and corresponding to their Toyo 88 Color Guide ink sample book. Like DIC, Toyo is primarily used in Asian countries, and isn't seen much in Europe or North America.

Trumatch. A process-color specifying system featuring small percentage changes from one process color to another. The Trumatch swatch book gives you a good set of printed examples for specifying process color.

Web. You can't count on everyone viewing your Web page to have the same video system you have. To compensate for the differences, most web browsers (Netscape Navigator and Microsoft Internet Explorer, for example) include a standard palette of colors. Use colors from this palette, and you can be assured that the colors in the files you export from InDesign will appear (more or less) as you intended.

InDesign's Color Controls

InDesign's controls for working with color are found in several palettes and menus. The most important palettes are the Toolbox, because it contains the Fill selector and the Stroke selector, and the Swatches palette, because it contains tools for defining, editing, and applying swatches (which can be colors, gradients, or tints) to objects.

You can also use the Color palette and the Gradient palette to create and apply unnamed colors and gradients—but, as I've noted earlier, you'll be better off if you use named color swatches. Everything you can do using the Color palette or the Gradient palette can be accomplished using the Swatches palette.

Fill and Stroke Selectors

Stroke selector active

Fill selector active

At the bottom of the Toolbox, you'll see the Fill selector and the Stroke selector. These aren't labeled in any way (unless you count the tool help I always turn off), but the Fill selector is the one on the left (here's proof that InDesign's user interface, while easy to use, is hard to write about). When you want to work with an object's fill, click the Fill selector; to work with an object's stroke, press the Stroke selector. InDesign shows you which selector is active by bringing it to the front.

Here are my favorite shortcuts for working with the Fill and Stroke selectors.

◆ Press X (this is another of those keyboard shortcuts that doesn't work when you're editing text) to toggle between the Fill selector and the Stroke selector.

◆ Press Shift-X to swap fill and stroke colors (this shortcut is the same as clicking the Swap Fill and Stroke icon.

◆ Press D to apply the default fill and stroke colors to the selected object.

◆ To apply the currently selected swatch to an object's stroke or fill, click the corresponding selector, then click the Apply Color button (or click the swatch itself). To remove a fill or stroke from the selected object, click the appropriate selector and then click the Apply None button (or click the None swatch in the Swatches palette).

Swatches Palette

The Swatches palette is InDesign's "color control center"—it's where you create, edit, and apply colors, tints, and gradients.

The Swatches palette often displays a bewildering array of icons and symbols. What does it all mean? To find out, take a look at Figure 9-3.

Press Command-Option/Ctrl-Alt and click inside the Swatches palette to activate the list. Once you've done this, you can select a color by typing its name, or move up and down in the list of swatches using the arrow keys.

Creating a color swatch. To create a color swatch, follow these steps (see Figure 9-4).

1. Choose New Color Swatch from the Swatches palette menu. InDesign displays the New Color Swatch dialog box.

FIGURE 9-3
Swatches palette

To display the Swatches palette, press F5.

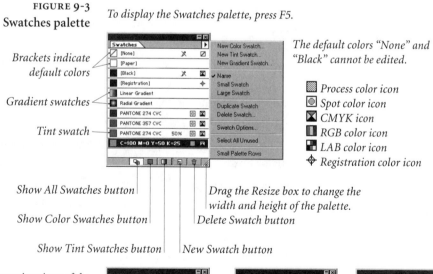

Brackets indicate default colors

Gradient swatches

Tint swatch

The default colors "None" and "Black" cannot be edited.

Process color icon
Spot color icon
CMYK icon
RGB color icon
LAB color icon
Registration color icon

Show All Swatches button

Show Color Swatches button

Show Tint Swatches button

Drag the Resize box to change the width and height of the palette.

Delete Swatch button

New Swatch button

Alternative views of the Swatches palette

Small palette rows

Small swatches

Large swatches

FIGURE 9-4

Creating a color swatch

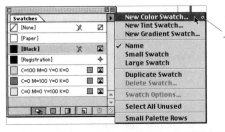

Choose New Color Swatch from the Swatches palette menu.

InDesign displays the New Color Swatch dialog box.

Enter a name for the color...

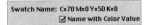

...or turn on the Name with Color Value option to have InDesign enter a color name.

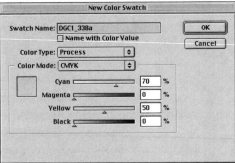

Set up the color type (spot or process) and color mode (the model used to define the color), then adjust the color values. Click the OK button when you're done.

InDesign adds the new color swatch to the list of available swatches.

2. Enter a name for the new color swatch (it's optional—InDesign will have filled in the Name field with a default name for the color), and define the color using the controls in the New Color Swatch dialog box.

3. Define the color using the controls in the New Color Swatch dialog box.

4. Click the OK button or press Enter to close the dialog box. InDesign adds the new color swatch to the list of swatches shown in the Swatches palette.

If you have an object selected when you choose New Color Swatch (or click the Add Swatch button), InDesign bases the color of the swatch on the color of the selected object (if the Fill selector in the Toolbox is active, you'll see the fill color; if the Stroke selector is active, you'll see the stroke color). If no object is selected, InDesign fills in the New Color Swatch dialog box with the definition of the default color (which is also the current color displayed in the Color palette).

This means that you can add unnamed colors (that is, colors you've applied to objects using the Color palette) to the Swatches palette. Select the object colored with the unnamed color, then click the New Swatch button (or choose New Color Swatch from the Swatches palette menu, then click the OK button in the New Color Swatch dialog box). InDesign adds the color applied to the object to the list of colors in the Swatches palette.

Adding Colors from a Swatch Library. Most of the time, I think you should add colors from swatch libraries. Why? Because your commercial printer wants you to (when they talk in their sleep, they call out Pantone numbers), and because it's the quickest way to add a named color to your publication. To choose a color from a color library, follow these steps (see Figure 9-5).

1. Display the Swatches palette if it's not already visible (press F5).

2. Choose a swatch library from the Swatch Libraries submenu of the Window menu. InDesign displays the swatch library in a new palette.

3. Select a swatch. To select more than one color, hold down Shift to select a contiguous range of color swatches, or hold down Command/Ctrl and click to select non-contiguous swatches.

   To "jump" to a specific swatch (as you'll often want to in the Pantone swatch libraries), press Command-Option/Ctrl-Alt and click in the list of swatches displayed in the Swatch library palette. Type the number of the color you want to select, and InDesign highlights the color.

4. To add a single color swatch to the Swatches palette, double-click the swatch (note that this *does not* apply the swatch to the selection or to the document default fill or stroke). To add more than one swatch, choose Add to Swatches from the swatch library palette's menu.

Adding Swatches from Illustrator or Other InDesign Publications. To add swatches stored in an InDesign publication or an Illustrator document, choose Other Library from the Swatch Libraries submenu of the Window menu. InDesign displays the Select a Library to Open dialog box. Locate and select an InDesign or Illustrator document, then click the Open button. InDesign displays the swatches defined in the document in a swatch library palette. At this point, you can add them to the current publication just as you'd add swatches from any swatch library.

FIGURE 9-5

Working with swatch libraries

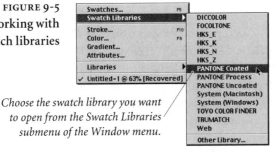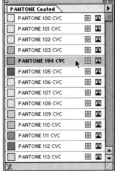

Choose the swatch library you want to open from the Swatch Libraries submenu of the Window menu.

InDesign opens the swatch library in a palette.

To select a swatch by number, hold down Command-Option/Ctrl-Alt and click in the swatch library palette.

You can use the swatch library palette just as you use the Swatches palette, but you might want to move swatches to the Swatches palette.

To get a swatch from the swatch library palette to the Swatches palette, double-click the swatch.

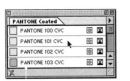

InDesign highlights the list in the palette (note dark outline).

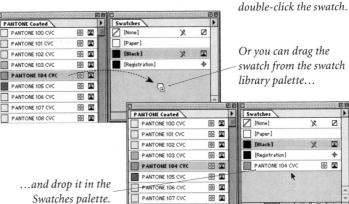

Or you can drag the swatch from the swatch library palette...

...and drop it in the Swatches palette.

Enter the number of the color you want to select, and InDesign scrolls to and selects the corresponding swatch.

...and then choose Add to Swatches from the swatch library palette menu. InDesign adds the swatches to the Swatches palette.

To move several swatches at once, hold down Shift to select a range of swatches, or Command/Ctrl to select non-contiguous swatches...

Creating a tint swatch. To create a new tint swatch, follow these steps (see Figure 9-6).

1. Select a color swatch in the Swatches palette. If you select a tint swatch, the new tint will be based on the same color as the existing tint swatch—you can't create a tint based on a tint.

2. Choose New Tint Swatch from the Swatches palette menu. InDesign displays the New Tint Swatch dialog box.

3. Enter a new value in the Tint field or drag the slider.

4. Click the OK button or press Enter to close the dialog box. InDesign adds the tint to the list of swatches in the Swatch palette.

FIGURE 9-6

Creating a tint swatch

Select the color you want to use as the "base" color for the tint.

Choose New Tint Swatch from the Swatches palette menu.

InDesign displays the New Tint Swatch dialog box.

Enter a tint value, then click the OK button.

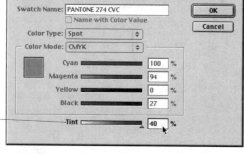

InDesign adds the tint swatch to the Swatches palette.

If you remove a color (see "Removing a Color Swatch," later in this chapter), all tint swatches based on that color will change to tints of the color you choose in the Delete Color dialog box. If, as you remove a color, you choose to convert the color to the default colors "None" or "Paper," InDesign removes all of the tints based on that color from the Swatches palette. This is also what happens when you remove a color swatch and choose the Unnamed Swatch option in the Delete Color option.

Swatch Shortcuts. When you're creating or editing a color swatch, you can take advantage of a number of shortcuts built into the New Color Swatch and Swatch Options dialog boxes.

◆ When you enter a value (or a mathematical expression) in one of the color value fields, you can hold down Command/Ctrl as you press Enter to apply the same percentage change to all of the color value fields.

◆ Hold down Command/Ctrl as you drag a color value slider to move all of the other sliders in tandem. Note that this does not affect color sliders whose value is zero.

Out of gamut warning

Out of Gamut Warning. When you have turned color management on, InDesign monitors the values of the colors you create. When a color swatch definition falls outside the gamut defined by the separations profile you've selected (in the Application Color Settings dialog box), InDesign displays an alert icon next to the color sliders in the New Color Swatch or Swatch Options dialog box. To adjust the color definition so that it falls in the gamut of the separations profile, click the alert icon.

Creating a gradient swatch. To create a gradient swatch, follow these steps (see Figure 9-7).

1. Choose New Gradient Swatch from the Swatches palette menu. InDesign displays the New Gradient Swatch dialog box.

2. Enter a name for the gradient, if you want (or use the default name suggested by InDesign). Edit the gradient's ramp and color attributes using any or all of the following techniques.

   ◆ To add a new gradient stop, click below the gradient ramp.

   ◆ To change the color of a gradient stop, select the stop, then adjust the color definition using the controls above the gradient ramp.

   ◆ To change the position of a gradient stop, drag it along the ramp.

   ◆ To delete a gradient stop, drag it away from the ramp.

   ◆ To change the midpoint location between any two gradient stops, drag the midpoint icon along the top of the ramp.

3. Once the gradient looks the way you want it to, click the OK button to add the gradient swatch to the Swatches palette.

Changing the order of the swatches in the Swatches palette. To change the order in which colors appear in the Swatches palette, point at a color name and then drag the color name up or down

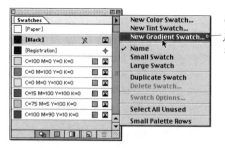

FIGURE 9-7
Creating a
gradient swatch

Choose New Gradient Swatch
from the Swatches palette
menu.

InDesign displays the New
Gradient Swatch dialog box.

Choose Linear or Radial
from the Type pop-up menu.

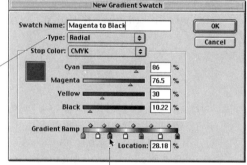

InDesign adds the
gradient swatch to the
Swatches palette.

To set the color of a gradient stop, select
the stop and then adjust the color values
using the controls above the gradient ramp.

in the Swatches palette. Once you've got the color where you want, drop it. This can be handy when you've got a long list of colors and want to position frequently used colors near the top of the palette.

Editing a Swatch. To edit a swatch, do one of the following:

◆ Double-click the swatch in the Swatches palette. (I don't use this shortcut—the first click will apply the swatch to the fill or stroke of any object I've selected, or will apply the swatch to the default fill or stroke if no object is selected).

◆ Select a swatch in the Swatches palette, then choose Swatch Options from the Swatches palette menu. Again, this method applies the swatch to the selection or to the document defaults.

◆ Press Command-Option-Shift/Ctrl-Alt-Shift and double-click a swatch to open the swatch for editing. This method does not apply the swatch to the selection or to the document default fill or stroke.

After any of the above actions, InDesign displays the dialog box appropriate to the type of swatch you clicked (the Edit Color Swatch, Edit Tint Swatch, or Edit Gradient Swatch dialog box).

Make changes to the swatch definition, then click the OK button to close the dialog box. InDesign updates the appearance all of the objects formatted using the swatch.

Deleting a Swatch. To delete a swatch from a publication, follow these steps (see Figure 9-8).

1. Select the swatch in the Swatches palette. To select a range of swatches, hold down Shift as you click the swatch names. To select non-contiguous swatches, hold down Command/Ctrl as you click the swatch names.

2. Click the Delete Swatch button (or choose Delete Color Swatch from the Swatches palette menu). InDesign displays the Delete Swatch dialog box.

3. If you want to replace the color you're deleting with an existing swatch, turn on the Defined Swatch option and choose the name of the swatch from the attached pop-up menu. To replace the swatch with an unnamed color, turn on the Unnamed Swatch option.

4. Click the OK button. InDesign deletes the swatch and applies the replacement swatch (if you selected the Defined Swatch option) or an unnamed color (if you selected the Unnamed Swatch option) to all of the objects formatted using the swatch you're deleting.

FIGURE 9-8

Deleting a swatch

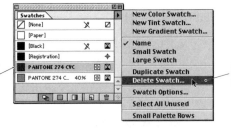

Select the swatch (or swatches) you want to delete.

Choose Delete Swatch from the Swatches palette menu.

To apply an existing swatch to the objects colored with the swatch you're removing, turn on the Defined Swatch option and choose a swatch from the pop-up menu...

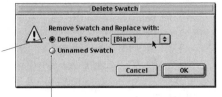

...or choose Unnamed Swatch to have InDesign apply an unnamed swatch of the same color to the objects.

InDesign deletes the swatch. If tint swatches were based on the swatch you removed, InDesign bases them on the replacement color you selected.

COLOR FIGURE 1

Overprint and knockout

Spot color 1 plate

Spot color 2 plate

Objects colored with spot color 1 set to knock out (Overprint Fill option off)

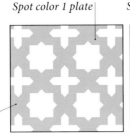
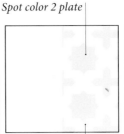

Spot color 1 knocks out spot color 2

Objects colored with spot color 1 set to overprint (Overprint Fill option on)

Spot color 1 plate

Spot color 2 plate

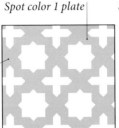
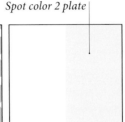
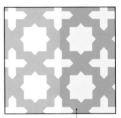

Spot color 1 overprints spot color 2

COLOR FIGURE 2

Trapping an open path

This cyan path needs to be trapped. Unless I've been very lucky, you'll see paper showing through around the stroke of the path.

Make sure you turn on the Weight Changes Bounding Box option on the Stroke palette menu—without it, your paths will change shape as you change their stroke weights (making manual trapping impossible).

To create a spread (as shown here), clone the path (by copying the path and then choosing Paste In Place from the Edit menu). Increase the stroke weight of the cloned path, then turn on the Overprint Stroke option.

To create a choke, clone the path and then decrease the stroke width of the cloned path. Set the stroke of the original path to overprint.

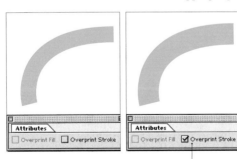

The original path knocks out objects behind it.

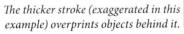

The thicker stroke (exaggerated in this example) overprints objects behind it.

Trapped path (without exaggeration)

Trapping closed paths and text

Again, unless I've been lucky, you'll see the paper showing through around the cyan circle in this example. To prevent the paper from showing, you need to trap the object.

Select the path you want to trap and press F10 to display the Stroke palette. Add a stroke to the object that's twice the width of the spread you want, and turn on the Overprint option.

If you could separate the fill and the stroke, you would see something like this.

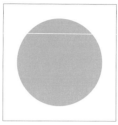

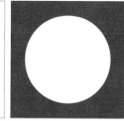

To create a choke, apply an overprinting stroke the color of the background rectangle to the ellipse.

The fill is set to knock out...

...the stroke is set to overprint.

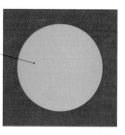

When you print, the the stroke of the circle overprints the background square, while the fill knocks out. This creates a spread.

This example has not been trapped, so you'll probably see paper showing through around the text characters.

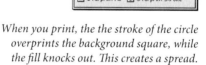

The cyan stroke overprints the background objects, creating a spread. In general, you want to spread the lighter color (cyan, in this example) into the darker color (magenta).

Trapped using a spread.

Because InDesign prints the fill of text over the stroke, I had to create a duplicate text frame containing characters with a magenta stroke and a fill of "None"

Trapped using a choke.

When you choke lighter characters, the apparent shape of the characters changes (not a good thing).

COLOR FIGURE 4
Overprinting and process colors

Background rectangle is 80C 20M 80Y 10K

0C 80M 0Y 40K

20C 80M 20Y 40K

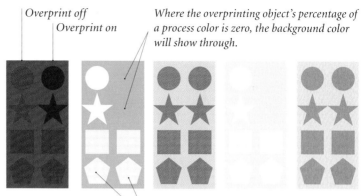

Overprint off
Overprint on

Where the overprinting object's percentage of a process color is zero, the background color will show through.

These objects contain percentages of each process color, so overprinting and non-overprinting objects print identically on each plate.

COLOR FIGURE 5
InDesign trapping

This (very beautiful) example was trapped using InDesign's default trapping settings (shown below).

Rich black (15C 15M 15Y 100K)

View Trap Style

Name: Default

Trap Width
Default: 0.25 points
Black Width: 0.5 points

Trap Color Reduction: 100 %

Trapping Thresholds
Step Limit: 10 %
Black Color Limit: 100 %
Black Density Limit: 1.6
Sliding Trap Limit: 70 %

Image Settings
Image Trap Placement: Center
☑ Trap Objects to Images
☐ Trap Images Internal
☑ Trap 1-bit images

OK
Cancel

COLOR FIGURE 6
Rosettes

We can't load our printing presses with millions of inks, so we fool the eye by printing patterns of dots of (at least) four inks when we want to print scanned natural images. The pattern made by these dots is called a "rosette."

In this example, I've enlarged part of the image (of my son, Max). Look at the enlarged sample from a distance, and you'll see how the dots blend together to create the appearance of more than four colors.

I've also pulled the sample apart to show the halftone screen angle used by each ink, at right.

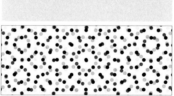

Rosettes for an area of flat color: 10C 10M 10Y 10K (a bland gray, as shown, but good for demonstration purposes).

Cyan

Magenta

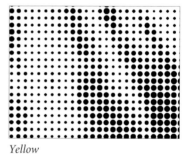

Yellow

Black

COLOR FIGURE 7
Duotones

Photoshop duotone.

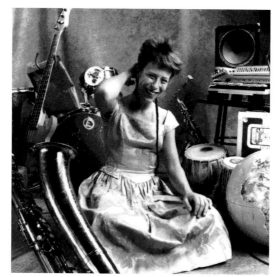

Two fake duotones: images in black ink over a background tint of cyan.

InDesign fake duotone: Two overlapping grayscale TIFF images colored with different inks(cyan and black).

100% cyan background

50% cyan background

To apply a color to an image (black and white or grayscale only), select the image with the Direct Selection tool

…and then click a color swatch in the Swatches palette.

Creating a "Neon glow" effect

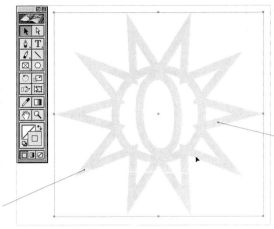

When you need to create a "glow" effect, you typically use a blend in Illustrator or FreeHand. But, with a little help from InDesign scripting, you can create blends in InDesign. Here's one of my favorite example scripts.

Select a path in InDesign.

The path should have a fairly thick stroke (3 points or more), and you should turn on the Stroke Weight Changes Bounding Box option (on the Stroke palette menu).

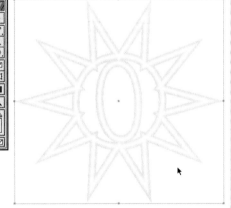

Run the script. The example Mac OS script on your InDesign CD doesn't have a user interface, but you can download the version shown here from Adobe's web site (the Windows version on the InDesign CD looks pretty much like this).

Enter the number of steps you want for the blend, then click the OK button. InDesign and the script work together to create the blend.

The "neon" effect looks better on a dark background.

We don't usually think of scripting as a creative tool, but this example script gives you a way to apply an effect that would be difficult to accomplish without leaving InDesign for a drawing program.

COLOR FIGURE 9
Separating color images

CMYK images as separated by Photoshop.

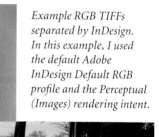

Example RGB TIFFs separated by InDesign. In this example, I used the default Adobe InDesign Default RGB profile and the Perceptual (Images) rendering intent.

Acrobat InProduction

For years, PDF has been
the best file format to
use when you're delivering
monochrome pages. Now
that InProduction exists,
PDF is a great format
for color publications, as
well. InProduction closes
the gap by providing color
separation and trapping in
a set of Acrobat plug-ins.

Acrobat InProduction
Separation Setup
dialog box.

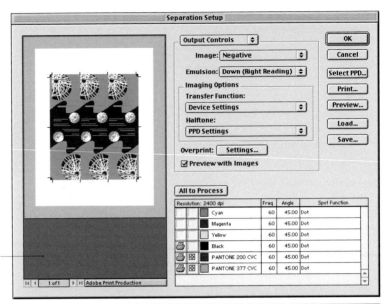

Previewing separations
in the InProduction
Separation Preview
dialog box.

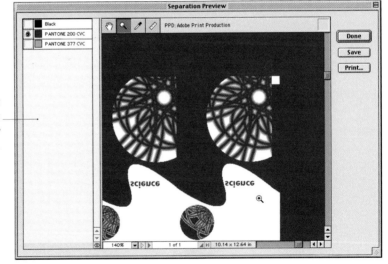

When you remove a swatch that you've used as a basis for tint swatches, InDesign bases the tint swatches on the color you specified (if you selected the Defined Swatch option), or an unnamed color (if you selected the Unnamed Swatch option).

Duplicating Swatches. If you want to base a swatch on an existing swatch, select the swatch in the Swatches palette and then choose Duplicate Swatch from the palette's menu. InDesign creates a copy of the swatch and assigns it a name (the default name is the name of the original swatch plus the word "copy"). At this point, you can edit the swatch.

The Color Palette

Given that I've already stated that you should use the Swatches palette instead of the Color palette, you might wonder why I'm bothering to write the next section. Over the years, I've come to realize that my methods are not necessarily for everyone, and that some people have very different working habits from my own. For some of you, working with the Color palette and unnamed colors might be better than the process of creating named swatches—and there's nothing wrong with that.

The Color palette is always *on*—whenever you adjust the controls in the palette, you're applying them to something (either the selected object or the document's default fill and stroke formatting). For a look at the Color palette, see Figure 9-9.

The Color palette does have one thing that the Swatches palette's methods for defining colors lack: the Color Bar. To apply a color, drag the cursor in the Color Bar.

Colors Palette Shortcuts

The Colors palette has shortcuts, too.

◆ To display the Colors palette, press F6.

◆ When you enter a value (or a mathematical expression) in one of the color value fields, you can hold down Command/Ctrl as you press Return/Enter to apply the same percentage change to all of the color value fields.

◆ Hold down Command/Ctrl as you drag a color value slider to move all of the other sliders in tandem. Note that this does not affect color sliders whose value is zero.

FIGURE 9-9
The Color palette

Fill and stroke selectors

Click this area to apply "none."

RGB mode

Enter color values using the fields and sliders...

...or drag the cursor in the color bar.

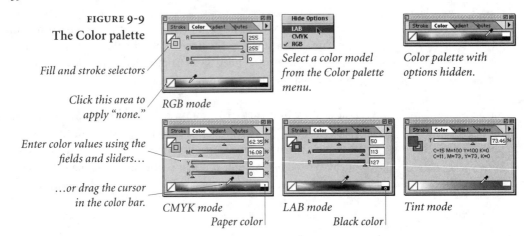

Select a color model from the Color palette menu.

Color palette with options hidden.

CMYK mode

Paper color

LAB mode

Black color

Tint mode

Out of Gamut Warning. When you have turned color management on, InDesign monitors the values of the colors you create. When a color definition falls outside the gamut defined by the separations profile you've selected (in the Application Color Settings dialog box), InDesign displays an alert icon above the Color Bar in the Color palette. To adjust the color definition so that it falls in the gamut of the separations profile, click the alert icon (see Figure 9-10). Note that you won't see this icon when you've chosen Hide Options from the palette menu.

FIGURE 9-10
Fixing out of gamut colors

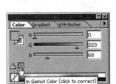

When the current color cannot be printed by the separations printer you've selected, InDesign displays the out of gamut warning.

Click the icon to redefine the color so that it falls within the gamut of the output device.

Applying Colors and Gradients

Once you've selected an object, you can use any (or all) of the following techniques to apply a color, tint, or gradient to the object (see Figure 9-11).

◆ Click one of the selectors (Fill or Stroke) at the bottom of the Toolbox, then click a color in the Swatches palette. InDesign applies the color to the object's fill or stroke.

FIGURE 9-11

Applying a color

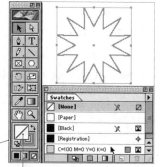

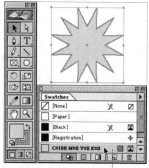

Press X to switch between the fill selector and the stroke selector.

Select the fill or stroke selector in the Tools palette.

Click a color swatch.

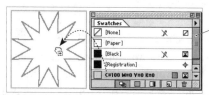

Press F5 to display the Swatches palette.

Drag a color swatch out of the Swatches palette (note that you do not need to select an object to apply a color via this method).

Drop the color swatch on an object's fill or stroke.

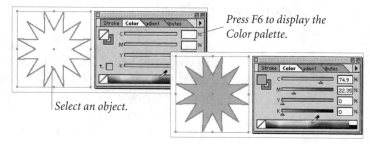

Press F6 to display the Color palette.

Select an object.

Click the cursor in the color bar, or adjust one of the color controls in the Color palette, and InDesign applies the color to the selected object.

◆ Click the Fill selector or the Stroke selector, then click the Apply Color button, Apply Gradient button, Apply None button, swap fill and stroke icon, or the default fill and stroke icon. Or press any of the keyboard shortcuts corresponding to the buttons.

◆ Select an object, then adjust any of the controls in the Color palette.

- Drag a color swatch out of the Swatches palette and drop it on the fill or stroke of an object.

- Use the Eyedropper tool to pick a color from an existing object, then click on another object to apply that color to it.

Applying Colors to Text

You can apply a fill or stroke to the characters of text in your publication. To apply a color to text, select the text with the Text tool and apply a color using any of the techniques described above. What happens when you select the text block with the Selection tool and apply a color? InDesign applies the color to the fill or stroke of the text frame.

Applying Colors to Imported Graphics

You can apply colors to bi-level TIFFs, and grayscale TIFFs. To apply a color to an imported image, select the image using the Direct Selection tool, click the Fill selector in the Toolbox, and then click a color swatch. When you try to apply an tint to an imported image, InDesign apples the color the tint is based on.

When you print, InDesign prints the image on the appropriate separation (for a spot color) or series of plates (for a process color). Applying a color to a color TIFF has no effect on the way that TIFF is separated by InDesign.

Creating Spot-Color Tint Builds

When you're working with spot-color publications, you often want to create tint builds (also known as stacked screens) of the colors you're working with to broaden the range of colors in your publication. Since you can't create a color containing percentages of two or more spot colors (20-percent black and 60-percent PMS 327, for example), as you can in QuarkXPress, it'd seem, at first glance, that you're stuck. You're not, though, as the following exercise demonstrates.

1. Open a new publication and add a spot color (create your own, or use one from the Pantone spot-color library). Next, create a 20-percent tint of black (if one doesn't already exist).

2. Draw a rectangle.

3. Without deselecting the rectangle, fill it with the spot color you created in step 1. Set the rectangle's stroke to None.

4. Clone the rectangle. To do this, copy the object to the Clipboard, then press Command-Shift-V/Ctrl-Shift-V. This displays the Step and Repeat dialog box. Enter 1 in the Repeat Count field and zero in the Horizontal Offset and Vertical Offset fields, then click the OK button to close the dialog box and create the duplicate of the selected object.

5. Fill the clone with the 20-percent tint of black.

6. Display the Attributes palette, if it's not already visible (choose Attributes from the Window menu). Turn on the Overprint option to make the rectangle overprint.

That's all there is to it. When you print, the gray rectangle overprints the spot-color rectangle, creating a combination of the two spot colors. Unfortunately, you can't see the tint build onscreen or on color printouts; you only see the color of the frontmost object.

Trapping

A "trap" is a method of overlapping abutting colored objects to compensate for the imperfect registration of printing presses. Because registration, even on good presses with good operators, can be off by a quarter point or more, abutting elements in your publication may not end up abutting perfectly when the publication is printed by your commercial printer. What happens then? The paper shows through where you don't want it to (see Color Figures 2 and 3).

Do I need to tell you what happens when you take your work to a press that's badly out of register or run by turkeys? Disaster. Before this happens to you, talk with your commercial printer regarding the tolerances of their presses and/or operators. Don't ask them if they're turkeys—it's considered rude.

Manual Trapping

If you can't (or don't want to) use InDesign's automatic trapping methods (In-RIP or built-in), you can still trap your publication—you'll just have to do it yourself. I'll describe the process, because I believe that you should know how to add and subtract, multiply and divide before you ever use a calculator.

Before I start describing manual trapping techniques, however, I need to state that InDesign's automatic trapping methods can trap your publications better than you can (assuming that you have both deadlines and a finite amount of patience), and if you use them, you usually won't even have to *think* about trapping.

Object-Level Overprinting. The key to trapping, in InDesign and elsewhere, is in controlling which objects—or which parts of objects—print on top of other objects as the printing press prints your publication. The only way to make manual trapping work is to control the overprinting characteristics of individual objects (see Color Figures 1 and 4).

Luckily, you can. Any InDesign path can be specified as an overprinting object (that is, it won't knock a hole in any objects behind it when you print), regardless of the object's color. The controls for object-level overprinting are the Overprint Fill and Overprint Stroke options found in the Attributes palette (see Figure 9-12). These controls, used in combination with InDesign's Paste Into command, can be used to create virtually any trap.

FIGURE 9-12
Attributes palette

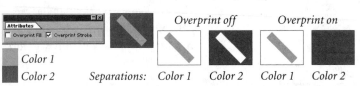

I have to stress the importance of the Weight Changes Bounding Box option on the Stroke palette menu. You cannot create traps when this option is turned off, so you'll have to make sure it's turned on as you follow any of the procedures in this section.

When you're working with trapping, you'll be creating *spreads* (outlines of objects, in the same color as the object, that are slightly larger than the object itself) and *chokes* (outlines of the object that are the same color as the underlying object's color). Spreads make the object larger so that the edges of the object print over the underlying object; chokes make the area knocked out of the underlying object smaller than the outline of the foreground object.

Use chokes when the foreground object is a darker color than the background object; use spreads when the foreground object is lighter. In other words, trap from light colors into darker colors. Sound subjective? It is. I use chokes when I'm trapping type—text characters often look distorted when you use spreads (the eye is very critical when it comes to text).

Overprinting Black. By default, all objects on an InDesign page knock out of all objects behind them—unless they're black. InDesign, by default, overprints black ink. Most of the time, this is a good thing. To turn off black overprinting, display the General panel of the Preferences dialog box and turn off the Overprint Black option.

Spot-Color Trapping. It's more important to trap abutting color fields in publications you're printing using spot colors than it is in process color publications. When you're working with process colors, you'll almost always see some ink between abutting objects, so you're less likely to see paper-colored gaps showing a poor trap.

The easiest way to demonstrate how spot-color trapping works is to show you some examples. As you work through these examples, you'll trap an ellipse into a rectangle by manipulating the color, width, and overprinting specifications of the path that surrounds the ellipse. First, draw the colored objects.

1. Create a rectangle. Fill the rectangle with a spot color ("Color 1"). Set the rectangle's stroke color to None.

2. Draw an ellipse on top of the rectangle. Make sure that the ellipse is entirely inside the rectangle. Fill the ellipse with a different color from that of the rectangle ("Color 2"). Set the stroke of the ellipse to None.

3. Save the file.

The ellipse needs to be trapped, or you'll run the risk of having paper-colored lines appear up around the ellipse when you print the publication. You can either spread or choke the ellipse, or both.

To spread the ellipse, follow these steps (see Color Figure 3).

1. Select the ellipse.

2. F10 to display the Stroke palette.

3. Choose Weight Changes Bounding Box from the Stroke palette menu, then enter a new line width in the Weight field.

The line width you enter in the Weight field should be equal to twice the trap amount—if you enter "2", you'll get a stroke of one point on either side of the path. If your commercial printer has asked for a trap of .5 points, enter "1" in the Weight field.

When you print, the ellipse is larger than the hole that's been knocked out of the background rectangle, which means that the outside of the ellipse slightly overprints the background rectangle. You've just created a spread.

After you're through looking at the objects, or printing, choose Revert from the File menu and revert to the version of the file you saved earlier. This way, you're ready for the next procedure.

To choke the ellipse, follow these steps (see Color Figure 3).

1. Select the ellipse.

2. F10 to display the Stroke palette. Make sure that Weight Changes Bounding Box option on the Stroke palette menu is turned on, then enter a new stroke width in the Weight field.

3. In the Stroke Inspector, choose Basic from the Stroke Type pop-up menu, set the line color to "Color 1" (the color of the background rectangle), type a line width for your trap in the Weight field. Finally, turn on the Overprint option in the Attributes palette.

When you print, the hole that's knocked out of the background rectangle is slightly smaller than the ellipse. This way, the outside of the ellipse slightly overprints the background rectangle. You've just created a choke.

Choose Revert from the File menu to get the file ready for the next procedure.

Trapping Across Color Boundaries. The techniques described above work well as long as objects don't cross color boundaries. If the objects do cross color boundaries (especially going from a color background to a white background), it's too obvious that you've changed the shapes of the objects. What do you do?

1. Drag the ellipse so that it's partially outside of the rectangle.

2. Clone the ellipse. To do this, copy the object to the Clipboard, then press. Command-Option-Shift-V/Ctrl-Alt-Shift-V. This creates a copy of the ellipse exactly on top of the original ellipse.

3. Without deselecting the cloned ellipse, press F10 to display the Stroke palette, if it's not already visible. In the Stroke palette, enter a stroke weight for the trap in the Weight field.

4. Turn on the Overprint Stroke option in the Attributes palette.

5. Select the ellipse, then note the values in the X and Y fields of the Transform palette. Press Command-X/Ctrl-X to cut the ellipse.

6. Select the background rectangle and choose Paste Into from the Edit menu.

7. Select the original ellipse and press Command-Shift-[/Ctrl-Shift-[to send it to the back.

8. Using the Direct Selection tool, select the ellipse you pasted inside the rectangle. If the ellipse did not appear in exactly the

same position as it occupied before you pasted it inside the rectangle, enter the X and Y values you recorded earlier in the X and Y fields of the Transform palette. InDesign moves the copy of the ellipse into the same position as the original ellipse.

At this point, the ellipse you pasted inside the rectangle spreads slightly, while the part of the ellipse outside the rectangle remains the same size and shape. Choose Revert from the File menu to get ready for the next trapping example.

What happens when the object you need to trap overlaps more than one other, differently colored object? In this case, you can run into trouble. The trap you use for one background color might not be the trap you want to use for the other. You might want to spread one and choke the other, depending on the colors you're using.

In these cases, you can use the same basic techniques described above for the overlapping and/or abutting objects. But, at this point, I have to urge you to save yourself some trouble and use either of InDesign's automatic trapping methods.

Trapping Lines. The trapping techniques above work well for filled paths, but what open paths? After all, you can't apply two different stroke properties to a single path. Instead, you clone the path and make the width of the clone larger or smaller to achieve the spread or choke you want. One of the strokes overprints; the other line knocks out.

Follow these steps to spread an open path (see Color Figure 2).

1. Draw a rectangle. Create a spot color and fill the rectangle with it.

2. Draw a path inside the rectangle. Create another spot color and apply it to the path. Do not set this path to overprint.

3. Select the path and clone it.

4. Press F10 to display the Stroke palette. Increase the stroke weight of the path by twice the amount of spread you need (remember, PostScript strokes grow out from their centers) and check the Overprint Stroke option in the Attributes palette to make the stroke overprint.

That's all there is to it. The original path knocks a hole in the background rectangle, and the clone of the path spreads to just a little bit beyond the edges of the knockout.

To choke the path, follow these steps (see Color Figure 2).

1. Draw a rectangle. Create a spot color and fill the rectangle with it.

2. Draw a path inside the rectangle. Create another spot color and apply it to the line. Set this path to overprint.

3. Select the path and clone it.

4. Display the Stroke palette. Decrease the weight of the path by twice the amount of choke you need. Leave the Overprint Stroke option in the Attributes palette turned off.

5. Use the Direct Selection tool to select the original path. Press Command-Shift-]/Ctrl-Shift-] to bring it to the front.

This time, the cloned path is narrower than the original, and knocks out an area that's slightly smaller than the original path, creating a choke.

Trapping Text. Text is usually the element in a publication that needs trapping the most. For whatever reason, it's easier to notice poor trapping around text than around other elements. At the same time, traps that are too large distort the shapes of the characters you're trapping. It's especially a problem with small type, especially serif type.

Here's how to create a spread for text (see Color Figure 3).

1. Draw a rectangle, create a spot color ("Color 1"), and apply it to the rectangle.

2. Enter text in a text frame. Position the text frame on top of the rectangle so that it's entirely within the area occupied by the rectangle.

3. Create a second spot color ("Color 2") and apply it to the text in the text frame.

4. While the text is still selected, display the Stroke palette. Enter the stroke weight you want (remember, it's two times the amount of trap you want) in the Weight field. Turn on the Overprint Stroke option in the Attributes palette.

The next example shows how you can choke text by making the shape the characters knock out of the background a bit smaller than the characters themselves.

1. Draw a rectangle, create a spot color ("Color 1"), and apply it to the rectangle.

2. Create a text frame. Position the text frame on top of the rectangle so that it's entirely within the rectangle.

3. Create a second spot color ("Color 2"). Select all the text in the text frame and apply "Color 2" to the fill of the text.

4. Without deselecting the text, press F10 to display the Stroke palette. Enter the stroke weight you want for the trap in the Weight field. Turn on the Overprint Stroke option in the Attributes palette.

If text crosses color boundaries, use the techniques described earlier for trapping overlapping paths.

Process-Color Trapping. Process-color trapping is a bit simpler than spot-color trapping, because it's usually less critical that process-colored elements have traps, but it can be far harder to figure out exactly what color to make the stroke for a process-colored object. And when you're talking about trapping two process-colored graduated fills, watch out!

The main thing to keep in mind, however, is that, for each of the process inks, the ink percentage used in the topmost object in any stack of objects always wins—they knock out all percentages of that ink behind them, regardless of any overprinting settings.

Unless, that is, the ink percentage is zero. If, for example, the percentage of cyan used in the fill color of the topmost object in a stack of objects is zero, turning Overprint off makes the path knock out any other cyan in the area covered by the path. Overprinting the fill, in this case, means that the area taken up by the fill disappears from the cyan plates—the percentage of cyan in the next object in the stack shows through the area where the objects overlap (see Color Figure 4).

Another way to think of this is to think of each ink in a process color as behaving like a separate spot ink.

Simple Process-Color Trapping. In process-color trapping, you've got to make your overprinting strokes different colors from either the background or foreground objects. Why? Because process colors have a way of creating new colors when you print them over each other. It's what they do best.

As in the spot-color trapping section above, I'll demonstrate process-color trapping techniques by example. First, create a couple of objects.

1. Create a rectangle that's filled with "Color 1", which is specified as 20C 100M 0Y 10K.

2. On top of this rectangle, draw an ellipse and fill it with "Color 2", which is specified as 0C 100M 50Y 0K.

3. Select both objects and set their stroke to None.

4. Save the file.

The ellipse needs to be trapped, or you run the risk of having cyan-colored lines appearing around the ellipse when the publication is printed—which could happen if the cyan and yellow plates aren't in good register, or if your paper stretches. Whether you spread or choke the ellipse depends on its color. If the ellipse is darker than the background rectangle, choke the ellipse. If the ellipse is a lighter color than the background rectangle, spread the ellipse. In this case, the ellipse is a lighter color, so you'll use a spread. To spread the ellipse, follow these steps.

1. Create a new process color containing only those colors in "Color 2" having higher values than "Color 1". Quick quiz: what component colors in "Color 2" have higher values than their counterparts in "Color 1"? If you said 50Y, you're the lucky winner. Specify a new color: 0C 0M 50Y 0K.

2. Select the ellipse.

3. Press F10 to display the Stroke palette, if it's not already visible. Enter the stroke weight you want for your stroke in the Weight field. It should be twice the width of your desired trap.

4. Apply the color swatch "Color 3" to the stroke of the ellipse and set it to overprint.

When you print, all the areas around the ellipse have some dot value inside them, and the new colors created where the objects abut won't be too obvious. Choose Revert from the File menu to get ready for the next example.

What if the ellipse is the darker color? If it were, we'd have to choke it. To choke the ellipse, follow these steps.

1. Select the ellipse and fill it with "Color 1". Select the rectangle and fill it with "Color 2".

2. Create a new color ("Color 3") that contains only the largest color component in "Color 1". That's 100M, so "Color 3" should be specified as 0C 100M 0Y 0K.

3. Use the Weight field in the Stroke palette to specify the weight of the trap you want.

4. Set the stroke color to "Color 3."

5. Turn on the Overprint Stroke option in the Attributes palette.

When you print, the stroke you applied to the ellipse guarantees that there's no gap around the ellipse, even if you run into registration problems when you print the publication.

Automatic Trapping

At this point, you've read your way through the manual trapping techniques, and are seriously considering hiring twenty house elves to take care of your trapping needs. But wait—InDesign includes two powerful automatic trapping methods: In-RIP trapping and InDesign built-in trapping (see Color Figure 5).

What are the differences between the two automatic trapping methods? InDesign's built-in trapping cannot do the following things (all of which can be accomplished by in-RIP trapping).

◆ Trap gradients created in InDesign.

◆ Use trap widths greater than 1 point.

◆ Be used with in-RIP separations.

◆ Create traps inside color images (using the Trap Internal Images option in the Edit Trapping Style dialog box). Built-in trapping can trap InDesign objects to the contents of image files (provided those images are saved as Photoshop or TIFF—images contained in DCS, EPS, or PDF files won't work). Note, however, that InDesign's built in trapping can trap bilevel images (i.e., 1-bit TIFFs) to InDesign objects and to other images.

◆ Trap imported vector graphics or type in PDF or EPS files. See "Built-in Trapping and Imported Graphics," later in this chapter.

Don't let the length of the above list discourage you—InDesign's built-in trapping can take care of the trapping needs of most publications and printing processes. If, however, you see an item in the above list that is crucial to your publication, then you'd probably better use in-RIP trapping.

Built-in Trapping and Imported Graphics. When InDesign elements overlap an imported EPS or PDF graphic, InDesign won't be able to trap the InDesign elements properly. If the elements don't touch each other, or don't need to be trapped, this isn't a problem. If they do need to be trapped, however, you can sometimes work around the problem by adjusting the frame that contains the graphic. If the InDesign elements overlap an empty area in the graphic, edit the shape of the frame containing the graphic so that it doesn't touch the elements.

Alternatively, you can copy and paste paths from Illustrator or FreeHand (or any other application capable of putting data on the system Clipboard in Illustrator-format), thereby converting the paths into InDesign objects—but this will only work for very simple graphics.

Specifying Trapping Settings. To set trapping options for a publication, or to create new trapping styles, turn to the Trapping panel in the Print dialog box (see Figure 9-13).

Choose Application Built-in from the Trapping pop-up menu to use InDesign's built in trapping, or choose Adobe In-RIP to use the trapping built into the selected printer. To turn trapping off, choose Off.

1. Click the Styles button. InDesign displays the Trapping Styles dialog box.

2. Select a trapping style in the list of available trapping styles and click the Edit button, or click the New button to create a new style. InDesign displays the Edit Trapping Style dialog box.

3. Set up the options in the Edit Trapping Style dialog box.

   Trap Width. The value you enter in the Default field sets the trap width for all inks except solid black—you set that trap width using the nearby Black Width field. If you're using InDesign's built-in trapping, the trapping width is never greater than one point (regardless of the value you enter in these two fields).

   If you're working with a rich black (that is, a color containing other inks in addition to black), the value you enter in the Black Width field also sets a kind of "margin" of black ink at the edges of a rich black object. This margin is known as the "holdback" or "holdback area."

   The holdback area comes in handy at the edges of a rich black object. If, for example, you've placed white text over a rich black area, the holdback area prevents the non-black inks from appearing around the edges of the white characters.

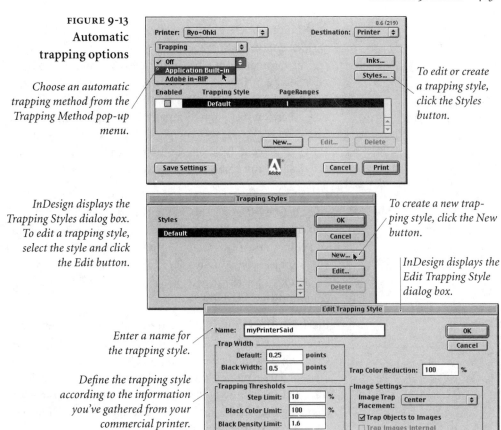

FIGURE 9-13
Automatic
trapping options

Choose an automatic
trapping method from the
Trapping Method pop-up
menu.

To edit or create
a trapping style,
click the Styles
button.

InDesign displays the
Trapping Styles dialog box.
To edit a trapping style,
select the style and click
the Edit button.

To create a new trap-
ping style, click the New
button.

InDesign displays the
Edit Trapping Style
dialog box.

Enter a name for
the trapping style.

Define the trapping style
according to the information
you've gathered from your
commercial printer.

Trap Color Reduction. The value you enter in this field defines the colors InDesign creates as it builds traps. When the value in this field is 100 percent, some color combinations can result in a trapping color (or colors) that is darker than either of the original colors. To avoid this, enter a smaller value in this field. Enter zero to set the neutral density of the objects created by the trapping system to the neutral density of the darkest color (note that this doesn't necessarily mean it's the same color).

Trapping Thresholds. Imagine that you have two process colors in your publication. Color 1 is defined as 60C 20M 0Y 0K, and Color 2 is 65C 15M 0Y 5K. Do these two colors need to be trapped if they happen to end up next to each other on your InDesign pages? That depends on you, your publication, and your commercial printer. The fields in the Trapping Thresholds panel of the Trapping dialog box control when and if InDesign traps the boundaries between colors in a publication.

Step Limit (In-RIP trapping only). The Step Limit field sets the percentage of difference between each color component to trigger automatic trapping. In the above example of Color 1 and Color 2, using the default value of 10 percent in the Step Limit field means that InDesign would not trap the two colors—there's not enough difference between the inks that make up the two colors. If you lowered the value in the Step Limit field to 5 percent, InDesign would trap the objects (because the C, M, and K ink components vary by that percentage).

Black Color Limit. How much black ink has to be used in a color before InDesign applies the holdback defined by the value you entered in the Black Width field? That depends on what you enter in the Black Color Limit field. Enter 100 percent when you want to apply a holdback to colors containing 100 percent black ink, or lower the percentage to apply a holdback to colors containing less black ink.

Black Density Limit. InDesign traps colors in a publication based on their ink neutral densities (see "Ink Neutral Densities," later in this chapter). Lighter colors typically spread into areas of darker colors, which usually produces a less obvious trap. You can manipulate the way that InDesign traps objects by changing the settings in the Ink Neutral Densities dialog box. Or you can use the Black Density Limit field to redefine the density InDesign thinks of as black. By default, black ink is set to an ink neutral density of 1.7.

The value you enter in the Black Density Limit field also affects InDesign's application of the Black Width holdback area—see Trap Width, above. By reducing the value in the Black Density Limit field, you instruct InDesign to apply the holdback to inks other than black.

Sliding Trap Limit (In-RIP trapping only). When gradients abut, the colors at the edges of the gradients vary along the border between the two gradients. You can't use a simple spread or choke for the entire length of the boundary between gradients—at some point, the trap will become too obvious.

One way to solve this problem is to use a centerline trap—a trap that extends equally on either side of the boundary between the gradients. Another method is to use a sliding trap—which changes from a spread to a centerline trap, and then to a choke, depending on the ink neutral densities of the colors used in the gradients.

The value you enter in the Sliding Trap Limit field defines the point (or points) at which the trap switches from a spread to a centerline trap, and from a centerline trap to a choke. This value is a percentage of the difference between ink neutral densities (note that this is unlike the percentage in the Step Limit field, which is the difference between the color components making up a color). Enter zero percent to force InDesign to use a centerline trap for the entire length of the trap, or enter 100% to make InDesign apply a spread along the length of the boundary between the two gradients. Other values (such as the default 70 percent) apply sliding traps.

Image Settings. The controls in this section of the Edit Trapping Style dialog box define the way that InDesign traps InDesign page items to imported graphics. Note that "image," in the context of this dialog box, means any imported graphic—not just bitmaps.

Image Trap Placement. Choose Center to apply a centerline trap (see "Sliding Trap Limit," above) to the boundary between the InDesign object and the imported graphic. Choose Choke to extend the InDesign objects into the area inside the imported graphic. Choose Neutral Density to apply the trap based on the ink neutral density of the abutting colors. Choose Spread to spread the colors from the image into the InDesign object.

Trap Objects to Images. Turn this option on to apply automatic trapping to areas where InDesign objects abut imported images. InDesign uses the trapping method you chose from the Image Trap Placement pop-up menu to trap the objects (see above).

Trap Internal Images (In-RIP Trapping Only). Turn this option on to apply in-RIP trapping to areas of color inside imported bitmap images. Most scanned images (photographs) don't need trapping—this option is for synthetic images (such as screen shots) containing abutting areas of flat color. Turn this option off for faster trapping.

Trap 1-bit Images. Turn this option on to trap bilevel images to InDesign objects. This affects images you've applied colors to in InDesign.

4. Click the OK button to close the Edit Trapping Style dialog box and save your trapping options.

Trapping Ranges. If the pages in your publication have differing trapping needs, you can use trapping ranges to vary the trapping styles used to trap the publication. To do this, click the New button in the Trapping panel of the Print dialog box. InDesign displays the New Trapping Page Ranges dialog box (see Figure 9-14).

Select a trapping style from the Trapping Style pop-up menu, then enter the page range you want to trap using the style using the controls in the Ranges section of the dialog box.

FIGURE 9-14

Creating a trapping range

Click the New button (below the list of trapping ranges) to define a new trapping range. InDesign displays the New Trapping Page Ranges dialog box.

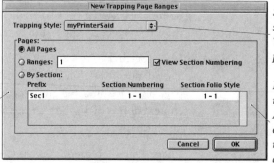

Select a trapping style from the Trapping Style pop-up menu.

Define a page range (click the All Pages option, enter a page range, or select a section).

Once you've created a trapping page range, turn it on by clicking the Enabled button in the trapping ranges list.

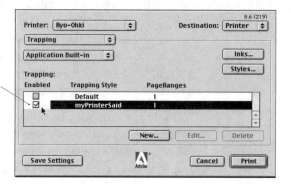

Editing Ink Neutral Densities. When you use either automatic trapping method, the trapping system (whether in InDesign or in a PostScript RIP) bases its trapping decisions on the inks used in abutting objects on an InDesign page. In general, the trapping system tries to spread lighter inks into darker inks. How can the system tell which inks are lighter or darker? By comparing the ink neutral density values between the objects.

In general, InDesign assigns ink neutral density values based on the CMYK values of the colors you've used in a publication. If you've used spot colors (inks), or have created colors using the RGB or LAB color model, InDesign uses the process color equivalent of the color.

Most of the time, this approach works pretty well. But I can think of three cases in which you might want to edit the ink neutral density values.

◆ Varnishes. A varnish should almost always be the lightest ink on the page, so set its ink neutral density to 0. This way, the trapping system will spread the varnish into abutting objects.

◆ Metallic Pantone inks. Metallic inks are more opaque than other inks, and they're also somewhat reflective. Spreading a metallic ink into an abutting area of some other color is almost certain to create an obvious trap. Set the ink neutral density of metallic inks to 1.7 (the value of black ink) or higher—that way, they will be considered the darkest ink on the page by the trapping system (and all other inks will spread into them).

◆ Pantone fluorescent inks. Like metallic inks, fluorescent inks are more opaque than other inks, and they're also very bright. In general, you want every other ink to spread into an area of fluorescent ink, so you set the ink neutral density to a high value. I think that 1.6 makes a good setting for fluorescent inks—that way, they'll spread into black areas, but most other inks will spread into the fluorescent ink.

◆ Pantone pastel inks. These are very light colors, and should be treated in much the same way as you'd treat a varnish. Set the ink neutral density value to .15—approximately the same value as that of process yellow ink.

To edit the neutral density value for an ink, follow these steps (see Figure 9-15).

1. Display the Trapping panel of the Print dialog box.

2. Click the Inks button. InDesign displays the Inks dialog box.

3. Select the ink you want to edit.

FIGURE 9-15
Adjusting ink
neutral densities

When you click the Inks
button in the Trapping panel,
InDesign displays the Edit
Trapping Inks dialog box.

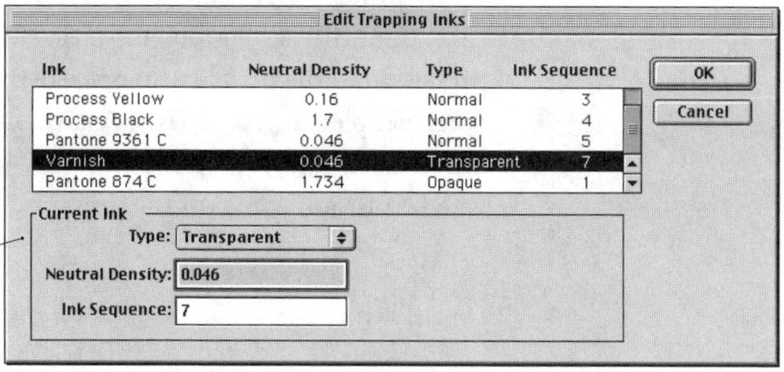

4. To set the ink type, choose an option from the Type pop-up menu. You use these options to declare to the trapping system that a specific ink doesn't follow the usual trapping rules. This can come in handy when you're working with certain types of spot inks: varnishes, Pantone metallic colors, Pantone fluorescent colors, and Pantone pastel colors. You can also control the inks trapping behavior by manipulating its ink neutral density, as in Step 5.

   ◆ Choose Normal for all process inks and for most spot colors.

   ◆ Choose Transparent for varnishes and very light spot inks (Pantone pastels, for example).

   ◆ Choose Opaque for very opaque inks, such as Pantone metallic or fluorescent colors.

   ◆ Choose Opaque Ignore for inks you want to have the trapping system ignore entirely.

5. Enter a new value in the Neutral Density field. Do this only if you've set the Type pop-up menu to Normal. Use this approach if your publication contains "specialty inks" (the ink types listed in Step 4) and you need to define the ways these inks trap to each other.

6. Click the OK button to close the Inks dialog box and apply your changes.

The Color "Done"

As you work with commercial printing, always remember that you're at the mercy of a series of photochemical and mechanical processes—from your imagesetter through the printing press—that, in many ways, haven't changed since 1900 (if that recently). Temperature, humidity, and ambient static electricity play large roles in the process, and the people who operate these systems are at least skilled craftspeople; at best, artists. Ask them as many questions as they'll answer, set your job up the way they want it, and then sit back and watch your job come off the press.

10

Printing

Printing is an ancient art, and has been invented and reinvented many times. You can print by rolling a carved cylinder over a sheet of wet clay, as the Mesopotamians did. Or you can smear a carved block of wood with ink and then press the block into a sheet of paper, as the Chinese started doing in the 8th or 9th century. With grease, water, and ink, even a slab of limestone can learn to transfer an image to paper, as Alois Senefelder of Munich found in 1798 (thereby inventing lithography).

Later, somebody (or, more likely, several somebodies) came up with moveable type—which, in turn, changed printing from a craft into an industry. Scribes the world over lamented the decline in the quality of written materials. The romance novel followed closely on the heels of this technological advance.

Printing—the ability to make dozens, hundreds, thousands, millions of copies of an image—flourished. For whatever reason, we humans will go to great lengths to get our pictures, text, and advertising into the hands of our willing or unwilling audience. In spite of the encroachments of the Web, printing is still the best way to do that.

A Brief Rant

To be entirely frank, InDesign takes a step backward in the design of its printing user interface. I don't mean that InDesign prints poorly (it doesn't), or that major printing capabilities are absent (they aren't, as far as I can tell). It's just that the process of printing a publication is more difficult, more of the time, than it is in other publishing programs (QuarkXPress, PageMaker, and FreeHand, for example). On the Macintosh, it's made even more difficult by strictures imposed by that system.

What makes me say this? InDesign's software designers chose to bind the program very tightly to the system's printer driver software. In other publishing programs you can choose a PPD without having to reconfigure the printer driver. But not in InDesign. In other programs, you can change output media (i.e., paper or film) sizes in the Print dialog box. But not in InDesign.

In my opinion, these two things—PPD choice and paper size—are decisions you make when it's time to print a publication, and should, therefore, be in the Print dialog box. Not in the Page Setup or Printer Properties dialog box. It should also be possible to make these choices without involving the printer driver. Printing to only one type of printer and to a single page size is something business users do—graphic arts professionals have to print to many different output devices.

Luckily, as I said, it does work, and has the features you need to produce your publications. It isn't bad—it's just a little less convenient than I think it should be. And, with the printer styles in InDesign 1.5, much of the inconvenience goes away.

Printing System Requirements

The *InDesign User Guide* states that InDesign *requires* a PostScript level 2 printer, but I've been able to print to PostScript Level 1 printers by installing and choosing the Microsoft PostScript printer driver on my Windows systems, and have been able to print to earlier PostScript printer (i.e., "LaserWriter 8") drivers on the Mac OS. I *think* that the *User Guide* is trying to tell you that you won't get all of InDesign's printing features if you use an older printer driver.

That said, InDesign *prefers* to print using the AdobePS 8.6 PostScript printer driver on the Mac OS, on the Windows side, you can use either the AdobePS 5.1 driver (in Windows NT4) or the AdobePS 4.3 driver (in Windows 98). On the Macintosh, InDesign 1.5

cannot print using a non-PostScript printer driver unless you download new versions of two plug-ins from adobe.com.

The InDesign Print Dialog Box   When you press Command-P/Ctrl-P, InDesign displays the Print dialog box. Never mind that it says "Printer 'printer name'" on the Macintosh instead of "Print." It's the Print dialog box and everybody knows it (or the Windows version of InDesign does, anyway).

Printing a Publication

The basic process of printing a publication is very simple. When you're ready to print, follow these steps.

1. If you're using a Macintosh, and want to print to a different paper size than the current default paper size, or if you can't remember what the current default paper size is, choose Page Setup from the File menu (or press Command-Option-P). You have to do this because there's no way to change the paper size within the Print dialog box. Checking first saves you the trouble of opening the Print dialog box, realizing that you need to change or check the paper size, cursing, and then closing the Print dialog box. If you're the type who might also punch the monitor, your desk, or a co-worker, this step can also save you bruised knuckles.

2. If you're not using a Macintosh (or if you are and you're certain that the paper size selected in the Page Setup dialog box is correct), Choose File>Print (or press Command-P/Ctrl-P) to display the Print dialog box.

3. Select a printer from the list of installed printers (on the Macintosh, you'll find the printer on the Printer pop-up menu; in Windows it'll appear on the Name pop-up menu). You do not need to go to the Choose (on the Macintosh) or to the Printers control panel (Windows) to select a printer.

4. Set up printing options using the panels of the Print dialog box (including, if you're a Windows user, the printer and paper setup options in the Properties dialog box for the printer). Most of the rest of this chapter will be spent discussing the meaning and intent of these options.

5. Click the OK button to print your publication.

General Printing Controls

There's a difference between the layout of the Windows Print dialog box (in Windows 2000, Windows 98, and Windows NT) and the corresponding dialog box on the Macintosh—in the Windows version, the Number of Copies and Collate options are always visible, regardless of which panel (or tab) you have displayed. On the Macintosh, these controls are in the General panel. On both platforms, the printer name and destination are constant (see Figure 10-1).

FIGURE 10-1

Print dialog box(es)

To view another panel of the Print dialog box, choose the panel name from the Panels pop-up menu, or press Command-Down Arrow or Command-Up Arrow to move to the next or previous panel (respectively).

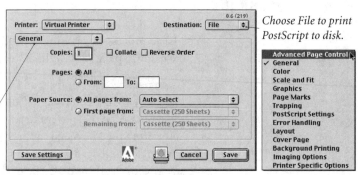

Choose File to print PostScript to disk.

Macintosh Print dialog box

Panels pop-up menu

Windows Print dialog box

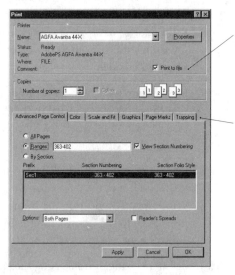

Turn on the Print to File option to print PostScript to disk.

To view another panel of the Print dialog box, click the appropriate tab.

Printer/Name   Select the printer you want to print to from the Printer pop-up menu (on the Macintosh) or the Name pop-up menu (in Windows). When you select a printer, the printer driver changes the options displayed in the panels of the Print dialog box to reflect that printer's capabilities (as defined by the PPD). You should, therefore, always select the printer first, before changing any other settings.

Print to File   Most of the time, you'll probably send your pages to a printer, but you can send the same stream of PostScript (it's just text) to a file. To do this on the Macintosh, turn on the File option; in Windows, turn on the Print to File option. If you're printing to a Virtual Printer (on the Macintosh) or to a printer on FILE (in Windows), you'll print to disk regardless of the state of this option. For more on printing PostScript to disk, see "Printing PostScript to Disk," later in this chapter.

Copies   Enter the number of copies of the page you want to print here. You can print up to 9999 copies of your publication. On the Macintosh, this option appears in the General panel of the Print dialog box.

Collate   When you turn on the Collate option, InDesign prints the range of pages you've specified (in the Advanced Print Control panel), in order, for each copy of the publication you print. This makes for much slower printing. When you print multiple copies of a page, your printer only needs to process each page once (and then prints multiple copies of the page using the same image); when you turn on the Collate option, your printer must process each page once for every copy of the print job.

Save Settings/Apply   On the Macintosh, you can click the Save Settings button to close the Print dialog box and save the current settings. In Windows, click the Apply button, and then click Cancel to close the dialog box.

Page Setup (Macintosh)/Properties (Windows)

On the Macintosh, a number of important printer setup choices are inside the Page Setup dialog box (choose Page Setup from the File menu)—which is a shame, because you can't open the Page Setup dialog box from inside the Print dialog box (as you can in Windows). If you frequently print to different paper sizes, you'll probably need to get in the habit of opening the Page Setup dialog box before you print—just to check the paper size (see Figure 10-2).

In the Windows Print dialog box, you can click the Properties button to display the basic setup of the selected printer (see Figure 10-3). The options in the Properties dialog box for the selected printer are very similar to those found in the Page Setup dialog box on the Macintosh. You use these options to define the paper size and orientation, polarity (positive or negative), and other options you want to use to print your publication.

FIGURE 10-2
Page Setup
(Macintosh Only)

Choose PageSetup from the File menu (or press Command-Shift-P) to display the Page Setup dialog box—where you'll find some important (and some not-so-important) printing options.

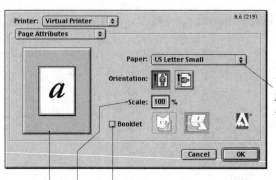

The most important option here: paper (or film) size.

Paper/page preview

This field is overridden by the controls of the Scale and Fit pane of InDesign's Print dialog box.

You can choose to print your publication as an imposed booklet—provided the page size of your publication and the paper size you've chosen allow it—but you won't be able to print color separations if you do.

A less important option—which still might be useful: "watermarks" are graphics or text that print on some or all pages of a print job. You can customize the text used in the watermark by selecting the Text option and then clicking the Edit button...

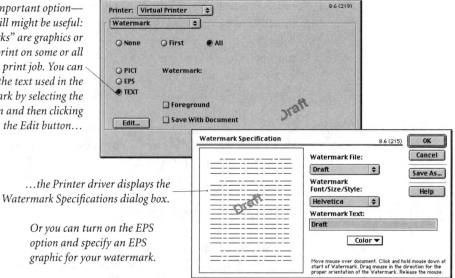

...the Printer driver displays the Watermark Specifications dialog box.

Or you can turn on the EPS option and specify an EPS graphic for your watermark.

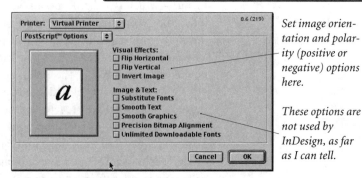

Set image orientation and polarity (positive or negative) options here.

These options are not used by InDesign, as far as I can tell.

FIGURE 10-3
**Printer Properties
(Windows only)**

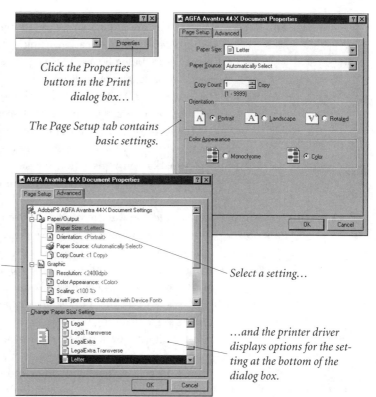

*Click the Properties
button in the Print
dialog box...*

*...to display the Printer
Properties dialog box. The
options in this dialog box
control paper (or film) size
and other printer-specific
properties.*

*The Page Setup tab contains
basic settings.*

*The Advanced tab contains a
more detailed set of printer
capabilities. All of the commands found in the Page
Setup tab are duplicated in
the Advanced tab.*

Select a setting...

*...and the printer driver
displays options for the setting at the bottom of the
dialog box.*

The options you see in the Page Setup panel of the Printer Properties dialog box are determined by the paper sizes and paper source
entries in the PPD for the selected printer.

Who's on First?   If you've been exploring the Page Setup (Macintosh), Printer Properties (Windows), and Print dialog boxes, you've probably noticed
that a number of the controls are duplicated in different places.

Some of the time, changing one of the controls changes the other.
When you enter a value in the Copies field of the Printer Properties
dialog box in Windows, for example, the printer driver will enter
that value in the Copies field of the Print dialog box.

In other cases, one control overrides another during the printing process *without* changing the settings visible in the dialog boxes.
You can find controls for Scaling in the Page Attributes panel of
the Page Setup dialog box (Macintosh) or in the Advanced panel of
the Printer Properties dialog box (Windows)—but the feature also
appears in the Scale and Fit panel of the Print dialog box. In this
example, InDesign ignores the controls in the Page Setup (Macintosh) or Printer Properties (Windows) dialog boxes when similar or
identical controls exist in the panels of the Print dialog box.

Page and Paper   When I talk about page size, I'm talking about the page size you've defined for your publication using the New Document or Document Setup dialog boxes. This page size should be the same as the page size of the printed piece you intend to produce. "Paper size," on the other hand, means the size of the paper or film you're printing on. There can be a big difference between these two sizes.

Try to print your publication on a paper size that is no larger than the publication's page size, unless you need printer's marks (crop marks and registration marks). For more on page size and paper size, see "Paper Size," later in this chapter.

Creating a Custom   Why would you want to create a custom paper size? It's simple—to
Paper Size   save time and money. If you're working at an imagesetting service bureau, you know that imagesetting film and processing chemicals cost money. And that if you can reduce the number of square inches of film or ounces of chemicals you use you'll have more cash left over to spend on the outrageously expensive equipment your customers are demanding you buy.

In addition, a basic concept of PostScript printing is that increasing paper size increases the amount of printer memory required to print your pages. Your jobs will print faster if you use a paper size that's no larger than your publication's page size plus any printer's marks you plan to use (which add about 60 points in each dimension).

Not all PostScript printers support custom paper sizes, but most imagesetters do. If you try to create a custom paper size and receive the PostScript error "Offending command undefined: 'setpageparams,'" your printer can't create custom paper sizes (you can still feed it any physical sheet of paper you can fit into its manual feed slot; but you can't print to the printer using a custom paper size).

To create a custom paper size in Windows, follow these steps (see Figure 10-4).

1. Open the Print dialog box and select a printer capable of printing on custom paper sizes.

2. Select PostScript Custom Page Size from the Paper Size pop-up menu. (Note that these user interface items are not only inconsistent with my terminology—they're inconsistent with each other, as well.) When you select this option, the printer driver displays the PostScript Custom Page Size Definition dialog box.

3. Enter the width, height, and paper feed direction, and other options for your custom paper size. Note that the printer driver

FIGURE 10-4

Creating a cutom page size in Windows

Click the Properties button.

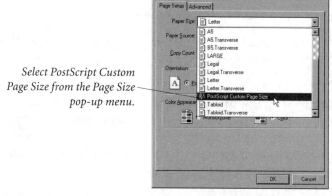

Select PostScript Custom Page Size from the Page Size pop-up menu.

Set up the custom paper size you want. If you plan to print printer's marks, don't forget to make the paper size a little larger than the publication's page size.

When you choose PostScript Custom Page Size, you'll print to the paper size you defined.

Note: These screen shots are from Windows NT4; Windows 2000 and Windows 98 dialog boxes are similar.

To view or edit the paper dimensions, click the Advanced tab, then select the paper size and click the Edit Custom Page Size button to return to the Custom PostScript Page Size dialog box.

displays the minimum and maximum paper sizes to the right of the width and height fields (in the current measurement units—you can change the units using the options in the Units section). In general, the Paper Type option is determined by the PPD you've selected. For printers that can accommodate custom paper sizes, there's probably no need to enter offset distances in the Perpendicular and Parallel Direction fields.

4. Click OK to set the properties for the custom paper size.

Does anyone see a shortcoming of this approach? The printer driver limits the number of custom paper sizes available per printer driver instance: one in Windows NT, or three in Windows 98 and 2000. If you're a busy imagesetting service bureau with a need for lots of custom paper sizes, you'll still need to create an edited PPD.

To create a custom paper size on the Macintosh, follow these steps (see Figure 10-5).

1. Open the Page Setup dialog box (choose Page Setup from the File menu or press Command-Shift-P).

2. Choose the printer from the Printer pop-up menu.

3. Choose Custom Page Default from the main pop-up menu. The printer driver displays the Custom Page Default dialog box.

4. Enter the width and height for your custom paper size. Note that you can view the minimum and maximum values for various paper attributes from the PPD Limits pop-up menu. For printers that can accommodate custom paper sizes, there's probably no need to enter offset distances in the Perpendicular Direction and Parallel Direction fields.

5. Enter a name for the paper size in the Custom Page Name field.

FIGURE 10-5
Creating a custom paper size on the Macintosh

Choose Custom from the Paper pop-up menu in the Page Attributes panel of the Page Setup dialog box.

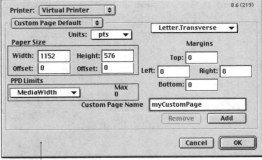

Choose Custom Page Default from the Panels pop-up menu. The printer driver displays the Custom Page Default panel (this panel is not available until you select Custom from the Paper pop-up menu).

Set up the custom paper size you want. If you plan to print printer's marks, don't forget to make the paper size a little larger than the publication's page size.

The new page size appears on the Paper pop-up menu.

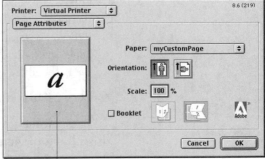

The printer driver displays a preview of the selected paper size.

6. Click Add to add the custom paper size. The name of the custom paper size appears on the paper size pop-up menu.

You can repeat this process to add more custom paper sizes to the printer type (there doesn't seem to be a limit to the number of custom paper sizes you can add—I've added more than 30). To delete a custom paper size, select the paper size name from the paper sizes pop-up menu, then click the Remove button (below the Custom Page Name field).

Advanced Page Control

I'm not sure what makes this panel more "advanced" than the others, but it's where you specify which pages you want InDesign to print (see Figure 10-6).

Page Ranges   Turn on the All Pages option to print all of the pages in the publication. To print a range of pages, turn on the Ranges option. Enter the page range in the Ranges field as shown in Table 10-1.

You can mix and match page ranges. To print pages one, three, six through ten, and 20, for example, you'd enter "1,3,6-10,20." The pages and ranges you specify must be in order (you couldn't, for example, print page 20 before printing page six), and you can't print a page twice in a single pass by entering the page number twice.

To print one or more sections of the publication, turn on the By Section option and select the sections you want to print from the list of sections. To select a continuous range of sections, hold down Shift as you click the items in the list; to select a non-continuous range, hold down Command/Ctrl as you click the sections.

TABLE 10-1
Printing page ranges

To print:	Enter:	Example:
A continuous range of pages	first page - last page	12-21
Up to a specific page	-last page	-5
From a page to the end of the document	first page -	5-
Non-contiguous pages	page, page	1, 3
Mixed page ranges		-3, 6-9, 12, 15-

FIGURE 10-6

Advanced Page Control

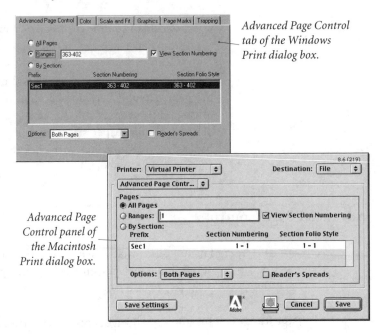

Advanced Page Control tab of the Windows Print dialog box.

Advanced Page Control panel of the Macintosh Print dialog box.

When you turn on the View Section Numbering option, you can specify a page in the Ranges field by entering section markers. For example, if you want to print pages 1 through 4 of a section you've named "FrontMatter," and pages 2 through 7 of the section "BodyPages," you'd enter "FrontMatter:1-4, BodyPages 2-7". If you don't turn on the View Section Numbering option, you'd have to enter these pages numbers using absolute numbering. If you turn this option off, you'll get an error message if you enter section markers in the Ranges field. This option affects the display of the page numbers shown in the Sections list.

Options   To print even and odd pages, turn on the Both Pages option; to print even pages, turn on the Even Pages Only option; and to print odd pages, turn on the Odd Pages Only. These options affect all page ranges, including page ranges you've entered in the Ranges field. If you've turned on the Reader's Spreads option, these options will be unavailable.

Readers Spreads   When you turn on the Readers Spreads option, InDesign tries to print each spread in the publication on a single sheet of paper (or other output media). If the spread is larger than the selected paper size, turn on the Scale to Fit option in the Scale and Fit panel of the Print dialog box and/or change the paper orientation.

Color

Do you want to print a composite version of your publication, or do you want to print separations? If you want to print separations, which inks to you want to print? Those are the questions you answer using the Color panel of the Print dialog box (see Figure 10-7).

Composite/Separations   Turn on the Composite option to print a grayscale or color rendition of your publication (if you're printing to a local laser printer, you'll see the colors represented by shades of gray; if you're printing to a color printer, you'll get color), or turn on the Separations option to print color separations.

If you turn on the Separations option, InDesign activates the Inks list and its associated controls (the In-RIP and Print This Ink options and the All to Process, Print All Inks, and Print No Inks buttons) and changes the options on the Screening pop-up menu.

Screening   What halftone screen frequency (in lines per inch) and screen angle do you want to use to print your publication? If you're printing a composite, you can choose either the printer's default (which is defined by the PPD you selected) or you can enter values in the Screen Frequency and Angle fields. When you do this, the Screening pop-up menu changes to read "Custom."

FIGURE 10-7
Color

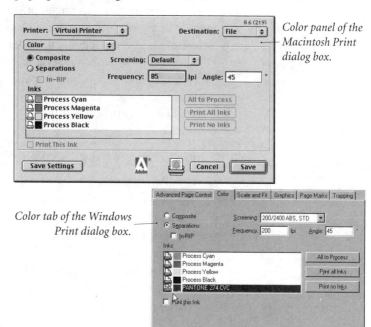

Color panel of the Macintosh Print dialog box.

Color tab of the Windows Print dialog box.

When you're printing separations, you'll see more choices on the Screening pop-up menu, and the values shown in these fields change as you select inks in the Inks list. Where the heck are these choices and values coming from? They're coming from the PPD. Every PPD contains a list of screen frequencies and screen angles optimized to avoid moiré patterns on the specific PostScript device described by the PPD. Because of the way that PostScript halftoning (or any digital halftoning, for that matter) works, a PostScript RIP cannot perfectly "hit" just any halftone screen.

On PostScript Level 1 devices, the screen angle and screen frequency you'd get would sometimes fail to match the frequency and angle you specified. This often resulted in serious output problems and severe moiré patterns. PPDs list combinations of screen angles known to be safe for a given printer at a given screen frequency and angle.

While the need for these optimized screen angles has diminished somewhat with newer versions of PostScript, I strongly advise you to stick with them when you're printing separations.

To override the optimized screen settings for an ink, select the ink in the Inks list and then enter new values in the Screen Frequency and Angle fields. Again, I don't recommend this, but you might have a very good reason for doing so that I simply haven't thought of yet.

The optimized screen angles only cover the process inks, however. When your publication includes spot inks, InDesign sets the screen angle of every spot ink to 45 degrees.

For spot-color work—especially where you're overlaying tints of two spot colors or using duotones from Photoshop based on two spot inks—you need to specify the screen angles appropriately. Here's how to set them.

◆ If the spot inks *never* interact, set the screen angle for the inks to 45 degrees (because a 45-degree screen is the least obvious).

◆ If you're creating lots of two-ink tint builds, or using duotones, you have a few choices, and two (somewhat contradictory) goals. You want both colors to print as close as possible to 45 degrees (especially the dominant, or darker, color), and you want as much separation between the angles as possible (the greater the separation between angles—45 is the maximum possible—the less patterning is visible where the screens interact). Table 10-2 lists some options.

TABLE 10-2 Screen angles for spot color work	Subordinate:	Dominant:	Notes:
	15	45	Traditional. Only a 30-degree separation, but neither angle is very obvious on its own.
	0	45	Avoids patterning. Ideally, the ink printed at zero degrees is a very light color—otherwise, the horizontal bands of halftone dots will be too obvious.
	22.5	67.5	The complete compromise. Both angles are more obvious than 45 degrees, but less obvious than 0, and you get the full 45-degree separation to avoid patterning.
	75	30	The dominant color screen is slightly less obvious than the subordinate screen. Full 45-degree separation.

◆ If you're printing with two spot inks and are not printing with process inks, use the default screen angles for Magenta and Cyan from the optimized screen you've selected.

Inks   When you turn on the Separations option, InDesign activates the Inks list. In this list, you'll see at least the four process inks (yes, they'll appear even if you aren't using process colors in your publication), plus any spot inks you've defined.

When you select an ink in the Inks list, InDesign displays the halftone screen properties for that ink in the Frequency and Angle fields (see "Screening," above).

Click the All to Process button to convert all of the spot inks in the Ink list to process colors. The colors created by this method are *simulations* of the spot inks, and probably won't match the spot colors you applied to objects in the publication (some colors are easier to simulate than others are). Clicking this button does not change the definitions of the colors in your publication—it only changes the way that they print. After you've clicked the button, the button's title changes to Revert to Spot. Click the Revert to Spot button to restore the spot inks to the Inks list.

Click the Print All Inks button to set all inks to print, or click Print No Inks to turn off printing for all of the inks in the Ink list.

Select an ink and turn on the Print This Ink option to make the ink print—or double-click the printer icon that's to the left of the ink name in the Inks list. Don't worry about inks that aren't used in your publication—InDesign will not generate a blank separation for them. If, for example, your publication uses only black ink and a spot ink, InDesign will not create separations for Cyan, Magenta, and Yellow, even though those inks appear in the Inks list.

Turn on the In-RIP option if the selected printer can create color separations (some PostScript Level 3 RIPs, such as Agfa's Taipan 3.0 software RIP, can do this) and if you want the RIP to do the work of color-separating your publication. If the PPD indicates that the RIP you've selected does not have the ability to create color separations on its own, InDesign will display an error message when you turn on this option.

Scale and Fit

If you want to enlarge or reduce your pages as you print them, or if you want to print an oversized publication (relative to your printer's paper sizes) as a series of tiles, or if you just want to view the way your publication fits on the selected paper, choose Scale and Fit from the Print dialog's pop-up menu (Macintosh) or click the Scale and Fit tab (Windows) to display the Scale and Fit panel of the Print dialog box (see Figure 10-8).

FIGURE 10-8
Scale and Fit

Turn off the Constrain Proportions option to scale the vertical and horizontal axes independently—this can help compensate for the distortions imposed by the flexographic printing process.

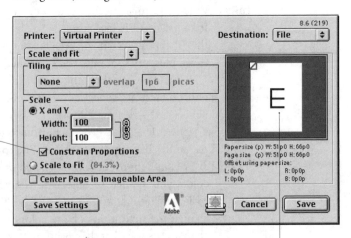

The page preview shows how the publication page fits on the selected paper.

Tiling   If your pages just won't fit on your paper, you've got to resort to tiling and (horror of horrors) tape, wax, or glue. InDesign offers two ways to tile documents—Automatic and Manual.

Automatic Tiling. When you choose this option, InDesign starts the tile at the upper-left corner of the page, and prints as much of the page as it can given the paper size. Then it starts the next tile, with an overlap as specified in the Overlap field. It goes across the page, then moves down the page by the height of the paper you're printing on (again allowing for overlap), and then goes across the page again.

At the bottom of the page preview, InDesign tells you how many tiles will be required to print each page. If you find that it's producing *lots* of tiles per page, try reducing the overlap. If you're just tiling together a proof, a slight reduction in the scaling percentage could save you a lot of time with scissors and tape.

Manual Tiling. When you choose Manual tiling, InDesign only prints one tile per piece of paper, using the zero point on the ruler as the upper-left corner of the tile. To print successive tiles, you have to move the zero point and print again.

I find manual tiling much more useful than automatic tiling—automatic tiling always seems to split the tiles right in the middle of an important text block, so you can't read it. Or, worse, splits a large image or other tinted area—have you ever tried cutting and pasting to get the halftone dots in a photograph to line up? With manual tiling, you can ensure that items that you want to be able to proof are positioned so they're easy to see and read.

Tiling: Just Say No. Now it's time for pure, unadulterated (no adults were used), talk-radio-style opinion. Any time anyone tells me that they plan to tile a publication, my sense of honesty and fair play forces me to ask them why they want to do that. Is it a masochistic streak they've had since childhood? A profound sense of personal inferiority? Something genetic?

If you can't find some way to print your publication without tiling, then use a copy camera or other photographic process to enlarge it to the size you want, rather than printing tiles and then trying to paste the printed tiles together. If you don't know if such a service is available in your area, get out the Yellow Pages. Even if you have to send the publication across the country to get it blown up to the size you want, do it. Sure—these services do cost money. But what's your time—or your sanity—worth?

Scale   You can scale the output of your pages, from as small as one percent to as large as 1000 percent of their actual size. You can specify a scaling percentage yourself, or ask InDesign to fit the page on the paper.

X and Y   Turn on the X and Y option to enter scaling percentages in the Width and Height fields. You can enter scaling percentages from 1 to 1000 percent. When you use large percentages, watch the print preview to see that the enlarged page will fit on the paper you've selected.

If you're printing using a commercial printing process that distorts the printed images (flexography, for example, typically stretches the image axis that's parallel to the rotation of the printing cylinder), you can compensate for the distortion by entering different values in the Width and Height fields. To do this, turn off the Constrain Proportions option, then enter the percentages you want in the Width and Height fields. When the Constrain Proportions option is turned on, any changes you make in one field are reflected in the other.

Scale to Fit   When you turn on the Scale to Fit option, InDesign calculates the scaling percentage necessary to fit the page (plus any printer's marks you selected in the Page Marks panel of the Print dialog box) onto the selected paper size, and uses that scaling percentage when you print the publication.

Center Page in   The "imageable area" of a printer is the area of the paper (for a given
Imageable Area   paper size) on which the printer can print. If you've done much snooping in PPD files, you've probably noticed a peculiarity: the imageable areas of some printers are not regular. They might be six points from the edge of the paper on the left, and twenty-four points off on the right, and other distances at the top and bottom of the sheet. These distances are sometimes imposed by the printing engine's hardware; sometimes by the printer's software. But they always add up to a set of hidden "margins" you won't know about until you try to print.

Why would you want to center the printed page in the imageable area of a piece of paper, rather than centering the page on the paper? I'm not sure—maybe you want to see a detail at the edge of your page that's being clipped off? Whatever your reason, you can reach your goal by turning on the Center Page in Imageable Area option.

Print Preview   InDesign displays a preview of the way your page fits on the selected paper size in two of the panels in the Print dialog box (the Scale and Fit panel and the Page Marks panel). This preview does not include a preview of the elements on your pages, unlike the print preview features found in Word, Excel, Illustrator, or FreeHand. The previews, however, do provide feedback that can save you from printing pages in the wrong orientation or printing pages that won't fit on the paper.

InDesign displays additional information below the print preview—such as the paper size, the page size, and the page offsets (values showing how much smaller—or larger—the page is than the selected paper). If the page is larger than the paper, InDesign displays the offset values in red.

These two preview windows are the only places in the Print dialog box where you can find the size of the paper you're printing on. To change it, you'll have to return to the Page Setup dialog box (Macintosh) or the Printer Properties dialog box (Windows—at least you can get to this on without having to close the Print dialog box).

Graphics

The options in this panel control the way that InDesign prints the fonts and graphics in your publication (see Figure 10-9).

Send Image Data   The Send Image Data pop-up menu affects what InDesign does with bitmaps in TIFF, JPEG, Paint, and other explicitly bitmapped file formats. It has no effect on images inside imported EPS or PDF graphics.

Do you want to print that 30-megabyte color scan every time you proof a document on your laser printer? Probably not. The Send Image Data popup menu gives you four options to control what InDesign does with images when you print. (If you want to prevent *all* imported graphics from printing, use the Proof Print option, which I'll describe later in this chapter.)

All   Use this option when you want InDesign to send all of the image data from the image file to the printer. I recommend that you always use this option when printing the final copies of your pages.

Optimized   This option tells InDesign to only send as much information from
Subsampling   the image as is necessary to produce the best quality on the given

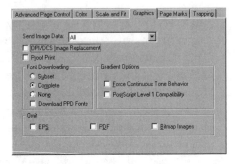

output device using the current settings. It reduces the amount of data that has to be passed over the network and imaged by the printer. It can speed up printing immensely.

How InDesign pares down the data depends on whether the image is color/grayscale or black and white.

◆ **Color/Grayscale images.** As I mentioned in Chapter 7, "Importing and Exporting," there's no reason for the resolution of grayscale and color images (in pixels per inch) to exceed two times the halftone screen frequency (in lines per inch). When you choose Optimized Subsampling from the Send Image Data pop-up menu, InDesign reduces the resolution of grayscale and color images to match the halftone screen frequency you've selected (in the Color panel of the Print dialog box). If you've set up a 75-line screen (for instance), InDesign won't send more than 150 dots per inch of image resolution. Note that InDesign does not change the resolution of the images in your publication—it just reduces the amount of data that's sent to the printer.

◆ **Black-and-white (bilevel) images.** When you're printing bilevel, black-and-white images, and have selected Optimized Subsampling from the Send Image Data pop-up menu, InDesign matches the images it sends to the resolution of the output device. So if you've got a 600-pixels per inch black-and-white TIFF, and you're printing on a 300-dpi laser printer, InDesign reduces the resolution of the image to 300 pixels per inch before sending it to the printer. For those who really want to know, InDesign gets the printer's resolution from the DefaultResolution keyword in the PPD.

The real value of the Optimized setting lies in laser-proofing jobs that are destined for high-resolution (hence high halftone screen frequency) output. If you're producing a job that will be printed with a 133-lpi screen, for instance, you may be working with images that have resolutions of 250 ppi. But for proofing on a 600-dpi laser printer (which has a 85-lpi default screen frequency), you only need 106 dpi—maximum. By subsampling to this lower resolution, InDesign is sending *less than one fifth* of the information over the wire. Obviously, this can save you a lot of time. With high-resolution line art, InDesign might send only a sixteenth of the data.

Printing an image using the Optimized Subsampling option produces a more detailed printed image than using the Low Resolution option, but doesn't take as long to print or transmit as the full-resolution version of the image.

While Optimized Subsampling might sound like the universal cure for perfect (speedy, high quality) printing, it isn't. Subsampling, by its nature, blurs and distorts images, especially in areas of high contrast. Therefore, I think you should use this option for proof printing, but not for printing the final copies of your pages.

Low Resolution

Choose Low Resolution from the Send Image Data pop-up menu to have InDesign send only the preview images it displays on your screen to the printer. Again, this is an option to use when you're printing proof copies of your pages, not for final output.

OPI/DCS Image Replacement

When you're printing through an OPI server, you can direct the server to replace the low resolution images you've used to lay out your document with the high resolution images you've stored on the server. To do this, turn on the OPI/DCS Image Replacement option as you print. This omits the images from the PostScript output, leaving only the OPI link information in their place.

To retain OPI image links to images stored inside imported EPS graphics, make sure that you turn on the Read Embedded OPI Image Links option in the EPS Import Options dialog box.

Proof Print

When you print with the Proof Print option turned on, InDesign prints all of the imported graphics in your publication as boxes with Xs through them. As you'd expect, this makes it print faster. Proof printing is great when you're copy-editing the text of a publication— why wait for the graphics to print?

Note that you can speed things up a bit, without completely eliminating the graphics, by using the Low-Resolution or Optimized Subsampling options on the Send Image Data pop-up menu. Also, note that you can turn off the printing of a particular type of imported graphic using the Omit EPS/PDF/Bitmap Images options in the Graphics panel of the Print dialog box.

Font Downloading

One of the best ways to speed up InDesign's printing is to manage dowloaded fonts sensibly. You can save many hours over the course of a day, week, or month by downloading fonts in advance, and by understanding how InDesign handles font downloading.

The basic concept is pretty simple: Fonts can be either "resident" (which means that they're stored in your printer's memory or on a hard drive attached to the printer) or "downloadable" (which means they're stored somewhere on your system or network).

When you print, InDesign checks the printer PPD to see if the fonts are available on the printer. If the font is available, InDesign sends a reference to the font, but does not send the font itself, which means that the text will be printed in the font available on the printer.

What happens when a font is not available in the printer's memory or on its hard drive? That depends on the option you've chosen in the Font Downloading section of the Graphics panel of the Print dialog box.

When you turn on the None option, you're directing InDesign to refrain from including any fonts in the PostScript it's sending to the printer (or to disk). If text in your publication has been formatted using fonts that are not resident on the printer, that text will be printed using the printer's default font (usually Courier).

When you choose the Complete option, InDesign checks the state of the Download PPD Fonts option. If this option is on, InDesign sends all of the fonts used in the publication to the printer's memory. If the option is turned off, InDesign downloads all of the fonts used in the publication that are not listed in the PPD (PPDs contain lists of fonts available on a given make and model printer, plus any you've added by editing the PPD). InDesign downloads the fonts once for each page that's printed. As you'd expect, this increases the amount of time it takes to send the job to your printer.

To decrease the amount of your printer's memory that's taken up by downloaded fonts, or decrease the amount of time it takes InDesign to send the fonts to your printer, turn on the Subset option. When you do this, InDesign sends only those characters required to print the publication. This can speed up printing tremendously.

Gradient Options

Turn on the Force Continuous Tone Behavior when you're printing to a dye-sublimation color printer, or turn on PostScript Level 1 Compatibility if you're printing to a PostScript Level 1 device.

Omit   When you turn on the EPS option in this section, you're telling InDesign not to print any EPS graphics in your publication. The PDF and Bitmap Images options do the same thing for imported EPS graphics and TIFF images, respectively.

Page Marks

When you print your publication, you can choose to include (or exclude) a number of printer's marks—crop marks, registration marks, and other information (see Figure 10-10).

All Printer's Marks   Turn on the All Printer's Marks option when you want to print all of the printer's marks and page information.

Type   Now here's an intriguing option—a pop-up menu offering only "Default" as a choice. The idea is that developers will be able to add different printer's marks at some point. I haven't seen any yet.

Page Information   Turn on the Page Information option to print the file name and date of your publication on each printed page or separation. This makes it easy to tell which of several printed versions is the most current. It can also make it easier for your commercial printer to tell which pieces of film in a stack of separations go together (it's easy for you to tell, but put yourself in their shoes for a minute). If the paper size is smaller than the page size, InDesign won't print the file name and date.

Bleed Marks   Turn on the Bleed Marks option to print lines outside the area of your page that define the area of the bleed. If your paper size is not larger than your page size, InDesign won't print your bleed marks.

FIGURE 10-10
PageMarks

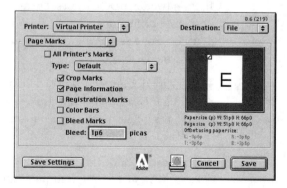

Crop Marks   Turn on the Crop Marks option to print lines outside the area of your page that define the area of the page. If your paper size is not larger than your page size, InDesign won't print your crop marks.

Registration Marks   When you turn on the Registration Marks option, InDesign prints little targets around the edge of your page for your commercial printer to use when they're lining up, or registering, your color separations for printing. If your paper size is smaller than your page size, InDesign won't print the registration marks.

Color Bars   When you turn on the Color Bars option, InDesign prints small squares outside the bleed area of your printed page. Your commercial printer can use these samples to calibrate and adjust their press as they print the publication.

Bleed   The value you enter in the Bleed field sets the real boundary of the printed page. When the value in the Bleed field is zero, InDesign neatly clips off any page elements extending beyond the edges of the page. This leaves little room for error in trimming the resulting printed pages—usually, when you want a page element to bleed off of a page, you should allow at least 24 points of bleed to compensate for inaccuracies in printing and trimming.

Print Preview   The preview window displays the effect (given the current page and paper sizes) of your choice of printer's marks options.

Trapping

The Trapping panel of the Print dialog box (see Figure 10-11) contains controls for InDesign's automatic trapping features—both built-in (where InDesign does the trapping) and in-RIP (where your PostScript printer does it).

Choose one of the following trapping options from the Trapping pop-up menu.

◆ Off. Use this option if you're done all of your trapping manually (using InDesign's fills and strokes) or if you plan to separate and trap the publication using a post-processing program (such as Adobe InProduction—see Color Figure 10).

◆ Application Built-In. Choose Application Built-In when you want InDesign to trap your publication as it's sent to the printer (or to disk).

FIGURE 10-11

Trapping

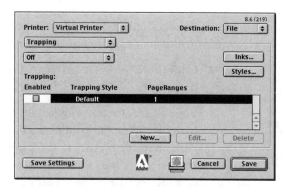

◆ Adobe In-RIP. Turn this option on when you want to leave trapping up to the PostScript Level 3 RIP in your printer or imagesetter.

If you've chosen Application Built-In or Adobe In-RIP trapping, you can specify trapping settings using the Inks dialog box (click the Inks button) or select or create a trapping style (click the Styles button). Again, refer to Chapter 8, "Color" for more on working with InDesign's trapping controls.

Printer Styles

I don't know about you, but I find I print a typical InDesign publication (at least) three different ways. I print a proof copy on my laser printer, a color proof on a color printer, and then I print my final copies on an imagesetter. In the first two instances, I print composites; when I print to an imagesetter, I typically print color separations. In InDesign 1.0, this process was painful—for each type of printing, I had to claw my way through the settings in the Print dialog box (and, on the Macintosh, the Page Setup dialog box).

In InDesign 1.5, however, I can define printer styles for each type of printing I do—which means that switching from proof to final printing is as easy as selecting the appropriate printer style.

Printer styles are like paragraph styles—they're bundles of attributes that can be applied in a single action. All of the attributes in the Print dialog box and in the Page Setup (Macintosh) or Printer Properties (Windows) dialog boxes are included in a printer style.

Creating a Printer Style   To create a printer style, follow these steps (see Figure 10-12).

1. Use the Print (and, on the Macintosh, Page Setup) dialog boxes to set printing options the way you want them.

2. Choose Define from the Printer Styles submenu of the File menu. InDesign displays the Define Printer Styles dialog box.

3. Click the New button. InDesign displays the New Printer Style dialog box.

4. Enter a name for the printer style, then click the OK button. InDesign opens the Print dialog box (it'll be filled in with the current printing settings). Click the OK button. InDesign returns you to the Define Printer Styles dialog box and adds the new printer style to the list of available printer styles.

To print using the settings in a printer style, choose that style name from the Printer Styles submenu of the File menu. InDesign displays the Print dialog box. Click the Print button (or the Save button, if you're printing to disk), and InDesign will print the specified pages.

To print without displaying the Print dialog box, hold down Shift as you choose the printer style name from the Printer Styles submenu.

Managing Printer Styles

You can use the Define Printer Styles dialog box to add printer styles, delete printer styles, rename printer styles, edit printer styles, or import or export printer styles.

◆ To add a printer style that is not based on the current print settings, open the Define Printer Styles dialog box, click the New button, enter a name for your new style, and then work your way through the panels of the Print dialog box to set up the printer style.

◆ To create a new printer style that is based on an existing printer style, open the Define Printer Styles dialog box, select a printer style, and then click the New button. Enter a name for your new printer style, then modify the settings in the panels of the Print dialog box. Note that this does not link the two printer styles—changes made to the "parent" printer style will not affect any printer styles you've based on it. It is, however, a little less tedious than working your way through all of the printing controls just to change a single setting.

◆ To delete a printer style, select the printer style name and click the Delete button.

◆ To export printer styles, select the style names and click the Export button. InDesign displays the Export Printer Styles

FIGURE 10-12

Creating a printer style

Set up the panels of the Print dialog (and Page Setup dialog box) the way you want them...

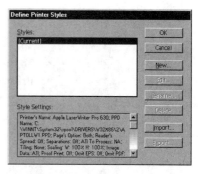

...choose Define Style from the Printer Styles submenu of the File menu.

InDesign displays the Define Printer Styles dialog box. Click the New button.

Enter a name for the new printer style and click the OK button.

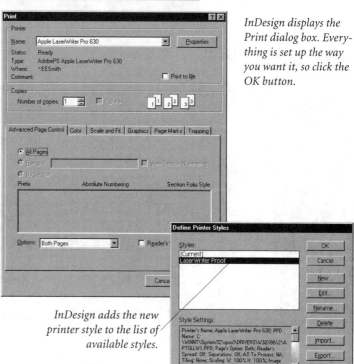

InDesign displays the Print dialog box. Everything is set up the way you want it, so click the OK button.

InDesign adds the new printer style to the list of available styles.

To print using the printer style, choose the style name from the Printer Styles submenu of the File menu.

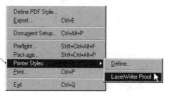

Hold down Shift if you want to print without displaying the Print dialog box.

dialog box. Specify a file name and location for the printer styles document and click the OK button.

◆ To import a printer style or set of printer styles, open the Define Printer Styles dialog box and click the Import button. InDesign displays the Import Printer Styles dialog box. Locate and select a printer styles document (or an InDesign publication containing printer styles), then click the OK button. If the printer styles you're importing already exist in the publication, InDesign will create copies of the styles (InDesign will append a number— usually "1"—to the duplicate printer styles).

◆ To rename a printer style, select the printer style name in the Define Printer Styles dialog box, then click the Rename button. InDesign displays the Rename Printer Style dialog box. Enter a new name for the printer style and click the OK button

InDesign and PPDs

PostScript Printer Description files (PPDs) describe your printer to InDesign and to your printer driver. PPDs are not, and should not be confused with, printer drivers—even though the printers drivers used with InDesign blur this distinction. Printer drivers are pieces of software that direct information from your system and applications to a hardware port—usually, your computer's printer port or network connection.

PPDs work in conjunction with printer drivers to give applications information about the printer (what paper sizes are available? what's the resolution of the printer? what do the printer error messages mean?) and to customize the printer's operation for the application (what PostScript routine does the application use to render halftones?).

InDesign and other applications use PPDs to optimize printing for a specific printer.

Rewriting PPDs   You can edit your PPDs to add custom page sizes, to add new sets of screen angles, to download PostScript routines automatically, and to do a variety of other things.

Editing PPDs   According to the Adobe PostScript Printer Description File Format Specification (version 4.3), the "official rulebook" of the PPD format, you're supposed to avoid directly editing the content of a PPD.

Instead, you're supposed to create a new PPD that includes the content of the PPD for your printer, then overrides parts of that content with your custom information or adds new features to the PPD.

The only trouble is—it doesn't work with the printer drivers that work with InDesign. All of them—AdobePS5.1 for Windows NT systems, AdobePS4.3 for Windows 98 systems, and AdobePS 8.6 for the Macintosh—lack the ability to use the "Include" keyword.

This means that you'll have to create your own PPD—usually by editing a copy of an existing one.

If you make changes to your custom PPD after you've chosen it in the Print Setup dialog box, you may have to switch to another PPD and back again to get the printer driver to update the information in the Print and Page Setup dialog boxes to reflect changes you've made to the PPD.

What's in a PPD?

Table 10-3 (on the following pages) is a listing of some of the keywords you'll see when you open a PPD file. I haven't tried to cover every keyword and entry you'll find in a PPD, mainly because InDesign doesn't use all of them, and because you can always refer to the PDF Specification on adobe.com.

InDesign uses PPDs conforming to version 4.0 of the Adobe PPD specification. If you can't see your PPD in the list of available PPDs, you've probably got an old PPD. You can probably find a new one at Adobe's web site.

Adding Custom Paper Sizes to PPDs

The main reason to edit PPDs is to add custom paper sizes. If you find yourself entering the same numbers in the Page Size dialog box over and over again, it's a job for custom page sizes. Once you've added a custom page size to a PPD file, the size appears on the Paper Size pop-up menu when the PPD file is selected.

If you're creating your publications on page sizes other than the paper size of the printed piece, stop (unless you're creating signatures, or have some other good excuse). Remember that paper size equals printer RAM—your jobs will print faster if you use a paper size that's no larger than your publication's page size plus crop marks (which adds about 60 points in each dimension).

You can add custom paper sizes to PPDs for any printer that can accept variable page sizes. Usually, imagesetters can accept variable page sizes and laser printers can't.

To add a custom paper size to a PPD file, follow these steps.

1. Open the PPD with your word processor or text editior.

TABLE 10-3   PPD Keywords

Keyword	Example	What is it?
*PSVersion	`*PSVersion: "(2013.108)"`	Version of PostScript in the printer's ROMs. Change this value if your printer has a different PostScript version than that listed in the PPD.
*DefaultResolution	`*DefaultResolution: 2400x2400dpi`	Default resolution of the printer. If you usually run your printer in a different resolution than the one you see here, change the resolution here.
*Resolution	`*Resolution 1200x1200dpi: "1200 statusdict /setresolution get exec"`	Sets the resolution of the printer, for those printers capable of switching resolutions via software commands (imagesetters, mostly). If you don't know the routine to change the setting on an imagesetter (they're all different), leave this value alone and change the resolution from the imagesetter's control panel.
*ColorDevice	`*ColorDevice: False`	Tells InDesign whether the selected printer is a PostScript color printer or not.

*FreeVM	`*FreeVM: "992346"`	Amount of the printer's virtual memory (VM) InDesign can work with before having to flush fonts, etc. If you know your printer has more—or less—memory available, increase or decrease this value. Usually, a printer's startup page shows you how much VM the printer has available. If yours doesn't—or if you've turned off the printer's startup page and don't feel like turning it on again—download the following code (your printer will print a page with the memory amount on it):
		`%%show FreeVM`
		`/Helvetica findfont`
		`12 scalefont setfont`
		`72 72 moveto`
		`/memString 256 string def`
		`vmstatus exch sub memString cvs show`
		`showpage`

*Password	`*Password: "0"`	Provides a password for the printer. Do not change this, or if you do, make sure you remember the password.

TABLE 10-3   PPD Keywords (continued)

Keyword	Example	What is it?
*FileSystem	*FileSystem True	Lets InDesign know if the selected printer has a hard disk. If this value is "True", InDesign checks the printer's hard disk for downloadable fonts before looking for them on the current system. If you have a hard disk attached to your printer, set this keyword to "True"; otherwise, leave it at "False."
*ScreenAngle	*ScreenAngle: "45"	Sets the default screen angle the printer uses to print halftones. Change this value if you want a different default screen angle for your printer. Any setting you make to the halftone settings in the Color panel of the Print dialog box overrides this value.
*DefaultScreenProc	*DefaultScreenProc: Dot	Sets the default halftone screen drawing procedure for the printer.
*ScreenProc	*ScreenProc Dot	Halftone screen drawing procedures for the printer. If you enter a different dot shape here, make sure you specify it using the DefaultScreenProc keyword.
*ScreenFreq	*ScreenFreq: "120"	Sets the screen frequency the printer uses to print halftones. If you don't like it, change it. Haftone screen frequency settings you make in the Color panel of the Print dialog box overrides this value.
*DefaultTransfer	*DefaultTransfer Normalized	Sets the default transfer function for the printer.
*DefaultPageSize	*DefaultPageSize: Letter	Sets the default paper size for your printer. The keyword for the paper size corresponds to the name of a defined paper size existing either in the printer's ROMs or in the PPD file. See the section "Adding Custom Page Sizes to PPDs," earlier in this chapter.
*PageSize	*PageSize Letter: "letter"	Sets up a paper size. If your printer has variable page sizes (imagesetters usually do; laser printers usually don't), this entry could be: `*PageSize Letter.Extra: "statusdict begin 684 864 0 1 setpageparams end"`

TABLE 10-3   PPD Keywords (continued)

Keyword	Example	What is it?
*DefaultPaperTray	*DefaultPaperTray: None	If you have a printer with more than one paper tray, change this to the tray you want as your default. The tray selection for your printer is defined in the "*PaperTray" section of the PPD.
*PaperTray	*PaperTray Letter: "statusdict begin lettertray end"	Defines available paper trays for your printer.
*DefaultImageableArea	*DefaultImageableArea: Letter	Sets the default imageable area (the area inside a paper size that the printer can actually make marks on) for the printer. The available imageable areas for your printer are set up using the "ImageableArea" keyword.
*ImageableArea	*ImageableArea Letter.Extra: "0 1 684 864"	Sets up the imageable area for a defined page size (in the example, a page size named "Letter.Extra").
*DefaultPaperDimension	*DefaultPaperDimension: Letter	Sets the default paper dimension for the printer. You set up paper dimensions using the "*PaperDimension" keyword.
*PaperDimension	*PaperDimension Letter.Extra: "684 864"	Sets up the paper dimension for a specific page size (in the example, a page size named "Letter.Extra"). Enter the width and height of the paper, in points. For a wide orientation page, the entry would read: "*PaperDimension Letter.Extra.Wide: "864 684"
*VariablePaperSize	*VariablePaperSize: True	Tells InDesign whether your printer can accept variable paper sizes. Most imagesetters can; most laser printers can't. If your printer can accept variable paper sizes, you'll be able to enter a custom paper size in the Custom Page Size Default dialog box (Macintosh) or PostScript Custom-Page Size Definition dialog box (Windows) and print to whatever size of paper you want (within the imagesetter's capabilities).

TABLE 10-3   PPD Keywords (continued)

Keyword	Example	What is it?
*VariablePaperSize (continued)		You can also add your own custom page sizes to PPDs of printers capable of accepting variable page sizes. Changing this value from "False" to "True" does not give your printer the ability to accept variable page sizes.
*DefaultInputSlot	*DefaultInputSlot: Lower	Sets the default paper feed for your printer, if your printer has more than one input slot. The available input slots are set up by the entries in the "*InputSlot" keyword.
*InputSlot	*InputSlot Lower: "statusdict begin 1 setpapertray end"	Defines the available input slots for your printer.
*DefaultManualFeed	*DefaultManualFeed: False	Makes manual feed the printer's default paper feed. Don't change this unless you habitually use your printer's manual feed.
*ManualFeed	*ManualFeed True: "statusdict begin /manualfeed true store end"	Sets up the printer's manual feed mechanism, if it has one.
*Font	*Font Times-Bold: Standard "(001.002)"	Lets InDesign know that a font is resident in the printer. Add fonts to this list if you're sure they're going to be on your printer's hard disk or memory. If InDesign does not find the font name in this list, it will download the font to the printer. To add a font to the list, type: *Font: PostScriptFontName: Standard "(001.001)" The PostScript name of the font can be a bit tricky to figure out. The best way to do it is to create a text block containing the font in InDesign and print the file to disk as PostScript or create an EPS. Then open the file with a text editor and look at the way InDesign cites the font names at the beginning of the file. The numbers following the font name are the font type and the font version. Most downloadable PostScript fonts are Type 1 (or

TABLE 10-3   PPD Keywords (continued)

Keyword	Example	What is it?
*Font (continued)		"001"). Unless you know the font version, just enter "001" for the version.
*DefaultFont	*DefaultFont: Courier	Defines the default font for your printer. This is the default font that gets used if InDesign can't find the font used for text in your publication. If you're tired of Courier, you can change it to any other printer-resident font you want.

2. In the section of the template file reserved for custom code, enter three lines defining your new page size. The lines are shown below. Variables you enter are underlined.

```
*PageSize PageSizeName: "statusdict begin x y offset orientation end"
*ImageableArea PageSizeName: "0 0 x y"
*PaperDimension : "x y"
```

PageSizeName is the name you want to use for your custom page size. This name should not have spaces in it.

x is the width of the custom page size, in points (if you're an inch monger, just multiply the inch measurement by 72 to get the distance in points).

y is the height of the custom page size, in points.

Offset is a value used to offset the paper size from the edge of the imagesetter's paper (or film) roll. This value should almost always be zero.

Orientation is either "1" or "0". "0" means normal orientation (with the height of the paper being measured along the length of the imagesetter's paper roll, and type in normal orientation printing across the roll); "1" means transverse (where the width of the paper is measured along the length of the imagesetter's paper roll). Here's a custom page size for a 576-by-1,152-point (eight-by-16-inch) paper size with a normal orientation.

```
*PageSize PageSizeName: "statusdict begin 576 1152 0 0 end"
*ImageableArea PageSizeName: "0 0 576 1152"
*PaperDimension PageSizeName: "576 1152"
```

3. Save the file as a text-only file, adding the ".ppd" file extension. Name the file something like "my_new_page_size.ppd."

4. Create a new instance of the printer driver using the edited PPD.

The new paper sizes should appear in the Paper pop-up menu (in the Page Setup .

Printing PostScript to Disk

When you print a publication, InDesign directs a stream of Post-Script code to your PostScript printer. This code, for the most part, is simply text made up of commands that tell the PostScript interpreter in your printer how to draw the objects on the pages. But you don't have to print to a printer—instead, you can direct the same PostScript commands and data to disk. This is called "Printing PostScript to disk," and it's a great way to save yourself time, trouble, and money.

Printing your pages to disk as PostScript offers the following advantages.

◆ The publication is "frozen" as it is on your machine. When you take the PostScript file to another system for printing, you don't have to worry about fonts or linked images—you don't even have to worry about whether the other system has InDesign installed.

◆ When you compress a PostScript file (using Zip or StuffIt compression), the file can shrink significantly in size, making it easier to transport or send via email.

◆ PostScript files are a good way to deliver your publication to an imagestting service bureau for print (see the next section).

◆ You can edit the PostScript with a word processor to learn about InDesign's PostScript, fix printing problems, add special design effects, or just goof around.

InDesign offers two different methods for printing a file to disk as PostScript: device-specific, and non-device-specific. If you know the type of printer or imagesetter you'll be printing to, and if you rely on some aspect of that printer (the ability to print on custom paper sizes, for example), use the Print dialog box to print device-specific PostScript to disk. If you *don't* know what printer you'll be printing on, or don't care about any special features of that printer, then export the file using the Prepress File export format. If you want to print separations to disk, use the device-specific PostScript route—prepress files are not separated (though you can separate them using a separation utility).

Device-Specific PostScript

When you want to print your publication (or pages from your publication) to disk as device-specific PostScript, choose File from the Destination pop-up menu on the Macintosh, or turn on the Print to File option in Windows (both options are in the Print dialog box).

When you've set all the printing options you want, click the Save/OK button. The Create File/Print to File dialog box appears.

Enter a name for the file, choose a drive and directory to save it to, and click the OK button.

Prepress File

When you want to save your publication file using a generic Post-Script format—which might be required by a the post-processing program you'll be using to prepare the file for printing—you can export the file as a prepress file. This format includes everything needed to print the file, but does not include printer-specific information. To save a range of pages as a prepress file, follow these steps (see Figure 10-13).

1. Choose Export from the File menu. InDesign displays the Export dialog box.

2. Enter a name and set a location for the file, then select Prepress File from the Format/Save As Type pop-up menu.

3. Click the Save button. InDesign displays the Export Prepress File dialog box.

4. Set up the export options you want in the two panels of the Export Prepress File dialog box (the options control image handling, font downloading, page ranges, and printer's marks), then click the Export button. InDesign creates a prepress file.

Preparing an InDesign File for Imagesetting

I've listened long and carefully to the grievances of imagesetting service bureau customers and operators. I've heard about how this designer is suing that service bureau for messing up a job, and I've heard imagesetter operators talking about how stupid their clients are and how they have to make changes to the files of most of the

FIGURE 10-13

Exporting a publication as a prepress (generic PostScript) file

Choose Export from the File menu. InDesign displays the Export dialog box.

Choose Prepress File from the Formats (Macintosh) or Save As Type (Windows) pop-up menu.

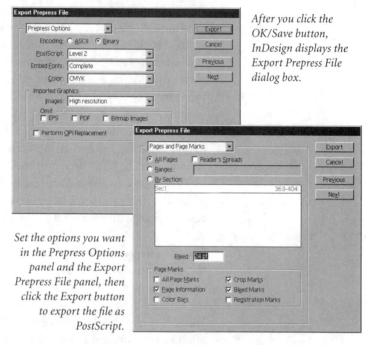

After you click the OK/Save button, InDesign displays the Export Prepress File dialog box.

Set the options you want in the Prepress Options panel and the Export Prepress File panel, then click the Export button to export the file as PostScript.

jobs that come in. I've listened long enough, and I have only one thing to say.

Cut it out! All of you!

There's no reason that this relationship has to be an adversarial one. I don't mean to sound harsh. I just think that we can all cooperate, to everyone's benefit.

Designers: You have to learn the technical chops if you want to play. That's just the way it is. The technical challenges are no greater than those you mastered when you learned how to use a waxer, an X-Acto knife, or a copy camera.

Your responsibility to your imagesetting service bureau is to set your file up so that it has a reasonable chance of printing and to communicate to your service bureau exactly how it is you want your publication printed (or, if you're delivering a PostScript file or PDF, to make sure that the settings in the file are correct).

Service bureau folks, you've got to spell out the limits of your responsibility. If you don't think you should be fixing people's files, don't do it. If you do think it's your responsibility, tell your customer up front you'll fix the files, and tell them what you'll charge for your time. And if you get customers who know what they're doing, give them a discount. This will encourage everyone else.

Okay, back to the book.

If you know what you're doing, one of the best ways to prepare your publication for printing at an imagesetting service bureau is to print a PostScript file to disk (the other best way is to deliver a PDF, provided your service bureau has Adobe InProduction). If you've set up your printing options correctly, the file will include everything that is needed to print the publication. This way, all your service bureau has to do is download the file—they won't need to open the file, set the printing options, or link to any images included in the file. The only things that can go wrong are related to film handling and processing—the wrong film's used, the film's scratched, or the film's been processed incorrectly.

This means, however, that you have to be dead certain of the printing options you want before you print to disk, because it's difficult to change things after that. Look out for the following:

Links to images. Make sure that any linked graphics in the publication are up to date, and that any embedded graphics are what you want them to be.

Tiling. If you're not tiling, make sure tiling (manual or automatic) is off. If you are, make sure you're tiling the way you want to. If you're using manual tiling, you'll have to print a separate PostScript file to disk for each tile you want to print.

Scaling. It's easy to forget that you've scaled things for printing on your proof printer. Make sure that this is set to the scaling you want (generally 100 percent).

Separations/Composite. If you want to get separations from your service bureau, make sure you choose Separations in the Print dialog box. An obvious point, but I've forgotten it at least once.

Printer Type. If you don't choose the right printer type, your publication may not print, and may even crash the service bureau's imagesetter. They hate this, so install a printer (a "virtual" printer on the Macintosh, or a printer on "FILE" in Windows) that matches their device. You might check with the service bureau to see if they have a custom PPD they'd like you to use.

Paper Size. Pick a paper size at least large enough to contain your page. If you're printing separations, pick a page size that's at least 60 points wider and taller than your page size so that printer marks (crop marks and registration marks) can be printed. Also make sure that you understand the page orientation you're working with—wide or tall; normal or transverse.

Printer's Marks. If you're printing separations, you can live without separation names and the file's name and date, but you've *got* to have the crop marks and registration marks if you want your printer to speak to you again. I turn them all on most of the time.

Negative/Positive Emulsion Up/Down. Are you printing negatives or positives? Emulsion up or down? Set it here.

Inks. Which inks do you want to print? If you don't set them to print here, don't look askance at your service bureau when you don't get an overlay/separation for the ink. If you don't want an ink to print, make sure you turn it off or expect to pay for an additional piece of film.

Preflight and Package

Are all systems "go?" Do you know the number of kilometers, meters, and centimeters it'll take to get your publication safely in orbit around Mars? Or is it miles, feet, and inches?

Preflight   To make sure that your publication is really ready for "prime time," you use the Preflight plug-in (choose Preflight from the File menu). When you do this, InDesign examines the publication for missing fonts, lost image links, and other conditions that might cause you problems and/or embarrassment when you take your publication to an imagesetting service bureau for printing. After it's done analyzing the publication, it displays the results in the Preflight dialog box (see Figure 10-14).

Package   Once your publication has successfully passed the preflight check, you can assemble all of the files needed to print the publication using the Package plug-in (this is similar to QuarkXPress' "Collect

FIGURE 10-14

**Preflight testing
a publication**

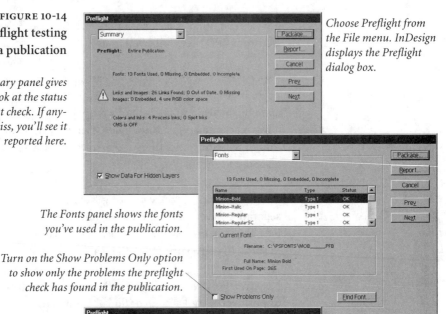

*Choose Preflight from
the File menu. InDesign
displays the Preflight
dialog box.*

*The Summary panel gives
you a quick look at the status
of the preflight check. If anything is amiss, you'll see it
reported here.*

*The Fonts panel shows the fonts
you've used in the publication.*

*Turn on the Show Problems Only option
to show only the problems the preflight
check has found in the publication.*

*This icon means trouble—in
this case, several images
saved using the RGB color
model that have not yet had
a color profile attached to
them.*

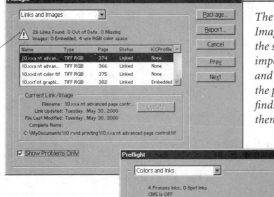

*The Links and
Images panel shows
the status of
imported graphics—
and any problems
the preflight check
finds with any of
them.*

*The Colors and Inks panel shows lists the
colors and inks used in the publication.*

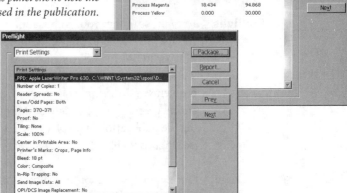

*The Print Settings panel pro-
vides a report on the current
printing settings.*

for Output" feature, or PageMaker's "Save For Service Provider" plug-in). To "package" a publication, follow these steps (see Figure 10-15).

1. Choose Package from the File menu. InDesign runs a preflight check on the publication and then displays the Printing Instructions dialog box.

2. Enter contact information in the Printing Instructions dialog box—this information will appear in the report (it's a text file) InDesign will add to the package you're creating.

3. Click the Continue button. InDesign displays the Package Publication dialog box. Set the options you want and enter a name for the folder that will contain the packaged publication.

    When you turn on the Copy Fonts or Copy Linked Graphics options, InDesign copies the files to the folder you specify.

4. Click the Package button. InDesign creates the folder and copies the publication and the files you specified into it.

FIGURE 10-15
Packaging a publication for remote printing

When you choose Package from the File menu (or click the Package button in the Preflight dialog box), InDesign displays the Printing Instructions dialog box.

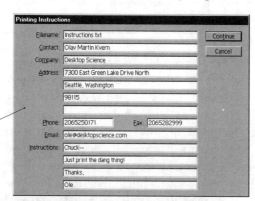

Enter your contact information and any notes you want to include in the fields— these instruction will be saved as a text file.

After you click the Continue button, InDesign displays the Package Publication dialog box.

Enter a name and location for the package (the publication file and any other files you choose to copy).

Choose the files you want to copy to the package folder.

If you're copying fonts, InDesign displays this message.

Printing to Non-PostScript Printers

When you print to a non-PostScript printer, what you get depends on the printer driver. Most of the time, InDesign objects and type print very well, thanks to InDesign's internal drawing model, the Adobe Graphics Manager (AGM). The printing options available also depend on the printer driver—you won't see any of the panels (Advanced Page Control, Color, or Trapping, for example) described earlier in this chapter in the Print dialog box (see Figure 10-16).

FIGURE 10-16
Non-PostScript Print
Dialog Box

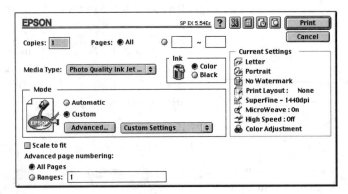

Macintosh Non-PostScript Printing. InDesign 1.5 for the Macintosh shipped without the ability to print to non-PostScript printers, but Adobe has just (as I write this) released updated versions of two InDesign components—AGM.rsrc and AGMLIB+Plugin—that add this capability. Download these from adobe.com (they're currently at http://www.adobe.com/support/downloads/829a.htm, but this URL is subject to change), then put them in your InDesign folder (you might want to back up the existing files before you do this). Restart InDesign, and you'll be able to print to your non-PostScript printer.

All the News that Prints to Fit

Printing is all about thinking ahead. From the time you press Command-Shift-N/Ctrl-Shift-N to create a new publication, you really should be thinking "How the heck am I going to print this thing?" By the end of the production process, you'll be tired, cranky, and less able to deal with any problems that come up—so make your decisions about paper size, color selection, and graphic file types as early as you can.

Scripting

Most of the time, we tell a program (an application, a plug-in, or our system software) what to do by manipulating the program's user interface—we click, drag, and type. Scripting is a way of telling a program to perform the same tasks and accomplish the same things. The difference is that, with scripting, we don't have to click the buttons, type the characters, or choose the menu items. The script does it for you. Scripting is what computing is supposed to be *about*: having your computer take over boring, repetitive tasks so that you can spend more time playing *Oni*. Er, I mean, concentrating on your creative work.

Scripting also gives you the ability to add the features you need to InDesign *now*, rather than waiting for Adobe to give them to you. Even better than that, scripting gives you a way to customize InDesign to match your publications and habits to a degree that Adobe is *never* going to provide.

I'm convinced that the reason many people have not taken up scripting is that they're scared. They think scripting is difficult, and is only for people with advanced computer science degrees. And they tell themselves that they're too "intuitive" and "artistic" to master the minimal analytical skills required to write a script.

Look. I'm practically a high school dropout, and my background is in illustration, not computer science. I have never taken a single class on programming. As a rebellious teenager I did my best to ignore the sciences and to panic at the sight of even simple equations (in psychoanalytical terms this makes sense: my father was a high school algebra teacher).

I got over it. These days, I write scripts. You can, too.

System Requirements

What do you need to write and run scripts for InDesign? Two things:

- The standard scripting system for your computer.

- The InDesign scripting documentation and example scripts.

Macintosh   On the Macintosh, all you need is AppleScript. You might or might not have it installed, but you've certainly already got it—it comes on the Mac OS installation CD. If you can't find your installation CD, you can download AppleScript directly from Apple (http://www.apple.com/applescript). What's the easiest way to tell if it's installed? In the Finder, search for a file named "Script Editor" (this is the application you use to write and run AppleScripts). If you can't find it, you'll have to install it from the CD.

A number of alternative script editors are available—and, if you're planning to do serious scripting, I strongly recommend you take a look at Scriptor, from MainEvent Software (http://www.mainevent.com) and ScriptDebugger, from Late Night Software (http://www.latenightsw.com). If you want to build user interfaces for your AppleScripts, you'll probably want to get FaceSpan (http://www.facespan.com/core.html).

Windows   On the Windows side, you've got a number of options. There are (at least) three slightly different scripting systems claiming to be the system standard: Visual Basic Script (VBScript), Visual Basic for Applications (VBA), and Visual Basic (VB). They're all from Microsoft, and they're all variants of the Basic programming language. All of them work.

The Cheapest Option: VBScript. Get the Windows Scripting Host if you don't already have it. To find out if the Windows Scripting

Host is installed on your machine, search for "wscript.exe." If you find this program, your machine is equipped with the Windows Scripting Host and can run VBScripts; if not, go to http://msdn.microsoft.com/scripting/ and download and install the program. Once it's installed, you can write scripts using your word processor or text editor.

This approach, while inexpensive, has a few drawbacks.

◆ The example scripts on your InDesign CD and in the Scripting Guide PDF were written using Visual Basic, not VBScript, and there are a number of differences between the scripting methods. You will not be able to use most of the scripting examples without modifying them.

◆ Troubleshooting (debugging) VBScripts can be difficult. You're not in a sophisticated programming environment (as you would be if you were using Visual Basic), and you can't step through the lines of your script. All you can do is run the script and then note any error messages that appear.

◆ It's hard to build user interfaces in VBScript.

Something You Might Already Own: VBA. If you own Microsoft Excel, Microsoft Word, Microsoft Access, or Visio, you already own a copy of VBA. If you plan to write scripts to move data from these programs to InDesign (Access for database publishing, for example), you might want to simply write VBA scripts to control InDesign from inside these programs. The disadvantages are similar to those of VBScript—you won't be able to use the examples from the Scripting Guide verbatim; you'll have a harder time troubleshooting your scripts, and you'll have a harder time building user interfaces than you would in Visual Basic.

Not Quite Free, but Worth Every Penny: Visual Basic. The last claimant to the title of "Windows Scripting Standard" is Visual Basic, and it's an 800 pound gorilla of a contender. Visual Basic is a complete programming environment capable of building applications of the size and complexity of InDesign itself. C++ programmers reading that last assertion might scoff—let them. They've got their jobs and esoteric knowledge to protect, after all. But the truth is that Microsoft has improved the lowly and ancient programming language Basic to the point that it can hold its own with the most modern, object oriented languages.

All of the Windows scripting examples on the InDesign CD were written in Visual Basic. This means it's easy to base your scripts on the examples—you can copy the examples right out of the PDF (we didn't lock it against text copying) and paste them into Visual Basic subroutines. It's easy to construct dialog boxes and other user interface items in Visual Basic, and the environment offers powerful debugging tools.

While some Visual Basic packages are very expensive, all you need to learn and use InDesign scripting is the Visual Basic Learning Edition, which is usually available for under $100.

If You Cannot Run the Visual Basic Scripts: It's because your system lacks the required Visual Basic resources. Go to http:// support.microsoft.com/support/downloads/ and search for the file "VBRUN60.EXE" (I'd give you an exact URL, but Microsoft keeps moving the file around). Download and install this package—it contains everything you need to get the scripts working on your system.

Learning about InDesign Scripting

Once you've gathered and installed the software you need to start scripting, you need to learn about how InDesign implements scripting. You're in luck—you'll find the *Adobe InDesign Scripting Guide* in the Scripting folder inside the Adobe Technical Information folder on your InDesign CD. This is a PDF file that contains an introduction to scripting, reference chapters for AppleScript and Visual Basic, and dozens of scripting examples (it's more than 250 pages long). In addition, you'll find eleven example scripts in the same folder. Even if you don't intend to write scripts of your own, you might find something useful in the example scripts:

◆ AddGuides. Draws guides around the currently selected object or objects. This script shows you how to get positioning information back from InDesign, and how to create ruler guides.

◆ CreateIndex. Creates a simple index by taking all of the words tagged with the character style "Index," adds the page number, and then creates a new publication containing a sorted list of the index entries. You can copy the text out of the new publication and paste it into the original document, or you can save the new document as your index. This script shows you how to traverse the stories in a document looking for text formatting attributes (in this example, the character style "Index"), how to extract text from a story, how to get the current page number from a text selection, and how to sort text alphabetically.

◆ CreateTOC. Creates a simple table of contents by extracting the text of all paragraphs formatted using the paragraph styles "heading 1," "heading 2," and "heading 3," and placing the text (and page number) in a new text frame in a new publication. The script also applies styles as it builds the table of contents. This script shows you how to traverse the stories in a document looking for text formatting attributes (in this example, the paragraph styles), how to extract text from a story, how to get the current page number from a text selection, and how to create and apply new paragraph styles.

◆ Neon. Creates a simple "glow" effect by duplicating the selected path or paths. Each copy of the path is slightly smaller than the original, and slightly lighter. The final duplicate path is a white hairline. The resulting group of paths is something like an Illustrator blend.

◆ RandomFill. Draws an number of rectangles, ellipses, or polygons and pastes them inside the selected path. You can control the object type, size, color, and stroke weight. This is a great script for quickly generating a random background for your publications.

◆ WordCount. Displays a count of the words in the selection.

◆ PathEffects. If you've used Illustrator, you've probably played with the path effects "Bloat" and "Punk." This script includes those path effects, as well as a few others. If you want to learn about scripting InDesign paths, path points, and control handles, this is a good place to start.

◆ FitFrameToText. InDesign can fit a frame to the frame's content—but only when that content is a graphic. If it's a text frame, the only way you can resize the frame to fit the text is to manually resize the frame. Unless you use the FitFrameToText script. When you run FitFrameToText on an unlinked text frame, the script resizes the frame so that it is no bigger than it needs to be to accommodate the text it contains. If the selected frame contains overset text, InDesign will attempt to increase the height of the frame to accommodate the text.

- CreateCharacterStyle. When you create a character style in InDesign by basing the style on the selected text, InDesign records only those attributes that differ from the default formatting of the surrounding text. While this is a powerful and flexible way of working with character styles, its also different from the way that other applications (QuarkXPress, FrameMaker) work. In those applications, character styles apply every formatting attribute. The CreateCharacterStyle script creates a new character style based on the selected text and defines every formatting attribute.

- TabUtilities. This script automates two tasks: setting a right tab stop at the right margin of a paragraph, and setting a left tab at the current cursor position. Select some text in a single-column text frame, then click the Tab at Right button to set a tab stop at the right edge of the text column (this will also remove any existing tab stops in the paragraph). Click the Tab at Cursor button to set a left tab at the current cursor position.

- SelectObjects. Selects all of the objects on a spread that belong to a specific object type (or set of types). This script is only slightly useful by itself, but it shows you how to traverse the objects on a spread to find objects based on their type or content. As such, it's a great starting point for any graphic "search and replace" operation you might want to implement. Want to make sure that all of the graphics in your publication are scaled to the same percentage or use the same color management profile? Modify this script (as shown below).

I wrote the *Scripting Guide* and the example scripts—they're not perfect (I forgot to account for paragraph space before and after in the FitFrameToText script, for example), but I do think that they:

- Add features to InDesign.

- Are fairly easy to read and understand.

- Demonstrate important InDesign scripting concepts.

- Provide a good base for scripts of your own.

- Are in some cases goofy and kind of fun. Who says scripting has to be dull?

Or that's what I was trying to do, anyway. The following are a couple of additions to the *Scripting Guide*.

Set and Copy (AppleScript)

AppleScript has two different methods for assigning an object to a variable: *set* and *copy*. These two commands do very different things. In the Scripting Guide, I used set almost exclusively, but now I think I should have used copy for some examples. Why? Let's look at an example.

```
Tell application "InDesign"
Set mySpread to active spread of active window
--Imagine that text frame 1 begins with the text
--"Sailors always welcome ladies…"
Set myWord to word 1 of text frame 1 of mySpread
Set myString to "British " & text contents of myWord
Set text contents of myWord to myString
--Text now reads "British Sailors always welcome ladies…"
--myString now contains "British"
End tell
```

If, instead, you had used *copy*:

```
Tell application "InDesign"
Set mySpread to active spread of active window
--Imagine that text frame 1 begins with the text
--"Sailors always welcome ladies…"
Copy word 1 of text frame 1 of mySpread to myWord
Set myString to "British " & text contents of myWord
Set text contents of myWord to myString
--Text now reads "British Sailors always welcome ladies…"
--myString contains "Sailors"
End tell
```

Variables whose values are assigned using *set* are dynamic: when the object they refer to changes, their values change as well. When you use *copy* to assign a value, that value is "frozen" and remains the same regardless of the state of the original reference.

On a Slightly Sheepish Note

The example scripts for Windows include Visual Basic projects— the source code you'll need if you want to base a script of your own on one of the examples. Due to naming convention differences between me (I put spaces in filenames) and Adobe's version control software (it doesn't understand spaces in filenames), some of the projects can't find their attendant forms. If you try to open a project and get a "Form not Found" error, simply add the form you'll find in the same folder as the project file.

Well, while we're here, we might as well run through the list of other problems with the example scripts:

◆ The PathEffects script will produce asymmetrical results when the action of the script moves some of the points beyond the edges of the pasteboard.

◆ The Neon script on both platforms *seems* to leave a number of the objects making up the glow selected. The objects are actually grouped together, but InDesign has forgotten to update the screen (in other words: it's not my bug). Redraw the screen (press Shift-F5) to see the correct selection.

Thinking about Scripting

Because scripting is a great tool for automating large, repetitive tasks, many of us think that that's *all* it's good for. But there's far more to scripting than that. Scripting is also good at little things— operations that might save you only a few seconds a day, but can make your work easier or more precise.

By "little things," I means scripts that save you only a few mouse clicks, drags, or key presses at a time. It's these tiny tasks, repeated in their dozens, hundreds, or even thousands day by day, that add up to fatigue, irritation, and repetitive motion injuries. When you take a common task that involves some number of actions and replace it with a simple double-click or keystroke (all it takes to run a script), you reduce the difficulty and complexity of your work.

Scripting, which many of us think of as being somehow *opposed* to the creative process, can be a powerful creative tool. I often imagine effects I'd like to use in a publication layout that would be difficult to accomplish by hand. When there's time, I turn to scripting for help. Frequently, in the course of working on a script, I'll find a variation on the effect that leads me in an entirely new creative direction. Scripting gives me time to experiment—and I think experimentation has a lot to do with creativity.

What I'm getting at here is that scripting is what you make of it, and how you think about it. If you only think of scripting as something applicable to massive projects, you're missing out on many of the benefits—and most of the fun.

Getting Started

For your first script, try the "Hello World" examples in the Scripting Guide. They're short, they show you how to create a new document, create a new text frame, add text to the text frame, and apply formatting to that text. After that, start thinking about what you'd like to do with scripting. Is there some task you do in InDesign every day that's driving you crazy?

Wait—I've got one! When you want to get an object or series of object *out* of a frame you've pasted them into, you can end up doing a lot of selecting, cutting, and pasting. A script that could remove all of the objects inside a frame (while maintaining the positions they occupied in the frame) would save you some time and trouble. Right? Let's go!

AppleScript   This script assumes you have an object selected, and that the object contains at least one other object or group. The script will not ungroup a group as it processes the objects. To create the script, follow these steps (see Figure 11-1).

1. Start the AppleScript Script Editor.

2. Enter the following text (note that ¬ indicates a long line—do not enter a line break in the Script Editor).

```
tell application "InDesign 1.5"
```

FIGURE 11-1
Cut contents script (AppleScript version)

Start the AppleScript Script Editor

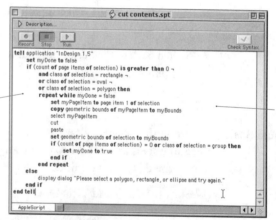

Enter AppleScript (don't worry about the indents or formatting—the Script Editor takes care of it for you).

Once you've entered a script, select an object you've pasted other objects into.

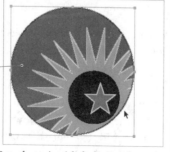

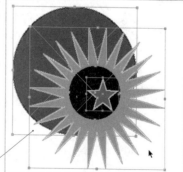

Run the script (click the Run button in the Script Editor), and InDesign will "un-nest" the objects while retaining their original positions.

```
set myDone to false
if (count of page items of selection) is greater than 0 ¬
and class of selection = rectangle ¬
or class of selection = oval ¬
or class of selection = polygon then
repeat while myDone = false
set myPageItem to page item 1 of selection
copy geometric bounds of myPageItem to myBounds
select myPageItem
cut
paste
set geometric bounds of selection to myBounds
if (count of page items of selection) = 0 ¬
or class of selection = group then
set myDone to true
end if
end repeat
else
display dialog "Please select a polygon, rectangle, ¬
or ellipse and try again."
end if
end tell
```

3. Switch to InDesign. Select a path that contains one or more objects.

4. Switch back to the Script Editor and run the script. InDesign will remove each nested object inside the frame and paste it into the same position as it occupied while inside the frame.

Visual Basic To create this script, follow these steps (see Figure 11-2). These are the same steps as you take to create any Visual Basic script, but I'll repeat them here as a reminder.

1. Start InDesign and Visual Basic.

2. In Visual Basic, create a new project. Choose "Standard EXE" as your project template.

3. Choose References from the Project menu. Visual Basic displays the References dialog box. Turn on the Adobe InDesign 1.5 Type Library option (in the Available References list), then click the OK button to add this reference to your project.

    If you can't see an entry for the Adobe InDesign 1.5 Type Library in the list, click the Browse button. Visual Basic displays the Add Reference dialog box. Locate and select the file "Scripting.rpln" in the Required folder inside your InDesign folder. Click the Open button. When Visual Basic returns you to the References dialog box, the Adobe InDesign 1.5 Type Library option should appear in the Available References list.

FIGURE 11-2

Cut contents script (Visual Basic version)

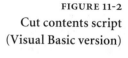

Start Visual Basic and choose New Project from the File menu. Choose Standard EXE.

Click the OK button.

Visual Basic creates a new project and displays a blank form.

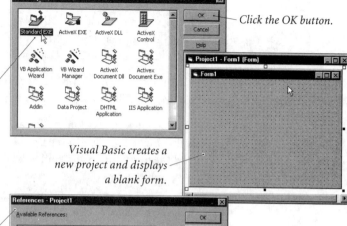

Choose References from the Project menu. Visual Basic displays the References dialog box.

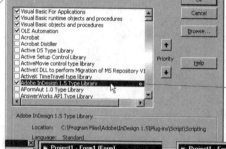

Turn on the Adobe InDesign 1.5 Type Library option and click OK to close the dialog box.

Click the Command Button tool.

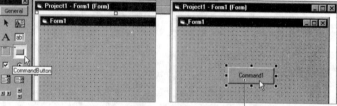

Draw a new command button on the form, then double-click the button.

Visual Basic displays the Code window.

Enter the code for the button (between the "Private Sub" and "End Sub" lines).

To run your script, choose Start from the Run menu (or press F5), then click the button. the result will be the same as that shown in the AppleScript example.

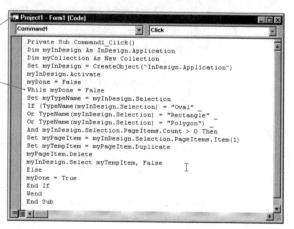

```
Private Sub Command1_Click()
Dim myInDesign As InDesign.Application
Dim myCollection As New Collection
Set myInDesign = CreateObject("InDesign.Application")
myInDesign.Activate
myDone = False
While myDone = False
Set myTypeName = myInDesign.Selection
If (TypeName(myInDesign.Selection) = "Oval" _
Or TypeName(myInDesign.Selection) = "Rectangle" _
Or TypeName(myInDesign.Selection) = "Polygon" _
And myInDesign.Selection.PageItems.Count > 0 Then
Set myPageItem = myInDesign.Selection.PageItems.Item(1)
Set myTempItem = myPageItem.Duplicate
myPageItem.Delete
myInDesign.Select myTempItem, False
Else
myDone = True
End If
Wend
End Sub
```

4. Create a new form. To do this, choose Add Form from the Project menu. Visual Basic displays the Add Form dialog box. Select the standard form template ("Form") and click the Open button. Visual Basic creates a new, blank form.

5. Add a button to the form. To do this, select the CommandButton tool and then drag the tool in the form.

6. Double-click the button to display the Code window. Enter the following text (between the line beginning with "Private Sub" and the line containing "End Sub" that Visual Basic will already have entered for you).

```
Dim myInDesign As InDesign.Application
Dim myCollection As New Collection
Set myInDesign = CreateObject("InDesign.Application")
myInDesign.Activate
myDone = False
While myDone = False
Set myTypeName = myInDesign.Selection
If (TypeName(myInDesign.Selection) = "Oval" _
Or TypeName(myInDesign.Selection) = "Rectangle" _
Or TypeName(myInDesign.Selection) = "Polygon") _
And myInDesign.Selection.PageItems.Count > 0 Then
Set myPageItem = myInDesign.Selection.PageItems.Item(1)
Set myTempItem = myPageItem.Duplicate
myPageItem.Delete
myInDesign.Select myTempItem, False
Else
myDone = True
End If
Wend
```

Now you're ready to test your new script. Go to InDesign and select a path that has another path or group pasted inside it. Return to Visual Basic and click the Run button. Visual Basic displays the form. Click the button you created in Step 5. If everything's working properly, you should see the script switch to InDesign (that's what the "myInDesign.Activate" line does). After that, the script should extract the objects inside the selected path.

This example script contains very little error checking code—so you'll get an error from Visual Basic if the script encounters a condition it's not prepared for. The script will fail if no publication is open, for example.

Why did I leave out error checking? It can make the script a lot longer, slower, and harder to read. For examples of proper (which is not to say foolproof) error checking, refer to the example scripts on your InDesign CD.

More Fun with Scripting

I'll limit myself to just one more scripting example, because I recognize that I'm a long-winded pedant, and because I want to finish this book sometime this decade. Illustrator and FreeHand both have drawing tools for creating spirals, but InDesign doesn't. Which means that when you want to wrap text around a spiral, you've got to either draw it yourself using the Pen tool (tedious) or copy and paste the spiral from another program (boring). Unless you use the following script (which, I'll immodestly point out, contains features not found in either Illustrator or FreeHand).

Note: This script involves a small amount of trigonometry—so I've had to add some handlers (subroutines) to the AppleScript section, because AppleScript has no built-in trigonometric functions. In addition, you should note that the Visual Basic functions return values in radians, rather than degrees, and that InDesign's vertical axis is upside down relative to traditional geometric plotting.

AppleScript

1. Open the Script Editor.

2. Enter the following code (the lines beginning with "--" are comments, so you don't have to enter them).

```
--DrawSpiral
--Set center point of spiral
set myX to 0
set myY to 0
--To set the distance between each "wrap" of the spiral,
--change the value x in x/4 in the following line (default
--value is in points).
set myDistance to 3 / 4
--Set the growth rate--values greater than 1 result
--in a logarithmic spiral. Try 1.05.
set myGrowthRate to 1
--Set the number of "wraps" around the spiral.
set myNumberOfIterations to 48
--You can change the position of the curve handles
--by changing the value in the following line. Try
--45 for a "square spiral" effect.
set myCurveConstant to 29
--If myPointType is true, the spiral will contain
--curve points; if it's false, it'll use corner points.
set myPointType to true
tell application "InDesign 1.5"
activate
set mySpread to active spread of active window
tell mySpread
--Create a new graphic line.
set myGraphicLine to make graphic line
```

```
--Set myPath to the path of the graphic line.
set myPath to path 1 of myGraphicLine
--Get the path points of the path.
set myPathPoints to path points of myPath
--Set the position of the first point in the path.
set myPathPoint to item 1 of myPathPoints
set anchor of myPathPoint to {myX, myY}
--Here's the loop that draws the spiral.
repeat with myCounter from 1 to myNumberOfIterations
set myAngleIncrement to myCounter * 90
set myRadius to myDistance * myCounter
set myX1 to myRadius * (my myCosine(myAngleIncrement))
set myY1 to myRadius * (my mySine(myAngleIncrement))
--myPhantomRadius is the distance to the control handles--
--it's a little greater than the actual radius.
set myPhantomRadius to myRadius / (my myCosine(myCurveConstant))
--Next, calculate the control handle locations.
set myX2 to (my myCosine(myAngleIncrement + myCurveConstant)) *
myPhantomRadius
set myY2 to (my mySine(myAngleIncrement + myCurveConstant)) *
myPhantomRadius
set myX3 to (my myCosine(myAngleIncrement - myCurveConstant)) *
myPhantomRadius
set myY3 to (my mySine(myAngleIncrement - myCurveConstant)) *
myPhantomRadius
--If the current path point is the first or second point on
--on the path, use that point--otherwise, create a new point
if myCounter is greater than 2 then
tell myPath to make path point at end
--Elbow myPathPoints so that it includes the new point.
set myPathPoints to path points of myPath
end if
set myPathPoint to item myCounter of myPathPoints
--Move the path point into position.
set anchor of myPathPoint to {myX1, myY1}
if myPointType then
set point type of myPathPoint to smooth
else
set point type of myPathPoint to corner
end if
--Set the position of the control handles.
set right direction of myPathPoint to {myX2, myY2}
set left direction of myPathPoint to {myX3, myY3}
--If myGrowthRate is greater than 1, increase myDistance.
if myGrowthRate > 1 then
myDistance = myDistance * myGrowthRate
end if
end repeat
end tell
end tell

--Trigonometric handlers follow
on mySine(x)
repeat until x ³ 0 and x < 360
if x ³ 360 then
```

```
set x to x - 360
end if
if x < 0 then
set x to x + 360
end if
end repeat
set x to x * (2 * 3.141615927) / 360
set answer to 0
set numerator to x
set denominator to 1
set factor to -(x ^ 2)
repeat with i from 3 to 40 by 2
set answer to answer + numerator / denominator
set numerator to numerator * factor
set denominator to denominator * i * (i - 1)
end repeat
return answer
end mySine

on myCosine(x)
repeat until x ³ 0 and x < 360
if x ³ 360 then
set x to x - 360
end if
if x < 0 then
set x to x + 360
end if
end repeat
set x to x * (2 * pi) / 360 -- 3.141615927
set answer to 0
set numerator to 1
set denominator to 1
set factor to -(x ^ 2)
repeat with i from 2 to 40 by 2
set answer to answer + numerator / denominator
set numerator to numerator * factor
set denominator to denominator * i * (i - 1)
end repeat
return answer
end myCosine
```

Visual Basic

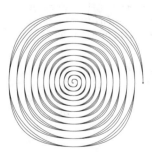

1. Set up a project, form, and button as described in the previous section.

2. Enter the following code in the button.

```
Rem DrawSpiral
Dim myInDesign As InDesign.Application
Dim mySpread As InDesign.Spread
Dim myLine As InDesign.Line
Dim myPath As InDesign.Path
Dim myPathPoints As InDesign.PathPoints
Dim myPathPoint As InDesign.PathPoint
Const pi = 3.14159265358979
myX = 0
```

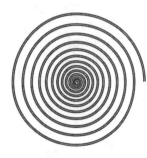

```
myY = 0
Set myInDesign = CreateObject("InDesign.Application")
Set mySpread = myInDesign.ActiveWindow.ActiveSpread
Rem To set the distance between each "wrap" of the spiral,
Rem replace x in CDbl(x)/4 with the distance you want.
Rem This default value is in points.
myDistance = CDbl(6) / 4
Rem The following values could be entered via text fields
Rem or radio buttons.
Rem Set the growth rate--values greater than 1 result
Rem in a logarithmic spiral. Try 1.05.
myGrowthRate = 1
Rem Set the number of times around the spiral.
myNumberOfIterations = 48
Rem You can change the position of the curve handles
Rem by changing x in myRadians(CDbl(x)).
myCurveConstant = myRadians(CDbl(29))
Rem If myPointType is true, spiral will use curve points,
Rem if it's false, spiral will use corner points.
myPointType = True
Rem Add a line to the current spread.
Set myLine = mySpread.Lines.Add
Rem Get the path of the line.
Set myPath = myLine.Paths.Item(1)
Rem Get the points on the path.
Set myPathPoints = myPath.PathPoints
Rem Get the path point of the path.
Set myPathPoint = myPathPoints.Item(1)
Rem Set the position of the first path point.
myPathPoint.Anchor = Array(myX, myY)
Rem Here's the loop that draws the spiral.
For myCounter = 1 To myNumberOfIterations
myAngleIncrement = myRadians(myCounter * 90)
myRadius = myDistance * myCounter
myX1 = myRadius * Cos(myAngleIncrement)
myY1 = myRadius * Sin(myAngleIncrement)
Rem "myPhantomRadius" is the distance to the curve handles--
Rem it's a little greater than the actual radius.
myPhantomRadius = myRadius / Cos(myCurveConstant)
Rem Next, calculate the control handle locations.
myX2 = Cos(myAngleIncrement + myCurveConstant) * myPhantomRadius
myY2 = Sin(myAngleIncrement + myCurveConstant) * myPhantomRadius
myX3 = Cos(myAngleIncrement - myCurveConstant) * myPhantomRadius
myY3 = Sin(myAngleIncrement - myCurveConstant) * myPhantomRadius
Rem If the current path point is the first or second point
Rem on the path, use that point--otherwise, create a new point.
If myCounter <= 2 Then
Set myPathPoint = myPath.PathPoints.Item(myCounter)
Else
Set myPathPoint = myPath.PathPoints.Add
End If
Rem Move the path point into position.
myPathPoint.Anchor = Array(myX1, myY1)
```

```
Rem Use the point type we specified above.
If myPointType Then
myPathPoint.PointType = idSmooth
Else
myPathPoint.PointType = idCorner
End If
Rem Set the position of the control handles.
myPathPoint.RightDirection = Array(myX2, myY2)
myPathPoint.LeftDirection = Array(myX3, myY3)
Rem If the growth rate is greater than 1, increase myDistance.
If myGrowthRate > 1 Then
myDistance = myDistance * myGrowthRate
End If
Next myCounter
```

3. Save the form file.

Testing the Spiral Drawing Script

To test the spiral drawing script, move the zero point to the point at which you want to locate the center of the spiral, then run the script (I recommend setting the publication's measurement system to points before running the script). If all goes well, InDesign will draw a spiral. I urge you to experiment with the settings in the script—the number of different types of spirals you can draw is practically endless.

Limits of InDesign Scripting

Some obscure (to the scripting team) or late-breaking InDesign features are not in InDesign's object library. Like what? Dashed line patterns (you can set the stroke type to "dashed," but you can't control the dash pattern). Another stroke-related feature, Weight Changes Bounding Box, is not supported. Path text objects are not supported.

If you're using Windows you can work around some of these limitations using the Visual Basic "SendKeys" function. Here's an example that sets the dash pattern of the first rectangle in a spread.

```
Dim myInDesign As InDesign.Application
Set myInDesign = CreateObject("InDesign.Application")
Set mySpread = myInDesign.ActiveWindow.ActiveSpread
Set myRectangle = mySpread.Rectangles.Item(1)
myRectangle.StrokeType = idDashed
myInDesign.Activate
SendKeys "%Wk{TAB}{TAB}{TAB}{TAB}{TAB}1{ENTER}"
```

Useful Scripting Utilities

As I said earlier, I like to use scripting to do small tasks in InDesign. Putting a ruler guide exactly at the left edge of the selected object, for example. This confuses my friends. How can you save time, they ask, when you've got to leave InDesign to go out to the Finder (on the Macintosh) or Explorer (in Windows) to run the script?

They're right—if you have to switch from program to program, you might as well limit scripting to lengthy, repetitive tasks. In the time it takes to claw your way through the volumes and folders on your hard drive to find and launch a script, you can accomplish most of the minor but annoying tasks that I've presented as good applications for scripting.

But they're missing the point. *Writing* the scripts is only one part of the solution. *Running* them is the other part. I don't switch out of my page layout applications to run scripts. Instead, I start them from inside the program, usually with the press of a key.

Most of the time, I do this using QuicKeys from CE Software (available for the Macintosh, Windows 98, and for Windows NT 4). There are also a number of *free* utilities that will also do the trick for you (you cheapskate).

OSA Menu   You might not know it, but you probably already have OSA Menu Lite—it comes on the Mac OS installation CD. (OSA, by the way, is short for "Open Scripting Architecture"—an Apple technology/ marketing ploy. OSA-compliant languages include AppleScript, UserLand Frontier, QuicKeys, tclScript, and MacPerl.)

If you don't have your installation CD handy, or if you want to download the most recent version of OSA Menu, you've got at least a couple of options:

◆ You can get OSA Menu from Apple—you'll find the version of OSA Menu Lite that came with MacOS 8.6 at http:// asu.info.apple.com/swupdates.nsf/artnum/n11402

◆ You can download the "full" version of OSAMenu from its author, Leonard Rosenthal, at http://www.lazerware.com/ software.html

I still haven't figured out what's "Lite" about the OSA Menu Lite, relative to the "standard" OSA Menu 1.2, so it probably has to do with features I'm not interested in or otherwise deem unimportant. Still, why not get the full package? A few extra scripting calories won't kill you.

Once you've installed OSA Menu, a new menu appears on the right side of the main menu bar—between the system clock and the Application menu. This is the OSA Menu, and it will appear on the menu bar in all of your applications (see Figure 11-3).

FIGURE 11-3

OSA Menu

After you install OSA menu, you'll see a new icon on your System menu bar.

When you put scripts in folders inside the Scripts folder...

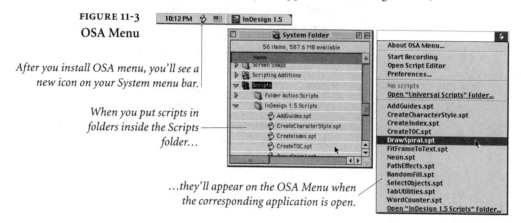

...they'll appear on the OSA Menu when the corresponding application is open.

Managing OSA scripts. The scripts that appear on the the OSA Menu are the compiled scripts stored in the Scripts folder in your System folder. When you store scripts inside a folder having the name of a specific application, those scripts will appear on the OSA Menu only when that application is active.

Assigning Keyboard Shortcuts to OSA Menu Items. You can assign keyboard shortcut to scripts by adding special characters to the end of the script's file name. The "\" character represents the Command key, "S" stands for Shift, "O" stands for Option, and "C" stands for Control. In general, these keyboard shortcuts will override any keyboard shortcuts in the application, so avoid giving scripts commonly used keyboard combinations.

It's Called the Taskbar for a Reason

Looking for a counterpart to OSA Menu for your Windows machine? You've had one all along—you can put your Visual Basic scripts (as either compiled applications or project files) on the Start menu.

QuicKeys

While there are other keyboard macro-making programs available, such as the excellent OneClick or the freeware KeyQuencer (both on the Macintosh), I use QuicKeys. QuicKeys is available for both the Macintosh and Windows, and a demo version is available for download at http://www.quickeys.com. QuicKeys gives you excellent support for automating user interface actions (menu choices, key presses, and button clicks), but it's also got excellent scripting support built in (on both platforms).

**QuickKeys +
AppleScript**

Want to run an AppleScript by pressing a keyboard shortcut? You can use QuicKeys, as shown in the steps below (see Figure 11-4).

1. Display the QuicKeys editor.

2. Choose AppleScript from the Scripting Tools submenu of the Create menu. QuicKeys displays the AppleScript dialog box.

3. Turn on the File option and then click the Select File button to select a file, or turn on the Text option and click the Modify Text button to enter a script directly in QuicKeys. In general, I think it's best to select a compiled script file using the File option—compiled scripts run faster. Enter a name and a keyboard shortcut for your AppleScript QuicKey.

4. Click the OK button to close the AppleScript dialog box.

5. Click the Close box to close the QuicKeys Editor.

When you're ready to run the script, press the keyboard shortcut you assigned to the QuicKey. All of InDesign's palettes will disappear momentarily—QuicKeys has to switch to a background application named "AppleScript Helper" to run the script. When QuicKeys returns you to InDesign, you'll see the effect of the script.

Here's an example script that draws crop marks and simple registration marks around the selected object. You can enter this in the QuicKeys Script dialog box or the ScriptEditor (your choice).

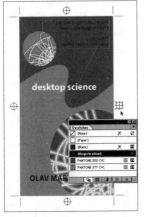

Crop and registration marks drawn by the CropMarks script.

```
--CropMarks
--Default values are in points--change them to
--match your measurement system, if necessary.
--myCropLength sets the length of each crop mark.
set myCropLength to 12
--myCropOffset sets the distance from the artwork.
set myCropOffset to 3
--myCropWeight sets the stroke weight of the
--crop marks (always in points)
set myCropWeight to 0.25
--myRadius1 is unused, but could be used
--for a "bullseye" in the center of the
--registration mark.
set myRadius1 to 3
--myRadius2 sets the diameter of the circle
--used in the registration marks.
set myRadius2 to 4.5
--myRadius3 sets the length of the cross hairs
--used in the registration marks.
set myRadius3 to 6
tell application "InDesign 1.5"
try
set myPageItem to item 1 of selection
```

FIGURE 11-4

QuicKeys and
AppleScript

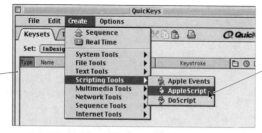

Display the QuicKeys editor.

*Choose AppleScript
from the Scripting
Tools submenu of the
Create menu.*

*QuicKeys displays the
AppleScript dialog box.*

*Enter a name and
a keyboard short-
cut for your
AppleScript
QuicKey.*

*Click the File option
to select a file...*

*Once you've
chosen a file or
entered a script,
click the OK
button.*

*...or click the Text option
to enter a script directly in
QuicKeys.*

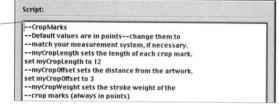

*Your new AppleScript
QuicKey appears in the
QuicKeys editor.*

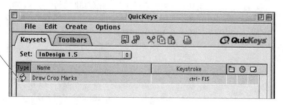

```
if myPageItem = {} then error
set mySpread to active spread of active window
set myDocument to active document
set myRegColor to color "Registration" of myDocument
set myBounds to geometric bounds of myPageItem
set myY1 to (item 1 of myBounds)
set myX1 to (item 2 of myBounds)
set myY2 to (item 3 of myBounds)
set myX2 to (item 4 of myBounds)
set myY3 to myY1 - myCropOffset
set myX3 to myX1 - myCropOffset
set myY4 to myY2 + myCropOffset
set myX4 to myX2 + myCropOffset
set myXCenter to myX1 + ((myX2 - myX1) / 2)
set myYCenter to myY1 + ((myY2 - myY1) / 2)
```

```
tell mySpread
--Upper left pair
set myY5 to myY3 - myCropLength
--Vertical crop mark
make graphic line with properties ¬
{geometric bounds:{myY5, myX1, myY3, myX1}, ¬
stroke weight:myCropWeight, stroke color:myRegColor}
--Horizontal crop mark
set myX5 to myX3 - myCropLength
make graphic line with properties ¬
{geometric bounds:{myY1, myX5, myY1, myX3}, ¬
stroke weight:myCropWeight, stroke color:myRegColor}
--Upper right pair
set myY5 to myY3 - myCropLength
--Vertical crop mark
make graphic line with properties ¬
{geometric bounds:{myY5, myX2, myY3, myX2}, ¬
stroke weight:myCropWeight, stroke color:myRegColor}
--Horizontal crop mark
set myX5 to myX4 + myCropLength
make graphic line with properties ¬
{geometric bounds:{myY1, myX5, myY1, myX4}, ¬
stroke weight:myCropWeight, stroke color:myRegColor}
--Lower left pair
set myY5 to myY4 + myCropLength
--Vertical crop mark
make graphic line with properties ¬
{geometric bounds:{myY5, myX1, myY4, myX1}, ¬
stroke weight:myCropWeight, stroke color:myRegColor}
--Horizontal crop mark
set myX5 to myX3 - myCropLength
make graphic line with properties ¬
{geometric bounds:{myY2, myX5, myY2, myX3}, ¬
stroke weight:myCropWeight, stroke color:myRegColor}
--Lower right pair
set myY5 to myY4 + myCropLength
--Vertical crop mark
make graphic line with properties ¬
{geometric bounds:{myY5, myX2, myY4, myX2}, ¬
stroke weight:myCropWeight, stroke color:myRegColor}
--Horizontal crop mark
set myX5 to myX4 + myCropLength
make graphic line with properties ¬
{geometric bounds:{myY2, myX5, myY2, myX4}, ¬
stroke weight:myCropWeight, stroke color:myRegColor}
--Left side registration mark
set myX5 to myX3 - (myRadius3 * 2)
make graphic line with properties ¬
{geometric bounds:{myYCenter, myX5, myYCenter, myX3}, ¬
stroke weight:myCropWeight, stroke color:myRegColor}
set myX5 to myX3 - myRadius3
set myY5 to myYCenter - myRadius3
set myY6 to myYCenter + myRadius3
make graphic line with properties ¬
{geometric bounds:{myY5, myX5, myY6, myX5}, ¬
```

```
stroke weight:myCropWeight, stroke color:myRegColor}
set myX5 to myX3 - (myRadius3 + myRadius2)
set myX6 to myX3 - (myRadius3 - myRadius2)
set myY5 to myYCenter - myRadius2
set myY6 to myYCenter + myRadius2
make oval with properties ¬
{geometric bounds:{myY5, myX5, myY6, myX6}, ¬
stroke weight:myCropWeight, stroke color:myRegColor}
--Right side registration mark
set myX5 to myX4 + (myRadius3 * 2)
make graphic line with properties ¬
{geometric bounds:{myYCenter, myX5, myYCenter, myX4}, ¬
stroke weight:myCropWeight, stroke color:myRegColor}
set myX5 to myX4 + myRadius3
set myY5 to myYCenter - myRadius3
set myY6 to myYCenter + myRadius3
make graphic line with properties ¬
{geometric bounds:{myY5, myX5, myY6, myX5}, ¬
stroke weight:myCropWeight, stroke color:myRegColor}
set myX5 to myX4 + (myRadius3 + myRadius2)
set myX6 to myX4 + (myRadius3 - myRadius2)
set myY5 to myYCenter - myRadius2
set myY6 to myYCenter + myRadius2
make oval with properties ¬
{geometric bounds:{myY5, myX5, myY6, myX6}, ¬
stroke weight:myCropWeight, stroke color:myRegColor}
--Top registration mark
set myY5 to myY3 - (myRadius3 * 2)
make graphic line with properties ¬
{geometric bounds:{myY5, myXCenter, myY3, myXCenter}, ¬
stroke weight:myCropWeight, stroke color:myRegColor}
set myX5 to myXCenter - myRadius3
set myX6 to myXCenter + myRadius3
set myY5 to myY3 - myRadius3
make graphic line with properties ¬
{geometric bounds:{myY5, myX5, myY5, myX6}, ¬
stroke weight:myCropWeight, stroke color:myRegColor}
set myY5 to myY3 - (myRadius3 + myRadius2)
set myY6 to myY3 - (myRadius3 - myRadius2)
set myX5 to myXCenter - myRadius2
set myX6 to myXCenter + myRadius2
make oval with properties ¬
{geometric bounds:{myY5, myX5, myY6, myX6}, ¬
stroke weight:myCropWeight, stroke color:myRegColor}
--Bottom registration mark
set myY5 to myY4 + (myRadius3 * 2)
make graphic line with properties ¬
{geometric bounds:{myY5, myXCenter, myY4, myXCenter}, ¬
stroke weight:myCropWeight, stroke color:myRegColor}
set myX5 to myXCenter - myRadius3
set myX6 to myXCenter + myRadius3
set myY5 to myY4 + myRadius3
make graphic line with properties ¬
{geometric bounds:{myY5, myX5, myY5, myX6}, ¬
stroke weight:myCropWeight, stroke color:myRegColor}
```

```
set myY5 to myY4 + (myRadius3 + myRadius2)
set myY6 to myY4 + (myRadius3 - myRadius2)
set myX5 to myXCenter - myRadius2
set myX6 to myXCenter + myRadius2
make oval with properties ¬
{geometric bounds:{myY5, myX5, myY6, myX6}, ¬
stroke weight:myCropWeight, stroke color:myRegColor}
end tell
activate
on error
display dialog "Please select an object and try again"
end try
end tell
```

QuicKeys + Windows Scripting Host = Fun!

While you can always use QuicKeys to launch Visual Basic programs you've compiled, the program works with VBScript files (these aren't quite the same as Visual Basic scripts) and the Windows Scripting Host to bring you a somewhat more casual approach to scripting.

Why do I say "more casual?" Because you can write VBScripts with nothing more than a text editor or word processor—heck, you can even use InDesign. You then direct the Windows Scripting Host to execute the content of the files—you can do this by double-clicking the files in the Windows Explorer, but there's an even better way—use QuicKeys. To create a shortcut for a VBScript, follow these steps (see Figure 11-5).

1. Display the QuicKeys Editor.

2. Click the Actions tab.

3. Choose Run Script from the System Tools submenu of the Create menu. QuicKeys displays the Action Properties dialog box.

4. Enter the file name and path of the VBScript file between the brackets in the Name field, or in the Select Script field. For some reason, the Browse button doesn't work for me—if it does for you, use it to locate and select the script file (much easier than remembering the full path and file name).

5. Assign a keyboard shortcut (or other QuicKeys "trigger," such as the QuicKeys menu or a toolbar button) to the script.

6. Close the QuicKeys Editor window.

At this point, you can run the VBScript by pressing the keyboard shortcut (or other trigger) you've assigned.

But wait—there's even more! You can even enter VBScripts as

FIGURE 11-5
QuicKeys and VBScript

Display the QuicKeys Editor and click the Actions tab.

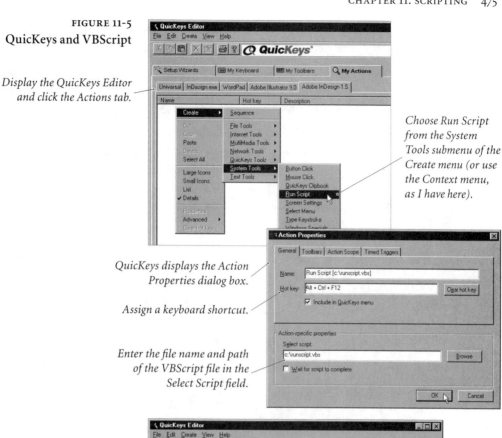

Choose Run Script from the System Tools submenu of the Create menu (or use the Context menu, as I have here).

QuicKeys displays the Action Properties dialog box.

Assign a keyboard shortcut.

Enter the file name and path of the VBScript file in the Select Script field.

QuicKeys adds the RunScript QuicKey to the list of QuicKeys in the QuicKeys Editor.

the text of an InDesign story, then direct the Windows Scripting Host to run the text as a script. Here's what you do.

1. Enter the following text in a text file.

```
Rem Run Script Script
Dim myInDesign
Dim mySelection
Dim myReturn
Dim WSHShell
Set myInDesign = WScript.GetObject("", "InDesign.Application")
Set mySelection = myInDesign.Selection
mySelection.Export "Text-only", "c:\MyDocuments\test.vbs"
Set WSHShell = WScript.CreateObject("WScript.Shell")
myReturn = WSHShell.Run("C:\WINNT\system32\wscript.exe
c:\MyDocuments\test.vbs", WshNormalFocus, true)
```

2. Save the script as a text-only file, giving it the file extension ".vbs".

3. Create a Run Script QuicKey and enter the name of the file you saved in Step 2 in the Select Script field of the Action Properties dialog box. Assign a keyboard shortcut (or other QuicKeys trigger) to the action.

4. Enter a simple VBScript in an InDesign text frame. Here's the "improved Hello World" script as a VBScript.

```
Rem hello world!
Dim myInDesign
Dim myPub
Dim myFrame
Dim myPara
Dim myBounds
Dim myIDCenter
MyBounds = array("3p0", "3p0", "63p0", "48p0")
Rem Note that the InDesign justification constant "idCenter"
Rem must be entered as its value (refer to the constant in
Rem the Object Library to get this value).
MyIDCenter = 1667591796
Set myInDesign = WScript.GetObject("", "InDesign.Application")
rem Set myInDesign = GetObject("", "InDesign.Application")
Set myPub = myInDesign.Documents.Add()
Set mySpread = myPub.Spreads.Item(1)
Set myFrame = mySpread.TextFrames.Add
myFrame.GeometricBounds = myBounds
myFrame.TextContents = "Hello, World!"
Set myPara = myFrame.Paragraphs.Item(1)
myPara.PointSize = 72
myPara.Justification = myIDCenter
myPara.Font = "Tekton Pro"
myPara.FontStyle = "Bold"
```

5. Select all of the text in the story, then run the Run Script QuicKey you created in Step 3. The script exports the selected text as a VBScript, then executes the script file. (This is one of my favorite tricks—using a script to write a script!)

Here's the VBScript version of the CropMarks script. This script will fail if you have more than one object selected. This code will work in Visual Basic with very few modifications.

```
Rem CropMarks
Rem Default values are in points--change them to
Rem match your measurement system, if necessary.
Rem myCropLength sets the length of each crop mark.
myCropLength = 12
Rem myCropOffset sets the distance from the artwork.
myCropOffset = 3
Rem myCropWeight sets the stroke weight of the
```

```
Rem crop marks (always in points)
myCropWeight = 0.25
Rem myRadius1 is unused, but could be used
Rem for a "bullseye" in the center of the
Rem registration mark.
myRadius1 = 3
Rem myRadius2 sets the diameter of the circle
Rem used in the registration marks.
myRadius2 = 4.5
Rem myRadius3 sets the length of the cross hairs
Rem used in the registration marks.
myRadius3 = 6
Rem Comment out the following line to use this script
Rem in a Visual Basic project
Set myInDesign = WScript.GetObject("", "InDesign.Application")
Rem Uncomment the following line to use this script
Rem in a Visual Basic project.
Rem Set myInDesign = CreateObject("InDesign.Application")
Set mySpread = myInDesign.ActiveWindow.ActiveSpread
Set myDocument = myInDesign.ActiveDocument
myType = TypeName(myInDesign.Selection)
Rem Is anything selected?
if myType = "Nothing" then
msgbox "Please select an object and try again."
else
Set myPageItem = myInDesign.Selection
Set myRegColor = myDocument.Colors.Item("Registration")
myBounds = myPageitem.GeometricBounds
myY1 = myBounds(0)
myX1 = myBounds(1)
myY2 = myBounds(2)
myX2 = myBounds(3)
myY3 = myY1 - myCropOffset
myX3 = myX1 - myCropOffset
myY4 = myY2 + myCropOffset
myX4 = myX2 + myCropOffset
myXCenter = myX1 + ((myX2 - myX1) / 2)
myYCenter = myY1 + ((myY2 - myY1) / 2)
Rem Upper left pair
myY5 = myY3 - myCropLength
Rem Vertical crop mark
Set MyGraphicLine = mySpread.Lines.Add
MyGraphicLine.GeometricBounds = Array(myY5, myX1, myY3, myX1)
MyGraphicLine.StrokeWeight = myCropWeight
MyGraphicLine.StrokeColor = myRegColor
Rem Horizontal crop mark
myX5 = myX3 - myCropLength
Set MyGraphicLine = mySpread.Lines.Add
MyGraphicLine.GeometricBounds = Array(myY1, myX5, myY1, myX3)
MyGraphicLine.StrokeWeight = myCropWeight
MyGraphicLine.StrokeColor = myRegColor
Rem Upper right pair
myY5 = myY3 - myCropLength
Rem Vertical crop mark
Set MyGraphicLine = mySpread.Lines.Add
```

```
MyGraphicLine.GeometricBounds = Array(myY5, myX2, myY3, myX2)
MyGraphicLine.StrokeWeight = myCropWeight
MyGraphicLine.StrokeColor = myRegColor
Rem Horizontal crop mark
myX5 = myX4 + myCropLength
Set MyGraphicLine = mySpread.Lines.Add
MyGraphicLine.GeometricBounds = Array(myY1, myX5, myY1, myX4)
MyGraphicLine.StrokeWeight = myCropWeight
MyGraphicLine.StrokeColor = myRegColor
Rem Lower left pair
myY5 = myY4 + myCropLength
Rem Vertical crop mark
Set MyGraphicLine = mySpread.Lines.Add
MyGraphicLine.GeometricBounds = Array(myY5, myX1, myY4, myX1)
MyGraphicLine.StrokeWeight = myCropWeight
MyGraphicLine.StrokeColor = myRegColor
Rem Horizontal crop mark
myX5 = myX3 - myCropLength
Set MyGraphicLine = mySpread.Lines.Add
MyGraphicLine.GeometricBounds = Array(myY2, myX5, myY2, myX3)
MyGraphicLine.StrokeWeight = myCropWeight
MyGraphicLine.StrokeColor = myRegColor
Rem Lower right pair
myY5 = myY4 + myCropLength
Rem Vertical crop mark
Set MyGraphicLine = mySpread.Lines.Add
MyGraphicLine.GeometricBounds = Array(myY5, myX2, myY4, myX2)
MyGraphicLine.StrokeWeight = myCropWeight
MyGraphicLine.StrokeColor = myRegColor
Rem Horizontal crop mark
myX5 = myX4 + myCropLength
Set MyGraphicLine = mySpread.Lines.Add
MyGraphicLine.GeometricBounds = Array(myY2, myX5, myY2, myX4)
MyGraphicLine.StrokeWeight = myCropWeight
MyGraphicLine.StrokeColor = myRegColor
Rem Left side registration mark
myX5 = myX3 - (myRadius3 * 2)
Set MyGraphicLine = mySpread.Lines.Add
MyGraphicLine.GeometricBounds = Array(myYCenter, myX5, _
myYCenter, myX3)
MyGraphicLine.StrokeWeight = myCropWeight
MyGraphicLine.StrokeColor = myRegColor
myX5 = myX3 - myRadius3
myY5 = myYCenter - myRadius3
myY6 = myYCenter + myRadius3
Set MyGraphicLine = mySpread.Lines.Add
MyGraphicLine.GeometricBounds = Array(myY5, myX5, myY6, myX5)
MyGraphicLine.StrokeWeight = myCropWeight
MyGraphicLine.StrokeColor = myRegColor
myX5 = myX3 - (myRadius3 + myRadius2)
myX6 = myX3 - (myRadius3 - myRadius2)
myY5 = myYCenter - myRadius2
myY6 = myYCenter + myRadius2
Set MyOval = mySpread.Ovals.Add
```

```
MyOval.GeometricBounds = Array(myY5, myX5, myY6, myX6)
MyOval.StrokeWeight = myCropWeight
MyOval.StrokeColor = myRegColor
Rem Right side registration mark
myX5 = myX4 + (myRadius3 * 2)
Set MyGraphicLine = mySpread.Lines.Add
MyGraphicLine.GeometricBounds = Array(myYCenter, myX5, _
myYCenter, myX4)
MyGraphicLine.StrokeWeight = myCropWeight
MyGraphicLine.StrokeColor = myRegColor
myX5 = myX4 + myRadius3
myY5 = myYCenter - myRadius3
myY6 = myYCenter + myRadius3
Set MyGraphicLine = mySpread.Lines.Add
MyGraphicLine.GeometricBounds = Array(myY5, myX5, myY6, myX5)
MyGraphicLine.StrokeWeight = myCropWeight
MyGraphicLine.StrokeColor = myRegColor
myX5 = myX4 + (myRadius3 + myRadius2)
myX6 = myX4 + (myRadius3 - myRadius2)
myY5 = myYCenter - myRadius2
myY6 = myYCenter + myRadius2
Set MyOval = mySpread.Ovals.Add
MyOval.GeometricBounds = Array(myY5, myX5, myY6, myX6)
MyOval.StrokeWeight = myCropWeight
MyOval.StrokeColor = myRegColor
Rem Top registration mark
myY5 = myY3 - (myRadius3 * 2)
Set MyGraphicLine = mySpread.Lines.Add
MyGraphicLine.GeometricBounds = Array(myY5, myXCenter, myY3, _
myXCenter)
MyGraphicLine.StrokeWeight = myCropWeight
MyGraphicLine.StrokeColor = myRegColor
myX5 = myXCenter - myRadius3
myX6 = myXCenter + myRadius3
myY5 = myY3 - myRadius3
Set MyGraphicLine = mySpread.Lines.Add
MyGraphicLine.GeometricBounds = Array(myY5, myX5, myY5, myX6)
MyGraphicLine.StrokeWeight = myCropWeight
MyGraphicLine.StrokeColor = myRegColor
myY5 = myY3 - (myRadius3 + myRadius2)
myY6 = myY3 - (myRadius3 - myRadius2)
myX5 = myXCenter - myRadius2
myX6 = myXCenter + myRadius2
Set MyOval = mySpread.Ovals.Add
MyOval.GeometricBounds = Array(myY5, myX5, myY6, myX6)
MyOval.StrokeWeight = myCropWeight
MyOval.StrokeColor = myRegColor
Rem Bottom registration mark
myY5 = myY4 + (myRadius3 * 2)
Set MyGraphicLine = mySpread.Lines.Add
MyGraphicLine.GeometricBounds = Array(myY5, myXCenter, myY4, _
myXCenter)
MyGraphicLine.StrokeWeight = myCropWeight
MyGraphicLine.StrokeColor = myRegColor
```

```
myX5 = myXCenter - myRadius3
myX6 = myXCenter + myRadius3
myY5 = myY4 + myRadius3
Set MyGraphicLine = mySpread.Lines.Add
MyGraphicLine.GeometricBounds = Array(myY5, myX5, myY5, myX6)
MyGraphicLine.StrokeWeight = myCropWeight
MyGraphicLine.StrokeColor = myRegColor
myY5 = myY4 + (myRadius3 + myRadius2)
myY6 = myY4 + (myRadius3 - myRadius2)
myX5 = myXCenter - myRadius2
myX6 = myXCenter + myRadius2
Set MyOval = mySpread.Ovals.Add
MyOval.GeometricBounds = Array(myY5, myX5, myY6, myX6)
MyOval.StrokeWeight = myCropWeight
MyOval.StrokeColor = myRegColor
end if
```

End Script

Scripting is all about *user empowerment*. Don't just sit around telling yourself that the reason you're working late is that InDesign can't do something you'd like it to do. Sure, there are things in every program we'd like the manufacturer to fix, but, with InDesign's scripting architecture, we've finally been given the tools we need to *fix them ourselves*.

By urging you to take up scripting, I'm urging you to take control of InDesign, your publications, your work, and your life. I know you can do it!

South East Essex College
of Arts & Technology